Praise for T

Through Esther's Eyes transported me back to the time of Jesus and helped me to experience the life, Death, and Resurrection of our Lord in a new way. Jacqueline's vivid depiction of the sights, sounds, and smells of Jewish life in first-century Palestine helped me to imagine what it would have been like to live among the people who first encountered the Messiah and witnessed His mighty works. It also helped me to appreciate the challenges these first believers faced in professing faith in Jesus Christ in a world that did not know Him nor accept Him. While the storyline of Jesus is familiar to the reader, the book takes some unexpected twists and turns as Esther's life unfolds and her faith grows through her encounters with Jesus. It is delightful book and very enjoyable to read!

– Anita Houghton
Author of *Kerygma 4 Kids* and *As For Me And My House*

Enthralling and captivating — a complete page-turner. *Through Esther's Eyes* will hook you from the start! You'll be transported back to when Jesus walked and preached in first-century Palestine. Though a work of fiction, Esther's character gives us an inside glance at life with Jesus, surely to open our eyes and our hearts. I highly recommend this unique novel!

– Donna-Marie Cooper O'Boyle
EWTN host and author of 35 books, including
52 Weeks with Saint Faustina

Through Esther's Eyes takes the reader on a journey through the life of Jesus from the perspective of someone very close to him. Jacqueline St. Clare's clear and dramatic style helps us to see many stories any reader of the Gospels would know well from a new vantage point, and provides a beautiful account of the humanity of Christ. This book is an excellent read for anyone who wants to think anew about the life of Jesus.

– Father Stephen Pullis
Graduate Pastoral Formation Director, Sacred Heart Major Seminary

Through Esther's Eyes is a beautiful story that brings the Gospels alive with well-developed and believable characters. I especially appreciate the author's research, which helped to transport me back to the first century. Kudos to this talented author. I recommend this book to everyone!

– **Ellen Gable**
Author of *Where Angels Pass*

Immerse yourself in the story of Jesus' life and ministry as told by Esther, His fictional cousin. This novel is steeped in Scripture; the words of the prophets, psalms, Gospel events, and many of Jesus' parables are skillfully interwoven throughout the story. A masterful and compelling debut: a must-read!

– **Barb Szyzkiewicz**
Editor, CatholicMom.com

Jacqueline St. Clare's *Through Esther's Eyes* is a well-constructed novel with defined and authentic characters. Their clear and dynamic dialogues are woven through swift actions moving from chapter to chapter and from scene to scene smoothly, creating a multi-faceted historical account relevant to our times.

– **Professor Edith Covensky**
Poet and author, Wayne State University

Jacqueline St. Clare has given us a richly-imagined life of a cousin of Jesus. With drama and deep feeling, Esther recounts her own story of hopes and disappointments, marriage and discipleship. From events spanning decades, in a complex web of relationships, Esther emerges as a real person, challenged to find God's purposes for herself and her people. And just as real, in her telling, is the playmate of her childhood and Master of her adult life, Jesus of Nazareth.

– **Kevin Perrotta**
Award-winning Catholic journalist and author

Jacqueline St. Clare delivers is 'a stunning, feminine, and faithful exploration of the Christ story. It was pleasure to read this well-researched and beautifully-rendered book. I'm eager to see what she writes next!

– **Megan Jauregui Eccles**
Author of *Where It Grows* and professor,
John Paul the Great Catholic University

If you enjoy the hit TV show *The Chosen*, you will love *Through Esther's Eyes*. An imaginative tale filled with suspense, it tells the story of a young girl who grows up in the shadow of her cousin, Jesus. Esther is with Jesus during key incidents in His life and provides an insightful onlooker's perspective on His rise from precocious child to revered Rabbi. Jacqueline St. Clare writes with an eye for telling detail and an ear for intriguing dialogue. I found myself absorbed in Esther's story and eager to discover where the tale would end. Riveting and realistic, it held me spellbound from the opening to the epilogue. I have to admit, it is rare for me to find a fiction work written by a 21st-century author that holds my attention. *Through Esther's Eyes* is that uncommon find!

– **Maria V. Gallagher**
Author, *Joyful Encounters with Mary:
A Woman's Guide to Living the Mysteries of the Rosary*

I give praise to our Lord Jesus Christ for calling Jacqueline St. Clare to share her gift for writing and her love for God. In *Through Esther's Eyes*, the reader will learn about what life COULD have been like for Jesus, His Mother Mary, St. Peter, and the Apostles. Her knowledge of biblical research and an active imagination filled with a poignant love for Jesus and Mary allowed Jacqueline to share a beautifully-expressed story that will challenge the reader to accept and embrace how much Jesus loves each one of us. This story will plant a seed, and as that seed is allowed to grow and bear fruit, the Holy Spirit will guide the reader to discover a fresh way of understanding Catholic Biblical history. What a beautiful journey to be on!

– **Catherine M. Lanni**
Spiritual Moderator and Foundress of the Shrine of Jesus
The Divine Mercy in Clinton Township, Michigan

THROUGH ESTHER'S EYES

A NOVEL

Jacqueline St. Clare

Jacqueline St. Clare

Available from:
Marian Helpers Center
Stockbridge, MA 01263

Prayerline: 1-800-804-3823
Orderline: 1-800-462-7426
Websites:
ShopMercy.org
Marian.org

Library of Congress Control Number: 2022908778
ISBN: 978-1-59614-568-9

Imprimi Potest:
Very Rev. Chris Alar, MIC
Provincial Superior
The Blessed Virgin Mary, Mother of Mercy Province
July 29, 2023
Feast of Saints Martha, Mary, and Lazarus

Nihil Obstat:
Robert A. Stackpole, STD
Censor Deputatus
March 19, 2022
Solemnity of St. Joseph

Cover and page design by Kathy Szpak and Curtis Bohner

MARIAN PRESS
STOCKBRIDGE MA 01263

Table of Contents

To my mother, Sharon

Palestine in the Time of Jesus

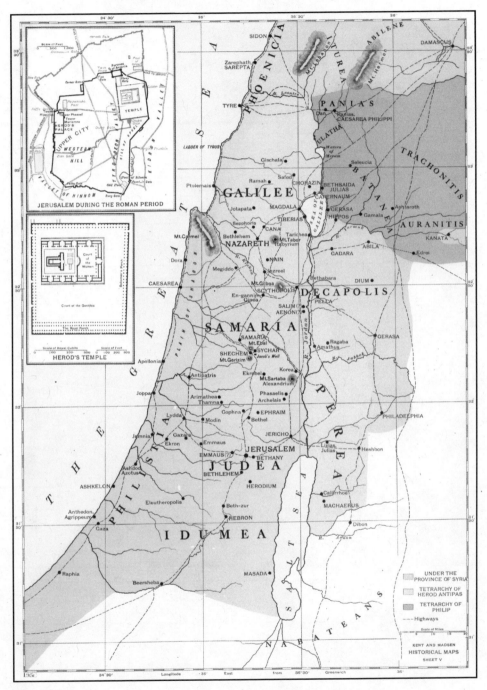

Family Trees

The House of Clopas

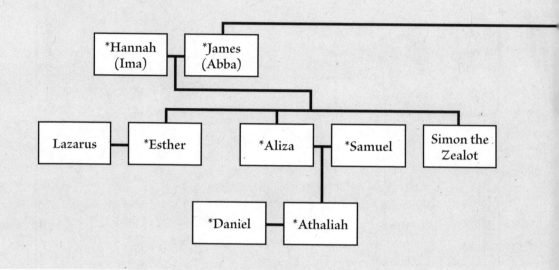

The House of Syrus

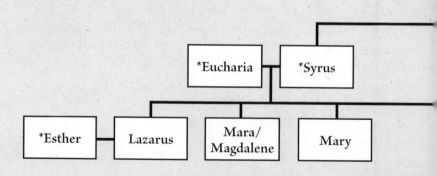

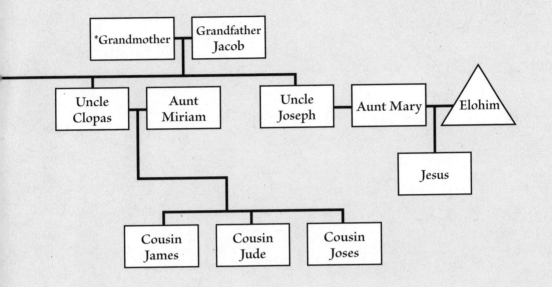

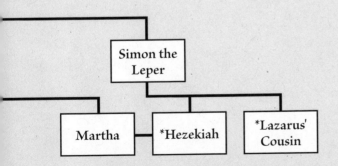

*Character not mentioned in the Bible

Preface

I am amazed to finally see my novel's publication, as the idea for it took seed over ten years ago. *Through Esther's Eyes* is a historical, biblical fiction story. I wrote it with piety and reverence, making sure to pray to our Trinitarian God: our Heavenly Father, Jesus of Nazareth, and the Spirit. The work is inspired by the Gospels and comes from my own relationship with Jesus, whom I love, serve, and worship as God.

I assure you that you were created out of love, in the Father's likeness, that you were captured by sin, but that Jesus of Nazareth has rescued you by the power of the cross and now you are impelled to respond with love and the sharing of the wondrous truth of the Gospel.

May you *experience* this through Esther's eyes and come into *relationship* with not only Jesus of Nazareth, but Mary Mother of God, St. Peter, St. Mary Magdalene, and all the Apostles and saints who are characters in the story.

However, this novel is not an exact copy of the depiction of the Gospels. As you will read in the Author's Note at the back of this book, I deviated from, extended, and/or reimagined the Gospels, by way of my intellect, insights, and creativity. I intend for it to be a meditation and, again, an *experience* for the reader; an experience that calls upon the many possibilities which history, combined with Catholic teaching and personal prayer, can give us. And since Jesus of Nazareth is the same yesterday, today, and tomorrow, I pray that in reading this historical fiction you find the current, outstanding love that the Father has for you. I hope you find a best friend in the famous Jesus. I pray that the Spirit works in you as you read, the way He worked in me as I wrote.

With Jesus, Mary, and Joseph,

Jacqueline St. Clare

Prologue

My mother, Hannah, favored me over my older sister, Aliza. I think as I was her youngest child, *Ima* thought I should be spoiled. I also think she hoped that my bright green eyes would catch me a rich husband.

Ima would wrap me in her mantle because it emanated her body heat. It smelled like Nazareth. Like soft warm bread, fresh wheat and barley, chickens, sheep, and mules. Like acacia, pine, cypress, and olive wood that rested in my father's carpenter shop. Like stone and mortar. Like burning olive oil, and even some of Aunt Miriam's aloe plant, all mixed in with the scent of human sweat and grime.

"Esther," Ima would say, leaning close to me so I could smell the watered wine on her breath. "Your name means 'star' in Persian. You are my star." She would pat my cheek with her calloused palm. "Shine brightly for Ima."

Now then, stand ready to witness the great marvel the LORD *is*
about to accomplish before your eyes.
1 SAMUEL 12:16

PART 1

THE
HIDDEN
LIFE

Chapter 1
4th Year of Our Lord

We see our sanctuary laid waste, our beauty, our glory.
The Gentiles have defiled them!

1 MACCABEES 2:12

The last time Ima carried me was the day that *Abba* died. I was only 4 years old when we lost him.

The day he died, our family was at the Temple in Jerusalem to celebrate the feast of *Passover*, as all pious Jews did yearly.

My little hands squeezed Ima's neck as she held me at her hip. We stood outside the southern wall of the Temple, close to the tomb of our prophetess, Huldah. Huldah's tomb was a grand structure by itself with a sort of miniature pyramid made of marble on top of it. Yet in comparison to the Temple, it was but one of many tiny crystals adorning a crown.

And it was the King of Kings who wore that crown. The very presence of *Elohim* resided in His Temple, most tangibly in the Holy of Holies. The Holy of Holies was the center of the Temple where only the high priest could enter once a year.

"Simon! Stay close to me," Ima called, taking a hand from my back so she could reach for my older brother. Simon gazed at the Temple. He was totally enamored by the pilgrims surrounding us, and in the marketplace behind us, singing and playing music, selling and buying goods. They rushed past us to walk up dozens of sand-toned stairs to squeeze through Huldah's gates. Worshippers roughly filed through the right gate, and those exiting the Temple took the left gate. I thought they looked like an army of ants, marching in and out of their hill.

"Ima! I want to go with Abba!" Simon insisted. His eyebrows raised in expectation as he stood on the tips of his toes. "I want to be a man and go to the Court of Israelites with him!"

"Your father is not in the Court of Israelites, Simon," Ima huffed. "He is…" She started mumbling to herself, "with his *companions*."

She said that last word with great dread.

Ima jolted backward as a body ran against her. I examined the crowds, my legs feeling sticky as they clasped Ima's hip.

From infants to hunched old men, all ages were present in Jerusalem. A variety of skin colors, pale to dark, revealed the faces of the Jewish people. They came mostly from the districts of Galilee and Phoenicia in the north of Palestine, and Judea, Perea, and then the tips of Philistia and Idumaea in the south. Even some Jewish Egyptians and Jewish Armenians were present, but Abba did not like those men. He called such men nomads who refused to live in the promised land of Israel, which Elohim had given to His people.

The women kept their dark locks tightly covered by their veils. The plain undyed veils of poor women were many, but the bright scarlet or violet of a rich woman's headdress stood out. Perhaps those bright silk veils belonged to the wives of merchants or the daughters of chief priests.

Men threw their small mantles, or *tallits*, lightly over their heads as was customary for prayer.

Tomorrow, when the feast began, fathers would take their sons to purchase an unblemished lamb for the Passover sacrifice. Next, they would take the lamb to the Court of Israelites, where women and *Gentiles* could not enter. There, the chief priests would sacrifice the animals.

Today, there were just normal sacrifices, be it pigeons or a goat. I could smell the heavy animal carcass, even with the thick aroma of incense, frankincense, cinnamon, and myrrh. I did my best to breathe through my mouth.

"I see him! I see him! It is Abba!" Simon called, jumping up, pointing at Huldah's Gates.

"I see him." Our cousin followed Simon, also bouncing excitedly. My aunt and other cousins stood near us.

"Where? I cannot see! I want to see Abba!" Aliza pouted. The 6-year-old was unable to see past her brother's waist.

I could not spot Abba, even at Ima's height. There were far too many in the crowd.

I adored my abba. His large hands, rough from years of carpentry would often pick me up and spin me around in the air. "My green-eyed beauty," he called me. His ink-black hair framed a handsome face made up of sharp curves. I loved the way he looked at Ima as if she were a pearl of great price. He would peck her on the cheek every morning before he started on his work.

I was so delighted the time Abba picked a poppy just for me when he came home from working in the neighboring city. It was such a small flower, but its bold red color was enchanting and may as well have been a ruby in my eyes.

"Out of my way!" A thundering voice boomed behind us.

Ima swung around to see two Roman soldiers who looked like mountains on their white horses. I gawked at them and their brilliant red capes. Each had a shield and spear at their sides, matching the glinting silver of their helmets. Their hard faces made me squirm, and I grasped Ima's tunic for comfort.

Ima hurried out of the way, ushering the children from the soldiers' path as they neared the Temple.

"Bastards," Ima murmured as they passed.

"Move it!" The soldiers yelled to the next person in their way. Jews stared, murmured, and glared darts at the soldiers who so closely approached the Temple.

"Hannah." I heard the deep, raspy voice of my uncle, Clopas, behind me. "Leave the Temple area. Go with my wife and children to the upper slopes of the city."

Ima swung around to face my uncle. His wife, Aunt Miriam, was beside him with her three sons.

"What is happening, Clopas? What is James doing?" Ima asked.

"My hope is that my brother does nothing." Uncle Clopas was a large man, just as my father was. His beard was black with a bald patch on his left jawline. "But he is strategizing with Judas the Galilean and the rest of those *Zealots*. I do not feel good about this, Hannah. Last thing we need is a repetition of Judas the Galilean's attack on Sepphoris."

A few years previous, when I was a baby and King Herod the Great died — or Herod the Beast, as my relatives called him — Judas the Galilean led a revolt on Nazareth's neighboring city, Sepphoris. Abba helped. Many Galilean revolutionaries died, and I was told that it was a wonder my father had not been killed. Several of our own Nazarenes had fallen when the governor of Syria quenched the revolt.

"If my husband was planning a revolt today, we would both know of it." I could feel the tense muscles beneath Ima's sweaty neck. I was partially cloaked within the veil that draped over her shoulders.

"Do you see how close the Romans are to the Temple? And with Passover starting tomorrow! Look at James and the rest of the men up there." Uncle Clopas threw his hand in the air. I still could not spot my father. "There is no need for a planned revolt. Those Romans take one step closer, then each man will act on impulse. We have experienced the likes of this too many times to count! *Get out*, Hannah."

Ima started to sputter. I slipped a bit down her hip so she lifted me higher. "Where are you going?"

"I am going to reason with my brother. I will join you, but first I must compel *your* husband to cease making trouble." Uncle Clopas' face fumed red. "James may think the rest of our nation does not care that the land does not belong to us, but I surely do. Only *I* will not act as a radical idiot! They are like bandits who will only be crucified by Rome."

Ima looked between Huldah's Gates and Uncle Clopas. Then her eyes fell on Aunt Miriam, who silently stared at her husband, mouth open wide.

"Get out, Hannah," Uncle Clopas repeated. "James and I will meet you shortly. Miriam," Uncle Clopas said, turning to his wife. "Take the children and leave."

Aunt Miriam pushed her sons toward the marketplace. After one last glance at Huldah's Gates, Ima followed Aunt Miriam, ushering the children through the thick crowds.

Clusters of people streamed against the back of Ima, brushing against my legs that dangled down her sides. Tambourines and silver horns played in celebration and people danced with liveliness. Men sauntered forward with their money bags so they could exchange their silver Roman *dinars* for *Hebrew shekels*.

Ima shifted me to her other hip and grabbed Aliza's hand. Simon was behind her and Aunt Miriam and her sons were at her left.

"Elohim be with them," Ima said to Aunt Miriam.

"Elohim is with the Messiah." Aunt Miriam's voice sounded as if a rock was clogging her throat. "It is the anointed one's duty to deliver us — not man's." Aunt Miriam shuffled forward, the soles of her feet maimed from accidentally stepping on hot coals as a child. It made her a slow walker and partially lame.

"*Miriam*," Ima said through gritted teeth. "I know you and Clopas find James rash. Yet James holds the greatest fervor for Elohim and seeks the establishment of Elohim's justice and righteousness. Something must be done while we await the Messiah. We cannot always bow our heads to Rome." Ima looked back. "Simon! Keep up, will you?" She turned back to Aunt Miriam. "Do not think I do not worry." Ima released a shaky breath as she hurried forward. "James threatens Rome. Anyone knows that no matter how much zeal he may have, Rome holds far surpassing power."

"Elohim has far surpassing power."

"I *know*, Miriam!" Ima huffed. My head grew dizzy as she jostled me up and down against the people, their yells louder than a legion's horses hooves pounding on the streets. "Do you think I have no faith? James and I have abounding faith. What would our father, Aaron, say to our submission to

24

idolaters? What would Joshua say? Without a doubt, they would both slay every last Roman; let them drown in their own blood. *Ohho!*" Ima ran into a petite woman. "Forgive me!" She raised me higher against her hip with one arm, pulling Aliza with her other hand. "Our village of Nazareth may be a petty inclusion of Israel, but dare I say it, Israel is a petty inclusion of Rome. Even if we are a village of peasants, at least we are starting to collaborate with other Galileans to stand against those who stain *our* land."

Aunt Miriam did not respond to Ima, but heaved, exerted from her effort to walk. Her sons held her arms to assist her.

Ima paid little notice to Aunt Miriam's struggle. "Even our Temple is defiled by Rome. They may let us worship the one true *El* there, but the late King Herod extended the Temple, modeling it after Roman architecture. Praise Elohim that king is now dead. But then again, Herod's scummy sons are now *tetrarchs.*"

"Ima! Look!"

Ima turned around to see Simon jabbing his finger toward the Temple. We stopped walking parallel to the Kidron Valley to see a clear view of the Temple and the thousands of pilgrims around it. The sun reflecting off the gold and white marble pricked my eyes.

"Elohim have mercy on us!" Ima almost dropped me. "They are throwing stones at the soldiers!"

Aliza started to cry at Ima's side, frightened by the loud noises.

I craned my neck to look at the Temple. From Huldah's Gates, men stood pelting rocks at the shiny helmets of Roman soldiers. Surely my father was there, though I could not see him. More men joined my father and his companions in their attack as the soldiers used their shields to block the falling rocks. Even more Romans on horses came forward. Leaping from their beasts, they started climbing the steps toward the men, their shields pressed in front of them. They drew their swords and screams of terror broke out.

"Do not look, Esther." Ima dug her fingers into my side. I released a cry as I saw men falling to the ground, injured. The musicians stopped and men scrambled. Animals were let loose, and the cages of birds were turned over.

"Abba is there!" Simon looked ready to run back to the Temple. "I see him!"

"No! Simon, come! Miriam, stop gawking! We need to keep the children safe — that is all the control we have." Ima turned and led us upward through the narrow streets.

People looked from the square windows and rooftops of their homes at the commotion down below.

Several ran past us, seeking to get as far from the Temple as possible.

"Hurry, children," Ima ordered, picking up her speed.

I strained my neck to look at Aunt Miriam behind us, struggling to keep the pace with her poor feet. Talk amongst the street of tightly packed houses increased as more people fled upward with us. Ima's veil flew off her head, but she made no effort to go retrieve it. Instead, her thick black hair scratched my face and neck.

Soon, Ima slowed her pace. Doubting herself, she said, "Perhaps we should return to Bethany. Syrus' house will be safe." Syrus' family had hosted mine for Passover since before I was born. Bethany was right next to Jerusalem, a perfect lodging spot for pilgrims.

"Clopas said to go to the upper city, Hannah," Aunt Miriam heaved.

Deciding to continue, Ima stepped forward, pushing through the crowd. Bodies jammed against me and I cried out.

"You do not start weeping, too," Ima whispered to me and then looked down at the sobbing Aliza. I let out no tears, despite the strain in my eyes.

Soon, we were on the wealthy side of the city. The houses were larger, though still tightly packed. People were everywhere because of the feast. Several fathers, mothers, and children ran upward to escape the chaos near the Temple, pushing others aside.

After crossing one more street, we reached the bordering wall of the city. Grass sprouted between the stones in the barrier. Ima slammed her back against the wall, slamming me along with her. I felt the tension vibrating through her body as she slid down the wall onto her bottom, and started to weep. She settled me on her lap, pulling Aliza onto her lap as well.

Aunt Miriam and her children followed and also sat against the city wall. Merchants passed us with camels and donkeys loaded with goods but they made way for a dozen Roman soldiers running toward the Temple, gripping their swords. They soon vanished between the lavish homes.

"James. James," Ima cried, roughly clutching Aliza and I. Aunt Miriam sat beside her, clearly troubled, but refused to shed a tear.

I shuddered with fear, although my young mind could not understand why or what was happening.

"Ima," Simon started. "Will Abba be all right?"

"Sit, son. Yes." She gulped. Her dark hair flowed freely with her missing veil. "Abba will be fine. Elohim is with him."

"But Ima...what if..." Simon spoke up.

"Hush. Enough from you. Be silent...and pray."

I squirmed in my mother's arms, wishing I could stand and walk, but she did not permit me. The sun was behind us, lowering in the cloudless sky so that the shadow of the wall totally covered us.

I was not sure how long we sat there, other than that it was a long time. I had the shadows of evening to look at and the wails from all around the city to listen to. Ima's sobs dimmed into a whimper.

"May each filthy soldier be struck down by Elohim!" a man yelled from his rooftop.

"Quiet! You will get us all killed too!" another man yelled from across the street. Others shouted, wept, and argued, giving my body no allowance for relaxation. I started to feel cold in the shade, so I burrowed closer to Ima.

"We...we should look for our husbands," Ima finally said.

Aunt Miriam slowly turned her head to Ima, her three sons close at her side. The small woman's mouth was open wide, as it nearly always was as if she was constantly pondering something. "Then...let us go."

"All danger should be passed by now," Ima whispered to Aunt Miriam as she scooched Aliza and me off of her. "If James and Clopas do not come for us by nightfall, we should return to Bethany."

"Walk to Bethany at night? Without our husbands?"

"Then we have to find someone. Syrus or some other man from our caravan has to still be in the city."

The women rose. Ima let me walk, though she tightly gripped my hand and Aliza's. We crossed the street.

Unlike the smiles of joy and wide eyes of excitement all pilgrims had when entering Jerusalem this week, their faces were now red with anger, their mouths twisted in grieving anguish. Curses howled from all about.

A woman looked out her door with timid curiosity. Men argued in the streets. Tears threatened my eyes as I saw a family of women and children walking up the street, sobbing.

As that family neared us, a figure pushed from behind them.

"Miriam! Praise Elohim!" Uncle Clopas stumbled past the family.

"Clopas!"

My uncle reached us, his beard glistening with the oil of sweat. His tallit loosely hung from his belt. His eyes were wide open like an infinitely long tunnel. "I found you. I found you. Praise Elohim, I found you," he whimpered like an abandoned animal. I had never seen him in such a state.

Aunt Miriam opened her short arms to embrace him, but he held up his hands.

"Stop! Do not. I have…" he looked at his hands. Bloody hands. Clopas swayed toward the limestone wall of a home.

"You are injured!" Aunt Miriam stepped toward him.

"No. No, *I* am not injured." His deep voice croaked as he fell to his knees, resting his head against the hard wall.

"Clopas," Ima breathed, bending down to his level. She pulled me with her, her hand gripping mine like a chain. "Where is James?"

"Is Abba coming?" Simon asked, stepping beside our uncle.

Uncle Clopas began to weep silently. His thick shoulders shook. He looked up at Ima, tears lining his cheeks. "You must forgive me, Hannah," he moaned. "I…could not…the Romans…they…killed…and James…" he gulped loudly. "He was one of the first ones stricken down."

Ima dropped my hand and almost threw herself at the wall. She screamed, banging her fist against the rough surface.

"Abba is dead?" Simon cried.

"Abba?"

"Uncle James?"

The other children added in their cries.

My lips quivered. They were mourning. I knew what mourning was. I had seen it on the face of Abba when his own father, Jacob, died. I had seen the tears and wails from neighbors in Nazareth when a son died of fever or a daughter was snatched by a Roman soldier. I had seen intense mourning when passing Golgotha, on the outskirts of Jerusalem; criminals hanging from trees as their families sobbed beneath them.

Yet this was quite different. I was no longer an observer.

Tears traveled down my face, creating a soppy waterfall before my vision. *Abba.*

Perhaps I cried simply because all of my relatives cried, but I recognized the despair in my mother's voice and the brokenness in my uncle's hunched figure. Aunt Miriam covered her face with her hands, finally weeping, herself.

Abba was not with us, and I missed him. I wanted him to come back to us as Uncle Clopas had.

A pair of Roman soldiers walked down the street toward us, their backs straight with purpose and feet strutting in a perfect line. We all stooped on the ground in misery as they passed us without even glancing our way.

I turned my whole body to stare at them as they walked further down the street. Abba hated those men.

Further comprehension dawned upon me as Simon uttered words of anger. "Abba…Romans…dead."

28

I took in a quick breath. Abba was in the land of the dead now; in *Sheol*. Because of those Romans, I was fatherless.

Chapter 2
5th Year of Our Lord

Father of the fatherless, defender of widows —
God in his holy abode.
PSALMS 68:6

I leaned over a steaming bowl of purple-toned beets, allowing the heat to wash over my cheeks and the sweet smell to enter my nostrils. I blew out a breath, savoring the warmth. It had been a cool day in late fall, and thankfully the rain had left us for the evening. All of the boys who were old enough went to work in the trade.

"Esther, get your face out of our supper!" Ima snapped as she filled a wooden platter with goat cheese. She had pretty eyes like mine but hers were a bright brown color. "Do you wish to make us all unclean?" Her eyes were between her wide forehead and sharp nose.

I leaned back from the food being prepared in the courtyard. Aunt Miriam had just finished reheating our leftovers of a fattened sheep we feasted upon earlier that week for the *Feast of Tabernacles.* I licked my lips, eager for the taste of meat as Aunt Miriam sprinkled salt upon it and Aliza added olives to a leftover dip.

"We get to feast all week!" I exclaimed, slapping my hands on my thighs. "Blessed be the name of *Adonai.*" I leaned back to look upward at the evening sky. I sucked in a deep breath. "From now and for…"

"Such provisions are almost finished, young one," Ima said. My sentences were usually cut off as I was considered too dramatic for a 5-year-old.

"Joses always takes too much lamb," Aliza complained about her cousin as she slapped her hands together. "I bet he will finish what is left before I have a chance to take a bite!"

"The men need more meat," Ima told her. "Is that not right, Miriam?" She called over her shoulder to Aunt Miriam who was now meticulously sprinkling the lamb with diced parsley. Ima then turned back to Aliza and me. "Your uncles, brother, and cousins work in the trade all day. Most of those days are spent building Sepphoris. They work hard so we can afford to share a fattened sheep with the villagers." The village had about fifteen families.

Understandably, Abba's death was terrible for my family. My mother was a widow, so her husband's brother, Uncle Clopas, adopted us, as was common. Simon, Aliza, and I were under the care of Uncle Clopas as if he was our father, though he was not very skilled at fatherhood. He was a rough, practical man. Not particularly sensitive. And certainly not loving, let alone amiable.

Aunt Miriam was sweet, but she was often set in her own particular and meticulous ways.

Ima raised us as most Jewish Galilean mothers did. She taught us the fundamental scriptures, the purity laws, how to work, how to follow the Sabbath regulations, how to pray, and how to treat others kindly. Simon, because he was a boy, got to study several days a week with *Rabbi* in the synagogue. He and all my male cousins did so, along with several other boys from the village. Of course, some farming families could not afford to let their young boys go to the synagogue at all, so their sons started working the trade as soon as they could walk.

When older boys became men at the age of twelve, they would either take on the family trade full time or become a scholar. But no one in little Nazareth had ever been known to do the latter. Our family were craftsmen of wood and stone, working as masons, builders, and carpenters.

"I wish I could study the scriptures," I would tell Ima. Along with the rest of the village I would listen to Rabbi speak and read the Torah on the Sabbath day in the synagogue. I would also hear my male relatives speak of the scriptures, and I was intrigued by their large words which were both fascinating and poetic; words like "firmament" and "alabaster;" "ravished" and "futility."

Ima just chuckled at my desire. "You must study what it is to be a daughter." She would point a finger at me. "So that you may study what it is to be a wife. And a mother who will care for many children. Remember that she who is without children is like one dead."

If I still complained to her, she would add, "Besides, even men do not need to be scholars to know the Word of Elohim. We all must know the Word so we may follow the law of Moses given by Elohim. That is how we live fruitful lives. *And*," she would continue, "that is why we turn from the presence of Samaritans, Romans, and any Gentile. Even our own blood if they are sinful or unclean."

Ima found one woman in particular to be sinful and deserving of foul treatment: my aunt, Mary. Being only a few years old, I did not know the details of Aunt Mary's sinfulness; only that she had many secret sins, especially the one regarding her pregnancy and her son, Jesus.

I was so young when Jesus and I first met, and the two of us lived in the same house for so long, that it felt like He was always a part of my family. Jesus, His father Joseph, and mother Mary were originally from Nazareth but lived several years in Egypt before returning to their home village. Which they did when I was 5. Jesus and I were the same age.

He was my closest friend.

I glanced at Aunt Mary working quietly behind us, drying out roasted chickpeas about three hands from the bedrock wall. Close to her was the awning of the carpenter shop. Between the shop and the *traklin* was Aunt Miriam's prized aloe plant.

Aunt Mary hardly spoke to anyone and few spoke to her, especially not Ima.

Catching me watching her, Aunt Mary smiled. I just stared back at her, blowing up my cheeks with air. Her eyelashes swept the tips of her cheekbones as she arranged the roasted chickpeas on a tray. She sat on her heels and her brown face was framed by a cream-colored veil that was tied tightly down her back.

"Ima!" Little Jesus hurried over to Aunt Mary from under the awning of the carpenter shop, which took up nearly a fourth of the small courtyard on the west wall. The courtyard was already tightly packed, and this was with only the women and children home.

Jesus squeezed behind one of our wandering chickens to get to Aunt Mary. Mother and son's faces were eye level. Jesus presented a small block of wood to His mother. "It is finished," He said.

"It *is* finished," Aunt Mary said, accepting the block of wood from Jesus so she might admire it. She placed a light hand on Jesus' shoulder, covered by His shapeless, stone-toned tunic. "You will show Abba your work when he comes home. He will be well pleased with you, my son." She returned the wood to Jesus.

"Esther, did you see?" Jesus turned toward me. I left my post by my mother to go to Him, meeting in the center of the courtyard. "Feel how smooth it is!" Jesus thrust the piece of wood forward for me to hold. I took it from Him and let my fingers glide over its surface.

Uncle Joseph had begun to assign small tasks to Jesus to train Him whenever He returned home from studying at the synagogue, in the early afternoon.

I held the piece of wood to my cheek, making a sound of awe. Jesus laughed, delighted by my appreciation. His hair, which was a dark, burnished color — almost the shade of a walnut — shot up from all directions. When there was more sunlight, his hair would even have hints of auburn in it. There was something forthright about His face. Plain, but not to the point of being artless.

"That is lamb I smell, is it not?" Uncle Joseph's voice carried into the courtyard. I turned around.

"Abba!" Jesus cried.

"As every house in the village is cooking it," Ima said, not looking up from her work as my male relatives walked through the open door. She stood, taking the platter of goat's cheese and kicked a chicken aside as she passed it. It squawked and rustled its feathers. Ima disappeared into the traklin where we ate our meals during the rainy season.

"Show Uncle Joseph, Jesus!" I returned the wood to Him.

Jesus happily gave the wood to His father.

Uncle Joseph had large, rough hands, just like my abba and Uncle Clopas. I thought that Uncle Joseph looked much more like Abba than Uncle Clopas did. Joseph had the same inky black hair and small beard as Abba, but hints of gray dotted Uncle Joseph's hairs. His arms could stretch to the length of an ox's yoke.

While Abba and Uncle Joseph's hair had a shine to it, Uncle Clopas had roughly textured hair, almost like wool.

Turning the wood in his hands, Uncle Joseph looked at his son. "Well done, Jesus. You are a natural at sanding."

"It once was coarse, but now it is smooth!" Jesus exclaimed, gazing eagerly at His father.

"And it is the same piece of wood," Uncle Joseph said, tapping it. "But with the hand of a carpenter, the same wood can shift from hard to soft."

"My Father in Heaven does that," Jesus said, gazing upward at Uncle Joseph. "He wants to take hearts of stone and make them hearts of flesh!"

"The prophet Ezekiel," Uncle Joseph said slowly with a grin. He gazed proudly at Jesus. "Has Rabbi already been reading the prophet's writings to you?" He rustled his son's hair.

"Your son is a little turtledove, we know it," Uncle Clopas grunted as he yanked off his satchel and plopped it on the compacted dirt ground by the many people who visited the court. "James! Take Balaam to the stable. Joses, help him unload the ass."

"But I had to do that yester..." Cousin Joses began to complain, but one hard glare from his father silenced him. Sighing, Joses followed his brother James, who guided our donkey across the small court. Uncle Joseph, Jesus, and I had to dodge out of the way so that we would not get run over.

Cousin Joses poked Aliza's head as he passed her, still by the oven with Aunt Miriam.

"Joses!" Aliza cried in fury.

Cousin Joses quickly disappeared into the inner stable before an adult could scold him.

"How were your studies today, Jesus?" Uncle Joseph asked, looking down at his son. His hair was thick with sweat from the day's work.

"Rabbi taught me what My Father in Heaven says to His people. That if you go out to war against your enemies and see horsemen and chariots, and the numbers of the enemy's army greater than yours, you shall not fear them. Because Adonai your El, who brought you out of the land of Egypt, is with you."

"You have nearly finished memorizing the Torah, then?"

"Yes! And Rabbi says that next we will read the writings of the prophet Samuel. And how My Father in Heaven chose David to be king."

"Joseph!" Uncle Clopas barked, settling his tools from the day's work in the carpenter shop. "I tell you, stop your son from calling Elohim His father!" Clopas waved a chisel in the air. The metal saw, ax, and pliers on the table glinted in the fading daylight.

"Jeremiah. Thus says Adonai, 'You shall call Me, my father,'" Uncle Joseph quoted, crossing his arms as he turned toward his brother.

"Adonai has reigned, let the people be angry. He that sits on the cherubim, let the earth be moved." Uncle Clopas rattled the wooden table with his large hand for effect. "We are sons of Abraham, Isaac, and Jacob. Adonai is their El and our El. Not our Father."

I just stood with my hands clasped behind my back, not understanding all of their words. Still, words like "chariots" and "cherubim" intrigued me.

"All of you wash up now," Ima commanded, re-entering the courtyard. She almost ran into Aunt Mary by the traklin entranceway. "Simon, see that the chickens are back in the stable." The traklin and stable doors were at the rear wall of the court. Steps leading to the rooftop were nestled between the doors. "Aliza, bring the rest of the food inside. Mary, get out of the way! Must you always be a nuisance?"

Aunt Mary walked across the back wall, past the doorway closest to the oven. It was a small room where she, Uncle Joseph, and Jesus slept. The little room was like their own private home.

Suddenly, my feet lifted off the ground. I squealed in delight. Uncle Joseph lifted me in the air and spun me around. He laughed, deep as a bass drum. I put my hand around his sturdy, hairy neck.

"Joseph!" Uncle Clopas barked from within the traklin. "Get in now. I am hungry as a wolf."

"And he sounds like a wolf," Uncle Joseph whispered good-naturedly as he set me down.

That night we had supper with our usual leisure. Wine was passed around freely, and the lamb went quickly. Cousin Joses did, in fact, steal a piece of lamb from Aliza, but Ima caught him and made him give it back. Lit clay oil lamps rested on the matted floor which our supper also rested on. Only one glowing lamp sat on the shelf fastened into the wall — we tried to conserve our fuel during the dark, cool months.

As the adults clustered on half of the ground, we children were on the other. Sometimes, we simply listened to our parents' talk. Sometimes we conversed with them. Other times — the times that I found most entertaining — were when we children conversed with each other.

"We saw Herod today!" Cousin Jude reported, licking his fingers, satisfied with his meal.

"I told you, before, Jude, seeing Herod is not a good thing!" Simon nudged his cousin with his elbow.

"We did not see *him*. We only saw his guards and slaves pass." Cousin Joses drank his watered wine from a wooden cup as if he were a grown man feasting.

"Herod *was* there, though," Jude persisted. "Probably riding a stallion between the clusters of guards."

"I suppose Herod wears a flowing purple cloak!" I smiled in contemplation, leaning backward. "Some say he has a dozen gold rings on his fingers!" The voices of others drowned my words. Jesus at least acknowledged me with the turn of His head and a smile.

"So that no zealous Jews would bother him," Cousin Jude said.

"So that *no* Jews would bother him. Zealous or not. We are all angry," Simon corrected him, his hands curled into fists.

"I thought Herod was a Jew," Aliza said, the muscles in her freckled face squeezing together in thought.

"He *is*, Aliza." Cousin Joses' voice bolted in superiority. "But Abba says he is more Roman than Jew."

"That is what our abba would say." Simon sounded resigned.

"But my abba said your abba was foolish." Cousin Joses turned and glared at Simon.

"Stop it!" Aliza cried. "I do not like it when you talk about him."

"My abba was brave!" Simon yelled, quickly standing up. His aim must have been to show strength with his position, but he almost fell over from his quick move.

"Simon, sit down," Ima commanded.

"Joses has insulted Abba," Simon complained, still standing, fists closed in tight balls.

Even in the dim lighting I could see Ima's face turn red. "Joses…" I could hear a growl nearly rumbling in Ima's voice.

"I will discipline my own sons," Clopas said. His normal tone of voice always sounded perturbed. "You discipline your own."

Ima's lips pressed together in fury. "Simon, I told you to sit back down," she said at last.

Simon obeyed but leaned over toward us to whisper, "It is the vile Romans who are at fault. For everything. Including Abba's death. I hate them!"

"Everyone hates the Romans. You are not a true son of Israel if you do not," Cousin Joses said, peering at the lot of us as if in challenge.

"I hate them," Aliza affirmed.

"As do I!" Cousin Jude declared.

"As do I," I said. After all, they killed Abba.

"James?" Cousin Joses looked at his brother, who had been silently rolling an olive in his hand for nearly the entire meal.

"I hate them," Cousin James said, to Cousin Joses' obvious satisfaction.

"I do not hate them." Jesus spoke plainly.

All eyes looked on Him harshly. Mine were blank with wonder.

"You *must* hate them." Aliza nearly pouted as she looked at Jesus through her thin eyes. "Elohim hates them."

"He is just a little boy who spent too much time in Egypt," Cousin Joses said, probably mimicking what he had heard his father say.

"You did live in a land of idolaters." Simon nodded his head in agreement.

"Ima taught us," I started. "That Elohim says we must not trust in wood or stone idols because they cannot hear or see or talk." I spoke in a loud voice, that was probably as loud as Simon's whisper. Though I was proud I had retained the information, no one seemed to pay attention to my display of knowledge.

As the others kept speaking, Jesus turned to me. "I pray with Abba and Ima. For idolaters to turn to My Father in Heaven."

I frowned. The Jews were not supposed to want goodness for idolaters, for they did not worship Elohim.

My eyebrows furrowed as I thought of Jesus' words. Anger boiled in my belly as I thought of the Romans striking down my father.

"I hate them," I repeated in a whisper. Jesus was the only one who heard. He looked at me with an expression that I could not define.

Chapter 3

7th Year of Our Lord

When I found your words, I devoured them;
your words were my joy, the happiness of my heart...
JEREMIAH 15:16

"Martha and Mary will arrive after the Sabbath!" Aliza exclaimed, as we gathered near the oven with Ima and our aunts. The chickens in the courtyard pecked and strutted behind us, their afternoon bawks loud as always.

Syrus of Bethany, Martha and Mary's father, had a great manor house on the outskirts of their village. It was a marvel to me. Since my earliest years, Martha and Mary were my beloved friends, though I saw them as exotic princesses. Indeed, a rich household from Bethany visiting a poor Nazarene home made an odd contrast and confounded many.

I sat on my heels, bouncing with excitement. "Do you think they will bring us a gift the way they did last time?"

Aliza and I exchanged looks of anticipation.

"Ah!" Ima gasped as she lifted the bread from the surface of the domed oven. "Hot! Hot! Hot!" She dropped it beside the other rounded loaves. We had made extra that day, since we would not be able to do any work after sundown, when the Sabbath began, through sundown tomorrow.

Ima put her fingers to her mouth and mumbled incoherently.

I could hardly pay attention to anyone. Martha and Mary would arrive in a mere couple of days! Last time they came they brought the finest and smoothest butter I had ever seen, touched, or tasted. The rich family brought other gifts for us, such as costly oil and fine olive wood from their own trees.

Our family was able to visit Syrus' family once a year when we traveled to Jerusalem for the feast of Passover. They would graciously host us and many other inhabitants of Nazareth and Cana.

They also had a large home in Magdala, near the Sea of Galilee. They would often visit relatives there and do business. Nazareth was the village they stopped in on their way north. Many children from my village asked me why such an affluent family from Bethany would stay with us of all people. Would it not be more reasonable for them to stay in Herod's rich city of Sepphoris, or at least set up their own camp in the outskirts of these towns?

"Perhaps that makes sense," I would tell them, imitating what Simon would say. "But Syrus is like our brother, and we are thus privileged with his presence."

Abba was the true reason for the friendship between our families. Whenever we asked Ima about how the friendship came about, she would tell us the same thing:

"Our people have always been oppressed, but Elohim has always come to our deliverance. Even in our own time, Elohim will deliver us. A savior shall come forth. He will be a second Moses. He will be a warrior like Joshua. He will be a messiah — an anointed one — like King David and King Cyrus — only greater. Elijah will come again and prepare the way for him. He will restore Israel, and this time we will have an everlasting kingdom and he will be our king. Our dominion shall endure from all generations, as was promised to our father Abraham. Rome will be beneath our heel. The land which Adonai promised us will be ours!"

Simon especially would take in these words with great interest.

I was more eager to hear about my father. "What does this have to do with Abba?"

"Your father was a great man. He understood what it meant to be a son of Israel and he took his duty as a Jew with utmost seriousness. See, many Jews have forgotten or dismissed what it is to be sons of Abraham. They do not worship Elohim according to the law of Moses. Rome is our ruler, and our leaders, like Herod, are influenced by the Gentiles. Even our chief priests in Jerusalem, the *Sadducees*, and some *Pharisees* are under the influence of Rome. They have turned from Elohim. Your father hated every rich Sadducee and every aristocratic Jew.

"'If he is rich,' your father would say, 'then he is to be struck down.' Abba believed every rich person has no zeal for Elohim. Only the poor do, like us, who have not indulged in the sins of Gentiles."

"But Martha and Mary are rich. Will they be struck down?" Aliza worried.

"Hush," Ima would say. "Your father believed this to be true, but then he met Syrus of Bethany. When James and Syrus became friends, your father's opinion of the rich changed. He claimed that most rich men were still vile and heinous, but there *were* men, like Syrus, who were commendable and zealous."

"But *how* did they become friends? How did the rich Syrus come across our poor family?" Simon plodded, his face muscles firm.

Every time he asked, Ima would lift her shoulders. "It was the will of Elohim."

That was always Ima's answer and that answer never changed. It did not bother me the way it bothered Simon. I was simply pleased to be friends with Martha and Mary.

"Get the wine from our storage caves, girls," Ima said to Aliza and myself. "Best get the almonds as well."

Aliza lit a small clay oil lamp from the fire beneath the oven and I fetched a new wineskin. I felt the straw crunch under my feet as I entered the cave-like structure of our stable. I patted our donkey, Balaam.

Two circular openings in the ground led to our storage caves. The cave to the left was for wood and stone carpentry supplies. The other — where I was allowed — was for food storage.

It was a bit of a jump to get down into the storage, but I was the smallest of the children and this was my duty. I was the child who entered the cave for supplies, and the larger children helped lift me out. As Aliza was ready to do after I fetched food and drink. She reached out a hand.

Just as Aliza lifted me up, Cousin Joses ran into the stable, his eyes bigger than Balaam's. "They have arrived! They are here!"

"Careful that you do not knock over our jars!" Aliza glared upward at our cousin.

"Who has arrived?" On my hands and knees, I panted from the work of climbing out of the cave.

"Lazarus! He is here. Syrus' family!" Cousin Joses ran back out.

My eyes met Aliza's. "Martha and Mary!" We exclaimed in unison.

"Quickly, girls," Ima whispered, bending into the doorway. "Syrus and his family have arrived! And far too early. Quickly! Bring out the provisions. We will need to make do."

Ima did not let us greet, let alone play with, our friends from Bethany, but insisted that Aliza and I help with our remaining Sabbath preparations.

Our guests gathered with the men in the courtyard and on the rooftop. Servants and slaves brought in provisions. We women worked with Ima in the traklin to finish preparing the meal.

A couple of Syrus' servants tried entering the traklin, but Ima told them to wait. I thought she liked being able to order them around.

After shaking out the mats we reclined on while eating, I saw Aunt Mary take the two candlesticks, hidden behind pots and jars of cooking utensils and spices, off the shelf of a sidewall.

Ima snatched the candlesticks from Aunt Mary and exhaled loudly as she plopped them on the ground, which served as our table.

I passed back and forth from the open door to the courtyard, and saw Martha and Mary. Mary looked ready to come inside and greet us, but her elder sister, Martha, held her back.

The sisters had two siblings. Lazarus, of course, their older brother, who was the same age as my brother Simon. He was kind but he scared me because he was very tall.

Then, there was Mara.

Although 6-year-old Mara was the youngest sibling, she scared me even more than Lazarus did. Mara's real name was Mary, the same as her older sister, but in Hebrew, "mara" is to be disobedient, rebellious, or bitter. Known for being all three — disobedient, rebellious, and bitter — the youngest Mary was thus called "Mara."

Ignoring her, I could think only of Martha and Mary. My ears ached from the excitement of hearing our guests' voices just outside of the room. "Ima! May we greet them now?"

"You may. Be sure you are all inside and ready for the Sabbath meal when the sun sets."

Aliza and I squealed with delight.

"If the Sabbath was not almost here, we would be able to run around in the dark tonight! I like that game where we chase and scare each other at night," Aliza said. Our feet pattered on the ground as we entered the courtyard.

It was so near sunset, my eyes easily adjusted to the light of the outdoors. This was the season of the late rains, when winter was ending and the sun finally shined frequently. The sky was clear, but of course I could not see the sun past the walls of the courtyard. Thankfully, I could not feel the heavy wind either. The wheat and barley harvest were upon us and the days would only get hotter from here on out.

"Aliza!" I whined as I realized that she was out of eyesight. She always went out to play without waiting for me!

I looked behind at the roof and saw two guards. One looked at the family gathered below and one at the length of the village that stretched out beyond the house. I sucked in a breath when I saw the swords roped to the guards' sides.

I surveyed the small courtyard, but did not see Martha, Mary, or Aliza. Bodies bunched together, elbows touching.

Aunt Miriam was with Syrus' wife, Eucharia, instructing the servants where to place what. Syrus and the men were in the center of the court, slapping each other's backs in greeting. Syrus' brother Simon—a Pharisee—and a couple of nephews, traveled with them. They were all heading to visit family in Magdala.

I stared at my brother Simon and at Jesus, who were speaking to Lazarus. Lazarus was a younger image of his father with his light brown hair that would wave in the breeze.

Mara stood by herself inside the carpenter shop. Uncle Clopas' shop! She scanned the shop with narrowed eyes. Her sharp eyebrows seemed permanently lowered toward her nose, yet her head was only a hand taller than the table itself!

My fear of the many people dissolved immediately when Aliza returned from the village with Martha and Mary at her side. The two sisters had olive-colored skin like the overflow of olives that piled on their father's property. Martha's eyebrows were sharp like Mara's but had a much more amiable curve to them, and Mary had eyebrows nearly as thin as a blade of grass. I could only see hints of their hair, as it was covered by their grey-blue veils, fit and durable for travel. Mary's hair was light, contrasting Martha's darker brown color.

Their eyes widened when they saw me. We ran to each other and Martha engulfed me in her arms. She kissed my cheeks. All of us girls giggled as Mary and Aliza wrapped their arms around us, joining in a big embrace.

"All of the fathers, mothers, and children were in the street! Staring and waving at us," Mary told me, looking back over her shoulder at the door. I saw a couple of Nazarene children peering into our doorway. They darted out of sight at our glance.

"They are envious of us, Mary," I said, tilting my head to the side. "That we have such wealthy friends. And behold! You are beautiful to look at."

Perhaps *I* was envious of her. The same age as I was, her soft skin did not have one hint of dirt or grime. She stood straight, as if she was the woman of our household. Though she was wearing plain clothes for traveling purposes, her tunic was nicer than any person's in our village.

"Abba paid your neighbors to see to our camels, Esther," Martha said. "I asked Mother and she said you would be old enough to try riding a camel. But only for a quick moment, she said. And I must be on it with you."

I gasped in delight. "Can we now?"

"Now? O Abraham, no. It is time for the Sabbath," Martha said, looking at the sky as a couple of birds flew over. She was Aliza's age, but much more mature.

"*I* already rode a camel." Aliza turned to me, proudly.

"Why are you here so early?" I asked the sisters, ignoring Aliza.

"Our caravan leader and guards thought the heavy winds would limit our travel," Martha explained. "But they did not."

"A path and a way will there be, and it will be called the holy way; the unclean will not pass over it, and this will be unto you a straight way, so that fools will not err therein," Mary said slowly and reverently.

I looked at her with awe — she spoke perfect Hebrew. I understood it but could not comprehend the meaning of the poetic words.

"Pride goes before destruction, and the spirit is lifted up before a fall," Martha said, raising her brows at her sister. Glancing back at Aliza and me, she said, "Mary has begun reading the scriptures and is using every opportunity to show it."

"I am not! Shall I explain to you how the prophet Isaiah —"

"You see her?" Martha raised her hands at Aliza and myself. "Silence yourself, Mary, before you make a fool of —"

"Girls!" Simon cried, interrupting Martha.

She looked over, her face turning red. She avoided looking him in the eye as he and the boys stood a short distance from us.

I noticed the adults already convening inside the traklin.

"Ima says it is time to come in for the Sabbath meal," Simon continued.

"Come on, now. Go inside," Cousin Joses yelled, pleased to give an order.

"You are not our father!" Aliza pursed her lips.

"Children come inside. Quickly now," Ima called.

Jesus was the first to hurry on inside.

"Mara, come," Lazarus called to his sister, who still loitered inside the carpenter shop.

"I will come when I see fit," Mara's young, high-pitched voice called. Without looking his way, she picked a wooden drill off the worktable and rolled it in her small hands.

"That is not yours!" Simon strode toward her.

"Mara, leave it be. Come," Lazarus repeated, stepping beside Simon and gazing into the dark shadows of the shop. "Go on in. I will get Mara." Lazarus looked at the rest of us. He crossed his arms and sternly looked down at his disobedient sister.

We obeyed the eldest boy and moved toward the traklin entrance. Lamplight poured from the door and laughter and chatter beckoned us.

"Mara!" Eucharia almost collided with me. She passed us, reached for her daughter in the shop, and grabbed her by the ear, pulling her out from beneath the awning. "Be thankful Elohim has not struck you down on the spot for toying on the verge of the Sabbath! Stop staring, children," she said as she passed us. "Get inside."

Rabbi joined us that night for the Sabbath meal. Surely because of our visitors, but also because of his favorite pupil, Jesus. After we ate, resting followed. Tomorrow would consist of even more resting.

That night, the men spoke within the traklin while the women and children were lounging in the main sleeping room. I could hear the men's excited murmurs.

"Where is Mara?" Aliza whispered, leaning toward Martha and Mary as we sat on our bundles of pallets. A fine silk blanket that Martha brought rested over Aliza's and my laps.

"She is supposed to be on the rooftop." Martha sighed, waving her hand in careless dismissal.

Her long brown curls tumbled down her back. They shined slightly in the very dim light, and I could not stop admiring them. I touched my hair, feeling the knots in it. I would have asked Martha to brush it for me if it were not the Sabbath.

"On the rooftop?" Aliza leaned back against the cool mudbrick wall. "It is far too cold to be up there at this hour."

"Mara will do anything that is contrary to normal behavior," Martha explained. "One of the guards is probably keeping an eye on her to ensure she does not wander around at night."

"Would she really do that?" I asked, putting fingers to my mouth. How could such a young girl be so defiant?

"She would." Mary nodded her head vigorously.

"Father once had her locked in her room," Martha said. She glanced at her mother, Eucharia, to ensure she did not hear her daughter's conversation. "She is a hard one to control and discipline. I am thankful she is on the roof. Let her stay up there, far from us. We will not miss her presence."

"…Esther was the one who was chosen…"

My head snapped toward the traklin door. *Esther.* The men were talking about me?

I looked back at the other girls. Was I the only one who heard my name being mentioned?

"Father might just leave Mara at our house in Magdala so that she is far away from us..." Martha continued.

"Esther...requested several banquets...her courage...asking the king..." The men said my name again!

"I am going to listen to the men speak." I informed them of my decision. Aliza made a sour face as the sisters looked at me curiously.

I bit my lip. Perhaps I should not if they disapproved.

"I have done so before," Martha told Aliza, and then looked at me.

"As have I," Mary said. "I do not always understand their conversation, but I listen nonetheless."

"You cannot go in the room!" Aliza cried loudly.

"Hush!" Martha said. "We will not go into the room. We will simply listen by the doorway. There is no impropriety in that."

"It is boring," Aliza complained.

"Then you do not need to join us." I smiled at Aliza, pleased that Martha and Mary liked my idea.

We lined up against the wall by the door and sat down.

Eucharia was speaking to Ima, Aunt Miriam, and Aunt Mary. Ima looked over at us with her usual sharp expression, yet she did not scold us. She only shook her head slightly, dismissing the silly ways of children.

"Adonai saved His people and delivered us from all these evils," Rabbi said, his voice sounding as if he spoke through his nose.

"If she was not a woman, Esther would have saved her people much sooner." That must have been Martha and Mary's uncle, Simon the Pharisee. "Fear held her back. She was fragile and weak, fainting at the thought of confronting a king."

"But did she not eventually confront him?" Uncle Joseph said. "And that led to the deliverance of our people."

Somewhat disappointed, I realized that it was not me they spoke of. They spoke of the great Queen Esther of Persia. Centuries ago, when our people were threatened by massacre under the king, Queen Esther was ushered by her cousin Mordecai to speak to the king and beg the salvation of the Jews. It took Esther several attempts to request that her people, the Jews, be left unharmed, for she was afraid of the king's fury. Yet she finally spoke to the king and it was declared that her people would be safe.

"No surprise that it was a man who made Esther do it. I tell you, we would have been delivered sooner if it was a man doing the task."

My mouth suddenly felt sour. I thought Esther was a beloved character. Not one looked upon as weak!

"Is this truly the case?" I heard Jesus' young voice. It was not loud, but it was very clear. "Did the leaders of our people not have the choice to return to My Father when he sent them judges? Or when he sent them the prophets?"

"Joseph, this is indeed a terrible habit you have taught the boy," Uncle Clopas' voice growled. "His language is far too familiar with Elohim, He who is not to be called by His holy name."

"Surely, Elohim is a better father than any of us," Uncle Joseph challenged.

"You think that since Jesus is an intelligent child, He can speak as He likes. Knowledge of the scriptures does not grant Him the right to preach what He sees fit."

"Come now, Clopas," Syrus said. "Jesus is...what is it? Seven years? He is harmless. We must not restrain Him in His search for knowledge and justice. What do you say, Rabbi?"

My head rested against the cool wall as I listened, strangely entranced.

"I say that Adonai is referred to as many things. Yes, He is a father, but He is also compared to a mother. Even as a husband. He is a builder, a maker, and it is we, the people Israel who have been made by Him and are espoused to Him."

"We are builders!" my young brother, Simon, exclaimed. "Carpenters!"

"And you must remember that Adonai designed you before you designed anything," Rabbi said gently.

I followed the conversation well.

"We stray from my point," Syrus cut in. "Be it Esther or Mordecai, Elohim is the wonderworker. No man can work wonders by his own authority."

"May I ask a question?" Lazarus said in a much deeper voice than I had last remembered.

"Speak, Son."

"By whose authority do the Zealots act?"

Quietude came, and I rubbed my fingers on the compacted dirt ground beneath me. Perhaps I stopped following the conversation.

"They...they say by Elohim's," Syrus said.

"They do! They do act by Elohim!" My brother Simon spoke excitedly.

"Calm yourself, Simon," Uncle Clopas warned. "Remember you are but a child and do not understand such things."

"If they are under the authority of Adonai, then why do they all die?" Lazarus continued.

Aliza made exaggerated sighs, obviously telling us she was bored. How could she be? It was like watching a brawl, but with my ears alone!

"They do not all die, Lazarus," Syrus explained.

"Indeed, they are more triumphant than you would think," Simon the Pharisee said.

"Besides, did not the prophets also die?" Syrus added.

"Careful how you speak, Syrus," Rabbi interrupted. "It was Adonai who called Samuel. It was Adonai who chose the young Jeremiah. It was Adonai who revealed Himself to Isaiah. The Zealots are radical rebels, not chosen prophets of Elohim. Think! Even Elijah was taken to Heaven on a chariot of fire and will return. He was not crucified as a criminal."

"I do not think Zealots are criminals," Syrus said slowly.

"In the eyes of Rome, they are," Uncle Clopas curtly responded.

"Only if they become bandits, pillaging rich Jews and Romans," Syrus said. "Zeal for our land and people warrants no condemnation."

Aliza grew bored. "I am leaving!"

"Then leave," I said, not giving her a glance. Turning to Mary, I asked, "Do you study such things?"

"Yes!" she whispered. "I do. I do love studying the prophet Elijah."

I looked at her as if she was a rabbi. Were such interesting discussions a result of studying the scriptures?

There was something beautiful about them; the Torah and the writings of the prophets; the psalms. The Word of Adonai was entrancing. It was complicated and mysterious, and I wanted to solve the mystery.

Chapter 4
11th Year of Our Lord

Do you have daughters?
Keep them chaste, and do not be indulgent to them.
BEN SIRA 7:24

We were traveling from the pale sandy mountains of Judea to return home to the green hills of Galilee. Passover was behind us, but we were still celebrating the lengthy *Feast of Unleavened Bread*. In total, our pilgrimage took two weeks — most of that travel — but I thought they were the most enjoyable days of the year. Our caravan traveled from Jerusalem along a major road that cleverly avoided Samaria by going around it. Thus, we were on the east side of the country, traveling close to the Jordan River.

Soon, we Nazarenes and other western inhabitants of Galilee would curve to the left, and those who lived in the north, by the Sea of Galilee, would continue straight toward Tiberias.

Our caravan had a Judean treasure traveling with us: The household of Syrus of Bethany. Syrus had hosted us for the feast and was now journeying north toward Magdala with us. Some other wealthier, priestly families traveled with us toward Galilee as well.

"Adonai has blessed me! Hallelujah!" I whispered to myself in a slight hum. "Blessed be the name of Adonai from now and forever. From the rising of the sun unto the going down of the same, the name of Adonai is worthy of praise."

It was the same tune as a song Uncle Joseph and I sang on our way to Jerusalem. Uncle Joseph had a deep, confident voice, while I whispered the words — afraid of what our fellow travelers would think of me. As we walked, Uncle Joseph would place his large hand on my head. The slight pressure of his warm hand made me feel secure and safe; comforted and defended.

Presently, I walked between Jesus and Martha. We were having all sorts of fun. We chased each other, hiding between different people and animals in the caravan. We read the signs of the weather in the wind and sky. We drew in the sand when we made camp.

One thing that threatened my joy was the sweat that flowed down my forehead, neck, and back. I felt that I looked like a child who had been spit upon by a dozen camels. I put a hand to my damp veil, tightly wrapped around my head for utmost sun protection. I glanced around to ensure no one noticed my state. My cousin James walked ahead of us with his new wife of only a few weeks.

Jesus walked on my left and was clearly sweating through His gray tunic. His unruly hair bounced as He stepped forward. Martha, on the other hand, appeared hardly fazed by the journey. She walked on my right, each step a sweep of grace. My eyebrows furrowed, wondering how her skin was smooth and soft as opposed to shiny and oily. She had chosen not to ride a camel so she could be with us.

I cast a glance over my shoulder. I did not actually see him with my quick glance, but I knew very well that he was walking behind us: Lazarus, Martha and Mary's brother.

"…simply put, no woman likes snakes," Martha said to Jesus, looking straight ahead of her.

"Or scorpions," I said immediately.

"Esther, scorpions have nothing to do with this!" Martha exclaimed, eyeing me as if my words were questionable.

"Surely scorpions were in the garden of Eden as well," Jesus said, and I was thankful for His warm smile.

"Scorpions *are* creeping things." Martha rolled her eyes. "And all of the animals were in Eden. Mules, and fish, and birds, and lions, and…never mind. We were discussing the most cunning of all the animals: The serpent."

Understanding dawned on me as I realized the conversation I had joined. They were speaking of the creation account in the Torah.

"Upon your breast will you go," Jesus recited.

"And earth you shall eat," Martha was quick to add.

"All the days of your life!" I finished enthusiastically, yearning to be as learned as Jesus and Martha were.

"Listen, Martha," Jesus said, "I will put enmity between you and the woman, and between your seed and her —"

"She will crush your head, and you shall lie in wait for his heel. I know! You see, women do not like snakes!" Martha said.

Jesus looked at her, waiting for her to finish.

"Do you hear a "messiah" being mentioned? Or salvation being given to us?" Martha continued, raising her slender fingers in the air.

"I hear the word, 'seed.' The *seed* of woman," Jesus explained. "It is a promise of a redeemer for fallen humankind."

"We were not even sons and daughters of Abraham yet." Martha plodded on. "Let alone, an entire nation."

"Yet we were sinners long before Abraham," I found myself saying. My lips curved slightly as I thought of what Jesus had taught me. He had taught me many things in the evenings in Nazareth about what He learned from Rabbi. I would also listen to my uncles and brothers speak intensely at meals about the scriptures and the law of Moses. And of course, when I was in the company of Martha and Mary, I devoured the Word.

Like the prophet, Jeremiah, the Word had become my joy and the delight of my heart.

"Adonai has been promising us a savior," I continued, relishing the attention both Jesus and Martha were giving me. "He has been promising us a savior from the moment we, who were created in His image and likeness, chose to be unlike Him." Of course, it was a pure repetition of what Jesus had taught me. "Behold, choosing to be unlike Elohim is a sin. It is evil. A choice which causes destruction. But Elohim is *life*." My vision blurred as I looked up at the sky, and contemplated the goodness of life. "The serpent is evil. But evil will be crushed by the woman's seed."

"Tell me, Esther." A deep voice startled me. It was Lazarus, now walking by Jesus' side. My face filled with a terrible heat, dreading what he could possibly say to me. No man besides my brother, cousins, and uncles addressed me. No man. "Do you think there are any other references to *the* Messiah in the Torah — even before Elohim's covenant with Abraham?"

I felt my blood pumping in my head as I tried to focus on what he was saying, and not on how odd I felt.

"I...I would say..." I had asked the same thing of Jesus. "I would say that...even the act of mercy that Elohim showed to Cain when he murdered his brother Abel, tells us of the merciful intervention of...Elohim in our lives. His mercy — well — His mercy indeed endures forever. Every historical account; every story we know; even of our first parents, gives the message that Elohim is bound to His people, Israel. And His covenants and prophets only strengthen such a message. Each sin we commit against Him, though we are indeed rebuked and punished, is followed with reconciliation, just as the prophet Hosea rebuked but remained faithful to his wife who was a prostitute, Gomer."

My face heated all the more at the word "prostitute." It felt too odd to say it in a man's presence.

"Well said, Esther," Jesus whispered to me, looking pleased.

I bit my lips, looking straight into His warm brown eyes. He knew very well that every word of knowledge I spoke was first from Him.

"And what is our sin, now?" Lazarus asked, but I did not look at him. I was too terrified to. "That causes our land to once again be taken from us? Is it the intermarriage of our people? The submission to Rome by our priests? The lack of reverence to the Temple?"

I took a quick breath. "I do not know," I admitted. "But," I found myself bravely saying, finally looking up at Lazarus. He was tall for a teenager and I was not sure what the look on his face meant. Only more heat rushed to my face. "But when Elohim reconciles with His people; when He sends us our warrior-king; the seed of Adam; the seed of Abraham, Isaac, and Jacob; the seed of Judah, Jesse, and David, I will give each of my sons to Him, to restore the kingdom of David."

"I will do the same." Martha gently but firmly grasped my hand, squeezing it. I smiled at her, my ally and friend.

She suddenly pulled me back from Jesus and Lazarus so the two of us could speak alone. Her mahogany veil made her young olive skin look very beautiful. "Esther, are you unwell? You look as red as a fox."

"I just feel overheated," I sighed.

She pulled her hand from mine, likely because it was sweaty and hot.

"I have news I have been waiting to tell you. I do not think I can hide it anymore." She tilted her head toward me. "Do not dare tell Aliza, for then the whole world will know, but when you see me next year..." she slowed, then finished, "I may be betrothed." She watched for my reaction.

I held in a gasp. "Betrothed!" I repeated quietly.

Martha put a hand to my back, leading me further to the side of the caravan where fewer people were walking. "To my cousin," Martha said, scanning those around us. "I do not know where he is at the moment...but — "

"One of your male cousins?"

"O Abraham! Of course, a male one!"

"What I mean is, you only have two male cousins."

"I will marry Hezekiah. The taller one. He is a Pharisee like his father and brother. Our marriage will profit my father Syrus' business."

"Hezekiah is the more handsome one." I smiled eagerly at her. Hezekiah lived in Syrus' house, so Martha would not even need to move homes when married. I tried to imagine her as a wife. A wife and mother.

"And Mary? Does Syrus know who she will be given to?"

"He is looking at a young man who lives in Emmaus."

"Emmaus!" I exclaimed. "Aunt Miriam is from Emmaus."

"But Mary is still young like you. She has time."

"What of your sister Mara? She is even younger. Does your father have any arrangements for her?"

Martha clasped my hand again, looking at me pointedly. "I will tell you, Esther, but remember that he that walks deceitfully reveals secrets, but he that is faithful, conceals the thing committed to him by his friend."

I recognized the proverb. "Truly, you can trust me, Martha, to not be a talebearer."

"There is...a secret mission in our visit to Magdala," Martha told me, her sharp eyebrows raised as she whispered. "Father is going to leave Mara there in his manor house. In truth, I do not see how Galilee is a good place for anyone to live."

My eyebrows shot up as she spoke of my province, which was known for unrest, rebellion, poverty, and a plethora of Gentiles.

"Forgive my insult" she added, "but Mara will stay there as woman of the household."

"But she is young and has no husband."

"Not yet. As you said, she is still too young, but she would bring dishonor on any man. All in Judea know of her defiant nature, her neglect of duties at home, her angry outbursts. She torments anyone she comes in contact with. Father hopes to get her off his hands."

"Is Mara truly that terrible?"

"I will not miss her presence. She sneaks out at night, unchaperoned. Mary thinks Mara is just buying all sorts of silks and perfumes, but there are rumors that she goes out to meet with older, promiscuous girls."

"Are they true?"

"O Abraham! I do not know." Martha put her thin fingers to her forehead. "Pray they are not. I would not be able to bear it and most certainly Father and Mother would not be able to bear it!"

"Your family is acclaimed by all," I assured her. Their family truly was. I thought about Martha and what it would be like to know the scriptures so well; to read and to write; to live with the respect of all; to have wealth and riches for both my comfort and the comfort of my whole family. And to marry a wealthy husband. Blessed indeed, Martha and Mary were obvious favorites of Elohim.

I wondered if it would be possible for me to be so favored; to have the acclaim of all and of Elohim Himself. Could I, like Queen Esther of Persia, a lowly Jewish woman, be lifted up to the palace of the king to be savior of my people? Could I, like Judith, singlehandedly save the nation of Israel from our enemies? Could I, like Deborah, become a great prophetess, forever known by men?

Even without riches, could I be like Sarah, the mother of Elohim's nation? Could I be like Rebecca, who birthed Jacob, the man who would become Israel? Could I be like Hannah, bearing Samuel miraculously and dedicating him to Elohim?

I would even willingly be like the great martyr during the time of the Hasmoneans: the mother of the seven sons. The mother who would let each of her seven sons die for the sake of Elohim and the land of Israel, and who would willingly die herself.

"Still, Mara could destroy that acclaim. She truly could." Martha sighed, interrupting my musings. "At least if she is in Magdala, no one down in Judea will hear of her deeds. That is Father's hope."

"Are you nervous to be married?" I asked her. It would only be a few years until I would be given to a man. Would he be a Nazarene? Someone who was well-loved and respected, like Jesus?

"Not at all. Why should I be nervous? I already know Hezekiah. He is a good man and a Pharisee like my Uncle Simon. It will be time for me to do what I was intended to do. To be a wife. To be a mother."

A flush of heat consumed my body and I glanced ahead, at Lazarus and Jesus talking.

"Esther?" Martha looked puzzled. "What is the matter with you?"

The next thing I knew, Aliza was at my side, peering into my eyes like an unwanted visitor peering into a private room.

"Your face looks like it is the exact color of blood." Her freckled nose wrinkled.

"We are walking through our desert country at the hottest part of the day." I turned my face from my sister.

"Are you ill?" Martha asked. "We should stop soon to rest for the afternoon. We will have the servants pitch tents for shade."

"I am fine!" I assured them. "It is just...sometimes heat rushes to my face."

Aliza threw her head back and laughed, which caused my lips to purse in irritation. "You know what she is doing, Martha? Esther is blushing!"

Blushing. I had heard the word used before, but I did not quite understand what it meant. Aliza explained. "It means you are in love."

That strange heat rose to my face again! It felt awful.

"Who are you in love with, Esther?" Aliza giggled.

"Stop it, Aliza. You are being childish, which is never a good thing," Martha scolded.

Aliza shut her mouth immediately, eager for the approval of Martha of Bethany.

We did stop in the shade shortly after that. The temperature had cooled as we reached the meeting point of the Jordan River Valley and the Jezreel Valley. We rested outside of the city, Beth Shean. By three in the afternoon, our family like most families, decided to stay in Beth Shean for the night. In the morning, we western Galileans would take the road toward Sepphoris, while the northern Galileans and the house of Syrus would take the road toward Tiberias. Our time with the treasure from Judea would cease until the next Passover.

That night I was in a sort of daze. I could not enjoy myself at all and claimed that I was merely exhausted and needed rest. As I sat in a tent, listening to music and laughter outside, I kept pondering what Aliza had said and could not stop touching my face. I needed to sort such concepts and words out for myself. What was blushing? And if I blushed, was I indeed in love?

Chapter 5
12th Year of Our Lord

When Ruth was back with her mother-in-law, Naomi said to her,
'My daughter, should I not be seeking a pleasing home for you?'
RUTH 3:1

We were journeying south, toward Jerusalem, for the Feast of Unleavened Bread. Our caravan took the eastern side-road along the Jordan River.

More palm trees appeared each day. The green, grassy mountains of Galilee slowly shifted into the yellow dusty hills of Judea. The dust crept into my sandals and fingernails, and my eyes, ears, and mouth. Of course, every few miles or so we would see the silhouette of crucifixes near the road, reminding all of us what happens to any who defy Rome.

"The designs of sand rippling on the mountains look like cooled wax," I observed aloud as we reached an area away from any executions. Jericho was far behind us. We were in a barren area with the occasional clump of thistle and rocks piled at the base of hills. "Do You think so, Jesus?"

Jesus nodded, wiping a bead of sweat from His forehead as we walked. He now had hints of whiskers. "I would say so. I *feel* more like melted wax at the moment." Natural to His character He added, "Blessed be My Father in Heaven. He gives some clouds to block the heat of the sun."

"Are you well?" I asked. Jesus' face was red and strained. "Have you drunk water recently?" I pulled at my tunic, drenched in sweat. The air was still and heavy.

"No."

My lips formed a thin line. I eyed the sack hanging over Uncle Clopas' shoulders. It held a flask of water so I hurried ahead toward my uncle, who was with Simon and my cousins. I swatted at a fly that landed on my chin.

"I feel like a hypocrite, that is what." Simon waved one hand in the air as the other held his tallit in place to block the sun.

"Uncle?" I announced my presence.

He either did not hear me or chose to ignore me.

"Then you are calling each of us a hypocrite, Simon," Cousin Joses said. "Sepphoris may be a Greco-Roman city, but it is still the Jewish capital—"

"Capital *by* Herod Antipas."

"But that does not mean we are serving Herod with each person we construct a building for."

"Yes, it does," Simon protested. "Each time I set foot in that city I am serving Herod. Each time I pay his taxes, and those of Rome."

"Our families would pay taxes to the government whether you worked in Sepphoris or not."

"But cities like Sepphoris and Tiberias and Caesarea are where they all reside—government officials, wealthy merchants, tax collectors. Herod himself has property in Sepphoris. I cannot keep working for that fool. My resentment of all forms of power is..."

"Then join the Zealots, Simon," Uncle Clopas barked, throwing a hand in the air. "Join them as your father did. Join the unorganized bunch of men who plot the world's destruction. Start a revolution. And prior to joining them, make certain you leave my household."

Uncle Clopas trudged forward with heavy steps. He had said such things before, but I was not sure if he meant them. He usually resorted to telling his nephews and sons to leave home if they disliked the way he ran the household.

I thought I heard Simon growl as he turned to Cousin Jude. I heard him say something about the Romans laughing at the Jewish Sabbath.

"Uncle," I called, my throat dry and my veil weighty.

At last acknowledging me, Uncle Clopas looked down at me with his usual scowl.

"May I have water?" I asked.

His expression remained the same, but he shrugged the sack from his shoulders. "Only what you need, understand?" He grumbled. "We need enough to reach Bethany today."

"Yes, Sir." I took the sack and fell back in step beside Jesus.

"Drink, Jesus," I told my cousin, handing Him the flask. "Martha always encourages us to drink water. She claims it is the solution to most ailments."

Jesus took the flask, popped off the lid, and drank a large gulp before handing it back to me. I took a small sip myself, noting that the flask was far less than half full.

"Simon is angry, as usual," I told Jesus. "He is angry every day. It makes *me* feel angry every day." I closed the flask roughly. My eyes searched for Uncle Joseph. When I found the broad back of Jesus' father, bitterness sunk into me at the thought of my own father.

My lost abba. It was Rome who killed him.

"Tell me why you are angry."

"No. You will only look at me with your innocent face and…and try to make me feel guilty for being angry."

Jesus' expression was not hard or condemning, and never showed any taking of offense. I was not even sure what His expression was. But I liked it. That was why I claimed Him as not only my brethren, but my dear friend.

Martha and Mary would say that I was in love with Him, but I hushed them, telling them not to speak such nonsense. Aliza could attest to the fact that I did not romantically love him. He was my brother. A brother I dearly loved, more so than my cousins James and Joses and Jude.

Aliza was just betrothed to a man down the street called Samuel. They would wed within a year! Eagerness settled in me to tell Martha and Mary the recent news.

"Esther, look!" Jesus exclaimed. My eyes searched in the direction he pointed. "It is a legion!"

Passing the caravan of hundreds from Nazareth, Cana, and other towns was indeed a legion of Roman soldiers. They plodded on horses, their red capes billowing behind them.

Simon spat at the ground as they passed us, and Uncle Clopas slapped him on the head. Thankfully, they did not look our way to see the harsh glares.

My body tensed with fear and rage. These were the men who killed my father. Horrendous, evil men.

"Do you think they go to Jerusalem?" Jesus asked.

"Probably for the feast. There will be thousands of us there," I said, watching the light bounce off of their silver helmets and gear.

"Imagine if we could ride a horse, Esther." Jesus smiled at the thought. "We would reach Bethany in three days instead of five if we rode one!"

My gut rolled at the near presence of those soldiers. I looked away and lifted my chin. "We would," I concurred. "But for now, we will arrive in Bethany in a couple hours."

"Esther, take these upstairs," Ima said, shoving a variety of rolled-up pallets and mats into my arms. They sagged with the awkward bundle.

Ima's lips were in a thin line as she looked at me, her dark veil falling down her back. She began to examine me, clucking her tongue. Reaching out, she tugged at the edge of my veil, raised it to my face, and wiped my forehead, cheeks, and chin with it.

My eyelids fluttered in irritation. When she released my cream-colored veil she tucked a few of my stray hairs into it. Leaning in even closer she said, "Lazarus is a handsome one."

I blushed, afraid to respond. We had been in the house of Syrus for only a quarter of an hour, and I had not yet seen Lazarus.

"Go and be my star!" Ima squeezed my shoulder as if to show affection, but it felt more like a pinch. She called out "Eucharia!" and left me for the wife of our host.

A shaky breath fell from my lips as I assessed the crowded courtyard of the affluent house of Syrus. This courtyard was as large as my uncle's home, and had a nice well right in the center of it. White limestone columns lined its rim. Juniper bushes and bay laurel shrubs sprouted from ceramic pots.

Olive groves and terraces were beside the house while other buildings housed the olive press and workrooms of the estate. On a previous visit, Martha and Mary had taken me inside those rooms so I could see the equipment.

Today, I had yet to see Martha and Mary, but I assumed they were at work in the kitchen. Shifting the array of pallets in my arms, I began weaving through the clusters of people who were exchanging festival greetings. I walked toward the stone steps that led to the second story.

I noted Simon of Bethany, Martha and Mary's uncle, speaking with Uncle Clopas and Uncle Joseph. The man's sons stood by their father. They were a handsome family, which I was certain pleased Martha, if she was indeed betrothed to her cousin.

"Joyous Festival, Esther," one of Eucharia's sisters said as I passed her. "You have grown! And your eyes. They seem to be a brighter shade of green each time I see you."

Smiling politely, I continued to the stairs. My lips twisted with uncertainty. How could I gracefully ascend them while I balanced the strange load in my arm? Shrugging to myself, I decided to call upon the determination that Elohim had when helping His people, Israel, cross the Red Sea.

I gave a huff and the pile almost fell from my arms. But I continued with the persistence of a beggar.

Victory surged through me as I reached the top of the stairs. I was in the hallway of the living quarters. I simply needed to reach the guest quarters at the end of the —

I suddenly slammed into another body. I gasped as the pile fell and the rolled-up pallets and blankets tumbled across the floor.

"Esther!"

I looked up.

"Lazarus!" My senses pricked to absolute attentiveness.

Lazarus bent down and began picking up my pallets and mats. I noticed the ripples of his light brown hair and his fine tunic.

"Forgive me." I crouched beside him, to help pick up the mess. My hands seemed to swell, making gripping anything a challenge.

He laughed slightly. "I was not looking. I walked out of my chambers to greet our guests and…"

Our eyes met as we looked up at the same time. Mine leaped away from his earth-brown ones.

I clutched some of the pallets to my chest, rising to my full height. He held the rest of them, standing up as well.

"Your journey from Nazareth was pleasant?"

I smiled. "Yes. And it was warm. Very warm." I blushed again, feeling warm indeed.

"The heat is heavy in the desert, yes. But we have a lot more vegetation in Bethany." His eyes shone with pride for his town, and his shoulders were held back and straight with confidence. "We have plenty of olive groves if you are in need of shade."

I gave another quick smile, my eyes unsure of where to look. His eyes? His shoulders? Behind him? The bundle in his arms?

"My sisters have not stopped talking about seeing you and Aliza." He smiled. "It was starting to annoy me," he added.

I opened — then closed — my mouth. Then opened it again. What did he mean by that? Did talk of me annoy him? "I will take those," I decided to say, looking at the pallets in his arms. "And I will put them in the guest quarters."

But he said that he might as well carry them.

Dread filled me, but I was resigned to follow him down the hall. Stumbling slightly as I went, we made it to the guest rooms.

He set the load against a wall of the room that was furnished with wicker baskets, colorful pillows, and small tables. A servant girl was arranging jugs and basins for guests. On seeing us, she came to take our assortment of pallets.

Lazarus and I looked at each other. His stature, as usual, intimidated me.

"Thank you," I said quietly, looking away. Then, before another uncomfortable moment could occur, I turned and left, hurrying down the hall and almost running back down the stairs. My hands slid against the smooth stone wall.

As I reached the bottom, a servant climbed up the stairs, her eyes on the basket in her arms. I touched my hand to my forehead, thinking about the event that just occurred.

Lazarus' image was a fresh painting in my thoughts.

"Esther!" Mary of Bethany pranced toward me. With a little bounce she reached and embraced me.

Martha came faithfully to her sister's side.

"*O Abraham,* it is good to see you." Martha took her turn to embrace me, her arms warm and firm.

"Tell me how you have been!" I squeezed Martha's shoulders, examining her sharp features. Turning to Mary's softer face, I touched the younger sister's arm.

"These past weeks have gone by in dreadful slowness." Mary's shoulders heaved as if bearing a very heavy burden. "These preparations for Passover! All of us women and the servants have been cleaning every corner of the house to rid it of all leaven. At last," she added, brightening, "tomorrow we celebrate."

When the day-long feast of Passover finished tomorrow eve, we would continue the Feast of Unleavened Bread; seven days eating bread without leaven as our ancestors had when fleeing Egypt. They had had no time to wait for the bread to rise.

"I saw Aliza briefly," Martha told me.

"She is glowing," Mary said, then called the girl who was giggling with a handful of friends. "Aliza!" she called again.

"She told you the news?" I asked, disappointed that I did not get to tell them first.

Aliza finally walked toward us. To me, her freckled face held more pride than joy.

"You are betrothed," Mary said, wrapping her arm around Aliza, who lifted her chin.

"Samuel is a very attractive man." She ran her fingers along the hem of her veil as if it were costly silk.

"Even if he is a little plump in the cheeks," I added, raising my eyebrows.

Aliza scowled. "You are jealous, Esther, that no man has taken a fancy to you."

I opened my mouth to tell her that the only man who had taken a fancy to her was a poor, meek Nazarene with a pitiful *mohar*, but Martha cut in.

"I would say that Samuel *is* attractive, with the large, strong build of a hard-working farmer. Every man in Nazareth is like that! All of your cousins and brother are as well."

Aliza smiled mischievously. "Do you fancy my brother, Martha? Our cousin James is taken, but say you married Simon — then, you would be my sister-in-law."

Martha blushed. "Of course not! I—"

"You could marry Simon, Martha, and Mary could marry Jude. We would all truly be family, then," Aliza continued.

"And Esther could marry Lazarus," Mary added with a laugh. "You could all move here to Bethany and live with us."

It was my turn to blush as I thought of my encounter upstairs with Lazarus. "You are being foolish, Aliza. Childish. Simon and Jude could never offer a mohar to satisfy Martha and Mary's family. Surely they would be embarrassed to be associated with our Nazarene family."

"Are we not already associated with you?" Mary pulled me toward her so she could settle one of her arms around me while the other was around Aliza. "I am thankful our fathers were such good friends so that we may be." She gave a huff. "Now, Martha, please tell them your news. You are deceiving them with your silence."

"I was trying to tell you!" Martha said. "I am betrothed to my cousin, Hezekiah. We marry in three months."

"How wonderful!" I responded. "If only I could attend! How would I ever be allowed or able to do so?" I looked at Mary. "Is it true that you are betrothed as well?"

"I…" Mary lowered her voice. "Father does not want me betrothed until I reach my time."

"Your time?" I said loudly.

"Hush!" Martha scolded me in a whisper. "Lower your voice, Esther, lest someone hears you. Mary has yet to reach maturity."

Aliza giggled as Mary looked away from us, embarrassed.

"Have you reached your time, Esther?" Mary looked up at me timidly.

"No," I stated. I was not sure if I wanted my time to be here or not. The sooner the time came, the sooner Uncle Clopas would look for a husband.

"You are blessed it has not yet come. It is truly terrible," Aliza assured Mary, although she appeared to be glad about her own maturity.

"Hush!" Martha's eyes widened in alarm. "If Mother catches us speaking of this, so close to public ear…"

"All of this talk of engagement," Aliza said, one eyebrow raised, "And we have failed to mention the name of Jesus."

"Silence, Aliza, do you only wish to poke fun at Him?" I narrowed my eyes. I found that Aliza only spoke of Jesus with the intension of teasing, if not insulting Him. He was odd with His unusual piety, but He was a good person, who had just reached His manhood.

"He is only 12, is he not?" Mary asked.

"Indeed. Only 12." I leaned toward Mary who was a small measurement shorter than me. "We are the same age," I added proudly.

"Tell me of Simon. Who is he to marry? Surely he is of age," Martha asked.

I thought of my 17-year-old brother with those all-too-becoming lines of anger around his eyes. "He has his eyes set on a girl from Cana." I looked around for her. "She is beautiful." I did not see her, however. My eyes caught a cluster of children near the well.

"A couple of men in their family are Zealots," I heard Aliza say, but I was too intrigued by the children chasing each other around the rim of the well to pay attention. "No wonder Simon likes them."

The young children were compelling, and I left my friends without so much as a backward glance so I could watch the dozen or so of them playfully push and tackle each other.

"Careful, little ones." I announced myself with a laugh.

"*Shalom*, Esther!" a few of them called as they chased each other. Their big eyes and short stature warmed my heart, making me laugh more.

"Shalom, everyone." I crouched down to their height, thinking that one day I would be the mother of many children.

I caught one boy in my arms before he looped around the well. His laughter rang high as I scooped him up and stood with him in my arms. I began spinning him around the way Abba and Uncle Joseph used to do to with me as a child.

"Esther, I am dizzy! I am dizzy!" The boy partly screamed, partly giggled. Feeling dizzy myself, I slowed down and set him on the ground.

Out of the corner of my eye I noticed Jesus cheerfully talking to someone. Lazarus. My gaze immediately left the two men.

"Esther! Do that to me! Please," a toddler begged.

With a playful huff, I picked up the girl, lifting her above my head.

The rest of the children stopped playing with each other and begged for my attention. They began to bounce as they surrounded me. "Esther! Esther! Do that to me!" they demanded. I set one down to pick up another.

"You forgot me, Esther!"

"What about me?"

"My turn!"

"Just wait a moment, everyone," I huffed, setting down another child.

"Do not hurt Esther!" I heard Jesus' laugh behind me. I turned to face Him, holding my veil in place with one hand as a child clutched the other.

"Jesus, have you come to play with us?" I faked naivety.

"Jesus, will you? Please?"

He teasingly charged at a child and scooped him up. The children cheered in response. With a child tossed over His shoulder like a sack of potatoes, Jesus whispered, "You have your hands full, Esther."

I beamed back at Him, feeling the soft curl of the girl's little fingers on my hand. Fresh air rushed through my lungs in my exhilaration.

"A child's love is the best," I quietly said. "They treat me like a queen."

"Ah yes, Queen Esther." Jesus smiled playfully as He tossed a little one in the air. "I agree with you." He stated matter-of-factly, "A child's love is the greatest."

Forgetting Him, I blinked several times, startled by the realization that Lazarus was watching me. Surely, he was looking at Jesus and the children. He was looking at *all* of us. I tried to convince myself of this.

Nevertheless, I felt terribly self-conscious. I decided not to dare look his way. But, oh, he still was at the center of my attention even if he was not the focus of my eyes.

Chapter 6

I will be a father to him, and he shall be a son to me,
and I will not withdraw my favor from him as I withdrew it
from the one who was before you; but I will maintain him in
my house and in my kingdom forever, and his throne
shall be firmly established forever.

1 CHRONICLES 17:13-14

Like a herd of animals squeezing into a pen, people squeezed through the tight, overflowing Huldah Gates of the Temple. Our caravan was no longer together — over one hundred people could not possibly stay in one group. Jesus was at my side and I saw the backs of Uncle Clopas and Uncle Joseph ahead of us. I was not entirely sure where Ima was, but she was likely with Aunt Miriam, still climbing the steps behind us.

The great crowds enthralled me, and I longed to enter the inner courts with the men and chief priests, just to get a sense of the detailed craftsmanship and the veil of the Temple that separated us from the Holy of Holies. Then again, I would likely drop dead on the spot for being so close to Elohim's presence.

Earlier that morning in Bethany, we ritually purified ourselves in a *mikveh* in Syrus' house so we would be ceremonially clean when entering the Temple. We took a route from Bethany, down the Mount of Olives which many pilgrims camped upon for festivals. At the base of the mountain was a beautiful garden of olive trees that Syrus owned. Martha told me it was called Gethsemane. From it, we had a grand view of the Temple.

As usual, we were not allowed to enter straight through the East Gate and were told by Temple guards to go around, through the Kidron Valley, and to the Fountain Gate of the city, so that we could enter the Temple from the southern side. Uncle Clopas muttered that they only wanted our money and wished for us to walk through the market before entering the Temple. We had little other option. After passing through the gate, we walked a long length toward the Temple Mount, past the many merchants selling anything from silk to oil to spices to jewels.

Now, with each step closer to the Temple, the walls of the massive structure seemed to double until I could not even see the top of it. I wondered if even the birds could reach the top. Passing under a large arch, we turned right toward the Huldah Gates, the gates where my father died.

Hate and rage boiled inside of me, but I pushed down those sickening feelings and continued through the right Gate of Huldah.

Wafting rich incense beckoned as we were thrust into a dark gallery. Lamps lined the stone walls. The ceiling curved in on us, making me feel like I was in a closed cistern.

"It is beautiful," I told Jesus, admiring the threatening yet elaborate carvings of the ceiling. I knew from our yearly visits that above these ceilings were the stretching floors of the Royal Porticoes.

The crowd pushed us forward through the tunnel's narrow passage. It was a relief to see light, and as we walked up the steps, more light. The crowds were even thicker out here.

As always it was like entering an entirely different world; one in which Jews were at the center. As we stood in the public square, the Court of Gentiles, the white gold and marble of the Temple itself stretched before me. Incense and smoke billowed upward from its inner courts. My nose scrunched in irritation at the smell of butchered animal. No matter the myrrh, frankincense, incense, and cinnamon that the priests perfumed the air with, nothing could cover the smell of carnage.

Close behind us, on the porticoes, were money changers and merchants. "You must not purchase an animal with a dinar," a man shouted. "Exchange it for the Hebrew shekel here, so you do not defile Elohim's Temple."

It must have been an entire hour before we wrapped around the southern corner of the court toward the East Gate — the gate Uncle Clopas originally wanted us to use. Though we were in a ceiling-less structure, the breeze was blocked by the walls of stone and by bodies, making the air heavy. Sweat formed on my brow and made my tunic leech to my skin.

"It *is* beautiful, Esther." I barely heard Jesus say beside me. His eyes were closed and He was facing the Holy of Holies. How could He find it beautiful if He was not even looking? People jostled against us, but He remained serene.

"Esther, stay close to me." Ima called in my ear, startling me. I had totally forgotten her. "I do not want you to get lost," she shouted over the noise, causing Jesus to open His eyes. "Miriam was almost trampled by the crowds!"

I looked behind me. Aunt Mary faithfully stood at Aunt Miriam's side. They looked like two little leaves floating in a deep storm at sea. Aunt Miriam's mouth hung open in her usual wonder as Aunt Mary's was softly closed.

Priests walked around in their turbans, flowing black and white garments, and tasseled cloaks, ordering men to go purchase their Passover sacrifice.

"Come, now." Ima ushered me through the large square and the Beautiful Gate that led to the Court of Women. It was one of the largest courts in the Temple, save the Court of Gentiles. It was one of the few courts in which women were allowed. Men, of course, could enter that court so they could pass into the Court of Israelites to offer sacrifice. Further in, only the priests could enter the Court of Priests, and the high priest alone could enter the Holy of Holies.

"A high priest chosen by Herod," Simon would say. "Even our religious leaders are determined by the Roman government. Herod is just a pawn in Caesar's hand, so Rome chose the rich Annas to be high priest! Despicable man. Probably the most affluent Jew there is. Does not faze him to make such a large Temple tax!"

I passed through the Court of Women, but could hardly see the neat stone pattern beneath me as it was covered by thousands of feet. Further in front of me, was a semicircle staircase that led to the other courts. There, the *Levite* choir blasted their horns, tambourines, and cymbals.

Jesus was gone from my sight. He probably went with the men to the stable on my right. Men emerged from it hauling Passover lambs on their shoulders as they headed up the steps to the inner courts. For the house of Syrus, there were only two Passover lambs needed for all of the family and guests. One lamb could feed dozens. Uncle Joseph and the other men witnessed the sacrifice that Syrus made, even if their immediate family did not need to purchase a lamb.

Tonight we would all feast in the actual city of Jerusalem, as prescribed in the Torah. Syrus owned a large household in the upper city like all the other rich inhabitants who had second or even third homes.

"We did not come all this way to Jerusalem to stand and do nothing." Ima yelled above the noise. She gripped Aliza's arm. "Let us pray to Elohim. Ask for mercy. Offer the Passover sacrifice so that He may look kindly upon you and grant you a husband who will give you many children in the years to come. Then beg Him to have mercy on our nation and to deliver us from the hands of our oppressors." She nudged me, and we made our way toward the side of the court, where several women either lay prostrate on the ground, or remained on their knees, facing the Holy of Holies.

It took me a moment to find a free opening. At last I found one, beside a woman who was rocking vigorously and practically shouting, "Blessed be Adonai, El of Israel."

I licked my lips nervously and dropped to my knees. Raising my hands reluctantly, I closed my eyes. Allowing myself to forget that people surrounded me, I began to whisper my prayers in Hebrew. No one could hear me over the noise, and the Word of Elohim dripped from my lips like honey.

"How lovely are Your tabernacles, O Adonai. You alone are Adonai! There is none like You. It is You who looks kindly on the righteous and smites the wicked. Give ear to my prayer. I bless You Adonai, Most High. Bless us from Zion. May we see the good things of Jerusalem all the days of our life. May we live long days and long lives. May we see our children's children. Shalom upon Israel."

The Psalms had such romantic words! "Give ear, O you that rules Israel. You who leads Joseph like a sheep. You who sits upon the cherubim, shine forth! Stir up Your might and come to save us. Convert us, O Elohim. Show us Your face and we shall be saved."

Lengthy sentences continued to roll off my tongue as I chose elaborate words to praise and bless Elohim.

"Remember not our former iniquities. Forgive us our sins for Your name's sake. Deliver us, pardon our sins." I thought of Rome and every Gentile who worshipped idols and ignored the one true El. "Adonai's foes shall be shattered. Smite the wicked. Curse those who so openly curse You. Show Your hate for those who hate You."

Two days later, we were back to walking. This time, toward home.

"That is Bethel up ahead." Simon nodded at the outline of the town.

"I am glad." I wiped the sweat from my brow. "For the love of Israel! This day has no end! First, with visiting the Temple again this morning, and then walking nonstop ever since."

"It makes me want *real* bread," Aliza added. "I grow sick of unleavened bread by the third day of the feast."

"Our ancestors went without leavened bread as they journeyed out of Egypt. We can do the same as we journey out of Jerusalem, leaving the Holy City behind us." Simon looked pointedly at Aliza. He wiped his forehead with his tallit. "And then Elohim provided them with bread from Heaven. Real bread."

The late afternoon sun promised that the hottest part of the day was behind us. We would camp in Bethel tonight, enclosed in the dust of the Judean mountains.

"I wish to taste manna," I mused quietly.

"Perhaps once or twice," Simon told me expertly. "Our ancestors found the bread sweet and pleasing at first, but they wanted no more of it after eating it every day."

"I would still like to taste it," I said. "Even if I had it every day, it would be bread from Heaven, after all."

I looked at Aunt Miriam ahead of us, riding on Balaam. Cousin James walked beside her, leading the ass.

"I already miss Martha and Mary," Aliza pouted dragging her feet as she walked. "We will not see them for at least a year now."

"Next time we see them, both you and Martha will be married," I said.

"We men get to visit them soon." Simon smiled proudly. "In just under two months' time for the *Feast of Pentecost*."

I clenched my teeth. The men got to go to Jerusalem three times a year for pilgrimage. We women were only required to go for Passover. Ima would say, "Why spend the extra money to travel if we are *permitted* to stay at home and work?"

My mind drifted to Lazarus, causing me to be squeamish. I stretched my hands in and out of fists as I tried to think of a different topic.

"My children." Aunt Mary's voice came from behind us. I turned, noticing a touch of anxiety on her brow. "Is Jesus not with you?"

"No." I looked back at the clusters of people in our caravan and spotted my mother far behind us.

"I have not seen Jesus," Simon said.

"When was the last time you saw Him? Is He further ahead?" Aunt Mary touched my arm.

"I have not seen Him since we entered the Temple this morning in Jerusalem," I told her, slowing my pace. "I assumed He was further back with you and Uncle Joseph." I examined the people in front of me. Men led mules that carried supplies. Many women walked with their children scattered around them while the little babes rested in their arms.

"Pray He is not still in Jerusalem."

My eyes widened. Aunt Mary hurried ahead in search of Him.

My cousins and siblings continued chatting. I bit my lip, and remained alert for any sign of Jesus' mound of disarrayed hair.

Uncle Joseph ran past us.

"Aliza," I murmured. "Aliza, I think Jesus is lost."

"He is 12 years old, Esther. Jesus is a man now. He cannot be lost." The smell of dust, mule dung, burnt shrubs, and animal wafted around us. Uncle

Joseph and Aunt Mary ran past us. I wanted them to acknowledge me, but they did not even cast their eyes in my direction.

Shame burst in my head. Jesus was lost and it was entirely my fault! Out of all my siblings I spent the most time with Him. How was it that I went this entire day without so much as giving Him a thought?

Word quickly spread in our caravan about our missing traveler. I tapped my fingers against my thighs. Was there nothing I could do?

"They are returning to Jerusalem."

"Now? It is nearing dark! They cannot go by themselves."

As I ran toward Ima, I bumped against a woman and did not bother to give an apology. "Ima!" She smiled, talking to some of the other women from Nazareth. "Jesus is—"

"Lost. I know, Esther." She glanced over her shoulder at Aunt Mary and Uncle Joseph who had stopped running and were speaking to Uncle Clopas.

"Who loses their own son?" Ima looked at the women, her fine eyes narrowed over her sharp nose. "First, it was a scandalous pregnancy — do not dare to forget it! Elohim surely does not! Now, they lose their son in Jerusalem? Perhaps He is lying dead on the side of the road somewhere. I favor my brother-in-law, but how did such a man get paired with Mary?"

"It must be an outward act," a friend of Ima decided, her back perfectly straight. "Anyone who would meet Mary would assume she is the kindest of persons. You could start to know her and find her personality pleasant. That is what I always found her to be. Until that bump appeared in her stomach before she entered Joseph's house as his wife. It all attested to her true self. She may have presented herself as a holy virgin, but her pregnancy proved she is a sinner."

"Perhaps losing her child is Elohim's punishment upon her," Ima said.

I could not help my mouth dropping. Was what she said true? Was Aunt Mary truly so terrible a person? Was Jesus dead? What must it be like for Him to be without His family? He was alone somewhere, without His father or mother.

"Ima!" An idea dawned on me. "May I go with my aunt and uncle back to Jerusalem? I could help them find Jesus. If I — "

"Absurd," Ima snapped. She looked at me harshly and then smiled mockingly at her companions. "No, Esther. That is a ridiculous, childish idea." She continued talking to the women. "I would never entrust my daughter to that woman. Ever. Even before they lost their son, I would not let any of my children travel with Mary. I tell you she is sly…"

Feeling like I was crushed by a pile of stones, I looked behind me to see Aunt Mary and Uncle Joseph walking quickly in the opposite direction of the caravan. Their image became smaller and smaller.

Soon, I was at the very back of the caravan.

"Do not slow your pace now, Esther." Uncle Clopas' deep, rough voice pushed me from my troubled thoughts. "We will camp in the shepherds' caves over there. Keep walking, girl." I did not dare look behind me again. As I faced forward, I saw the stone watchtowers that the farmers and owners of vineyards looked out of at night to ensure that no one stole their crops. If I could not help Uncle Joseph and Aunt Mary in Jerusalem, then what I could do was pray. Jesus told me that prayer was essential to all things.

Elohim! Come with haste to my help! Turn Your ear to my plea. Do not abandon Your servant, Jesus. Blessed are You, Elohim of Israel. Keep Him safe under Your wings. Hasten to the needs of Jesus! Bring Him to His father and mother. Bring Him home to our family.

"Jesus," I gasped, dropping the grinding stick for the grain mill. He was walking behind His parents, up the hill Nazareth rested on. I clumsily climbed down the steps from the flattop roof to the courtyard, tumbling slightly when I reached the ground. Passing my relatives at work, I exited our home and bounded down the rocky hill. I narrowed my shoulders so that I could fit between the tightly packed houses, and squeezed past a young woman carrying a sack.

"Jesus!" I cried as my aunt and uncle appeared behind the corner of a house.

Aunt Mary and Uncle Joseph moved aside so I could greet their son.

I embraced Him quickly and then pulled away, breathing heavily. "Jesus! I have never been so pleased to see You!" I put my hands on my head. I wanted to say so many things to Him but grew shy under the gaze of His parents.

As if reading my thoughts, Uncle Joseph said, "We will meet you two in the house." Aunt Mary looked at him agreeably and the couple took off.

I allowed myself to speak freely and dramatically. "These past days have been torture, Jesus. Where have You been? I have felt paralyzed with fear for You. Every morning, I woke up hoping You would be here, and You were not! The Feast of Unleavened Bread is already behind us. It has been a week since I last saw You and I did not even know if You were alive. You could have been beaten by bandits! Or...or taken captive by Rome and forced to be a slave. So many things could have happened. How…why have You done this to me?"

Short of breath, I took a moment to study Jesus. His hair was obviously knotted and sweat shone on His forehead. Yet His face was healthily flushed with no sign of injury or pain.

All I could hear was my own rapid breathing as Jesus calmly returned my gaze, appearing unfazed by my outburst. I looked at Him expectantly, waiting for Him to defend Himself.

Finally, He spoke. "I was in Abba's house the whole time, Esther."

I made a small sound of surprise. "*Abba*…the Temple, You mean?" I shut my mouth to let Him finish.

"I like being in the Temple. It is home because My Father is there. You know I enjoy spending time with Abba. Did you not realize I would naturally be with Him?"

The skin on my face prickled with annoyance. I knew Jesus to speak of Elohim as His father, but never so close as an abba! And never with such disregard for His true father by blood: Uncle Joseph.

We slowly walked up the hill, the smell and sound of goats and chickens in their pens. "Did *You* not realize that we were leaving Jerusalem to go home? You are not usually so careless. Did You not think of all of us? Of me? And Your parents!"

"I did not try to worry you or cause you any distress." Jesus spoke calmly, His face sincere. He did not seem troubled by my distress, which distressed me all the more. "Simply where My Father is, there also I will be."

I lifted my hands in exasperation. He was acting like a little child!

I narrowed my eyes at Him as we walked. "And Your abba is Joseph as my abba was James. I worry that Elohim will strike you down for over-famil-iarizing Him as Your Father."

Jesus smiled softly, looking ahead. "He is your Father, Esther. Call Him 'Our Father.'"

I clasped my hands together, twisting them in anxiety. "I do not speak to Elohim as Father when I am in the Temple," I admitted, still glaring.

"How do you speak to Him?"

"As Ima taught me," I said, as we passed a couple of women grinding grain on a compacted clay roof. "I bless and praise Elohim like the psalmist. I ask Him for mercy. I ask Him to look on me with favor. I ask Him to punish the wicked. He is high and mighty, Jesus. Not an abba."

"He created man and woman." Jesus smiled at me warmly and scratched His temple, His eyes squinting from the sun above us. "As a father creates children, so Abba created Adam and Eve and each one of us. He delivers our people as He delivered us from the hand of the Egyptians. He provides for us like a father as He gave us manna in the wilderness." Jesus wiped His hand on the back of His neck. "He pardons us as He pardoned David, but not without reproach. Even the scriptures say, 'I will be to him a father, and he shall be to Me a son.'"

I raised my eyebrows. After a few thoughts, I lifted my shoulders, shrugging aside Jesus' words.

"I was angry with myself," I decided to tell Him. "For losing You. Now, I am angry with *You*. This whole affair is Your fault." My throat tightened. "You should have known better, Jesus. I shall die from Your treachery!" I dramatically stomped ahead of Him, reaching the house.

Aunt Miriam shuffled out of the open door, her arms outstretched.

"Jesus!" she called. "I thought I heard Esther call Your name! And then Joseph and Mary arrived. Come here, dear boy."

My brother and cousins would have come running out of the house as well, but they were with Uncle Clopas working in Sepphoris. Ima was probably disappointed Joseph returned with His family. I had heard her say she wished they would return to Egypt where they belonged.

Jesus embraced our aunt. With a dramatic sigh, I returned to the roof of our home to finish grinding the day's grain, which would take at least another hour. I watched Jesus enter the courtyard. The chickens frolicked, as if they had missed Him as well. He smiled at them and tapped one on the head.

He was acting like His normal self. My anger did not seem to faze Him.

Cousin James' wife stood in the court, rocking her child in her arms as she started to speak kindly to Jesus. Aunt Mary was already at work by the oven.

Relaxing my shoulders, I decided to forgive Jesus. Was that not what He always told me to do? I did not understand why He acted so foolishly, but He was a good man.

I tossed the grinding stick from right to left hand as I focused on Jesus, who was now laughing hysterically with Cousin James' wife as He made faces at the child.

Chapter 7
13th Year of Our Lord

...he went down and spoke to the woman. He liked her.

JUDGES 14:7

It was Simon's wedding feast. I was one of the ten bridesmaids to his betrothed, a girl from Cana. Lazarus was a groomsman, along with Jesus and
Cousin Jude. Cousin Joses had recently been married, as well.

As usual, it was a seven-day feast. I tended to enjoy dancing, but I was so
aware of Lazarus' presence that I feared making any move. I was so frightened
of my feelings for him that I wanted to hide in a storage cave until he left for
Bethany.

He had wavy locks the same brown color as that of his sister Mary's.
When I looked at him, I thought of one of Solomon's songs. He was the
perfected image of the groom in the greatest love poem ever written. His
shoulders were perfectly straight and his chin was slightly raised.

I stood against the exterior wall of Uncle Clopas' house, observing the
dancing in the street. Lights glowed down the thinning paths between houses.
The celebration was practically bursting from the village, every Nazarene a
part of it.

"Esther, come dance!" Mary of Bethany called to me as she spun around
with the other dancing women. Young and old men danced beside them,
clapped their hands, jumped, and kicked their feet.

I smiled and threw a hand in the air as dismissal. I had lost sight of Lazarus
and I was thankful for it. Still, I did not dare go out to dance. Although it was
a young woman's time to meet a man, I was terrified. Ima would scold me if
she saw me just standing here, but I escaped her notice.

"Esther," a deep voice said beside me.

I started and looked at Lazarus, my face suddenly hot.

He held out a clay cup of wine for me and my trembling hand took it.

"Elohim reward you," I croaked, looking at his own cup. I looked up to
his soft brown eyes and attempted a smile, but my lip was twitching.

"Your brother is pleased," Lazarus said, leaning against the wall beside
me.

"Simon?" I asked quietly.

He laughed. "Simon, of course." He tilted his head. "*The bridegroom.*"

I blushed again. He must have thought I was a stupid ox!

"Yes, he is." I chose to take a sip of my wine so I would not have to say more. It was much more bitter than anticipated. I fought any sign of a grimace.

Lazarus took a sip as well and almost coughed out the wine. "This may as well be vinegar." He held the cup away as if it could hurt him.

At wedding feasts, we served the best wine first. When everyone was drunk and had had their fill, we served the lesser wine. I wondered if Lazarus ever drank lesser wine. Surely his family could afford fine wine for their whole lives and beyond.

He surprised me when he spoke. "Jesus was telling me the story of how Simon was stung by a scorpion just last week."

I let out a short, loud laugh. "Did He?"

Lazarus smiled. "He would tell the tale far better than I could, but the best part came when you tried wash Simon's wound with vinegar instead of water."

I bit my lip. "It was an accident."

"Was it?" His eyebrows raised teasingly.

"As it was an accident when Simon kicked me in the nose because of it!"

"Ah, I was getting to that part."

"Well, I poured vinegar on the wound on his foot…" I remembered Simon's yelp and kick. "It was a natural reaction, I suppose."

"You deserved it, Esther."

It felt strangely satisfying to have him say my name.

"Eye for eye, tooth for tooth, hand for hand, foot for foot." I quoted the law of Moses. I blushed yet again, realizing no man would find a woman attractive who stated the Mosaic law so freely.

He laughed. "Burning for burning, wound for wound, stripe for stripe."

My eyes widened, comforted by his continuing recitation of the law of Moses. I took a sip of wine.

"Esther, tell me what you think: Did Moses write the Torah?"

I almost spat out my wine. "Forgive me?"

"Do not fear. I am not blaspheming, I assure you. I merely want to know what you think. Of course, we hold true that Moses wrote the Torah, as the voice of Elohim spoke directly into his ear. It is just that I have been studying with some Pharisees and scribes. A few radical ones suggest that it was not logically possible for Moses to have written the entire Torah."

"By what logic?"

"That it was compiled over the course of hundreds of years and by many different authors. The scribes say this because the writing style and language shifts."

"And you agree?

"I did not say that. I am simply curious. I wonder if some scribes study for the sake of scholarship instead of the sake of Elohim."

"Why do *you* study?"

"Because my father wants me to be trained in the Word of Elohim, not simply the world of business and trade." He twisted his lips, as if embarrassed. "I am fully trained," he said to defend himself. "That is, I know what I am doing, and I work beside my father as a businessman. When he passes, I will be head of the trade." He straightened his shoulders all the more.

I wondered if he was trying to impress me. Whether or not he was, he was enjoyable to listen to.

"Now tell me what you think, Esther. The authorship of the Torah."

"Perhaps I agree with these Pharisees and scribes that Moses did not write the Torah." I started.

"Really? I did not expect…"

"Because Elohim is the author of the Torah." Splendid excitement shot through me. "As Elohim created man, then even man's ability to write is due to Elohim. Moses was a man who was incoherent in speech. He grew up as an Egyptian, killed a man, and would eventually doubt Elohim."

"And what of the plagues sent to Pharaoh, the splitting of the Red Sea, the reception of the Ten Commandments, the leading of our people — all the miracles he worked?"

"Indeed, those were great things, but it was Elohim who accomplished them *through* Moses." I looked at Lazarus. "I think," I added quickly to not sound too authoritative.

"You think…" Lazarus drawled waiting for me to finish.

We looked into each other's eyes as I had never looked into a man's before. "I think," I said softly, "that Elohim accomplished all and Moses simply needed to say 'yes.' Man only has the power that is given to him by Elohim."

I felt empowered by Lazarus' attention and continued. "Samson was strong, but only with Elohim's power. So too, David killed Goliath with one stone by the power of Elohim. It seems to me that *logically*, the Word is not a matter of who the author is and when he wrote it, so much as the knowledge that the Word is from Elohim Himself. Is that not why we worship the one true Elohim? The Elohim of Israel. Man has failed us. Man breaks our covenants. Elohim is ever faithful."

He looked at me as if waiting for me to finish. I had. "But man has some power," he finally said. "Moses was a son of Abraham. He inherited the covenant that Elohim made with Abraham. Surely that gave him powers."

I remembered a Psalm. "Adonai, my allotted portion and my cup, You have made my destiny secure. Pleasant places were measured out for me; fair to me indeed is my inheritance. But I say to Adonai, 'You are my Adonai, You are my only good.'"

Lazarus relented. "Well said, Esther. I agree with you, but only in part. Though Elohim is the, eh, instigator of the Torah, a man still wrote it — or several men. Would not learning who indeed wrote it aid us in knowing more fully who Elohim is?"

One side of my lip curved upward. "Yes," I said, "but I would still be cautious as it is easy to lose sight of Elohim's hand."

"Where did you learn what you say?"

My eyebrows raised. I was not sure what he meant.

"Does someone teach you?"

Now I understood. "Yes. Jesus." I smiled, embarrassed at how consumed I could be by the scriptures. "I...I often make Him tell me everything He learns." How I wished to study the scriptures the way Jesus did. And Lazarus, Martha, and Mary did.

"And He learns from a rabbi?"

I tilted my head to one side. "Yes...but...but Jesus is very intelligent. He...has His own opinion and...interpretation."

"And you agree with His opinion?"

"Yes. Because of my confidence in Him more than my confidence in what He says." I took another sip of the bitter wine.

"You are good friends," Lazarus observed. "It is a dear friendship."

"Yes, but...He is my cousin and...He is only...He is my brother...I... He can annoy me at times...Jesus is still so much like a young boy..." It was not entirely true, but I did not want Lazarus to think that I had any romantic interest in Jesus. Especially if it was possible that Lazarus had a romantic interest in me.

"I would like to know Him better. He is not like, say, Simon or Joses."

"Not at all," I agreed. I decided to say nothing else about Jesus, lest Lazarus have a misconception.

Fortunately, he changed the subject. "I saw you playing with the children earlier. You looked...as amused as they were."

I blushed. He was watching me? What could that mean? "Children are a woman's joy," I said cautiously, not looking him in the eye.

"And a woman's crown of beauty."

Was he calling me beautiful? Or calling me hideous because I had no children of my own? I forgot such questions for the time being as we conversed for at least another hour. We talked about the classic story of Tobit and his wife and child, Tobias. This led us to speak of angels, fish, miracles, Babylon, and demons.

I was enamored. And I prayed that he was as well.

Soon after Simon's wedding feast, the young women of Nazareth stormed up to me.

"He certainly had an interest in you, Esther."

"It must be your eyes! They would entrance any man!"

"Did he ask your uncle for marriage?"

"Imagine you as the wife of a rich Judean!"

The women of our village had never given me such notice before. Though I never considered myself to be one who liked attention, I decided that I did enjoy it to an extent. I myself felt awe at Lazarus' interest in me.

Others were more skeptical. And realistically so.

"He was probably bored at the feast," Aliza told me. "He had no wealthy women to entertain him. You were all he had. At most, he would give a pretty poor girl attention for a couple of days and forget all about her when he returns to Bethany. At most. Besides, a man like Syrus would be foolish to let his son even suggest marriage to a Nazarene. Men like him need to make alliances. They need women of high social class to further their station. Lazarus will probably marry a daughter of a Pharisee or chief priest or some wealthy landlord."

Still, others like Ima were hopeful. "We will need to plan accordingly when we visit the family for Passover next year," she said. "I believe that a man in love will not care how much money a woman's family has. If he has truly found a star who is respected by her kinsmen and proves dignified, useful, and devout — all of which you have become with age, Esther — there will be no stopping the man!"

"Pray and pray for good fortune!" she continued. "Syrus was good friends with your father and this will only help your case, Esther."

As for my thoughts on Lazarus' attention, I think I was truly "sick with love," as the phrase went. I daydreamed about him and wondered what would happen if he did seek to betroth me. Then I would scold myself for thinking such a thing, for it would be impossible. Yet every part of my heart ached with the desire for it to be so.

14th Year of Our Lord

At the next Passover, Lazarus and I spoke at greater length and intensity than at the wedding. We spoke of all sorts of topics, from chariot races to farming to Herod Antipas' politics. He told me about the architecture of the Temple, explaining which parts were made immediately after our exile from Babylon and which were added by the previous king, Herod the Great. He even spoke to me of springtime and of turtledoves and fig trees and foxes. I thought that he may have been referring to a Song of Solomon, hinting at his affection, but told myself I had imagined it.

Yet he seemed so interested in what I had to say and think. He held my opinion in esteem — more so than Jesus. Lazarus praised me and agreed with nearly every word I spoke.

I wondered if he truly meant to take me as his wife.

"You may actually become my sister-in-law!" Mary of Bethany told me, and I laughed with her, that night of Passover.

Martha, Mary, and I were in Mary's bedchamber, resting on the cushions and pillows on the floor.

"What…do you think he intends…" I began, unsure of how to speak of such things to the sisters of Lazarus.

"It is truly hard to say," Martha said, leaning on a violet pillow with tassels the color of gold. "Father and Lazarus travel so often on business, and when home, they are consumed with work. I hardly speak a word to them. There is no way to tell what they may be planning."

"But you agree, do you not, Martha, that Lazarus is in love with Esther?" Mary was practically bouncing with excitement. She threw a pillow in the air and caught it.

Martha's lips settled in a thin line. "He is interested, yes. But I truly cannot say for certain."

"Well, I can!" Mary exclaimed, reaching for my hand. "And I will do what I can to sway him toward you."

I pulled my hand from her. "Please, Mary! Do not embarrass me! I…let Lazarus do what he wills…"

"Do *you* love him?" Her eyes were round and large and expectant.

Unsure of what to say, I fiddled with the corner of a cushion.

"Do not make her answer, Mary," Martha said. "A matter such as this takes time and subtlety — you do not want to throw Esther at Lazarus — "

"I do not want to *throw* Esther at him, but this cannot take time and subtlety. What if a Nazarene is interested in Esther? What then? She could be taken before Lazarus has a chance."

"My point is not to meddle!" Martha leaned fiercely toward her sister.

"Martha! Mary!" I cried out to get their attention. They looked at me. "I must confess something," I said slowly.

They turned their ears to me.

"I...I have not yet reached my time. I know I am already fourteen years of age, but...it has not come...I do not know why...Aliza had hers far before this age...I am not even...able..."

Mary's mouth opened wide as Martha made a sound of understanding. "Lazarus can wait," Mary finally said, earning a hard look from Martha. "I was betrothed before my monthly bleeding started and now I have it and will be married in a few months!"

"No," I said. "Lazarus cannot wait. If...if by the miraculous hand of Elohim, Lazarus did ask Uncle Clopas for me...he would have to be denied. Our whole family would be embarrassed by such a thing — that I am still just a girl — but...I cannot help it, Martha and Mary...I do not know why...or how..."

"Fear not, Esther," Martha said. "You are still young. I have a friend who did not get hers until she was fourteen. Surely yours will arrive soon."

I clung to that assurance.

But toward the end of the feast, I had another conversation with the two sisters.

"Lazarus was ready to ask your uncle," Mary admitted, sliding her hand around my arm. She looked over her shoulder then pulled me into her chambers. "Martha did not wish for me to tell you, but I think I must. Lazarus spoke to us last night and told us he intended to take you as his wife."

Heat exploded throughout my entire being, and all parts of my body felt like they had stopped working. I could no longer breath. I could no longer move. My heart could no longer beat. He wanted me as his wife!

"But that is when Martha told him about...that you are still a..."

"A girl," I finished for her, finding my breath. My cheeks flushed. Tears pricked at my eyes. "Oh, Mary...this is...shameful!" I did not think I could even look at Lazarus again knowing that he knew...

"Are you angry with Martha?"

"Rather she tell him before he spoke to Uncle Clopas."

"Do not weep, Esther. He may wait for you to reach womanhood."

"Surely he has fifty delicately adorned maidens at the ready. There is no telling when I will blossom."

"But, Esther," Mary said, touching my cheek. "You look more woman than your sister! And you have greater knowledge than most young women. I think that is why Lazarus likes you!"

"Knowledge does not get one a husband, Mary." My voice was shaky. "I thank you for what you have done for me, and for your comfort, but...we will not be sisters-in-law."

Chapter 8
15th Year of Our Lord

You made Adam, and you made his wife Eve to be his helper
and support; and from these two the human race has come.
You said, 'It is not good for the man to be alone; let us make
him a helper like himself.'

TOBIT 8:6

I was terrified to go to Judea and see Lazarus during the next Feast of Un-leavened Bread. In fact, I wished to never look at him again. My heart was broken. So I was relieved to discover, when we were on pilgrimage to Jerusalem, that Lazarus was away from his father's house. Apparently, he was in the vicinity of Judea, but was seeing to his business. I wondered if he was out seeking a wife or had already found one and was settling the arrangements with the blessed girl's family.

Then. It happened. During the feast, my womanhood came. I cried fitfully, for if it had been but a year earlier I could have been betrothed to Lazarus.

Martha and Mary learned of my womanhood during the festival, and rejoiced, but I think they saw the pain in my eyes. I blessed them for not speaking of my circumstances, nor of Lazarus.

Martha already had her first child and Mary was happy with her new husband. I was thankful we could focus so much attention on the two of them and their exciting lives, while I avoided my own sorrows.

But once we returned to Nazareth, I wept nearly every day. "I may as well die!" I moaned dramatically, between sobs.

"Hush now, Esther," Ima snapped. "You will get over him. We will find you another man."

"B-but I do not want another man! There is none other like him. Oh, if I but heard him coming across the mountains and bounding across the hills!"

Ima threw her hands up in the air. "She will get over it," she told Uncle Clopas, who was appalled with my emotions.

By the time the wine harvest arrived a few months later, I convinced myself that Lazarus had forgotten me. Of course, since I did not hear any word of his marriage arrangements, a part of me hoped that he would still come to Nazareth and beg Uncle Clopas for me. But it was a foolish notion.

Indeed, Uncle Clopas searched for a suitable husband for me in our region. I would have preferred Uncle Joseph to be my guardian, for he considered my feelings and sensitivities, while Uncle Clopas was quick to decide, and would easily cast aside my preferences.

"It is a pity," Ima assured me. "But it is time. We cannot delay these matters any longer. We must find a man with a fitting mohar for you. I would personally prefer him *not* to be a Nazarene, or from Cana, or some other minuscule village, but there is little we can do on that matter. We must take what is in our reach. You are still my star, Esther. Fear not."

One particular day, as we harvested grapes for the wine, I was having a dreadful time. I carried that wondrous but sorrowful weight of a babe — Aliza's second child, Athaliah — in my arms. The little body of my dear niece pressed against my breasts. My mantle draped over my shoulder so that her head was covered and protected from the midday sun.

A stone's throw away, the women of Nazareth danced and sang as they crushed the grapes with their bare feet. They held hands and laughed as the juice sprayed.

The whole village assisted in the wine harvest. Even my family, who were not farmers nor had business with vineyards, assisted. In exchange for our contribution, we received a year's worth of wine.

The men were in the vineyards plucking the fruit, while others hauled the pressed grapes back to the village to ferment for 40 days.

Near me, the wives of Simon, Cousin Joses, and Cousin Jude held their babies. Cousin James' wife pressed grapes alongside her children, showing them how to crush the fruit with the soles of their feet.

Aunt Mary gently eased in beside me, a basket of fresh grapes in her arms. "Look, Esther. You are a mother."

I glanced at her, then focused on the baby resting beneath my mantle. "I am no mother, Aunt. This is not my child." Athaliah's actual mother was drinking wine and playfully pressing grapes instead of holding her newborn daughter.

My breath became shallow at the thought. "I do not understand. Aliza has been married for nearly two years now. Yet she acts as if *she* is still a child. How can a child take care of a child?"

I lifted the baby slightly, eyeing Aunt Mary. Despite the sweat that slid down her forehead, she still looked clean and healthy.

"I know. It is not Aliza who I am irritated with." I rocked Athaliah gently. Aunt Mary did not need to say anything. "All the young men in Nazareth have taken wives," I said, my voice, wavering at the last word.

I looked to the terraces and fields that stretched out before us. Between the hills, the men were hard at work harvesting. I could see their strong figures from here.

"Aunt Mary." I lowered my voice. "The women…Aliza and…my friends have been teasing me. They say I will marry the farmer, Abijam. He just lost his wife and now he needs a new wife to care for his seven children."

I looked at the brightness of the sky. Spotting the sun, I shut my eyes, focusing on the strange orange blur I saw behind my eyelids. "You know children are one of my greatest joys but…I want my own children, Aunt Mary. Not…not some old farmer's children."

And I wanted a good husband. A *young* husband. An image of Lazarus popped into my mind. I opened my eyes, trying to shake it away.

"Esther! Esther!" Aliza skipped across the dry grass toward me. I felt my arms tense beneath Athaliah's weight.

Aunt Mary left us to give the women more grapes to press.

"How is my Athaliah?" Aliza licked juice from her fingers then pulled aside my mantle to look at her child's face.

"Keep your voice down," I muttered. "She is sleeping." I knew it was a silly demand when there was so much singing and loud laughter around us.

"You should lay her down back at home, Esther, if you think we are so loud." Her freckled face was red from the heat, movement, and consumption of last year's wine.

"Perhaps I will." I turned from her to the path up the hill to Nazareth.

"Oh, Esther!" Although she put an arm around my shoulder, she was not being affectionate. "There is one thing I must tell you." I smelled the old wine on her breath.

"Word is that Abijam has been working very close to Uncle Clopas today." Aliza could not help the giggle escaping her mouth. "The women and I are betting that the farmer will ask for a betrothal by sundown tonight!"

I pulled away and hurried toward the hill, not caring to look back. "For the love of Israel! Not Abijam!" I whispered, tears in the corners of my eyes.

I was little Esther of Nazareth, last child of the failed rebel, James, with a dowry of a few cedar utensils and a wooden chest. A temptation for no young man, I would be left with the poorest man and oldest widower of the village.

My calves screamed in irritation. I grunted, realizing I had just walked into a cluster of purple thistles. Tearing away, I continued onward.

I did not care to take the donkey's path up the hill. It was an elongated, less steep path for mules. I took a route that was straight. Sweat rolled down my back. I avoided thistles. My sandaled feet scraped against rocks that had clumps of grass growing between them.

When Athaliah moaned, I decided to slow down for her benefit. I was carrying a child, after all.

I looked behind at the scene of women dancing while pressing grapes.

"Elohim." I clenched my teeth as I continued my journey up the hill. "If You are indeed our Father as Jesus says, then I beg You that Your daughter is given a good husband! One that is comely and beautiful and young."

A grunt escaped me as I reached the top. Perhaps Elohim would not give me a husband at all. Perhaps I would make a terrible wife and mother. What woman carried a child roughly up a steep hill?

"I am sorry, Athaliah," I whispered to the babe, touching her forehead. "We are almost there. I will lie you down in the shade of our home."

The sun burnt my forehead. It was not humid in Nazareth, though it certainly was hot. A few olive trees surrounded the synagogue along with a few yellow and white wildflowers. As I ascended the gentle slope of our village, a young man, recently married, hurried down with a wooden wheelbarrow, off to get more sacks of grape juice for fermenting.

When I entered Uncle Clopas' house, I passed through the traklin and into the bedroom. My hands felt sticky as I gently eased Athaliah into her wooden crib. Thanks be to Elohim, she was asleep.

I released a sigh. As I looked down at her, all I felt was a gnawing at my heart for one of my own. Instead of simply taking care of a child because Aliza or my sisters-in-law needed it, I wanted to care out of my own love and motherly responsibility.

I set to work on weaving in the traklin until the rest of my brethren returned.

I heard unfamiliar male voices in the courtyard. They were not the voices of my uncles or male relatives. Leaving the loom, I gazed into the bedroom and saw that Athaliah was still asleep. Then I tried to decipher whose voices I had heard. They sounded joyful. They could not be Roman soldiers, could they?

I shook my head. Of course, they were not Roman. They spoke *Aramaic*, not Greek.

Collecting myself, I ventured out into the light of the courtyard.

My eyes widened. Lazarus was there, speaking to his father Syrus. A group of servants carried their provisions inside our little home.

Heat rushed to my face as Lazarus turned, obviously startled at the sight of me.

"Esther," he mumbled nervously.

"Ah, there is the woman with the famous green eyes," Syrus exclaimed, warmly.

I did not know that Syrus even knew my name.

Athaliah's cry alerted me. "Excuse me!" I hurried back indoors.

As I entered the bedroom to pick up Athaliah, I noticed my hands were shaking. I tried to breathe as I took the child into my arms.

This was the most unexpected visit of my life. I had not seen Lazarus in over a year and did not think the sight of him would make me jitter like a butterfly. I had told myself that I had forgotten any fantasies involving him, but now all those fantasies came flooding back.

Athaliah stopped crying. Speaking courageous words to myself, I decided to go back to the courtyard to greet our guests. I needed to entertain them until my family returned from the fields. At least carrying Athaliah helped me feel guarded.

I entered the courtyard to see the servants piling some trunks, mats, and jars inside. Our home was so small, it would be a challenge to fit it all.

"There is room on the roof," I said, carefully rocking Athaliah.

Lazarus looked at me as if he wanted to say something, but he did not. His brown eyes took in the child in my arms and he looked…I was not sure what his look was. I thought he was troubled and disgusted. He turned to his father. "I will help the servants." He quickly announced, walking out of the house.

I blinked, finding it odd that a rich man would help his servants.

"Esther," Syrus said, taking a step toward me. His long face was tense, and his dark hair fell neatly at his shoulders, attesting to his wealth. "Is…" he spoke hesitantly. "Is this child…yours?"

A sort of shock went through my insides. My eyebrows shot upwards and I flushed.

Syrus cleared his throat. "Forgive me…what I mean is…are you married?"

My eyebrows reached higher. "No," I gasped, embarrassed and confused. "This child is…this child is my sister's."

Syrus' mouth opened in understanding. In the corner of my vision, I saw Lazarus walk in, carrying a trunk. I did not dare look at him straight on.

Lazarus' father let out an uncomfortable laugh. "Ah. I see. I see. Of course. I…of course. Forgive me, dear girl…I did not mean…Lazarus! Esther is holding her *niece*. How kind of her to tend to her *sister's child*." He moved toward his son and told him, "I will take that." Syrus pulled the trunk from Lazarus' arms and walked toward the steps to our roof.

I looked down at Athaliah, too frightened to look anywhere else.

Syrus apologized as he brushed past me. "You two best go outside. I do not want to run you over."

I pressed my lips together as Lazarus obediently followed his father's command. I reluctantly followed, keeping my focus on Athaliah.

My feet felt the transfer from flat to rocky ground.

Lazarus wore an orange and red striped vestment over his dark tunic. Typically, I would wait for him to say something, though he seemed to be at a loss for words.

"Are Martha and Mary with you?" I asked cautiously.

"No," he said quietly. "No, they are not."

I could think of nothing else to say.

"We passed by the grape-pressing on our way up," he finally said. His hair was perfectly wavy over his brow and he was clean-shaven, but his chin was lowered instead of raised with his usual confidence.

"Your mother told us to go to your home," he said. "She is probably on her way here as we speak."

I gave him a shy smile.

"I did not realize you would be up here." An odd shake was in his voice. "You do not enjoy the wine harvest?"

I twisted my lips. What was I to tell him? That I usually did but the women were teasing me? That I could not sing and dance when I would have to marry Abijam? That I desperately wanted to be a mother and thus stole some of Aliza's motherhood?

"I do," I said, opting for honesty. "But this child is mesmerizing." That was very true.

Lazarus smiled, leaning toward me. I did everything in my power not to pull away in fear.

"I agree, Esther. She is beautiful."

My stomach flipped at the way he looked at the child. Or was it the way he said my name?

"Are you journeying to Magdala?" I asked. "To visit your relatives?"

"No, my...my destination is Nazareth, which I am pleased you mention...I...Esther..." He struggled for words. "I am glad you are here so we can speak briefly in private before I would...would speak to your uncle."

In that instant, I was certain what was coming. The joy and thrill that coursed through me were nearly unbearable.

"Jacob once passed by a well, and there he saw Rachel. He knew from his first glance that she was his beloved."

I focused on him, clinging to his every word.

"And he gave seven years of work to Laban so that he could take Rachel as his wife," Lazarus continued. "And then, finding that Laban had tricked him and given him Rachel's sister Leah instead, Jacob waited another seven years for his beloved, Rachel."

I started to beam. I could not help it.

"I come here like Jacob, Esther," he said.

I thought I would fall over. My arms started to sag with Athaliah's weight. It was then that Uncle Clopas and my relatives bounded up the hill.

"Lazarus!" Simon shouted, eager to see his friend.

"Where is your father, boy?" Uncle Clopas asked in his deep voice as he approached us.

The rest went by in a blissful blur. As Syrus, Uncle Clopas, and Lazarus spoke of the arrangements, Ima, my aunts, Aliza, and my brother's wife and children surrounded me, discussing and marveling over the great wonder Elohim had worked that day.

"Jesus, there were so many people! Are there usually that many for a betrothal ceremony? The synagogue was bursting!" I pressed my hands to my cheeks as we spoke on the rooftop. It was the night after Lazarus and Syrus returned to Bethany to prepare a place for me. Our other relatives were spread out across the roof for sleeping as it was too hot to sleep indoors.

"They were eager to see the great blessing of one of their own village daughters," Jesus said in the darkness. I could just see His shadow as He looked up at the stars. Behind me, Ima mumbled to Aunt Miriam who was likely asleep. Uncle Clopas and Uncle Joseph were speaking below in the courtyard.

I thought of how Uncle Joseph put his large warm hand on my head and smiled down at me at my betrothal. "I take pride in this arrangement, Esther," he said. "But I will miss your presence, my girl."

I thought of the rest of the betrothal ceremony. "And I mean no pride or loftiness, Jesus, but did You see the mohar he gave to Uncle Clopas? It was outstanding!" I let out a giggle. My heart was so full I felt it would bound from my chest.

"Good olive wood."

"Of course, that is the part that would catch a carpenter's eye." I laughed freely. "But he gave olives and olive oil," I said. "And nard, myrrh, sheep, and a *colt*." I was still in disbelief. "And a year's worth of wages. Three hundred and fifty dinars! And I cannot forget my favorite gift. Lazarus gave me olivine jewelry," I told him. "It is a green gem that matches my eyes. Lazarus requested that I wear it for our wedding day!"

Perhaps it was odd that I was gushing my womanly joys and excitements to a young man, but Aliza was jealous and would not speak to me. Many of the Nazarene women seemed jealous. Martha and Mary were not here to rejoice with me.

But Jesus listened and was genuinely happy for me.

"I do not know how I will wait a year to enter his house. I wish it were only a day." I pulled my mantle tighter around my shoulders; my knees were pulled up to my chest.

Jesus adjusted his position to sit cross-legged. "Jacob waited seven years for Rachel, but it felt like a few days because of the love he had for her."

"And then another seven years after that! You are right as usual, Jesus. I thank Elohim for the blessings and miracles he has bestowed on me. I am certain the year will be swift. I will need to prepare myself, weave my trousseau and...and learn from my mother what a wife's place is." I frowned at the thought. I was not entirely pleased with the idea of listening to Ima tell me all that was right and wrong in a wife's world, as she tended to grow finicky.

"What is a wife's place?" He asked, His voice soft but clear — and much deeper than it used to be.

"Primarily to please her husband," I said, resting my chin on my knees. "Which comes from bearing many sons, willing whatever the husband wills, raising the children, working hard and generously, praying for the family, keeping peace in the household, hosting and serving guests and relatives, and anything else Lazarus may wish of me. Of course." I added an afterthought. "Being the wife of a rich man must be different than being the wife of a poor man. After all, I will have servants...I...I do not even know if I will have to grind any grain or cook! I have seen Martha and Mary cook in the kitchen, though. Perhaps they do so more out of propriety and hospitality than necessity. Surely, whatever they do I will do.

"I can hardly believe they will be my new sisters and that we will be close to Jerusalem — the Temple. Jesus, imagine it! I could visit the Temple every day. And Lazarus knows so many important people, Pharisees, Sadducees, *Essenes*, and rich merchants and government officials. I know some are envious of me, but regardless of his wealth I am gaining the fairest of all the sons of men." I laughed. "My heart has uttered a good word. I speak my works to the king. My tongue is the...what is it that comes next?" I looked at Jesus.

"My tongue is the pen of a scribe that writes swiftly."

"My tongue is the pen of a scribe that writes swiftly. You are beautiful above the sons of men; grace is poured abroad in your lips; therefore has Elohim blessed you forever. Your sword upon your thigh, O you most mighty. With your comeliness and your beauty set out, proceed prosperously, and reign."

I blushed, just thinking of *him!* "I know this is not a *royal* wedding, but I feel it might as well be! Do you agree? The 45th psalm is perfect for the occasion. Lazarus may as well be a king."

I could not tell if Jesus was smiling or not. "He is the *son* of the King of Kings."

"You mean, Elohim?"

"Yes."

"But I thought the 45th Psalm was a love song." I pursed my lips and leaned back to look at the stars clearly dotting the warm sky.

"It is."

"What you are saying then, is that we are to sing such a love song to Elohim. The way Elohim is like the bridegroom and Israel is like the bride, an unfaithful bride — but a bride, nonetheless. Is that not magnificent and beautiful? Jesus, You always make it seem like I am the one who discovers these truths in the scriptures, but in actuality, it is You!" I waited for Him to say something, but He did not.

"I am sorry, Jesus. I have spoken to You at great length. You must be finished hearing my careless words. I hardly let you take a breath — I hardly take a breath myself! I just...I feel like every problem in my life that I ever had is erased. All of this is nearly too wonderful to be true! Is this not a most miraculous event? I get the husband I love. The sisters I desire. And I will want for nothing and my children will want for nothing."

Jesus agreed, but added, "There will be many hardships, Esther. Even with so lofty a husband."

"But hardships do not matter, Jesus," I told Him. "I will take them all willingly. So long as I am with him and we love each other, I care not for any suffering that I encounter. For that suffering will become sweet if it is for my dear Lazarus."

Chapter 9
16th Year of Our Lord

How beautiful you are, my friend, how beautiful you are!
Your eyes are doves behind your veil.
SONG OF SOLOMON 4:1

I could not wait any longer. I cried inwardly to Elohim. All I had done was wait! Why had Lazarus not come for me?

My heart wept as I looked about the little room. All ten of my bridesmaids were there, holding their torches or oil lamps, ready for the announcement of the bridegroom's coming. I tried to understand. *Expect Adonai, do manfully, and let your heart take courage, and wait for Adonai.* I clenched my hands. *As the deer pants after the fountains of water, so my soul pants after You, O Elohim.* I felt the olivine necklace that rested above my breasts. *Why are you sad, O my soul? And why do you trouble me? Hope in Elohim, for I will still give praise to Him, the salvation of my countenance.*

I did not dare exclaim such words aloud. These foreign women would think I was acting like a leper dying in a cave. Yet I clung to the hope that Lazarus would understand my references to the psalms. Surely, he would.

If he came.

One of the young virgins adjusted the weighty red veil on my head. It was woven with scarlet and violet thread. I did not even remember the girl's name.

I sat on a depleted cushion in the stuffy room. It was hotter here than in Galilee, even at this late hour.

We had expected Lazarus and his groomsmen to arrive *last* night. I had been in this wedding garb, including my jewelry, for over a day and a night. This early evening, my ten bridesmaids once again assisted me in rubbing more oil on my skin and perfuming my hair with myrrh. Praise to Elohim, Aunt Mary was wise enough to bring along extra olive oil, which she generously provided for me, as I had to keep filling my lamp.

Five days ago, a caravan from the house of Syrus arrived in Nazareth. It included a litter for me to rest on. Never would I have imagined being carried all the way from Galilee to Judea by four servants, although it was not very comfortable, despite the pillows and cushions that were arranged for me. I think I was too nervous to shift my position on the litter, lest I become too much of a burden for the servants carrying me.

We stayed at the home of a distant relative in Bethlehem while we waited for the wedding procession. My father's family was originally from Bethlehem, the City of David, where the Messiah would come from. Typically, the bride would wait for the bridegroom in her father's house, but as my uncle's house was five days from Jerusalem, Uncle Joseph arranged for me to prepare myself in Bethlehem, just a couple of miles' journey to Bethany.

Only my closest relatives traveled with me. Most Nazarenes could not afford to spend over two weeks away for the sake of one girl's wedding. At least I had Ima, Aunt Miriam, Aunt Mary, and Aliza. I wished they were in this overheated room with me but instead, they waited outside with the men.

I had the customary ten virgins as my bridesmaids, although I did not know these wealthy young friends of Syrus' family — who did not seem fond of me. From the way they spoke of him I wondered if a few of them were themselves in love with Lazarus. They arrived the day before to prepare me — for something that never happened.

At one point at least five of the bridesmaids slept as if Lazarus were not coming. The other five whispered complaints to one another about the situation. It was a hot summer, and no one knew why the bridegroom was delayed.

"Caesar Augustus died last night," I told a couple of the women. "Surely the Romans are grieving, and the Jews are rejoicing." I felt the twists of my braided hair. At least I was attempting to converse with the women but they looked at me with wide eyes, as if they did not know Augustus had died and therefore Tiberius was now Emperor.

"I wonder if that would delay the…Lazarus…" I said, trying to explain myself to them. "Rebels act when a power is weak."

"Lazarus is not a rebel," one girl said. "You should know that he comes from a just family, but certainly not a violent one. He is not…not a bandit like *poor* men!" Her voice dripped with disdain. Was she referring to my brother Simon whom some accused of being a bandit?

"That was not what I meant," I said in my defense. "Surely Syrus and Lazarus know many a violent man through their travels and business." My father had been one of them, but I did not dare tell them such a thing. They thought little of me already.

"You still hardly know your betrothed," one virgin said to me. "Repeat all this about Lazarus if — and after — you are wedded to him!"

My stomach knotted. If? How could she say "if"? Maybe I would not have felt so miserable if he had joined us on time. I found myself missing even Aliza and her complaints. At least she was my sister and I knew her. And Ima, ever hopeful, would tell me that I was her star.

"It is a strange situation," Aunt Miriam had said the night we left for Judea.

"Very strange." Aliza eyed me and wiped at her freckled cheek. "Usually, the procession to the bridegroom's house takes five paces. Not five days!"

I was certain all the others thought the bridegroom had changed his mind. Both the women in that small room with me and my relatives waiting outside.

Our Father in Heaven. Feeling desperate, I decided to test out praying the way Jesus always did. I addressed Elohim as my father. It did not seem too ludicrous, for my abba was no longer with me. *Praise to Your name…Father… see that Your handmaid is wed. May the bridegroom come in haste!*

It was then that I heard the deep voice of Jesus. The shofar blew, sending a jolt through my entire body. My kohl-lined eyes looked at the virgins around me. They jumped up at once, grabbing their lamps, torches, and jugs of oil. When one of the sleeping girls woke she spilled her oil.

It was not my time to care for such a thing.

"Behold the bridegroom comes!" Jesus called out. "Go forth to meet him!"

Other male voices joined as the shofar continued to sound a deep, prolonged note.

I got up as well, feeling faint, aware of the adornments, vestments, and the heavy veil on my head. I had as many as the high priest!

One bridesmaid settled fresh garlands around my neck: bold-colored flowers of purple, red, and deep pink. Another bridesmaid settled a thin translucent veil over my head while another opened the door.

"Go, Esther! Go on!" Someone practically pushed me out the door where fresh air in the outer room greeted me. I passed through, seeing my aunts, uncles, and siblings holding torches, ready to process. They were all singing a Song of Solomon.

"The voice of my beloved,
behold he comes leaping upon the mountains
skipping over the hills."

"To the courtyard!" Ima directed me as I passed by her, my hands clasping the thick handle of my oil lamp. I walked into the dust of the court to see many people I did not recognize.

Cymbals, flutes, lyres, and drums played. The shofar sounded even clearer outside. It all felt surreal and hazy as I passed the guests. It felt like I was walking through fog, but that must have simply been the veil over my eyes.

I walked out of the courtyard.

And then I saw *him*, surrounded by gladdened groomsmen. The moonlight was a fitting crown for him.

The torchlight that Jesus held by Lazarus' face offered perfect lighting for Lazarus' soft brown hair, pushed back with oil. His beard was trimmed so it covered his skin, without excess. He smiled, showing his straight white teeth.

His gown was covered in a striped coat of sea purple, violet, blue, and scarlet. I did not know if the buttons that lined his coat were plain metal or gold.

He held out his hand to me and I took it, my fingers adorned with gold and silver olivine rings.

"Arise, make haste, my love," Lazarus sang to me. "My dove, my beautiful one."

I smiled. "Hardly had I left them when I found him whom my soul loves," I said, standing beside him. He was about a head taller than me. We turned to face northeast. All the villagers of Bethlehem came out of their homes to watch, clap, cheer, and sing.

"Your eyes are doves behind your veil." He squeezed my hand and whispered, "Please forgive my delay in coming."

"You are here now and that is all that matters." I silenced myself should he wish to tell me more.

When a woman screamed I whipped around and saw Roman soldiers striding down the street toward us. My mouth dropped when the lead, likely the *centurion*, jumped off his horse.

I let go of Lazarus' hand so both of my hands could cup my oil lamp.

Many of the villagers disappeared into their homes. The centurion gestured with his hand and the dozen soldiers with him dismounted and began entering the houses, roughly shoving aside people and goods.

I sucked in a breath, praying they would not come near me. Lazarus stood in front of me like a barricade.

The centurion headed toward our procession. "You can carry on. . ." the Roman called out to us in Greek. ". . .once we search the town for some *Sicarii* who stole from a treasury in Jerusalem." He snatched a torch from the hand of a bridesmaid who stood motionless in fear.

"And that gives you the right to interrupt a wedding feast?" my brother Simon yelled.

"I do not see a wedding feast. I see a bride ready to go to a wealthy prig's home," the centurion replied dryly, eyeing me.

Lazarus stepped forward and I wondered if he meant to attack the Roman, but Simon ran toward the centurion and Lazarus charged after Simon, grabbing his arm and forcing it behind his back. "No!" Lazarus cried. "Simon! Do not act foolish! You will get yourself killed!"

"This is my sister's procession!" Simon yelled and glared back at Lazarus, struggling against him. He pulled free, but Aliza's husband grabbed Simon's other arm to help Lazarus.

"And I am the wealthy prig that she is marrying," Lazarus said through gritted teeth. Then to Simon, "No blood tonight! You know a cross is waiting for you if you do anything."

"At least tell them who you are. The great Lazarus of Bethany!" Simon raised his voice, looking at the lot of soldiers sauntering toward us. "Son of Syrus, owner of the finest olive oil factory in Judea!"

I put a hand to my veiled head, embarrassed by Simon's display and anxious about the Romans' response.

"And who are you?" The centurion walked toward Simon.

"Simon of Nazareth. Son of James," he growled.

"Nazareth?" The centurion looked back at his soldiers. "I have never heard of the place."

"Sir, it is a small village close to Sepphoris," a soldier explained in a hard voice.

"Ah, a Galilean." The centurion examined Simon's fuming face. "No wonder."

"He is no threat to you," Lazarus said loudly in flawless Greek. "Just one angry man. We have a procession to Bethany tonight if you would kindly let us proceed."

"Do not fret, dear bridegroom. You shall proceed. I pity you for gaining such a relative as this Simon. But he is nothing more than a barking dog on a chain, it would seem." The centurion gave a cold smile at the bound Simon, who panted loudly.

"Continue searching," The centurion decided, looking back at his men. "Anyone who sees this fugitive band of Sicarii is obliged by Caesar Tiberius to alert his procurator." The Romans began walking amongst our crowd, inspecting us. They entered my brethren's home.

"Jesus!" Lazarus called out. "Will You lead us out of here? In haste!" Anger flashed from his eyes. He softened as he returned to my side, putting a hand on my arm. "Continue the music!" Lazarus shouted at the musicians behind him.

We started walking to the Roman road that led north toward Jerusalem. The Romans gave one-sided smiles and mock bows as we passed them.

"That was out of the ordinary!" Lazarus whispered to me. "They should not be interrupting wedding processions."

"I am all too used to them interrupting our daily events," I admitted. "Lazarus, what is 'sicarii'? I have never heard the word and my Greek is not fluent."

"They are a sort of extreme sect of Zealots. Sicarii is a Greek word for bandits. It is a term the Romans created to refer to any rebels. Sicarii tend to use short, curved daggers. After they strike, they put their daggers beneath their cloaks and blend in with the crowds."

My lips twisted as I thought of Simon and then of my father. "I am grateful you stopped Simon from attacking. He is rash and angry and...zealous."

"Legions of soldiers are tightening their reigns under the new Emperor. Men like Simon are acting out all over."

I thought to ask Lazarus about his delay and what could have held him up an entire day. But he changed the subject. "Would you like to ride in a litter? I have servants who can carry you."

"No. I like walking." And walking beside *him*.

Perhaps it was good he changed the subject. We should have been talking about romantic, blissful topics. Not violence and politics. "How long of a walk to Bethany?" I asked. Some oil from my lamp dripped down my hands.

"Less than an hour. Are you certain you can walk? You have," he said, looking me up and down. "You have quite the attire."

I put a hand to my heavy veil. Did he not like the way I looked?

But then he said, "I look forward to that veil being lifted. Then I can see your eyes."

Immediately after arriving in Bethany, I went into the bridal chamber with Lazarus. He had prepared the room himself and furnished it. After we consummated the marriage covenant, we came out and celebrated with our guests. The wedding feast lasted the traditional seven days.

Many important men who I did not know came and gave extraordinary gifts of jasmine perfumes, chickens, a brass mirror, gold, and exotic plants. We received furniture and pillows, silk blankets, and alabaster vessels.

My favorite gift was the small wooden wash table that Jesus made for us. He used fine olive wood and on the sides of the table, He engraved star designs and told us that each of the stars was for the children He wished Elohim to bless us with.

I was now a member of the house of Syrus. One day, it would be the house of Lazarus. At least twenty people lived in the household as relatives. The rest were servants and slaves who had their own chambers near the back of the lower courtyard. A maidservant was even assigned to me!

I quickly discovered that life as a rich man's wife could be monotonous. That is, my help was not needed. If I helped in the kitchen, it was out of hospitality and the pleasure of serving, not because the servants could not work. Martha seemed to keep herself very busy with a variety of tasks, and I decided to aid her in preparing the evening suppers.

I found myself missing seeing Jesus every day. And Uncle Joseph. I had not realized how much of a father Uncle Joseph had been to me until I left him. Now Syrus, my father-in-law, was my new father, but the man was nothing like my abba or Uncle Joseph. Syrus was jolly and good-natured. He seemed to have no care in the world, and no caring for me.

One late afternoon, only a couple weeks into my marriage, I was working in the kitchen with Martha and the servants. The men were seeing to their business. I had glimpsed Lazarus at work that morning as he oversaw the transferring of the first and finest pressed oil into jugs.

I looked at Martha as I cut celery. "I wonder if I am pregnant already! How soon will I be able to tell? I hear that it is a feeling — an instinct."

"You must not romanticize pregnancy, Esther." She stirred the pot on the stove. "If you miss your monthly bleeding, then we will know. It took a few months after my wedding for me to conceive."

"And now you have two little ones," I said, plopping the celery into a dip of mint sauce. "Two little girls. Mary told me that she knew she was pregnant the morning after making love with her husband. She woke up feeling different."

I saw Martha's eyes roll to the side. "Surely, she did," she said, a bite of sarcasm in her voice.

"She also said that she knows her child will be a girl." I moved down the polished wood counter to grind pepper with a small peg and bowl.

"Because instinct told her." Martha groaned. "It sounds just like Mary. We need you, Esther, to have a son, that he may be an heir for Lazarus and take the property and trade."

What if I only had girls? What would happen?

Martha chopped walnuts, mint leaves, dill, and parsley.

Eucharia bustled in. "You almost done, women? The men have finished their work, and you know how hungry they get."

"Yes, Mother," Martha said, and told a servant to take the bread out of the oven. The smell of the fresh leavened bread made my stomach roll in hunger.

"I made some pomegranate juice earlier today," Martha said. "Esther, will you fetch it from the wine cellar?"

"Yes," I responded. I turned from my work with the pepper, wiped my hands on my apron, then hung it on a hook.

I opened the wooden door on the floor and shivered as I made my way down the cool steps. "Elohim," I whispered. "Do not let there be any scorpions."

It was dark and I could hardly see, so I was thankful for the light from the kitchen. I looked at the supply of food and drink, searching for the dark red liquid. Peeking at different bottles, I finally found the pomegranate juice.

I took a quick sniff from the jug to ensure I was correct. The sweet smell overloaded my nostrils. I felt something brush against my foot and I squealed, dropping the jug. It splattered across the floor. All of it.

Some of it soaked the hem of my beige tunic.

I groaned, throwing my hands up in the air. "It is but the first month that I am a wife!" And it was no scorpion that brushed against my foot. It was merely my foot brushing against a sack of potatoes!

I bit my lip, dreading the fact that I now had to go back upstairs and announce the embarrassing news. I looked around for something to wipe up the mess but could not find anything.

"Esther," Martha called, making me start. "Are you well down there?"

"Yes, yes," I yelled back. "I will be right up."

I straightened the brand-new green veil on my head, that was a gift from Lazarus, and shakily stepped over the spilled juice. My sandals stuck to the ground and I began wiping the soles on the stone floor, unsure of what else to do.

At least the jug did not break. "Hear O Israel, I promised that I would not make void my covenant with you!" I thought of the scriptures.

Once I had cleaned my sandals, I made my way back up the stairs.

"Did you not find it?" Martha asked, settling her slender hands on her hips.

"I did...I just...forgive me, Martha, but I...I dropped it and...it spilled upon the floor."

She sighed and her pretty, sharp features tightened in annoyance. I bit my lip hard enough to draw blood. "Alright," she said. "Have a servant clean it up, then."

It was distressing to ask a servant for help. First, I did not even know her name. Second, I was humiliated that I needed someone to clean up my mess. I felt as if Eucharia, Martha, and the other servants were watching as I asked a young girl to go to clean up my spill in the cellar.

I told myself it was only pomegranate juice. I had to stay calm and not weep. Why did this one event make me feel like I had failed as a woman? And I had irritated my sister-in-law!

"Let us begin supper," Eucharia announced, walking out of the kitchen. I looked down at the hem of my tunic. The stain made me wince, but I could not leave and change my tunic now.

What would the family think of me? I could not be late for supper!

So I straightened my veil once again and pulled down my sleeves, which I had rolled up. I walked out to the evening light of the courtyard and passed into a large banquet room. There was one main table in a horse-shoe shape for the family. When hosting guests, only the most honorable would sit at the table, while the women and the others scattered about the floor at small, short wooden platforms. Today, like most days, the women reclined on the right half of the cedar table against the back wall, drapes and curtains behind us. The men sat at the left. As I ritually cleansed my hands, I tried to keep my focus off my stained tunic. It looked like blood.

What would they think of me? That I was unclean?

Lazarus smiled warmly as I passed him. I gave him a quick smile as I sat on a cushion opposite. I feared my insides would collapse from embarrassment and I looked at my lap, trying to hide my tunic beneath the tablecloth. If only I had kept my apron on when I went to the cellar. That would have protected me from pomegranate stains.

I looked up, smiling again, trying to show that nothing was wrong. Yet the side of my lip was twitching.

The meal began and the servants brought out different dishes, placing them at the center of the short table. Fine bread with mint sauce and cheese dip, olive relish, fish poached in white wine, and carrots with cumin. One servant brought out mango juice — likely a replacement of the pomegranate.

As a woman, I did not have the right to speak during meals unless I was spoken to by a man. Family discussions had not been as rigid in Nazareth, but with such a wealthy and prominent family, my status strangely felt lowered. I was now even more unworthy of leading a conversation amongst the important men.

The men spoke about the upcoming winter and cooling weather that would be a fair refreshment after the burning sun of summer.

"Lazarus," Syrus said, leaning toward his son. "Tell me of your conversation with Shecaniah."

"We discussed the security for Gethsemane. We agreed that the watchmen on the Mount were not enough to keep pilgrims from camping there without permission and picking the olives from the trees," Lazarus said, ripping a piece of bread apart so he could dip it in olive relish. "We hired more men to guard the garden during feast days."

"Will they begin this new system for the Feast of Tabernacles?" Syrus asked good-naturedly. One hand rested on his belly as the other smeared cheese dip onto a small piece of bread.

"Yes, we will ensure we are not cheated." Lazarus' voice rose in irritation as he grabbed a fish for himself. "One would think that visiting Adonai in the Temple would encourage one not to steal. Instead, they act mad and greedy."

"We have the oldest olive tree in Judea, there," Hezekiah proudly exclaimed. He was even taller than Lazarus. As Martha looked at her husband I wondered if she was annoyed by his boasting.

Syrus dipped his finger in the cheese dip that had dripped on his plate and licked it. "I do want to ensure that the poor can take the scraps that the workers miss."

"But only the poor and widows," Hezekiah said. "Not just any selfish pilgrim."

As we neared the end of the meal, a servant placed an orange on my plate. I looked up at the servant curiously. Why was I the only one given an orange?

I looked at Lazarus, who was smiling at me from across the table. "For you, my bride," he said, leaning forward. His eyebrows danced upward.

I blushed, smiling back at him, then eagerly looked at the orange. I had never had one before but heard it tasted like fruit from Eden.

I touched the cool textured surface of the exotic fruit and wondered how I was supposed to peel it. I decided to grab a small knife from the center of the table. How hard could it be to peel an orange?

I started to cut the skin from the fruit in a circular motion.

The knife hit my thumb.

I looked up to see if anyone had noticed and none had to my great relief. But my thumb began to bleed. I placed the orange on the table and covered the cut with my other hand. When I moved my hand in order to look at it, bleeding continued down my wrist, making the cut appear much worse than it actually was.

I looked up again. Lazarus was staring at me questionably and Martha gasped beside me. Drips fell on the lap of my tunic. I closed my eyes, wishing the scene would disappear.

"Esther," Martha whispered. "You are bleeding!"

I nodded, unsure of what to do. I needed a bandage but where were they?

"Forgive me." Martha cleared her throat. "Father, may Esther and I be permitted to leave? She has cut her thumb."

I winced. Did she have to tell my father-in-law what I had done?

"Is she well?" Syrus looked at me, removing his hand from his stomach. More heat rushed up my neck.

I nodded. "Yes…it is only…only a little cut…"

Syrus gave his approval and Martha grabbed my arm, pulling me toward the kitchen.

My legs wobbled.

"It is as you said. It is just a little cut." Martha told a servant to fetch a bandage. "I will have to show you how to peel an orange sometime." She let out a long sigh. "I suppose you never learned."

I looked down at my hand, clasping my other hand. "I did not think I needed a tutor for peeling fruit," I said dryly.

The rest of the night went all too slowly. I was unable to help with the dishes since my thumb continued to bleed, making me ritually unclean.

Later that night, I was in Lazarus' chamber. Fresh lilies in clay vases were placed about the room, replacing the ones from our wedding feast a couple of weeks ago.

"Did you get to finish the orange?" Lazarus asked as he lay beside me in bed. I made sure he could not see my face as I rested my head beneath his arm.

"Yes," I said. "It was my first orange! It tasted delicious. Thank you."

"Let us look at that thumb." He gently took my hand to examine it, then kissed the small linen bandage.

"Forgive me, husband," I whispered. "I fear I dishonored you and Elohim tonight with my many faults."

He dropped my hand, giving a soft chuckle. "You and my sister Mary should compete for who is the most dramatic."

I frowned, not finding it humorous. "Until I give you a child, I must make myself useful in serving the household. I noticed your cloak has a loose thread in it. I will mend it tomorrow."

"If you insist. We can always have one of the servants do so."

I frowned again. "What would you like me to do, then?" Besides loving him when he came home at night?

"Perhaps Martha can teach you how to read."

I jumped upward and looked at him. "Read?" I exclaimed. My hair fell across my face as I leaned toward him.

"Is this excitement or fear?"

"Excitement, but…but Lazarus…" I pushed some hair behind my ear. "What would I do with such a skill?"

"Do you need it as a skill? What if you simply enjoy it? What if it pleased your husband? It cannot hurt you. Imagine if you could read the Torah and study the writings and the prophets."

"I would feel so selfish learning."

Lazarus lifted a lazy hand. "Give an occasion to a wise man, and wisdom shall be added to him. Teach a just man, and he shall make haste to receive it."

"I am not a man."

"I hope not."

"Lazarus," My voice lowered in frustration.

"Esther." He playfully mimicked me. "Pursue it as your pleasure and my pleasure. As you said, until we have a child. It will serve me and the household. I want you to read from the prophet Ezekiel, Esther. I think you would like his imagery and metaphors. He is very dramatic, like you. And I want you to tell me what you think of him; his thoughts on death and dying. You will be awed that all that you think you know is but a drop in the ocean compared to what you can learn."

The idea was so foreign to me. Never in my life had I considered *me* studying the law of Moses and the scriptures. That was only for the rich who had time and means to do so.

But now I was rich. And Martha and Mary studied the scriptures. Perhaps an education would help me become a closer relative in this household.

I would be educated in the way of the wealthy and fulfill my purpose as a rich, pious man's wife.

"Why did you choose me?" I settled back down into the crook of his arm.

"You have wounded my heart, my sister, my spouse, you have wounded my heart with one of your eyes." He spoke of the Song of Solomon.

"I thought your father would find some princess for you to marry." My lips protruded. I settled a hand on Lazarus' chest. "Would it not have benefited your family to make an alliance?"

"If you have not noticed, Esther, we tend to marry in the family. Martha married our cousin. Mary, a very distant relative in Emmaus. Even Mara married a relative in Magdala."

"Because Mara was found with the man! Unmarried. What else was to be done?" It was the shame of the whole house of Syrus. "But you, Lazarus! I thought you would want a daughter of a Sadducee or a wealthy Levite. Not a Nazarene."

"The last thing I want is an alliance with a Sadducee." Lazarus sounded annoyed. "They are defiling our Temple." He spoke quickly. "It seems every man who makes more than a dinar a day supports Rome. If Adonai has given the Sadducees the wealth of Solomon then let them act with Solomon's wisdom."

My eyebrows lowered as I pondered his words.

"Besides, Esther. I found you and I wanted you. I was growing anxious for a while there. Praise Elohim you finally started…you know…"

He was speaking of my late menstruation.

I never could have suspected that my monthly bleeding would be my perpetual curse.

Chapter 10
21ˢᵗ Year of Our Lord

One alone is my dove, my perfect one, her mother's special one,
favorite of the one who bore her.
SONG OF SOLOMON 6:9

"Let my eyes shed down tears." My fingers dug into my tan cheeks, pulling downward. "Night and day! Without rest!" I cried out the words of the prophet Jeremiah. "The great affliction with an exceedingly grievous evil!" I beat my fist against my breast.

Jeremiah cried such words when we were overtaken by Babylon. Jerusalem had been destroyed. The people of Judah were in exile. A repercussion of sinning against Adonai.

"My sin is always before me." I flailed on my knees on the tiled floor of my husband's bedchamber. I reached for the rug in front of me, across from the bed, and squeezed the coarse, red-dyed wool.

"Woe to me, my mother, that you gave me birth. This star that does not shine! I am far worse than the strife and contention to the land." My bare feet slid against the polished tiles. "Adonai, You have cast me from Your presence." I lifted my head. The ceiling was painted white for greatest light, as we had but a lone square window in the large room. Red and orange frescos decorated the walls, matching the colors that Lazarus and I wore on our wedding day.

"Your words were found, and I did eat them." I shook my head, eyes shut tight. "Your Word was to me a joy and gladness of my heart!" My voice boiled louder.

Over the past five years, the scriptures were indeed my favorite pastime; the loveliest song to listen to; my joy to study and learn; the excitement of my prayers.

"My El! My El! Why have You forsaken me?" I cried. As terror spiked through me, I banged my fist on the ground. "It is I who have forsaken You! You turned Lot's wife into a pillar of salt. That is all my womb is made up of: Salt!"

"Esther!"

I started, totally unaware that Lazarus had entered the bedchamber. My head whipped toward him, my thin black hair slapping my face.

"What are you doing, woman?" My husband closed the wooden door behind him and looked at me warily. I could see the indecision in his expression. Should he approach me, a dishonorable wife? Or call for a guard to cast me into the streets?

I panted like a dog as he decided to slowly approach.

"I do not think I have ever seen you in this state," he said.

I gazed up at him. He looked so tall from down here. His firm shoulders that usually relayed an air of superiority were clearly stressed. His brown beard was a shadow on his face. His oiled hair curled just below his ears.

I put a hand to my head knowing I must have looked horrible. I sniffled, starting to fidget under his gaze.

"Esther...tell me what ails you." His brown eyes that I used to sigh over, terrified me now. He was a good man, handsome, wealthy, strong, and devout.

And he was trapped with *me* for a wife!

"My ailment..." I whimpered. "Is actually what ails you."

Lazarus' face paled but he listened, nonetheless.

"I am barren," I raised my voice, but not too loudly, lest Lazarus' family or the servants heard me.

Barren. I finally said the word aloud. Until then, I had kept it in my head. Surely Syrus, Eucharia, and the whole household spoke of it. The whole town surely knew. I could almost hear the word "barren" on their lips as I passed them when journeying to Jerusalem. I could see it in the faces of the servants and slaves as they waited on me. They gave me looks of pity, but behind closed doors, they must have curled their lips and jeered at me.

I looked at Lazarus, trying to figure his reaction, but his face was blank. "Let us call for the midwife again," he finally decided.

I wanted to throw the rug in my hands at him, but I would not dare.

"She has worked with me for years now. She has given up on me." I heard the shake in my voice. "She gave me everything her profession taught her. Cleansing herbs to pure oils...to...to a massage to release tension — *anything* that would increase my fertility. She is the most renowned midwife in Judea. If she cannot help me then only Adonai can!" I raised my eyes to the limestone ceiling.

"We will call the physician — "

"Lazarus! Lazarus," I mumbled. "It has been f-five years. Almost five years since our wedding n-night!" I clenched my teeth together as more tears cascaded down my face. "How can you even look at me? I do not see why you have not divorced me — "

"Enough, Esther!" He said sharply, but not loud enough to be a shout. "I do not want to hear your self-pity. I am the face of this…this…"

Family. If we had children, he would have been able to say "family."

"Should you even be weeping like this? Surely the stress will only prevent conception. Esther, I am the only son of my father. I do *not* have any sons of my own." He put his hands to his head, wringing his fingers through his hair. "I will not hear of your…laments…" he waved his hand in the air. "I am doing everything I can to *not* lament and everything possible to give us a son."

I stiffened, feeling unable to breathe.

"I have not broken one rule from the law of Moses. As for my family history…my father has done some questionable actions." He paced back and forth between the wash table and the bed.

"What actions?"

"They are not to be repeated," he said. "The only other sin I can point to is my sister's, though she is far away at Father's home in Magdala. Mara is a sly, seductive woman, filthy as a prostitute. Can a woman's sin and my father's sin stain *me*?" He stopped for a moment to look straight at me. "Then you… we have searched your family history…"

"I…" I gulped. "My father was a Zealot, and my brother Simon is one as well, but they have only acted in the name of Adonai. If they killed, it was only for the sake of Elohim's kingdom."

"Which as you know, I consider to be a crime." Lazarus sighed, his hands clasped tightly behind his back.

I knew it well. He often spoke of his dislike for the Zealots and their methods. "And then…" I continued, a new thought forming. "This has not come to mind until now…" Should I have told him and given him greater cause for grief? "Do you know that my Aunt Mary conceived Jesus when she was betrothed to my uncle Joseph? It was before she entered Uncle Joseph's house as his wife."

"I have heard the rumors," Lazarus said curtly. I tried to decipher if he believed their sin could make me barren, but I could not tell what was on his mind. Crossing then uncrossing his arms, he sat on the bed, covered in red and orange blankets of silk and wool.

I had examined myself as well. I always ritually purified myself after touching any animal or food that was unclean, after menstruation, intercourse, and before entering the Holy Temple. I was devoted to the Torah, the writings, and the prophets.

However, I coveted much of my neighbors' possessions. I coveted the children of my sister and cousins; the children of my sisters-in-law. I coveted every woman who was looked upon with favor for doing the task she was created for: Motherhood. I coveted the life that dwelled in the womb. Whether Adonai graced me with a little son or a daughter — I cared not.

I may have held babes against my chest as an aunt. I may have taught children or watched over boys and girls in the town as a neighbor and friend. Yet I would never hold a babe against my chest knowing that he was mine to love, care for, and protect. I would never teach children out of my duty to them as my Jewish sons and daughters.

And my husband would never look at me as a true woman. I was incomplete.

"Well, rise," Lazarus said, quickly standing. "To battle against it." The strain in his voice was evident. He spoke the words that Adonai said to the prophet Obadiah; words that Lazarus and I had begun to repeat to each other during moments of trial as encouragement. Yet Lazarus looked anything but encouraging.

I looked at him quizzically.

His shoulders slouched as he exhaled. "What I came up here to tell you in the first place was that your family has arrived for Passover. They are already asking for you."

My eyes expanded in horror. "Why did you not say so?" I asked, though my stomach rolled at the thought of seeing them. Ima's eyes now held only condemnation. Uncle Clopas' roughness had not changed. My sister's carelessness. My brother's zealous statements. Aunt Mary's annoying quietness. Even those who I looked upon with more favor. I did not want to see Aunt Miriam and her sweet ways. I did not want to see Jesus with His consideration for me; I was not deserving of anyone's kindness. I did not want to see Uncle Joseph, so much like a father to me. I did not want to see Cousin James and Cousin Jude with their beautiful and large families.

"*Why did I not tell you?* You were — *are* — sobbing on the floor!"

"I cannot go downstairs to greet them," I said, quietly as he rigidly stepped closer to me.

"You must. For their sake. You have not seen your mother in nearly a year." He bent down and snatched the rug out of my hands, making my fingers burn.

"It is for her sake that I do not." I blew out the long black hair stuck to my mouth. "Look at me, husband."

He did so, likely deciding whether he should comfort me, scold me, or leave me be.

"Compose yourself, then." He stepped away. "We will..." He began, only to toss his hand in the air in disregard then pour water in the washbowl on our table. As he splattered the water on his face, I tried to finish his sentence for him.

We will...discuss this later? We will...smile for our brethren? We will... perform another fast? Another sacrifice?

After drying his face with a white linen towel, he slapped it on the table. Grabbing his sandals, he strapped them on, then left the room without another word. At least he eased the door gently to a close.

I took a shaky breath, only to let out a moan. This was an agonizing grief! I had not lost a child. Rather, I had not had one in the first place. Not even for a moment.

I clawed at my womb. What kind of woman was I if I had no children? What honor could I give to my husband and his family? What would I occupy my life with in this manor house — rich, affluent, and noble — if I were childless?

I stood up on shaky legs, stumbling toward the wash bin. I clasped my metal mirror and gazed into it, only to cringe.

Red splotches marked my face and the whites of my eyes. My hair would serve better as a swallow's nest. My green eyes, though, were as vivid as ever. It was as if my tears had watered them, only deepening their color. Olivine colored. I wore the linen green veil that Lazarus gave me because it brought out the color in my eyes. I wore it often to please him, though I did not like the attention I received from others because of it.

I thought my eyes were a sign of beauty that attracted my husband, but perhaps they were a sign of my curse. So all would know that the green-eyed woman was barren. The tired wrinkles around my eyes were like raisins. If I stopped weeping and lined them with kohl, I would have looked closer to my 21 years of age. Yet since my marriage to a rich man, my face thickened, and my body as well — not from bearing many children — but from rich delicacies and little activity. I set the mirror down on the table, turned away, and held myself with my arms.

What was I?

If I just had one healthy son, my appearance and my sins would be cloaked, and I would be honored and forever satisfied.

"Adonai." My tears blurred the room around me. "Give me a child. I beg You, oh Elohim, El of Abraham. El of Isaac. El of Jacob. El of Sarah. El of Rebekah. El of Rachel. Let me fulfill the duties and yearnings of a woman. *Make me a mother!*"

I stood hunched over the wash bin, but raised my head at the sound of joyful chatter and the greetings of my family downstairs. Was that the deep voice of Uncle Clopas? Was that Aliza's squeal? Was that the cry of my cousins' children?

"My nephews," I whispered solemnly. "Always an aunt. Never a mother." I swiped the hair from my face. "Elohim, give me the strength to move." My legs felt immobile. "Enough, Esther," I told myself. Straightening, I felt aches strain the whole length of my body, yet I could not stay up here mourning. My family was asking for my whereabouts.

My heart felt like a block of heavy stone as I swept my straight, thin hair over one shoulder. I poured water into the bowl from a stone pitcher, splattered the cool water on my face, and patted it dry with a white linen cloth.

Grabbing a comb, I started dragging it through my ink-black hair.

I threw my veil around my shoulders and raised it over my head so it draped down the sides of my face and past my shoulders. When I was hard at work in Nazareth, I would tightly wrap my veil around my head, tucking every strand of hair away, but now I wore it more for style. I flipped one side of it across my neck and over the opposite shoulder.

I searched for the little alabaster jar holding my perfume and found it on a lowest shelf. Opening it, the smell of jasmine and violet filled my nose. I hoped its scent would soothe my woes. Instead, it felt like my stone heart had dropped to the pit of my stomach. Nevertheless, I dipped my finger into the liquid and dabbed it behind my ears and on my wrists.

Pushing aside my emotions, I exited the room. Voices carried from every direction in the household and it felt like I had plunged myself into a storm at sea — above me; on the third floor; below me; outside. It was unusually busy, with three times its usual occupancy because of the pilgrims we hosted for Passover.

I wiped my eyes, sniffing loudly. Servants hurried back and forth as I made my way to the staircase. When I reached the bottom, I would face my whole family.

I turned the corner to the staircase and started, my hand bounding toward my chest. "Jesus," I breathed. I lowered my hand. Normally, I would be ecstatic to see my old friend, but I still had no wish to see anyone. Not even Him.

"Esther," Jesus said gently. "Shalom." His voice was clear. Deep, but not grainy. His dark brown beard was full and His youthfulness eminent. His eyes were a mixture of browns and bronze. As for His hair, it was still rather unruly, sticking up in different directions like an unpruned vine.

His undyed tunic was loose, the sagging sleeves reaching above His elbows. The tunic could not hide the firm muscles He had from years of hard labor. His arms had splinters and scrapes on them because He worked with stone and wood.

Not particularly handsome, He had an ordinary appearance. Despite this, He still had the same intriguing mannerism that had been with Him as a child.

"What..." I began. "What are You doing up here?" I expected the visitors to all be downstairs in the guest wing. Not here in the family quarters.

"My mother sent Me up here with our gift."

I looked to the basket in His arms. My nose crinkled as I looked at the assortment of barley, peas, and lentils which must have just been harvested. It was strange for a man to be the bearer of such a gift. And for Him to be the one to carry it instead of one of the women or servants. Still, whatever Jesus' mother said, He did.

"How is Your father? And mother? I miss You all," I said mundanely, trying to muster some enthusiasm to see Uncle Joseph. I was ashamed that he too knew I was barren.

"They are eager to see you. We all are," Jesus said, warm as ever. A servant hurried up the steps with a sack over his shoulder.

I put a hand to my head, patting my veil.

"Tell Me how *you* are," Jesus said.

I lifted my shoulders slightly. The stone heart that seemed to fall down to my stomach was pressing deeper into my gut. "I am...well. It is always a joy to see You and everyone from home." I displayed my teeth in a wide smile for extra emphasis.

Jesus looked at me expectantly as if I were not finished speaking. He could see right through me. To that very stone in my gut!

"And..." my eyes bounced off the walls as I frantically searched for something to say. "I must greet my mother. I miss her terribly." It was a lie.

With that, I hurried past Him, down the flight of stairs. Perhaps I should have taken the gift from Jesus and not left Him standing there, but I did not think I could stay near Him without breaking into tears.

After a few strides, I was in the courtyard. It was bubbling with people — far too many people that I knew.

"Esther. At last!" Ima swayed toward me, her arms extended. I would have rather walked into the doors of my room and hide, but I walked into her arms.

"Shalom, Ima. Your travels went well?" I felt the worn material of her maroon veil as my hands settled on her back.

"As well as a five-day desert journey can be," she said simply. "Now." She stepped away so that she could look at me. Her gaze glided over my body, resting near my abdomen. "Do you bear news for us?"

It was exactly as I feared. Could there not be one moment in which my state was not evident?

"No. I bear nothing, Ima."

"Esther," she whispered, reaching for my hands. I reluctantly let her take them. Her worn, calloused hands were surprisingly soothing to touch. She looked at me softly, concern encrusted in the crinkles at the corners of her eyes.

All will be well, Esther. She could have said. *I have faith in Elohim, and I will not cease praying that He bestows children upon you. I will never reject you, Esther. This is not your fault. I am here, and I will help you through this.*

She said, "Are you certain you and Lazarus are doing everything the proper way?"

"Are we doing…" I mulled over her question. "Ima!" Alarm sparked through me as I realized what she meant, blood rushing to my face. I looked around, hoping no one could hear her words. "Mmh…I…of course we are!" I mumbled. "I…Ima, we have been married for five years. Lazarus and I know…what we are doing."

"You must be doing *something* wrong. If not physically, then spiritually. You are ritually clean, are you not?"

"Yes. Lazarus' family has their own mikveh. We live right by Jerusalem. I follow all the purification laws."

"Elohim does not punish for no reason, child — "

"Please, can we…" I started, trying to find words, putting a hand to my head. I feared I would go mute from distress. "Can we…discuss this later?" I looked up at the relatives nearing, waiting for Ima to depart so they might greet me.

"You do not look well," Ima stated, squeezing my hands roughly.

Of course I did not look well! "I am fair."

She released my hands and stepped aside.

Aliza bounded toward me, one of her children at her hip. "Ah, the queen. Queen Esther." She slapped her free arm around my shoulder. She did not mean that as an endearment. Ever since I married Lazarus, she called me a queen. Sometimes she said it light-heartedly, but I could hear the envy in her voice. Envy that I lived in a home that was like a palace, as she still resided in a home that was like a cave.

"Take this one for me, will you?" She shoved her youngest son into my arms. "Be good to Aunt Esther."

I clenched my teeth at the wretched word "aunt." But then, my heart could not help warming with longing and love as I felt the softness of the toddler. I pulled my nephew against my chest.

"Aliza, you have at last found our sister?" Simon strode toward me.

Aliza stepped away from us to speak to some of the women. I noticed both of my sisters-in-law, Martha and Mary, with them. Martha glanced at me, raising her sharp eyebrows. She certainly knew of my predicament but was kind to me regarding it.

I swayed back and forth with the child in my arms. "Brother. Welcome back to Bethany." I saw Simon more often than my mother and sister because men were required by the law to come to Jerusalem for three different feasts a year.

"If only it were not crawling with Sadducees." He crossed his arms over his chest. "There likely are a legion of Romans sleeping in each of their houses, just waiting to spring out and desecrate all that we know to be holy."

My shoulders sagged. Simon could never keep away from politics. But I could not blame him. A few years ago, his wife was taken by Roman soldiers as payment for taxes. Simon did not know if his wife was a slave or dead.

"Rejoice that you are here, then," I said, trying to divert his mind from his pain. "You will not see more priests until you get closer to the Temple. Rest for now. You have been given a drink, I see?"

I noticed the goblet in Simon's hands. He raised it with a smile. "Always the finest wine. Syrus never disappoints. Where is he? I have been wanting to speak to him about some pressing issues in Galilee...It all shoots from Jerusalem." He raised a thick finger. "It all shoots from Jerusalem."

"Jerusalem or Rome?" I ask dryly.

"Jerusalem *is* Rome." Simon lightly smacked my shoulder with the back of his hand. "That is why we must give it back to Elohim." Simon strode away in search of Lazarus' father. Simon's recklessness and anger had grown with his years. Losing his wife was the climax.

I let my face fall into the crook of my nephew's neck. His hands curled around my shoulders, and he let out a moan which Aunt Mary must have heard, because our eyes met. I bounced my nephew in my arms and went to my aunt.

"Shalom, my child," she said as I approached. She embraced me and my nephew. "I see you are already caring for Aliza's son. You are a natural mother."

I frowned deeply, pulling from her embrace.

Her dark blue mantle draped over her one shoulder.

"I saw the gift you brought for Lazarus' family," I said. "Thank you. You know I like peas."

"I do. You saw my son, then?"

"Yes, I saw Him." I thought of how quickly I left Jesus' side.

"We were talking about you on the way here, Esther."

"We?"

"Joseph, Jesus, and I."

"Why is that?" I bit my lip, nervous. Uncle Joseph was a bit behind Aunt Mary, speaking to friends from Cana. For the briefest moment, our eyes met. He gave me an endearing, loving look, like a father who was proud of his daughter.

I glanced away.

"I asked if they would pray with me for you," Aunt Mary said.

Heat rushed to my face. I looked down at my nephew, his brown hair a mound of curls. "I am not worthy of your prayers." My voice was strained.

"Job did nothing to merit pain or suffering, Esther. Neither have you."

"Aunt Mary," I whispered, tears pricking at my eyes. "Do you know of the sorrows that fill me?" I found myself saying.

Aunt Mary removed her blue mantle from her shoulder and gently wrapped it around my shoulders. I stiffened, but warmth filled me. Warmth from Aunt Mary's mantle and warmth from my nephew's little body.

"You are in the hollow of my mantle," Aunt Mary said quietly but clearly. Pulling me into an embrace she placed her hand on my head. Instead of tears rushing from me, my shoulders sagged in relief. The tension in my forehead broke up.

"You, Esther, are in the crossing of my arms."

Chapter 11

A woman of worth is the crown of her husband,
but a disgraceful one is like rot in his bones.

PROVERBS 12:4

It took every bit of my strength to get out of bed this morning. My eyes were horribly sensitive. They continually watered, but thankfully had not spilled over since my fit of crying yesterday, when our guests arrived for the feast.

"My father was up all-night speaking to your brother," Lazarus told me as a manservant assisted him in putting on his henna-colored vest.

"What for?" I asked, feeling my dry lips.

"Business," Lazarus said testily, as the servant smoothed the vest and then adjusted the collar.

Lazarus sat down at a cedar wood table, imported from Lebanon, so the servant could oil his brown wavy hair. A lamp that my maidservant had lit earlier hung from the ceiling, giving us light.

My servant had gone in search of balsam for my chapped lips.

"Why would Syrus do business with my brother?" I asked walking toward the wash table to pluck the metal mirror from it. "Is he in need of a carpenter?"

Lazarus blew out a long breath. "No. He...never you mind, Esther."

I looked back at his tense facial muscles, pain pinching my heart. Ignoring it, I looked at the mirror. I inspected my green eyes, as usual. The eyes that were meant to make me a star.

Lazarus' father was a wealthy man who owned this countryside manor house. Its property stretched all the way to the main village of Bethany. Syrus owned several olive groves, pressed the oil on his own property, and sold and distributed his variety of oil products. His goods were exported throughout Judea, Galilee, and even as far as Persia. As his only son, Lazarus would inherit the business from his father in due time.

My husband already worked hard beside Syrus, traveling as a merchant to major cities like Caesarea and Tiberias. He wore his father's signet gold ring which marked him as the heir of Syrus of Bethany. He sealed papers and documents with it.

Lazarus gave me a plethora of fine clothes and comforts. If only they truly did comfort me.

"We leave in the hour," he said stiffly, rubbing his temples. "Your Aunt Miriam may have trouble walking into Jerusalem. I would give her a litter to assist her, but it could turn upside down in the crowds. What do you think of a colt?"

"A colt would do," I said, patting my hair, twisted in a fancy updo that my maidservant created. On one hand, the finery attested to the celebration of today's Passover. On the other, it disguised my inner turmoil.

I walked over to the sofas and settled on a yellow and green cushioned bench.

"Rejoice greatly, O daughter of Zion! Shout for joy, O daughter of Jerusalem," I said quietly. Mention of the colt had made me think of the Messiah. If I were a mother, perhaps my son could be the Messiah. "Behold your king will come to you, the just and savior. He is poor, and riding upon an ass."

"Upon a colt the foal of an ass." Lazarus finished Zechariah's prophesy, fiddling with his thick ring as the servant finished grooming his hair.

Our common love for the scriptures was our greatest bond. Yet even that bond seemed to be wearing as of late.

A knock sounded at the door.

"Enter," Lazarus said.

My maidservant walked in, carrying a small jar.

"May Elohim reward you," I told her as she gave me the bronze jar filled with oiled balm. I stuck my finger in the creamy texture and spotted my lips with the vanilla, cinnamon, and clove ointment.

Lazarus dismissed his manservant and turned to me. "You look fair," he said. It sounded more dutiful than loving. We had not spoken a word about my outcry yesterday.

With that, he left the room. I dismissed my servant as well.

I let out a shaky breath now that I was alone. "Adonai, do not permit my tears to show." I looked at the eastern wall to see the smallest hint of morning light traveling through the window.

Another knock sounded and I groaned quietly, but before I could answer, the door opened and my sister-in-law Mary, from Emmaus, walked in. A fine rose-colored veil was draped on her head. She and her husband were also staying with us for Passover.

"Esther," Mary said quickly, looking at me with her soft, mild features. Much softer than Martha's sharp ones. "I was talking about you. With Martha."

"Dear Israel!" I released a breath. "Does every person speak *of* me?" I rose from my seat and crossed my arms over my stomach. I wore a grey-blue linen tunic with a rich brown sash.

"We worry for you, Esther." Mary walked toward me.

"There is nothing to worry about!" I raised my voice at her. I lowered my arms and fiddled with the dangling end of my sash. "Forgive me, Mary..." I looked back at her. "I am anxious, but...as you can see, there is nothing to be anxious about."

"Esther?"

I explained. "I am a rich man's wife. And I live in a devout Jewish household. I am in good health. Except..."

"Except," Mary finished for me. She did not drawl on the sentence as I had but stated it as complete. She knew very well that I was as barren as a desert, dried out to the point of my existence withering away.

"Esther." Mary reached her hand toward me. I stiffened as it rested on my arm, my sleeves tight so as to flatter. "I know it is hard for you to have your brethren here when you are...when you are feeling this way."

I bit my lip, my teeth sliding against the balm on them. "Yes, well...I am trying to not let my wounds break open and bleed. Lest my emotions get the best of me." My voice cracked. "Of course, there are no wounds that even need binding. I am well, Mary. I am well."

"Esther..." Obviously, Mary did not believe me. "Perhaps there is a way you can stay at home while we travel to the Temple. Stay here and rest while we go to offer our Passover sacrifice."

"It is Passover, Mary! I cannot do such a thing. This is the one day a year I am required to enter Jerusalem. And I am more spoiled than the rest of the nation as I am in walking distance to the Holy City."

"But if you are ill — "

"I am *not* ill." I let out a humorless laugh. "Though, I agree. Perhaps Adonai will strike me down if I enter His presence."

"Esther!"

"Perhaps the Levites and priests will throw me out. Surely I reek of harlotry and blasphemy."

"Esther! You are no harlot. I know this to be true. Be careful speaking such."

I lifted my shoulders slightly. "Tell me then if Israel is a harlot or not. Has *she* ever had relations with a man? And still, Elohim calls her a prostitute — worse than a prostitute. That is what Ezekiel says."

"If you must compare yourself to Israel, Esther, then you must remember that though Israel breaks her covenant with Adonai, Adonai remains faithful. He calls you back. He will make with us an everlasting covenant. Is that not true?"

"Yes!" I crossed my arms. "No." I began again. "I…" How hard it was to find any words to express my grief and utter despair. "You know me to be dramatic, Mary. Forgive me…I…misuse the word of Adonai."

"Stop condemning yourself."

"If I were the one to condemn myself, then I would be dead!" I responded stiffly. I sniffed as I looked at her reaction. Her face was shadowed in the dim light.

"I think," she started. "I think that because you are grieving the absence of motherhood, that your thoughts are clouded and prone to…to drift to puzzling places. Esther." Her hand firmly gripped my arm, but not without softness. "I am here. I love you. Martha loves you. Our family loves you. Lazarus loves you. Elohim loves you."

Tears threatened to spill over.

"We do not have time for this, Mary," I told her. "Let us go downstairs to the kitchen. We have guests to host and serve. They must all be awake by now. Let us prepare for our pilgrimage. We want to arrive at the Temple gates early."

Our Passover guests left us yesterday, to my relief. I thought I would vomit if I spent another moment in their presence. I made sure to avoid Ima, lest she complain and insult me. I made sure to avoid Jesus and Aunt Mary as well, lest I weep all of my woes on them.

Instead, I occupied myself with the children. It was a bittersweet experience. I longed to be with them but playing with a child only dug a knife deeper into my broken heart.

"Where were you all day?" Lazarus asked as he walked into the bedroom that night.

I looked up from the papyrus scroll I was reading. I had been studying the prophet Amos. He was a shepherd who cautioned the northern kingdom of Israel against their corruption. My fingers rubbed against the thin paper. I rolled it up and set it gently aside in a wicker basket.

Lazarus rarely asked me about my day. Truly, there was nothing much to tell about it. "I was at the Temple, praying."

"And?"

My lips started to tremble as I thought of the incense I watched rising from the inner courts. I watched the whisking billows travel upward toward the heavens. I wondered if my prayers truly did rise up like incense. Or did Elohim turn His face from me?

"As usual, our guests were pleased with their stay here for the feast," I told him, changing the subject as I rose. "Martha never disappoints with her hospitality."

Lazarus threw off his vest and tossed it in a large basket. He did not look at me.

"Did you enjoy the feast?" I asked slowly, taking a wary step toward him.

"Well enough. But I am troubled by the commotion in Galilee."

"Galilee?"

"Magdala."

I frowned, thinking of the small but wealthy fishing town. "Is it about your sister?"

"No, it is not about Mara. It is…one of my men's daughters — a wealthy man — his daughter was attacked last week." He leaned against a pillar in the center of the large bedchamber.

"For the love of Israel," I gasped, my eyes widening. "Is this all we hear about these days? Who attacked her?"

Lazarus let out a humorless laugh. "A Roman."

I winced. "Who is this woman? What did the Roman do to her?"

"He raped her, Esther," Lazarus said sharply, not caring to be gentle with words.

"Oh, for the love of Israel," I repeated quietly.

"What I do not understand is why *this* woman." My husband beat a clenched fist against the limestone pillar. He pushed himself away from it. "She was on her father's property. She is the daughter of a merchant. Her father committed no crimes and her family was in no debt. Was the Roman after her just for the fun of it? These…" Lazarus waved a hand in the air. "These pigs are stepping over the line. They cannot come into our homes for no reason and defile our women."

I twitched at his words. Disgust and wrath boiled within me for the Gentiles. "The poor woman. What is her name?"

"Susanna."

I shook my head as I processed the meaning of this. "Was she married?"

"Betrothed. To one of my relatives in Magdala, actually. He divorced her immediately."

I took in a quick breath. "She did no wrong."

"But she is unclean. No righteous Jew wants a defiled woman."

I twitched again. Was he thinking of me? Did he find me defiled? Was I so defiled that I bore no children? I tried to pull my mind from such thoughts.

"Her father did not cast her out, did he?" I asked, my voice shaky.

"No. He did not. But she will surely remain unwanted. By Adonai's mercy, she has her father's riches to keep her."

I bit my lip and moved closer to him, my bare feet cold against the tile floor. "I do not want to think what my brother Simon would do if…when he finds out."

"Oh, he knows, Esther," Lazarus said through gritted teeth. He walked toward the wash bin. "Simon's wife was taken by Rome as a payment for his taxes. This just reopens his wounds."

I shuddered at the memory. His wife was a good woman from Cana and we had no idea what had become of her. After she was taken, Simon attacked a soldier. By the mercy of Elohim, Simon's rage caused no mortal harm. He was not sentenced to death but he was scourged by a centurion. Simon had yet to take a second wife.

"Simon is not fighting or…attacking anyone, is he?" Many poor Jewish men had resorted to attacking aristocrats in the name of Elohim, trying to strike terror.

I watched Lazarus wash his face. He waited for several moments to answer me.

"Of course not."

"Because when my father rebelled…"

"Simon does not believe a little rebellion like your father's would aid his cause. He believes in the Messiah. That Rome can only be defeated by the anointed one."

"And if the Messiah does not come in Simon's lifetime?"

"Then he intends to prepare the *way* for the Messiah."

Lazarus always seemed to know more about my Zealot brother than I did.

"By doing what?" I persisted.

"Whatever means he wishes, Esther. I do not know." Lazarus turned toward me, but he did not make eye contact. He pulled his outer tunic off in a swift motion and cast it on the floor.

I watched his tense shoulders. "Something about this is troubling you."

I approached him again, but he walked away, toward the bed. "Men like your brother do trouble me," he said stiffly. "But I do not agree with their methods."

I walked toward the bed where he now sat and tossed my long black hair behind me. I felt nervous, something I had not felt around Lazarus since we married.

"Does something else trouble you?" I asked quietly as I slowly sat beside him.

Lazarus took in a quick breath. Horror and guilt pulled at my heart.

"Beloved," I started, wondering what I could do to help his mood.

"Many things trouble me, woman," he said sourly. He looked at the tiled floor.

I gently lifted my hand to his back. He got up quickly. He had been avoiding me whenever I came near him.

"Esther, go to bed. It is time," he told me as if I were one of his servants. I jolted, the harshness in his voice surprising me.

Perhaps if my emotions were not so torturous, I would tell him what Adonai said. *He that dwells in the aid of the Most High, shall abide under the protection of the El of Jacob.* Lazarus and I had said our shared love for the Word of Elohim was how we fell in love. *He shall say to Adonai, "You are my protector, and my refuge: My El, in Him will I trust."*

But how could I speak words of comfort to him? When I thought I knew the truth behind his frustration?

Me.

I crawled under the blankets. Lazarus sat on one of the sofas and called a servant to bring him wine. Lazarus did not make a sound as he drank.

Nevertheless, my mind heard him say, *Cursed are you, woman. You have shamed me. I cannot look at you and I cannot love you. You have disdained the ways of the household and you eat the bread of idleness. You have no children to rise up and call you blessed. I too cannot praise you.*

My back muscles felt tense and sore as I tried to stop my thoughts. What if he threw me out or divorced me? Would he never have relations with me again? Would he send me away in exile to Magdala the way Mara was sent before me? Would he hide me from the world so that he would not be ridiculed?

Chapter 12

Queen Esther, seized with mortal anguish,
fled to the Lord for refuge.

<small>ESTHER C:12</small>

My lips trembled as I kneeled on the tiled floor of the Woman's Court in the Temple. The stench of incense and slaughtered lamb made me nearly gag. It used to comfort me, that smell. It used to remind me of our covenant with Adonai.

What felt like prickling in my head made my eyes roll backward. Surely, I was possessed by an unclean spirit.

But of course, I was not possessed, I argued with myself. I simply felt…

"Woe is me! I am doomed," I breathed my prayer, masked by the hundreds surrounding me. My fingers covered my lips as I rocked forward, the extra material of my veil and mantle tumbling to the polished floor.

The tears that had been building up all morning spilled over. Lazarus was cold to me again last night. Colder than he had ever been. *O you frost and cold, bless Adonai. Praise and exalt Him above all forever. O you ice and snow, bless Adonai. Praise and exalt Him above all forever.*

I thought of the words of the three young men who praised Adonai even when they were in the fiery furnace.

"I bless you, Adonai," I mumbled bitterly, trying to imitate them. But this was a furnace I had created myself! Adonai would not take me out of the fire of my own wickedness!

Still, Adonai had not struck me down as I thought He would. I gazed upward, my neck stretching as far back as possible so that I could look at the height of the Temple walls around me. I could not even see the top. Only large stone built upon large stone. On my knees, I shuffled toward a pillar. I felt like Jonah hiding from Adonai when I hid behind these columns.

"Where will I go from Your spirit? Or where shall I flee from Your face?"

I was in Elohim's own house. I could not hide from Him.

"Your words were found, and I did eat them, and Your Word was to me a joy and gladness of my heart." I wept the familiar words of Jeremiah, my hands pressed against my stomach. "Why is my sorrow perpetual, and my wound desperate so as to refuse to be healed?"

For the past five years, I had studied as Lazarus requested. I could read and I could write Hebrew. I could even read some Greek, since many of the sacred texts were now written in that Gentile language. I had late night conversations with Lazarus and Martha about the law of Moses and the prophecies. I enjoyed the discussions at first and reveled in the new knowledge, although I soon discovered that for everything that I learned about the Torah or about Adonai, there was so much that I did not know.

Now, every word that came from my lips seemed powerless, useless, and crumbling.

I had thought studying the scriptures would reap blessings, not curses! For learning Adonai's statutes should have made my ways steadfast. With eyes fixed on his commandments, I should have had no shame!

I recited the entirety of the 119th psalm. The longest of all the psalms of David. I started sobbing as I said, "I cry with my whole heart, hear me, O Adonai! I will seek Your justifications. I will! I will…keep Your commandments…I cry to You…s-save me!"

As an idea formulated in my mind, my weeping stopped and I straightened, gasping for breath. Before me were other women, consumed in their own prayer. I put a hand to my trembling lips, glad that no one seemed to care about my weeping.

I knew what I had to do. Desperation rushed through my blood as I rose. Dizzy, I almost fell.

I had to follow the statutes of Adonai more closely. In that, I would find perfection. In that, I would have children and be valued by my husband. In that, all people would see me as the star I was meant to be.

I set to work immediately, finding the scroll containing the Proverbs in Syrus' library. It was on the third floor of the manor home, where cabinets held a Torah scroll, the writings, and prophecies in both Hebrew and Greek.

After cleansing my hands so as not to soil the sacred writings, I stood at an acacia wood table in the center of the room. Several windows behind me on the eastern wall provided the perfect midday light. I gingerly unrolled the papyrus scroll of Proverbs, as my heart made a racket within me. I searched for the end of the document where I knew the praises of a good wife were written. They were praises for King Lemuel's mother.

"Who shall find a valiant woman?" I read, my hand skidding over the carefully inscribed words. The Hebrew letters were made of straight lines, creating boxed shapes and sharp angles.

"Far and from the uttermost coasts is the price of her. The heart of her husband trusts her."

My gut dropped. How far I was from a good wife! I forced myself to push aside my feelings of guilt and continue. "She will render him good and not evil, all the days of her life."

I read with desperation. "She has sought wool and flax and has wrought by the counsel of her hands."

My lips twisted. I had stopped spinning wool and weaving because there was no need. Would starting again bring good to Lazarus? "She is like the merchant's ship; she brings her bread from afar."

Perhaps I should have gone to the market in Jerusalem and bought exquisite foods for the house of Syrus. I could purchase dates from Jericho. I could have a goat slaughtered and roll it myself in salt, hyssop, and mustard.

"And she has risen in the night, and given a prey to her household, and food to her maidens."

I needed to take hold! I could not be idle as I had been these past years! I could not only study and sit and eat. I had to work as a woman should, even if I had every bit of wealth at my reach.

I read the rest of the passage, creating a mental list of what I must do. I had to work in the fields and terraces. I had to always be at work, never letting my lamp go out. I had to open my hand to the poor and needy and never fear any misfortune. I had to make fine garments and sell them. I had to speak wisdom and proclaim kindness.

Something burned in my chest as I read the passage over and over again. Longing, desire, pain. But hope. Hope as well. "Her children rose up, and called her blessed," I said, trying to firm my shaking voice, "her husband also, and he praised her."

I let out a few hard breaths. My eyebrows creased in determination.

"Rise up," I said aloud. "To battle against it."

Chapter 13
23rd Year of Our Lord

*He said, 'They trust in weapons and acts of daring, but we trust
in almighty God, who can by a mere nod destroy not only those
who attack us but even the whole world.'*

2 MACCABEES 8:18

One day, during the late winter season, we ate a small meal of cheese, salted quail, pistachio nuts, bread, and olive and hummus dip seasoned with hyssop. It was noon and I ate with the women and children in the rectangular banquet hall. Mats, pillows, and cushions covered the mosaic floor, the center of which had a circular design, shiny with shades of scarlet, brown, bronze, and gold tiles.

We had a treasure with us today. My sister-in-law, Mary, and her young daughter and baby son were with us from Emmaus. Her children were happy to play with Martha's sons and daughters.

"When do you suppose Lazarus will return with my father?" Mary asked. "I have not seen either of them since the year of Solomon!" She rolled her shoulders back as she spread goat's cheese on a squared chunk of quail.

I lifted my shoulders slightly. "A week? However long it takes for them to make a profit." Bitterness ebbed from my voice as I added, "In Herod's newly dedicated port city." My stomach was growling, but I feared being a glutton after I fasted this morning. Furthermore, I did not want the other women to judge me for overindulging.

"You mean the city *Tiberias.*" Martha muttered the name in disdain. Named after Caesar. "O Abraham!" She shifted her legs.

"I think this winter is the coldest it has ever been," Mary said, tapping the cheese with fingertips as if she were playing a pipe. I did not know if she changed the subject because she did not want to dive into politics or because she was not paying attention to the conversation.

"My husband said that *Gehenna* is flooding, strange as it sounds." Martha stuck a thick piece of bread in the dip at the center of the table.

"Where is Gehenna…" I began and then stopped myself. I did not want to sound unlearned in front of them. I had heard the name before, but I did not know where it actually was.

"It is a valley southeast of us, near Bethlehem," Martha expertly explained, nibbling on her bread. "It is ironic." She pulled the bread away from her lips. "Most men call it the valley of fire as they burn waste in it. Which is why it is so strange the valley is flooding. Is it Elohim drenching us with mercy?"

"They are calling it the same place as Sheol." Mary looked up at us. "My husband says that all of the Pharisees in Jerusalem are trying to prove a point to the Sadducees. That there indeed is a resurrection from the dead. Yet the wicked will be thrown into Gehenna when they die..."

I removed my mind from their conversation, overwhelmed with my own busy day. My scriptural routine had been in effect for nearly two years. It had been long and difficult, and my determination was still not rewarded! I woke before dawn, even before Lazarus — that is, if he was even home — and I recited, "Hear, O Israel! Adonai is our Elohim. Adonai alone!"

Immediately after, I cleansed myself in the mikveh to make myself ceremonially clean when I entered the Temple. Even if I knew I was already clean, I ritually purified my whole self to ensure I had no soil that could displease Adonai. I fasted the whole first half of the day. My hope was to further purify myself for Adonai. I then walked to Jerusalem with a manservant and my maidservant so we might enter the city just as the East Gate of the Temple opened.

Within the Women's Court, I beseeched Adonai for about an hour, asking Him for mercy and blessings as the light of the sun slowly emerged behind the pillars. I begged Him for children, and I offered five *prutahs* to the Temple treasury.

Next I went to the marketplace, just outside of the Temple. The two servants and I bought fresh fruits, depending on the season — pomegranates, grapes, or figs. We bought fresh vegetables, beans, lentils, and fine wine. Of course, the servants did not need me to make their daily purchases, but I hoped that my presence in buying goods aided the household. I was sure to purchase linen, wool, and scarlet and violet thread to make clothing.

I usually saw at least one beggar or blind man on the side of the street. I gave him bread, cheese, and one prutah. After doing so, I looked to the looming Temple behind us, hoping that Adonai saw my good deeds and offerings.

By midmorning, I returned to the house and set to work on weaving, sewing, cleaning, cooking, or baking. If it was the season for harvesting olives, I went out to the groves to pick the fruit myself beside the many workers.

At noon, I ate with the women and children. Immediately after, I began my studies. That afternoon, I had to study the law of Moses. I had been focusing on the purity laws to ensure that I followed every one to the last letter. I had also read of Sarah, Rebekah, Rachel, Tamar, Judith, Esther, Hannah, Deborah, and the other women of our history. Like Hannah, I made a pact with Elohim, declaring that if he gave me a son, I would dedicate that son to Him, the same way Hannah dedicated Samuel to Elohim.

By the ninth hour, I prepared supper with Martha and the servants. I helped serve the meal before I ate, and afterward I cleaned up.

If Lazarus wished, I spent time with him and loved him. Yet he wanted my presence less and less. He was often doing business or having heated discussions with his father in the late hours. Otherwise, I wove for the household, also giving my weavings to my family in Nazareth, to the poor, or I occasionally sold a fine tunic. Of course, during my monthly bleeding, I stayed in the bedchamber as I was perpetually unclean. For that impure week, I spent my whole day prostrating myself in the room, facing the Temple in Jerusalem. I blessed Adonai and I begged Him for assistance.

In truth, I did not see His assistance. Indeed, I had a fantastic fortune. I had moved up in the world and in society, but then I moved far down now that I was…

"Esther!" Mary slowly repeated my name, drawing me from my busy thoughts.

My head snapped toward her soft face, lined by her rosy veil. "Yes?"

"I was asking if you noticed any unrest in Jerusalem."

"Besides the usual?" I ate a small dry piece of bread and looked to my left, where Eucharia spoke to her cousins, nieces, and grandchildren.

"They say Greeks and Romans are disappearing," Mary said.

"They are not disappearing, Mary," Martha cut in. "Their attackers are disappearing. The Romans are found dead in the middle of the streets. They say the Sicarii kill them and then vanish into the crowd. Caesar is blaming Caiaphas for the violence — it has increased since he entered the high priesthood."

"I have not witnessed this," I said dryly. A small piece of bread seemed stuck in my throat. "Only the usual soldiers standing watch at every corner."

"They found a couple of daggermen," Mary said. "I saw them crucified outside the city."

"That is why I am thankful to enter through the East Gate of the Temple," I said, "far from Golgotha."

"Why *were* you near Golgotha?" Martha's eyes narrowed as she looked across the table at her sister. The lower city was poor and just outside it was a quarry and garden of graves.

"My husband is funding the restoration of David's Tower — the citadel in the northwest corner of the city," Mary explained, raising an eyebrow at Martha. "He is a good Pharisee, and a good wife aids her husband when she can. Even if I am only providing meals for the workers."

My gut swirled. I did not think Mary's husband liked me. Nor did Martha's husband, Hezekiah. Or Simon, their uncle. They were Pharisees, strictly following the law of Moses. To them, I was unlearned and unclean. The household would be better without me.

Lazarus' uncle, Simon, rushed in. All of us women started at his ragged breath and red face.

"Simon, what is the matter?" Eucharia asked, settling Martha's toddler down beside her.

"I have news. Word has spread from Tiberias."

"The city?" Martha was quick to question. "Good news?"

"No." Simon stepped forward, clutching each side of his vest. "Five Jewish merchants have been found." I watched him gulp. "Found dead in Tiberias."

Lazarus! My eyes raised as my hand touched my neck.

"Who are these men?" Eucharia's voice shook.

"I do not know. I have sent a man to Tiberias to find out." Simon wiped his face with his hand. "Pray to Elohim that Syrus and Lazarus are not among them."

I blinked, attempting to process this information. Father and son, wealthy merchants of oil. "Were the men murdered?" I asked. "Or was it a natural cause?" I thought I already knew the answer, but I had to make certain.

"Killed."

"By whom?"

"They say Sicarii."

I refrained from throwing my arms up in the air with despair.

"Father and Lazarus are truly the perfect target for daggermen," Mary whispered.

"I know it, girl," Simon said. "He is traveling. Traveling in the testy region of Galilee. Traveling in Galilee as an *aristocratic* Jew!"

"But Lazarus is always guarded when he travels." I rose to assure them and myself. "He has never mentioned any danger to me. He and Syrus are esteemed by all. Even by the Zealots." Like my father. Like my brother. Surely, if my brother Simon knew these Sicarii, he would warn them not to hurt his dear friends.

But Tiberias was far from Nazareth. There were probably dozens of Sicarii who Simon the Zealot had never encountered.

I put a hand to my lips, knowing that I would have to wait and see. And the waiting would be excruciating.

Two days later, I woke up from my night's sleep. I yawned, and while shifting myself I felt my knee brush against something.

I jolted and gave a quick yelp.

"Lazarus!" I looked down in the darkness. I could hardly see his shadowed body, but I could easily recognize my husband's presence.

"Esther..." He was obviously still laden with sleep.

I fell down on him, my hands pressing all over him, assuring myself that he was real and well.

He turned. I touched his face, my hands skidding over his beard. I pushed my fingers through his hair. "You are alive!"

"Woman, of course, I am alive," he muttered. "And I am exhausted from travel."

My palms rested on his cheeks. "When did you get here? Why did you not tell me?"

"It was late, and you were asleep. You look so tired these days. I did not want to wake you."

Was that truly his excuse? "I have been waiting for news of you and... and...I thought that *Sicarii* had *killed* you and your father! We did not know if you were dead or alive!"

Lazarus took my wrists and held them away from his face. I fell on my bottom on the soft bed. "There is no chance a Sicarii would kill me, Esther! Trust me."

"Trust you? Trust you! It is not in your hands if a man will *kill* you or not. It is not man's power to stop the spirit, neither has he power in the day of death." I was just reading of this as Solomon's own words.

He sat up, pushing the covers away. "I am telling you, woman, that there was no chance!"

"Why do you sound so angry?" I glared at him. In the darkness, I hardly saw his profile.

"You know what makes me angry, Esther? You!"

Of course. My insides melted. Right when I forgot about my own wickedness, it was thrown in my face again.

"You, Esther, and…and your petty attempts at quoting the scriptures. You and your somber moods hidden behind false smiles. You and your non-existent womb!"

I was shocked. "Lazarus…" I mumbled. "I…I know you married a poor — "

"Enough of the poor Galilean woman, Esther! Your sister is more successful than you! How many sons does she have? Seven? And she is living on a dung hill. I would rather live in a little farming village with a wife who bears me seven sons than…than…"

"Than with me," I finished for him. A multitude of tears mounded behind my eyes. They would be let out. But not now. I could not let them fall now.

He was silent for a moment, then he cursed. "Esther…I…that was harsh — let me explain…I…I was talking to Jesus when passing through Nazareth on my way to Tiberias…I told Him…of our troubles and…and He told me to go home to you and be true with you. I — I know this is not what He meant, but…it is the truth, Esther. *I am* mourning over the sons we will never have."

"Lazarus, you are true. You are true. I — I wish I could give you…I know. I know you have no lineage. I know you are the only surviving son of your father. I know your men have laughed at you and scorned you because of me." I sucked in a quick breath and continued. "It hurts your pride. And… and that is why…why we will go to the elders and request a…a divorce. You can divorce me…and marry a good woman…a woman of Elohim who is fruitful. You have every reason to. They will grant your request."

"Do not be foolish, Esther."

"It is because of my love for you, Lazarus. And I will leave if that is what is best for you."

"Esther…" he almost growled. "Stop your dramatics. This is not some gleeful story about Queen Esther saving our people from Haman. I will not divorce you. Abraham did not divorce Sarah because she was barren."

"But he had relations with Sarah's handmaid instead!"

"Think of Jacob who did not divorce Rachel because she was barren."

"He had four wives. It did not matter! And do not start telling me about Hannah. As you said, I am no Queen Esther, and I certainly am no Hannah, mother of the great prophet Samuel!"

"My point, *wife,* is that I will not divorce you! If there is anything I hold with conviction, it is the covenant between Adonai and His people! And our marriage is a covenant. My father taught me that. Adonai does not break the covenant with Israel. Israel is the one who wanders. I will *not* break the marriage with you, Esther. Do not break it off with me. We are yoked together."

"I am…I am wasting away, Lazarus. I have truly tried to please you. I have tried to the best of my abilities to be the good wife who is praised by the Proverbs. Yet it is all dust if I have no seed. I pray hours a day to Adonai and offer all that I am. When was the last time we made love and slept peacefully the whole next day? How can we even hope for a son if you will not even look at me? You are always busy, always overseeing the olive groves and the olive press and the selling and the negotiating and the traveling — "

"I understand. But a man needs to do his work to keep this house running. And my father has only grown lax in his work — as I suppose he deserves due to his age — but he — he has other types of work he cares more deeply for. He — he…"

"*He* what?"

"*He* is a Sicarii!"

My mouth opened wider, my hair sticking to my lips. Every part of me stilled like hard granite. I saw the shadows of Lazarus putting his hands behind his head as he fell back on his pillow. I felt the breeze he stirred and the wave of the bed beneath me as he fell.

"Sicarii are poor bandits," I said quickly. "He is not poor."

"He is not a Sicarii exactly — else he would be caught. But he oversees the men — not usually doing the ox's work himself."

"Syrus?" I said in disbelief.

"Syrus is my father," Lazarus drawled.

"What does he do?" I breathed a whisper.

"You will not tell anyone, woman, do you understand? He could be crucified if you show one sign — "

"Then why are you telling me?" He always called me "woman" when he was stern with me, as if to remind me that I was the reason for the fall of our race.

"Because I am trying to be true! If we are indeed yoked together, then I must tell you of the nature of my business." Lazarus removed a hand from behind his head and rested it on his stomach.

Is this what he and Jesus were discussing? "*You* are involved with *Sicarii?*" I looked down at him.

Lazarus gives a short, humorless laugh. "More than I want to be. It is a complicated knot, Esther. Lie down and I will explain."

I fell back beside him, trying not to breathe too loudly, lest I miss something he said.

"You…I take it you do not know the reason your father and my father were such good friends," he began.

"They admired each other, but — "

"It was more than admiration, Esther. They were allies." Lazarus turned on his side to look at me. "My father saw fire in James, a man willing to claim the land as Israel's. James saw that my father was not like the Sadducees and the wealthy merchants and the tax collectors and the landowners. I *will* say that my father is noble," he said with pride. "His riches have not covered his eyes to the poor and the oppressed. His station has only aided him in seeing the brutality of Gentiles. I see it too, Esther — their opulence and idolatry, firsthand. With the funds that my father has, he is able to help the poor bandits do their work. That is why we were not killed in Tiberias. My father was the one who made the killing and Gentile robberies possible. He supplies the weapons, plans, disguises; the secret lodgings necessary to do the deed."

I put a hand to my forehead trying to hold such information. Surely Lazarus would not help kill a man! He was too righteous. "And you help your father?" I asked cautiously.

"No — I — this is where the knot is, Esther. My father wants my help. My whole life, he has been trying to train me to take his place but…no…I cannot do it. Not in right judgment." He fell back once again.

"I praise Adonai for that," I said. "My husband is not a criminal of Rome."

"But my father is. And I am under his roof."

"Does your uncle Simon know of this? Or Hezekiah? Do they help your father?"

"They cannot do anything about it. If my uncle speaks out against his brother, the whole house could be crucified. And my father is the firstborn son, the head of the household. He could throw Uncle Simon out if he wished."

"What does he think to accomplish by…by supporting bandits? Was he not witness to my father's death? Rome crushes any spark of rebellion."

"He sees your father as a martyr, and all the Zealots who went before him."

"What is the point, Lazarus?" I asked, trying to remove the shaking in my voice. "A few Jewish aristocrats killed here, and a few Roman soldiers killed there. All it results in is unrest in our cities, Roman legions hunting for rebels and hundreds of men posted on trees outside of Jerusalem for us all to see. How can your father see any chance that — "

"That is where I disagree with him, Esther. It is foolhardy to play with Rome when we have no Messiah in sight. We need an anointed one who is a warrior-king like David. He will renew the twelve tribes and give us our land."

"And your father does not see reason?"

"He thinks he is preparing the way for the anointed one. He says it is his duty to strike fear and terror; to remind us and Rome that we will not be conquered. *I* want them defeated like anyone. You do not have to be a peasant to feel the loss from taxes *and* the Temple tax. Father agrees that we need the Messiah, but he argues that we need an underground army ready for his arrival."

I bit my lip. "He truly thinks the Messiah will come in our lifetime?"

Lazarus let out a long breath. "I do not know what he thinks. But it is up to the Messiah to choose his warriors. He is the chosen one of Adonai — not my father."

"I never could have imagined your father as…as a man involved with…"

"Killing and terror," Lazarus finished for me.

I shook my head. "He is a good-natured man. Peaceable. Friendly. Pleasant. I never would imagine him as a secret rebel against Rome. *And* your family has so many connections with Gentiles. You do business with so many. And with our own Pharisees and Essenes and the holy sects."

"Not the Sadducees," Lazarus said dryly. "When the Messiah comes, Pharisees, Essenes — I believe all Jewish people — will rally for the cause. But not the Sadducees. For the chief priests fear a messiah will take away their own power — which he will, mind you."

I put a hand to my forehead, feeling like my mind was piled full of grain. It suddenly made sense to me why my brother Simon spoke to Syrus so often. It explained why Lazarus and his father would have arguments deep in the night.

"You must hide this secret, Esther." Lazarus took my hand. I twitched in surprise at the warm, soft skin that pressed against mine.

"I will," I told him solemnly.

"You should know, wife," he said slowly. I tried to read his eyes, but the darkness did not allow. "You should know that my delay on our wedding day…"

My breath hitched as he mentioned the wedding.

"It was because of my father's actions in Jerusalem." He sighed. "I feel better telling you. I was delayed by my father's…business…That is why I was late."

My eyes widened.

"Those Sicarii the soldiers were searching for — my father was harboring them in his own house."

My breath fell. "Well, I…I suppose that explains it." There was silence between us until I said, "I was starving, you know. And my bridesmaids were awful."

Lazarus kissed my hand, his beard brushing against my fingers. "I was starving too. I had everything prepared for you, you know. I was ready. But I refused to harbor Sicarii in our cellar during our wedding feast."

I blinked, firmly grasping his hand.

"That does in part ease my emotions," I admitted. "I remember fearing you forgot me. Yet I would not want Sicarii in the cellar any more than you would." I closed my eyes, trying to calm my racing mind and heart. "There are none in the cellar now, correct?"

"None." Lazarus breathed in relief.

Chapter 14
29th Year of Our Lord

Now I am sending my messenger — he will prepare the way
before me; And the lord whom you seek will come suddenly to
his temple; The messenger of the covenant whom you desire —
see, he is coming! says the LORD of hosts.

MALACHI 3:1

"Mistress," my maidservant called from outside Lazarus' bedchamber. A quick knock on the door followed. I turned my head and rose. I felt dizzy from so quickly rising from prayer.

"Enter," I said.

"There are three men here," my maidservant said, looking at the ground rather than my eyes. "They wish to see you."

My eyebrows furrowed. I brushed down the linen material of my tunic, walking toward the open door. "Why me?"

"You are the woman of the household," my maidservant said plainly.

She did not need to say anything else. Three or so years ago, Lazarus' parents, Syrus and Eucharia, contracted leprosy. Both had recently died from the disease.

My elevated position was new to me.

My sister-in-law Mary had lost her husband and daughter due to leprosy as well. Mary lived with us now in Bethany with her only son.

Simon, Lazarus' uncle, had also caught the dreaded disease but was alive, living in the caves outside of Bethany. "Simon the Leper" is what family and villagers now called him.

As the eldest and only son of Syrus, Lazarus inherited his father's goods and business. He was the master of the household, the owner of the olive groves, gardens and the factory; the presses, the shops, the laborers, the exports, and, well, everything. It would seem I had everything as well. Except for a child.

Yet Lazarus was not here. He was still away in the desert region of Judea by the Jordan River. It was Lazarus' hope to meet the famous John the Baptist, who lived in the desert, wore a camel-hair garment, and a leather belt about the waist. The Baptist preached aggressively about the kingdom of

Heaven as many preachers had before him. Yet something in the Baptist's manner intrigued Lazarus, and he wanted to see this man.

Customarily, when the master of the house was away, his wife was in charge. I rolled my sleeves down and carefully draped my green veil over my head. After thanking my maidservant, I hurried out of the bedroom and into the hall.

That was when I saw Martha bolting toward me like a shot from a sling. "Esther," she hissed loudly. "Esther!"

"Speak, Martha," I urged.

"Three men are here. They wait for you in the courtyard." She stretched her hands out, displaying her slender fingers.

"I am aware. I am about to go down — "

"They are Sicarii, Esther."

My shoulders became rigid. "S-sicarii…" I put my hand over my mouth; looked at my maidservant. "Why-why were these men let in the house? Foreigners should not enter without permission from me. The guards should have turned them away." I tried to sound confident but did not feel so.

"They are not foreign to the household," Martha said firmly. "They are partners and allies of my late father — may he rest in the bosom of Abraham."

I let out a sound of disbelief. "Save your servant, O my El, that trusts in You," I whispered. "How did…I was not aware that you knew of…"

"Of my father's business?" Martha put both of her hands on her pointy hips. "I know what happens in this household, Esther. Even when the men try to hide it."

When I thought of it, it did not surprise me that Martha would know all about the funding and associations Syrus had with Zealots. Martha was an intelligent, observant woman; she knew every nook of this house and must have known every action that took place.

"Does Mary know?" I asked.

"No. No, and we shall keep it that way. She is still in bed as we speak, grieving all of her losses."

Though at least she still had a son, I thought.

If only Lazarus were here to deal with such an issue. It was my husband's intent to rid us of all connections with Sicarii after his father's death. But it would not be a simple task, as Syrus had been an ally and benefactor to those bandits for over thirty years.

"You must order them to leave the property," Martha decided, crossing her arms over her stomach. "They likely have weapons. Daggermen are ready to slaughter anything from a pigeon to a person!"

135

"They will not harm the daughters of Syrus," I said, hearing the quiver in my voice. "They respect your father too much and honor him as a leader and benefactor."

"But these are also men of anger and violence," Martha said firmly.

"O Israel! Hush your tone, Martha," I said, afraid they would hear our conversation from downstairs. "It is because they are angry, violent men that I must go down and see them." It was the most logical option. Surely, the men wanted to do business with Lazarus, but there were other reasons they could have come here. Hiding from soldiers. Cleansing and storing of weapons. Lodging for the night. Money for an operation.

"Then I will join you," Martha decided. "And aid you in all your needs."

"No. The fewer women present, the better. Especially so they do not know you are about your father's business." I bit my lip, feeling my heartbeat accelerate.

"I am at least sending a guard to accompany you." Martha swiftly turned down the hall.

I ran down the stairs and as I reached the bottom, stopped to take a few deep breaths. I was assailed by all sorts of horrific and dreadful thoughts but could not give them any notice. Deciding I was as collected as I could be, I entered the large courtyard. Early afternoon light shined into the court, illuminating the stone pillars and finely trimmed juniper bushes that lined the outskirts of the rectangular yard.

The three men turned to me as I approached.

"May shalom be upon you." I greeted them quickly. I fiddled with the hem of my veil, then forced myself to keep my arms pinned to my sides.

"And upon you, shalom," the man in the middle said. "Shalom. Shalom. Shalom." He spoke each word of peace very slowly and with his hands clasped behind his back. I immediately saw the hilt of a dagger saddled at his waist.

The other two men nodded. The one on the right stared at me intensely while the one on the left looked bored and restless to be here. They all wore plain garb — undyed — and tallits over their heads. Each wore a wide cloak about his shoulders, falling down to his ankles.

I heard a guard walk into the courtyard behind me. I did not need to turn around to verify that was who it was. Two more guards were stationed at the entrance of the house. Their quiet but alert presence gave me a burst of confidence.

"I am Esther, wife of Lazarus of Bethany."

"The barren one. Your eyes gave that away," the man on the right said with a sharp laugh. He stared at me even more fiercely.

I blinked several times and forced my lips into a little smile. "The light of the body is the eye," I said, lifting my shoulders in a shrug. "If the eye is single, the whole body will be lightsome."

"Where did you get a phrase such as this?" The one in the middle asked. His fingers casually danced on the hilt of his dagger.

"A friend of mine." *Jesus.* "It is of little importance. Will you tell me who you are?"

"Reuben, son of Joseph," the man to the right said.

"Elisha son of Aaron," said the one on the left.

"And I am Jesus son of Abbas." The man in the middle stepped forward. "Call me Barabbas. I was told by your servants that your husband is away."

"He is." It took much effort to remain calm.

"Travelling so close to the death of his own father," Barabbas said. "Which we are all grieved over."

My lips twisted. "It is far past the customary time for mourning." Which was seven days. "And Lazarus does not travel for pleasure or party. His first act as master of the house after his father *and mother's* death is to visit the man called John the Baptist."

"He thinks the Baptist is some messiah?" Barabbas asked, rubbing his thumb over his dagger. I could not help glancing back at my guard to ensure he was there and watching.

"That is what he went to find out," I said. I lifted my shoulders. "Your accent sounds Galilean. Is that where you come from?"

"From Joppa, yes," Barabbas answered. "And your accent is Galilean as well."

"I am daughter of James of Nazareth."

Barabbas quirked a brow. "I know of your father. He was one of the Jerusalem martyrs. This means that you are also the sister of Simon the Zealot?"

"Yes," was all I could think to say. Typically, I would invite these men into the banquet hall for food and fine wine. Yet I knew all too well how much Lazarus despised Sicarii. If he were here, he would demand that Barabbas and these men get off of his property.

Still, it was not my place to break an alliance that had existed far before I was fashioned from the dust. This was a delicate situation. Violent men such as these were easily angered.

"If only Lazarus were here to entertain you. Yet even then, I fear he is still overcome with grief. Surely you understand the loss of a brethren." My hands were shaking. I clasped them tightly at my waist.

Perhaps I should have had Martha with me so I would not deal with these men alone. Hezekiah, her husband, would have been helpful, but he was in Jerusalem.

I may as well not have a husband, Martha would say. *Hezekiah is always in Jerusalem with the other Pharisees in the Temple doing what only Father Abraham knows.*

"We had a long journey from Japha. Syrus was always quick to welcome us into his home." Barabbas was not asking for hospitality. He was expecting it. "Down in the caves, that is. To keep our work secret, even within this household."

I tried not to look surprised that there was a series of caves below the house.

"You have nothing to fear from the rest of the household," I said. "My servants are loyal, and our men are out on business." Perhaps I made the wrong decision, but at that moment, extending hospitality seemed the most acceptable action.

I did not want to go down in some cave I had never been in, so I brought them to the open banquet hall and had our finest wine brought out. They ate fresh bread with a choice of almond and herb sauce made with our own olive oil. I had a servant bring in nut-cakes filled with dried pitted dates, cinnamon, and walnuts.

"They say the Baptist's mother was barren until a very old age," Barabbas said, scarfing down his nut cake.

So they all concentrated on my barrenness. I forced a smile as I sipped wine. "Elizabeth. The Baptist's mother was called Elizabeth. She was cousin to my Aunt Mary."

"Some are saying the Baptist is an Essene," Barabbas said as his companions devoured their food. I clenched my teeth in disgust, trying to avoid staring at their sweat, greasy hair, and slimy-looking skin.

"I would think not," I said. "The Baptist lives alone, while the Essenes live in community by the Salt Sea. The reason they went to the desert in the first place was because they think the Temple in Jerusalem is defiled, although it is true that many Essenes live in Jerusalem. I have heard that the Baptist is also displeased with the leadership in the Holy City."

"They say he has disciples," Barabbas said. "I will be eager to hear your husband's report. The Baptist has greatly angered Herod Antipas and many a Pharisee. It may be an opportunity to come together and save our beloved Jerusalem from Roman puppets and Rome itself.

"The new procurator is our greatest concern as of now." Barabbas leaned back, pulling at the short hairs of his black beard. "*Pontius Pilate*. Began his reign parading the image of Caesar's head through the streets of Jerusalem. Perhaps it is Adonai's timing that the Baptist step forward while Jerusalem's power is in this blasted transition."

"But the Baptist is not the Messiah. Word is that the Baptist's own lips have declared that he is not the one we are searching for." I was in no mood for wine but I pretended to take a sip.

"Yes, but he has preached that he is preparing the way for the Messiah." Elisha leaned across the table to get more nut cake. "He will have many a supporter from the likes of us."

He meant Zealots, Sicarii, and bandits.

"John preaches a baptism of repentance for the forgiveness of sin," I said. "He says the kingdom of Heaven is at hand. *The voice of one crying in the desert: Prepare you the way of Adonai. Make straight in the wilderness the paths for our El. Every valley shall be exalted and every mountain and hill shall be made low.*" I spoke of Isaiah's prophecy of Elohim's comfort to His people.

"You know the scriptures well." Barabbas had pale crumbs of cake stuck in his dark beard.

"I have much time to study them."

"You could be useful to us, Esther." Reuben kept staring at me, with a rude and unnerving intensity. "With your studies. And if you are anything like your brother, you hate the Roman Empire as much as we do."

"And you think John is Elijah returned?" Barabbas asked. I was relieved he changed the subject, for what if I really was like my brother Simon?

"It is not for me to know. We must see what fruit he bears. John himself said that every tree that does not bear good fruit is cut down and thrown into the fire."

Barabbas grabbed a handful of Jericho dates and ate them, one by one. "The Baptist has spoken out against Herod marrying his brother's wife," he said. "Disgusting man. Herod — not the Baptist," he quickly added, spitting out a pit.

"Some would say John's words are treason," I said dully, wondering how I could dismiss these men from my house. They were filled with food and drink, which would hopefully help my case.

"I bet you," Barabbas said, raising a sticky finger in the air. "That John would burn down the whole Roman Empire and every false Jew who pretends to know and serve Elohim."

"Tell me about the Magdalene." For the first time during our meal, Elisha son of Aaron spoke. And blatantly off topic.

I frowned, thinking of Mara. I had not seen her since she was a young child.

"Syrus never explained much to me in regard to her," he added.

"As she was like one dead to him," I said in my father-in-law's defense. "Not one to speak of."

"Still, word traveled. That she divorced her first husband and married another in Magdala. Now both men are dead, they say." Elisha looked at me expectantly.

I lifted my shoulders slightly. "I have nothing else to say on the matter. She is as much a stranger to me as she is to you."

Reuben cocked a laugh, wiping his mouth with his sleeve. "Oh no! Elisha here is more familiar with her than you would think."

I jerked backward, surprised at the suggestion behind his words — and spoken in the presence of a woman. Could not my dear Lazarus return today? *Adonai is my light and my salvation. Of whom shall I fear?*

"Rumor has it that demons killed both of her husbands," Elisha said. "Demons that were inside of the Magdalene."

"Rumor has it," I repeated stiffly, gut rolling.

I opened my mouth again, then closed it, then opened it again. "What is your reason in visiting my husband's house?"

"Syrus' death has grieved us greatly," Barabbas said. "Of course, we could not come to the burial lest…lest we were discovered. But now, his son holds the power and is in a position to continue Syrus' legacy."

"Which is?"

"To bring about the kingdom of Elohim. To claim this land as Israel and Israel alone. To stomp on Pilate's face. Rid our nation of Sadducees and wealthy hypocrites."

"You know the scriptures, Esther," Elisha said. "*You shall be my people, and I will be your El. Thus says Adonai: Behold! The whirlwind of Adonai! His fury going forth, a violent storm, it shall rest upon the head of the wicked.*"

I continued. "*The wrath of Adonai will not return till He execute it, and till He accomplish the thought of His heart.*" I set my full cup of wine on the wooden table. "*In the latter days you shall understand His counsel.*"

"These are the latter days. Your father knew it, Esther. As does your brother, Simon."

My eyes widened at yet another mention of my abba. No one had ever spoken so fondly of him before, as if he was a hero instead of a madman.

I nodded slowly. "David did sing that Elohim will break the heads of His enemies; the hairy crown of them that walk on in their sins." The fear I initially felt at these men's arrival was quickly turning to anger. Real, righteous anger. The wrath of Elohim. Not for these men, but for the Gentile men they hated. It was one thing to know men of violence. It was another to know that the men of violence were my allies.

"Revenge is Mine, says Adonai." Lazarus stood in the doorway. "And I will repay them in due time." His arms tightly were crossed over his chest as he leaned against the doorframe.

"Husband!" I stood, immediately. Ah, the relief!

"Adonai will judge His people." He moved closer to the large horseshoe shaped table and continued reciting Torah. "I will kill and I will make live. I will strike, and I will heal. And there is none that can deliver out of my hand. For He will revenge the blood of His servants, and will render vengeance to their enemies, and He will be merciful to the land of His people."

Almost coughing on his cake, Reuben took a swig of wine.

"Lazarus, son of Syrus!" Barabbas rose and opened his arms. "Welcome. We were just — "

"I will not be welcomed by you into my own home," Lazarus said stiffly.

I smoothed my veil as I eased over to my husband. "Lazarus, these men just arrived from Japha." I glanced between him and the Sicarii. I wanted to be certain that Lazarus found no ill intention in me because I let them into our home. Yet I also wanted the Sicarii to see that I did not hate them. Something about their passion and zeal intrigued and beckoned me.

"Where are you men headed?"

"Jerusalem," Barabbas said.

Lazarus responded forcibly. "There are several hours till sunset. I suggest you be on your way. We are but a Sabbath day journey away from the city."

"Your wife was just hosting us." Barabbas said.

"And you shall be hosted no more. Get out of my home and do not return." Lazarus stepped forward, a sword at his own side. Our guard stood by the entranceway.

"Your father always welcomed our presence. You do not understand! We *need* to spend the night here. It is too dangerous for us to enter the city at this hour. Especially with the new procurator. For our safety's sake — "

"It is a danger you have put on your own head. And one that you will not bring to my household. Get out."

I stepped against the scarlet drapery.

Barabbas pulled out his dagger. Reuben and Elisha followed his example. Each dagger had a sharp, curved blade.

"Have you so little honor that you will attack a man in his own house?" Lazarus drew his sword. Three more guards stepped behind Lazarus, weapons drawn and pointed at the three Sicarii.

"You are nothing like your father! You bring the great Syrus of Bethany dishonor, and you will be cursed for it!"

The guards flanked Lazarus as Barabbas moved closer to him.

"As you so say and as the Torah says," Barabbas growled. "I will not be the one to curse you. I leave that in the hands of Elohim!"

Lazarus glared. "Understand me well! Whatever connection or alliance you held with my father is broken. I step on it. I cut it. I will not support you and your fellow bandits in *any* way. The kingdom of Heaven suffers violence, and the violent bear it away!"

I felt my blood pumping as I watched Lazarus and the guards clear the door so the Sicarii could leave.

Reuben spat on Lazarus, who swiftly sliced the top of Reuben's left brow with his sword.

I gasped.

A line of blood dripped down Reuben's forehead and into his eye.

"I would take care of you myself, you wealthy hypocrite!" Barabbas yelled. "Be grateful you are the son of Syrus, lest you would be first on my list to vanquish." The guards pushed him out of the room with the rest of the men.

Finally, our house was quiet. My lips trembled as I approached Lazarus and began explaining my reasoning for hosting the Sicarii; that they came to the door as familiar visitors; that I wanted to be cautious with the violent; that it was not my place to break the bond our family had with them.

"I should have broken it before I left here," Lazarus said, dropping his sword to the ground. A few of drops of blood smeared the carpet, but he did not care. I grabbed a linen napkin from the main table and wiped his hands. We both were unclean and would need to purify ourselves in the mikveh.

I hugged my husband. "What is done is done," I said. A part of me, though, could not blame the Sicarii for their anger against Rome. It was the same anger my father had.

"I will post extra guards at our doors and even purchase a large, strong guard to secure our safety. Sicarii would not dare attack us in our own home, but when traveling, we could be in danger."

"But Barabbas said that he would not harm you because you are Syrus' son," I put a hand to his arm.

"It is not something I can rely on, Esther." He sighed. "Barabbas is a leader among them." Lazarus glanced at the main table. "I see you have a nut cake. And that they ate almost all of it!"

I smiled. "But look: there is one piece left for you! Blessed are You, Adonai, El of Israel our Father, from eternity to eternity. Riches and glory are from You, and You have dominion over all." I looked upward at the ceiling. Dozens of oil lamps dangling from metal chains gave the room a festive early evening touch."

Lazarus reclined at the empty table and blew out a breath.

I hurried to my husband who had been gone for nearly two weeks. "Woe to you who subject the kingdom of Heaven to violence," I said quietly. "Where did you learn this saying?"

"John the Baptist."

"So you spoke with him!"

"Indeed, he baptized me."

"Baptized?" I leaned back, surprised. "Why would you do this? Baptism is for the Gentiles."

Lazarus' eyebrows furrowed as he picked at crumbs of the nut cake. "I know! But this was a baptism of repentance. Even for the Jews."

"I know you to be a proud man, Lazarus. You would humble yourself to baptism?"

"Yes! You should have heard his message. He said that whoever has two tunics should share with the person who has none. And that whoever has food should do likewise." Lazarus rubbed crumbs from his fingers. "His words and his message are mesmerizing. He speaks of the coming of the anointed one."

"All of Judea seemed to be there," Lazarus continued. "There were Phoenicians, Syrians, Galileans, Pereans, Idumeans and even Egyptians. I saw your cousin Jesus there briefly."

"And what did you and Jesus speak of?"

"Nothing. I was unable to reach Him in the crowd, let alone speak to Him."

I remembered speaking to Jesus when He came with all of the men to Jerusalem for the Feast of Pentecost. He had told me how much He enjoyed travelling and meeting so many people. But He also admitted He enjoyed His time in solitude.

"We have half a dozen little apprentices, Esther," Jesus told me during that visit a couple months ago.

"Well, even Cousin James' children are having children," I said. "I imagine Uncle Clopas is not thrilled to have his house crawling with them," I laughed, thinking of my gruff uncle. My heart warmed as I remembered how Jesus treated the little ones. "You do love children," I said. "Just like your father." A trait I thought Uncle Joseph passed on to Him.

"And you love them too," Jesus said, looking me straight in the eye without a blink.

But there was a difference between us. I thought it but did not dare to admit it. I was a married woman; my task was to have children. Jesus was an unmarried man; unmarried by choice, no matter how odd of a choice it was. He chose to have no children.

Jesus held my gaze. I looked away, afraid that He could read my thoughts.

"We are very prosperous, Esther," Jesus said. Not proudly, but with sincerity. "Our family has never had so much income. And Sepphoris only continues to grow and need our work."

I bit my lip, feeling guilty for their poverty compared to our fine household. Perhaps I should have given them more oil when they last visited Bethany. "Your mother looks well," I decided to say. "As if she has not aged a day past forty. And your father?"

"He is slowing down," Jesus said, which caused me to frown. Would another father figure of mine pass away? "He has lived a long life and worked hard. He is a good and faithful servant to My Father in Heaven."

I held in an exasperated sigh. "Yet my dear family of carpenters is still prospering?" I said, choosing to drift from the topic of death and Elohim as Father.

"Enough so that My father and I could retire and the family would still prosper."

"Your father and You?"

"I am not retiring from My work, Esther. Do not fear. My work is just beginning."

"So it is."

Jesus was still young and healthy, but not that young. Many poor men often did not make it past forty. Yet Jesus was hardly what I would call impoverished.

"Many are expecting the Baptist to restore the kingdom of Israel," Lazarus said.

My head snapped toward him. I blinked several times, focusing on my husband.

"But John insists he is not the Messiah," Lazarus continued.

"Then what did he preach?"

"Repentance. The coming of the kingdom of Heaven." Lazarus turned his head to the side, cracking his neck. "John said that upon entering the water of the Jordan, we should show our confession of guilt and willingness to put the life of sin behind us, so that we may start a new life of righteousness in the eyes of Elohim. But…I…I did not find any sin in me. I follow all of the commandments and have done so ever since I was a youth." His shoulders were straight and his chin up with his usual aura of pride.

I bit my lip — I had so many sins! Once I made my husband unclean without telling him. My monthly bleeding was longer than usual, and I did not realize I was still spotting, making Lazarus and all that we touched unclean! I did love Adonai, but I did not think I loved Him with my whole heart. If I did love Him with my whole heart, then I would not feel so angry and dreadful when in His presence. I feared I did not love Him at all. I did not love Him with my whole soul, else, others would notice my good deeds and rigorous prayer and study. They did not. They still saw the sin in me; my barren womb was the sign exclaiming it. They glared and turned their faces from me. I did not love Adonai with all of my might. Sometimes I grew relaxed during my prayers in the Temple or I almost fell asleep. And I did not clean or cook or weave as quickly and diligently as I should. And the command to teach the law to my children? I did not even have the chance. Adonai surely had found stain in me. If only my sin which was like scarlet could become white as wool and snow.

And this spare tunic John the Baptist spoke of? Was this a new sin I had to avoid? Would ridding myself of a spare give me children?

"I want to be baptized," I said.

"Perhaps, in time, you shall be, my wife. By John or by one of his disciples. Or whoever the one is who is coming next."

"Coming next?"

"John said to me when I emerged from the Jordan that he baptized me with water, but there is one mightier than him," Lazarus said, swallowing the last piece of nut cake. "Whose shoes he is not worthy to bear. He will baptize us with the Holy Spirit and with fire."

PART 2

THE
PUBLIC
LIFE

Chapter 15
30th Year of Our Lord

*Go, eat your bread with joy and drink your wine with a merry
heart, because it is now that God favors your works.*

ECCLESIASTES 9:7

Lyre, harp, tambourine, flute, and pipe mixed to create a celebratory tune
of quick, looping notes. We were on a mat on the roof of the bridegroom's
father's house. I sat beside Ima and Aunt Miriam.

Looking down at the courtyard I saw my niece, Athaliah, dance with
the innocence and happiness of a true bride. Her bridesmaids and the other
young girls turned, clapped, and kicked.

All of these children were growing up, marrying, and having their own
children. My discomfort was typical, for me, for weddings.

The bride was Aliza's daughter Athaliah, who I held when she was a
babe. And now she would have babes of her own! Cousin Joses and Cousin
Jude were searching for spouses for their growing children. Cousin James
already had grandchildren. Martha's children were reaching marriageable age.
Even my sister-in-law Mary's only son was already a man and would seek a
bride in but a few years.

Martha and Mary were not attending the wedding feast as Cana was a
long distance from Bethany. Lazarus and I were, of course, attending because
it was my sister who was the mother of the bride, and...we had little better
to do. No children of our own to see to. We might as well drink for the
celebration of other men's children. Besides, Lazarus could always expand his
business with men over a cup of wine.

We had arrived on the second day of the feast and it was now the fourth
day. Athaliah married Daniel, son of Daniel of Cana. A family of carpenters
like my own.

I moaned inwardly, imagining what it would be like to see my own
daughter dancing at her wedding. Perhaps she would have Lazarus' light-colored hair or even my green eyes.

The walls of the courtyard below were decorated with fine drapery and
flowering plants; various lilies. Torches lit up the night, and the stars sparkled
clearly above. In the rooms beneath me, wine and food were prepared by ser-

vants and then brought out on platters to serve. The atmosphere was bright and hopeful.

Ah, but we were missing Uncle Joseph's presence. It was almost a year since he died. Even though I rarely saw him once I married Lazarus, I remembered life with him as a child. He was so loving to me compared to Uncle Clopas. Uncle Joseph was a fitting father figure. He filled the absence of my own abba. Now I mourned the loss of both fathers.

And Jesus infuriated me! He went on all sorts of travels and attended weddings within the first year of Joseph's death — clearly *against* the law of Moses. One was not to celebrate within a year of losing a parent. And Jesus did not even call Uncle Joseph His father. He now had only His Father in Heaven.

Nevertheless, I was intrigued. It was unusual and unlawful, but I was curious, and compelled to discover the meaning behind Jesus' actions. Especially when I knew Jesus to have a heart as large as Elohim's. What could it mean to have such a good man dismiss the law?

A gust of early spring wind came from behind me.

"This town is as windy as the sea," Ima complained, straightening her veil.

I looked out to the south. I could not see them in the night, but I knew well the wheat and barley fields that stretched for miles. Nazareth was one of the far-off hills behind those fields.

Other clusters of women sat near us on the flat roof. Laughter rang and each woman drank wine as if it were water.

"I despise the journey here," Ima continued, the corners of her eyes surrounded by wrinkles. "We walk through fields and fields with no sign of shade. The sun threatens to burn through my veil!" She tapped the cup of wine encircled by her hands. "And the olive grove owners will not even let us rest amidst their plethora of trees." She brushed her legs, glancing at Aunt Miriam. "Not to mention the thistles. My ankles are scratched as if I spent the night in chains."

I listened to her but did not say anything. Aunt Miriam rode on the donkey due to her poor feet. That left Ima envious.

"You think I am foolish to complain," Ima said to me, as my stomach spun with my depression and infuriation. "I did not always feel so rustled from journeys, but I am old, Esther. You are right behind me and will feel the toil of a day's walk soon enough."

"What you say is right, Ima," I said quietly, but with teeth clenched in resentment. I decided not to tell her about the camels Lazarus and I rode to

Nazareth. After that, we walked with the caravan to Cana like everyone else. I picked up my cup and took a sip, tasting the spiced wine. I set it down and rested my hands on my knees.

Standing by a side of the courtyard, Lazarus caught my eye. He was speaking with my brother Simon. Our eyes met for a moment and he raised his cup to me with a smile on his lips.

"You have seen that man, Jesus?" Ima drawled, setting her cup down and stretching her back.

She acted as if Jesus were not her own nephew.

"I have seen Him." My throat felt like it was closing in irritation. With Jesus or Ima? I was unsure. "I was able to give Him a quick greeting when He arrived, but every instant He has been surrounded by people."

"The boy has made many friends. If 'friends' is the word to use." Ima cleared her throat.

"There He is!" Aunt Miriam tilted her head as she looked into the court-yard.

Jesus was indeed there. I could see only a portion of His face, the rest hidden by His dark hair.

I looked back at Aunt Miriam, trying to appear nonchalant as I searched for gossip. "Aunt Miriam, tell me what Jesus has been doing."

"I have demanded the same thing of Mary, and she will not clearly state what her son is doing," Ima heaved. "It is ridiculous. A carpenter leaving home and disappearing for months."

"He did not disappear. He was in Judea," Aunt Miriam said simply.

"Doing *what* exactly? Can you tell me, Miriam?" Ima asked. "I thought not. Clopas would never allow this of his own sons and James would not have allowed my Simon to do this. As for Joseph — "

"Joseph is dead," I stated sourly.

"Which makes Jesus' actions all the more appalling," Ima continued. "Jesus should not have started traveling within a year of His father's death. It is unlawful and it is embarrassing me! Jesus should be living at home, helping His widowed mother."

Yet my mother did not even care for Jesus' mother.

"Hannah, my dear," Aunt Miriam said softly, her round cheeks over-shadowing her small mouth. "She is still our kindred and she is my sister. You know that Mary is safe under my husband's care."

"So, Jesus gets to leave all family responsibilities and go wandering around aimlessly! He refuses to marry, and now He is refusing to work. And do you know whose doorstep He will be on when He is hungry? Ours." Ima readjusted her veil over her shoulder as more wind blew.

I would have stopped this conversation to end Ima's ridicule and complaints, but my curiosity overpowered that impulse. "They say that this past month, Jesus has been in Galilee. But near the sea — not Nazareth."

Aunt Miriam gave a smile, showing the teeth she hardly had. "Yes. He is a special boy. I have told you so before, Hannah."

Ima opened her mouth to speak, but I quickly talked over her. "All night, I have noticed about half a dozen men following Jesus around. A specific five or six men. They are very...distinguishable." I looked back down at the courtyard.

"They look like a herd of sheep who have never had their wool sheared," Ima said. "A shaggy lot."

Now that Jesus was in the open of the courtyard, it was easy to observe Him and His friends. I twisted my lips. The men's attire was in sharp contrast to those elegantly dressed for the wedding. I knew the one called Bartholomew was from Cana. He was the one with the overly long beard that fell down his chest. I did not recognize the others, but they all had noticeable characteristics. One's tunic appeared older than himself. Another was quite large, and his voice clearly carried up to the rooftops. One had the bushiest eyebrows I had ever seen, and they were falling toward his eyes as if in irritation. Still, another was extremely young, making me wonder if he was any older than thirteen.

"As I said, Jesus' friends are very distinguishable," I chose to say. Especially ill-groomed for a wedding feast. Aliza would no doubt be bothered by that.

"They are not friends, Esther." Aunt Miriam's voice was firm. "They are disciples."

My gut clenched at the word. I had been yearning to hear confirmation of that word from my relatives. Yet now that I heard, I felt like running away.

I put a hand to my forehead and rubbed.

Jesus' face turned in our direction. His hair, which used to be in terrible disarray, was combed but still frizzy. The dark, fluffy waves of hair rested just below his ears and His beard was full but neatly trimmed. His height was average, and His build was strong. The simple carpenter I knew.

The carpenter with disciples.

"You believe He is becoming..." I looked to Aunt Miriam whose mouth was usually hanging open. "You believe He is a teacher. A rabbi."

"A teacher? He has nothing to teach!" Ima leaned back as she finished her cup of wine. "He is a petty Nazarene just like the rest of us."

"Yet our own rabbi in Nazareth always found Him wise." I found myself rising to His defense. "He knows the scriptures as well as any Pharisee."

"Esther, get me more wine, will you?" Ima lifted her empty cup to me.

"You can finish mine, Ima." I handed her mine, my stomach feeling sour.

She took it and sipped. "The rabbi we had when you were a child, Esther, liked Him. But now we have a different rabbi teaching us Torah, and he does not like Jesus."

"I think Jesus could be a rabbi and teacher — for Nazareth. I have always thought so." I adjusted my legs. "He will one day become an elder of the village, I am sure."

"No, Esther, no. He could have stayed in Nazareth, but He did not! He probably left the village because none of us want Him there. So He goes looking for other places where people will listen to Him. That is why He is traveling to Capernaum and such. And He has absolutely no authority. He did not study in Jerusalem or with a renowned Pharisee. He is a poor peasant. His education is nothing more than the average Galilean."

"No, Jesus studies more than the average Galilean," I said. "He knows the scriptures as if He wrote them Himself."

"He *acts* like he wrote them Himself! He is an arrogant boy who — "

"And some say He did learn from a renowned teacher." Fire scorched through my entire being. "They say He was a disciple of John the Baptist." I frowned. Why was I trying to defend Jesus? I did not even know what the man was aiming to do with these travels and disciples.

"And now they say Herod is seeking to kill John." Ima always had to stir the pot and drag out any disagreement. "Jesus ought to be careful." She gulped more wine, finishing the cup.

"For the sake of Israel! I hope not." I swallowed roughly, my throat feeling scratched. "Herod will just issue warnings. He does not like that the Baptist spoke out against his marriage to Herodias."

"Why are the waiters not coming to the roof with food and wine?" Ima looked around, apparently bored with our conversation. "They were refilling our cups constantly, but they have ceased."

"I will get you more," I told her through gritted teeth. Ever since she realized I was barren, all she did was disagree with me on all accounts. I could not remember the last time she called me her "star."

I rose, taking the cup from Ima, then glanced at Aunt Miriam. She drank very little as she was a frail small woman.

I took the thin staircase down to the court, one hand on the rough stone wall at my side. The thump of music echoed off the courtyard walls, growing louder as I reached the bottom. I smiled longingly when I saw Aliza dancing whole-heartedly with her daughter as if she were one of the young women. If only I were not raging with envy. And I used to think it was Aliza who was envious of me.

"Esther." Lazarus was beside me. I turned and smiled at my husband. His face was softly aglow in the torchlight, making me think of our own wedding. His beard was now fuller than that day, his hair lighter, and his earth-brown eyes were a shade darker. His shoulders were straight and held back, still showing authority. But I knew them to be tight and rigid. Despite our marital relations being better than they were, he was still not satisfied. I did not blame him. I had not seen him truly happy in nearly a decade. At least the wine gave him some superficial joy.

"*We*," he said, turning the cup in his hand, "are going to speak with Jesus."

I looked at my brother Simon who stood beside him, his arms crossed over his chest.

"May I join you?" I asked. It was an opportunity I could not ignore.

"You may." Lazarus took my elbow and ushered me forward.

"Looks like He is coming to us," Simon remarked from behind as a giggling young couple nearly ran into me. I swiped at the wine they spilled on the sleeve of my tunic. Not caring, I expectantly looked to Jesus.

"Lazarus! Esther!" He exclaimed as He trotted toward us. "Simon!"

"Jesus," I breathed, taking in His healthy, joyous face. I grew nervous as I noticed His disciples standing close behind Him, observing us.

"Shalom, my friend." Lazarus smiled, gripping Jesus' arm good-naturedly.

Jesus gripped Lazarus' arm in return and kissed him on the cheek. "It is indeed good to see my family. I have missed you," He said sincerely.

His eyes fell on mine. Kind eyes. Dark, but ever warm, the colors of burning wood and rich soil. "Esther," He spoke my name dearly.

"I have missed You, as well," I said, my lips spreading into a large smile. I was so taken by His presence that I forgot why I was infuriated with Him.

Simon stepped forward and awkwardly patted Jesus on the shoulder.

Jesus chuckled. "I would like you to meet My disciples," He said, stepping slightly aside and gesturing toward the six men.

Disciples.

"Here is Andrew of Capernaum." The man with the terribly worn tunic nodded at us in greeting. "And Andrew's brother, Peter." Peter gave a quick tilt of his head. He was the one with big eyebrows, dark as soot and thick as caterpillars. "And this is James Zebedee." Jesus motioned toward the largest and tallest of the men; James had a jolly smile on his face. "Then John, who is the brother of James." He was the very young lad, much smaller than his brother. "Here is Philip." Jesus pointed at the man with excessively curly hair. "And, lastly, Bartholomew. You know him, do you not? He is a fine leather-worker who travels in our caravans, yes?"

I tried not to stare at Bartholomew's outrageously long beard.

"Bartholomew." Simon curtly nodded his head. Yes, he knew Bartholomew.

"I have been wanting to meet you all," Lazarus said. "You have made quite an impression on us and the other guests."

I nodded in agreement, already having forgotten some of their names, and definitely not able to remember which were brothers. Most had pleasant expressions and looked at Jesus almost the way a child would at his abba.

I returned my gaze to Jesus, my eyes narrowing in curiosity.

"And this is Simon, My cousin and brother. We are a family of carpenters, we are. And Simon's sister, Esther. She is wife to My good friend Lazarus of Bethany."

"Shalom," the men said in unison. One of the voices was much louder than the rest. I believed he was the one named James Zebedee. I bit back a smile at the way they uncomfortably stood. The one who I thought was Andrew did not even lift his face from the ground.

"The Zealots of Galilee have discussed You much, Jesus," Simon said, his arms tightly crossed. My face grew red with embarrassment. Simon had never been subtle about his beliefs. "They are begging me to tell them what Your purpose is, but I tell them I have not seen You in at least three months."

"You are a Zealot?" James Zebedee asked loudly.

"Yes." Simon straightened, raising his eyebrows as if challenging any of them to comment.

"A radical, then, eh?" The curly-haired disciple said.

"Yes…" Simon spoke slowly.

"Philip," Jesus said, turning to the curly-haired disciple. "You are right. If Simon is a radical as he says, then he must follow Me."

Simon chuckled anxiously. "B — become a disciple? Cousin Jesus! We both know You are no prophet. You are no teacher."

I dared not blink lest I miss anything in the expressions of Jesus and Simon staring at each other. But then, I saw the other disciples. Their frowns and grimaces said they did not like the idea of a Zealot joining them.

"What is your purpose, Jesus?" Simon pressed.

"The kingdom of Heaven."

Cheers and laughter from the wedding party vibrated around us, but we were as silent as the dumb. Simon stared at Jesus so hard, I feared his eyes might crack.

The other disciples looked extremely uneasy as well. Bartholomew nervously rocked back and forth as if terrified of what Jesus might say next. He played with his unruly beard, pulling at it as if he were yanking grass out of the ground.

As for me, I too began to fidget, gripping the cup in my hands with greater force than necessary. Unsure of what to think or make of Jesus' words, I looked to Lazarus. He studied Jesus with his eyebrows knotted in confusion.

"That is a radical statement," Simon finally said.

"It is, Simon." Jesus had a pleasant confidence. He seemed to be the only one at ease among us. "Come follow Me."

Jesus continued looking confidently at Simon as Aunt Mary quickly walked up to Jesus and placed her gentle hands on His arm. Her eyes were soft and calm, but she stood straight, purposefully. She wore her widow's black garments with her usual dark blue mantle hung over her shoulder.

"Excuse me." Aunt Mary looked at us. "Please forgive me." She lowered her tone and murmured just loud enough for me to hear. "They have no wine."

Shocked, I put a hand over my mouth. The men made long sighs of dread and embarrassment for Daniel and Athaliah's families. The night was still young, and it was only the fourth day of the feast. Aliza would be horrified. I turned to look at the dancing crowd in the center of the courtyard. Aliza was in the middle of the group with her husband, likely ignorant of what was occurring. I remembered the wine cup in my own hand that I told Ima I would refill.

Jesus turned His head toward Aunt Mary. "Woman," He said calmly but adamantly. "What is that to Me and to you?" His expression was serious. Aunt Mary looked deeply into her son's eyes. "My hour is not yet come."

There was a moment in which neither Jesus nor His mother spoke, but instead communicated with their eyes.

I looked back and forth between the two.

Jesus gave a curt nod to His mother and the two of them walked toward the inner household. His disciples followed, like shaggy little sheep, as Ima had remarked — they looked on the verge of ridiculousness!

Ridiculous as they were, I turned to Lazarus. Without a word, we agreed to follow Jesus as well. We squeezed through the jubilant crowd.

Once we were indoors, we were able to walk briskly after the lot of them. We turned into a back room that served as a kitchen. The smell of pastries and fruits grew incredibly strong as I took in the sight of three plainly garbed waiters and one finely dressed waiter speaking to each other in hushed tones.

Bounteous platters rested on the platform in the center of the kitchen. Finely salted goat's cheese, a fattened calf, and thick stews spiced with cumin, sage, hyssop, and saffron. Sweet deserts of apple, almonds, cinnamon, raisins, and honey. Stone water jars for ceremonial washings lined the back wall. We used them to purify our hands before eating. The waiters peered into a large jar empty of wine.

The one I assumed was the headwaiter, due to his air of authority and colorful band on his forehead, spoke to the servants in a soft voice. "I will alert the bridegroom." He put his head in his hands, clucking his tongue. "What a terrible shame for such a blessed feast!" He went off in search of Daniel.

Jesus approached the remaining servants with Aunt Mary at His side.

"Whatever He says to you, do it." Aunt Mary kindly but firmly ordered the servants, then took a step back as if she was an audience watching a play.

I was curious. Jesus was not typically one to order servants around. Few recognized or acknowledged His presence, but He was acting and speaking with authority.

"Fill the waterpots with water," He commanded, motioning at the purification jars.

"We will have to fetch more from the cistern."

"Go on, then." The waiters hurried back and forth between the kitchen and water cistern in the back of the house. They took buckets and water jars and began carrying the water from the cistern and poured them into the enormous jars.

I found myself beside the curly-haired disciple, Philip. "Do you know what He is doing?" I asked.

"I have no idea," Philip said but did not seem at all distressed by the fact. His curly hair swept over his eyebrows. "You never know with Him, though, do you?"

I blinked, returning my gaze to Jesus, who supervised the waiters' work.

Philip seemed more familiar with Jesus than I was, although I was the one who spent years living in the same household as Him! I knew Him to be favored by Elohim and act in unusual ways, but He did so in silence and secret — not in public and with so many witnesses.

Muttering and hushed conversation flowed between the disciples and servants as the servants filled each jar to the brim.

"Now draw some out," Jesus told the waiters when they had completed their task. "And take it to the headwaiter."

Using a ceramic ladle, a waiter obediently poured some of the water into a deep serving bowl. After a last glance at Jesus, they left the room.

As they did so, I studied Jesus. His expression was calm, and His warm eyes glowed in the lamplight.

Irritation gnawed at me as I failed to comprehend anything. Filling water jugs for no reason. Jesus and disciples. The kingdom of Heaven.

The headwaiter came running back in, his lips moving, but no words coming out. Brushing past me he asked, "How can this be? Where has this come from? Out of my way! Please, leave the kitchen. We have wine to serve."

I took a step back, trying to give the waiters room. They hovered over the stone jars and drew more water out, except it was not water that they drew. Rather, it was burgundy colored — wine!

"I spoke with the bridegroom," the headwaiter told the waiters. "He is speechless…no idea where this comes from. Mind you, he is drunk as a…"

"How can this be?" Lazarus mumbled into my ear beside me.

I looked at him as the headwaiter continued speaking in his fussy tone, "Every host sets out the good wine at first, and when guests have well drunk, then lesser quality wine. But you have kept the good wine until now! They did not even tell me they had it in storage. Where did this new wine come from? A neighbor?"

I heard gasps and exclamations, but I could no longer see the water jars or Jesus as people crowded around the jars.

The disciples of Jesus, the waiters, and my brother spoke at once with enthusiasm.

"It was water but a moment ago."

"Wine!"

"Impossible!"

"I tell you, He turned water into wine. It is a miracle!"

My face was surely an expression of excitement and shock. Terror as well.

Lazarus' face was in his hands. I could not tell if he was frightened or happy.

People swarmed in the room, making a dizzy blur before my eyes.

I could not deny my own eyes. I had witnessed water changed to wine as clearly as our ancestors in Egypt saw Moses change the water of the Nile to blood.

My mind jumped to alternative conclusions that I could only regard as ludicrous. Perhaps someone else turned water into wine or they had extra wine in a storage cave that they overlooked. Maybe the water jars were filled with wine in the first place.

"Out! Let us work. Get out of the kitchen," the headwaiter gave a finicky shout.

I left the kitchen and made my way back out into the open courtyard, thankful for a breeze.

"Esther." Aliza grabbed my arm. "I cannot believe it! How could they run out of wine? What type of family is my daughter marrying into?"

"No…no, Aliza," I breathed. "They have not run out…there is more… Jesus turned water into wine."

She tapped my cheek. I think she meant for it to be a light tap, but it felt more like a slap. "Are you well? Or are you the culprit who consumed the rest of the wine? I know you have always favored our odd cousin, Esther, but I have not heard you come up with such a foolish notion in — "

"Mistress." A waiter with a bowl and ladle interrupted the mother of the bride. "Have some more wine."

He poured the rich red liquid into Aliza's cup. He then filled my empty cup I nearly forgot I was holding. When he left, Aliza narrowed her eyes.

"It is as I said, Aliza." I leaned toward her. "Jesus turned water into wine."

I took a sip from Ima's cup. "Taste it, Aliza! It is exquisite. I have tasted nothing like it. It is complex and of fine fruit."

She took a sip. "It is wine. Nothing more and nothing less."

I bit my tongue. Surely, she was lying and simply refused to accept its opulence.

"Do not speak of Jesus anymore," Aliza demanded, straightening her shoulders and lowering her cup. "You would think He was the high priest Himself with all of the attention He is getting from His mysterious travels and…disciples. This is Athaliah's wedding. Think of *her*."

I glanced at my niece in the center of the courtyard with her husband. They laughed merrily, each holding a wine cup. Jesus must have still been in the kitchen.

"It is Athaliah's wedding." I agreed, forcing a smile. "Excuse me, I forgot that Ima was waiting for me."

As I turned from my sister, I frowned. Murmurs of excitement grew as the splendid wine was passed about. Shouts of celebration and enjoyment increased, ringing from all directions.

I returned to the rooftop to find that my mother and Aunt Miriam had already been served their share of the miraculous wine. Ima did not care that I neglected coming to her. I decided not to try and tell her what I witnessed. Aunt Miriam might have been intrigued, but now was not the time.

Instead, I went down to the courtyard in search of my husband. I spotted him speaking rapidly with one of Jesus' disciples. I bit my lip wondering if I should approach the men or not. My curiosity was bulging, and I decided that it would be appropriate to politely stand beside Lazarus until spoken to.

After thanking a waiter for filling my cup again, I proceeded to my husband's side. His eyes turned to me, lighting up.

"Esther, you have tasted the wine, then?" His shoulders looked relaxed and his mannerism carefree.

"It may be superior to Caesar's finest wine," I said, glancing at the disciple; the one with the terribly worn-out brown tunic.

"I was asking Andrew how he first met Jesus," Lazarus explained.

Andrew. I repeated his name in my mind.

"I was a disciple of John the Baptist, originally," Andrew said and took a gulp from his cup.

"Ah, the Baptist," I said quietly, unsure of what to say in regard to the controversial man.

"Jesus was in Judea and…John told us…that Jesus is…" Andrew's words slowed as if he was deciding if he should continue or not. He did not make eye contact with either of us. "He told us Jesus was the one we should follow."

"John himself said this?" Lazarus breathed. "I — was baptized by him. I will admit, Jesus resembles the Baptist with His words. They both speak of the kingdom of Heaven."

My stomach cramped as I thought of John the Baptist and his message. Was Jesus intending to take the place of John? What danger would that put Jesus in? What title did Jesus have, then? Dare I think prophet?

"John lives in Judea, but you have come to Galilee," Lazarus observed, looking at Andrew with earnest.

I drained my cup.

"Yes, we came to Galilee and are staying in Capernaum. We stay in the house of my brother, Peter."

"Capernaum is your hometown, then?" Lazarus asked.

"Yes, well, our father is originally from Bethsaida, but we found even more business in Capernaum. The town is closer to the shore than Bethsaida."

"I assume you are fishermen?"

"Yes. Peter and I work with the sons of Zebedee, James and John. John was a disciple of the Baptist with me." Andrew scratched at his chest, continuing to look at anything but our eyes. "And you are from Nazareth, then?" Andrew asked.

I glanced at Lazarus. Andrew was not looking at either of us, so I could not tell who he was speaking to. Deducing it was me, I said, "Yes. My hometown is Nazareth."

"He told us about you." Andrew smiled, not quite lifting his gaze to mine. "You are the same age, He said, and were good friends as children."

I blushed, surprised and embarrassed. I could not help feeling a bit of pleasure that Jesus mentioned *me*.

"Jesus was the," I searched for a word, "the angel of the two of us, for certain." I decided to divert the attention from myself. "Andrew, you have been a disciple for how long?"

"Only a month, I would say. Only a month."

"And you will return to Capernaum after the feast?"

"I believe so. Wherever Jesus tells us. Passover is upon us, so we may go back to Judea."

"You are all welcome at my home for Passover," Lazarus was quick to say. "It would be my pleasure and my wife's pleasure to host you. We live in Bethany and also have a house inside the Holy City that my cousin Hezekiah runs."

"And you and your wife are welcome to visit us in Capernaum. You can spend some time with us and Jesus."

Lazarus put a finger to his chin, mulling over the invitation. "I am a busy man. A businessman. But I often work in Magdala, so perhaps I will."

There was silence.

"He has made disciples quickly," Lazarus commented, leaning back.

"John and I are the ones who introduced our brothers to Jesus. I have known Philip for a while now, and he was eager to join us. Philip, then, was the one to convince Bartholomew to follow, and now, your brother Simon may be next."

I raised my eyebrows, looking over my shoulder for my brother. Not seeing him, I turned back to Andrew.

Lazarus glanced at me and then at Andrew. "Who...what is...what is Jesus truly doing?" He shifted his feet.

Andrew smiled, showing yellow teeth behind his scraggly beard. His eyes focused more on Lazarus' chest than his face as he spoke. "I have been... grappling with that question and...after this," he said, raising his cup, "I have come to believe more and more that He is the one the scriptures foretell. The one John the Baptist prepared the way for." Andrew turned his head toward me. "You know Jesus well. This should make sense to you." He lowered his voice, "That Jesus is the prophet like Moses! The prophet who is the Messiah."

I closed my eyes at the final word. It was not foreign to the tongue of a Jew, but it certainly was regarding Jesus.

"You believe this…" Lazarus started.

"Do not deny it. You just saw Him turn water into wine. I will tell you. I have witnessed other, more private, miracles."

I tilted my head, wanting to hear more of these private miracles, but did not summon the courage to ask.

"He is a son of David, no?" Andrew continued.

"Yes," I said, "but Jesus…I know Him as a carpenter."

"And David was only a shepherd boy, no?" Andrew looked at the wine cup in my hands and then at his own cup. "Look at me." Andrew looked down at his worn tunic, apparently very aware of its poor condition. "It seems Adonai chooses the humble to do His work. He chose Judith, a woman, to save Israel single-handedly. He chose young Jeremiah to prophesy. Whosoever will exalt himself will be humbled: and he that will humble himself will be exalted. This is the way of our Father in Heaven."

Chapter 16
31ˢᵗ Year of Our Lord

Rich and poor have a common bond:
the LORD is the maker of them all.
PROVERBS 22:2

The wedding feast at Cana was nine months ago. Three pilgrim feasts passed since: the Feast of Passover, the Feast of Pentecost, and the Feast of Tabernacles. A non-pilgrim feast, *The Feast of Lights*, finished last week. We commemorated the rededication of the Temple by the Hasmoneans after they defeated the Greeks. Then farmers sowed their peas, lentils, and flax. Winter rains came and remained with us.

We had still not seen Jesus since Cana. What occurred at the wedding felt like a strange dream that was with me for a few days and then disappeared from memory. My monotonous life as a barren wife resumed immediately upon our returning to Bethany.

One afternoon, Martha surprised me as she walked into the workroom on the first floor of the house. "Esther, dear Esther."

"Martha." I inclined my head at her, my fingers resting on the cloak I was weaving. The wool gently scuffed my fingertips. A spindle and wicker basket rested beside me. Against the wall was a collection of material, thread, flax, and wool and different dyes, neatly compiled in wooden cabinets.

Martha rested her hands on her hips. She walked toward me, her mahogany veil draped behind her. "Now that the Feast of Lights is behind us, and Jesus has…well, Jesus has spoken so adamantly these past months throughout Judea…I have a request for your husband that I *need* your assistance for."

My eyebrows furrowed as I wove. "You have listened to Jesus preach?"

She hesitated, then spoke. "No." Her long torso straightened. "But I have heard of what He preaches."

"And?"

"The kingdom of Heaven is at hand."

My lips formed a thin line. This was all I heard of Jesus. Was the summary of His preaching that one phrase? I took a fresh yellow wool thread and began weaving a new line in my cloak.

"I do not understand," I said. "You have not seen Jesus in nearly a year."

"And I am grieved that I did not see Him or hear Him teach when He was in Judea. O Abraham knows."

"Lazarus was not grieved; he was insulted." Word was that Jesus was spending the feasts within the city of Jerusalem, near the Essene Quarter. Martha's husband Hezekiah reported that Jesus was hosted by a Pharisee, Nicodemus. No one was supposed to know of their whereabouts, but Jesus was now an acclaimed rabbi and an acclaimed rabbi could only be so secretive.

"I know Lazarus was insulted that Jesus did not stay with us," Martha said. "Which is why I need your help."

I looked up at her as she rested her arms upon the top of the wooden frame. "I have decided to build a hospice."

"A hospice." I tested out the word.

"For the sick and dying of Judea."

"What inspired this idea?"

"Jesus." She smiled, more to herself than to me as she dipped her pointed chin. "Listen, here, Esther. They say Jesus speaks of helping the afflicted and those who are lost and forgotten in Israel. O Abraham knows we have several of those in Judea. Even some in Bethany. I think of Jesus and how He has always paid much attention to the weak and the sick." She drummed her fingers on the frame, her nails long and shiny. Her eyes sparkled as she looked upward, as if into another world. "Think of Uncle Simon and his leprosy — even my own parents, when leprosy struck them. Jesus was kind and generous to us. Particularly with the *time* He spent with them."

"But Martha," I said, craning to look at her. "You already do so much for the sick and the poor. You and Mary take bundles of food and supplies to the lepers."

"But we never go directly to the leper caves."

"I hope not. You would be unclean."

"What is unclean can be made clean by purification and sacrifice." She straightened her shoulders.

"You give to the poor already. I witness it myself. Your hands freely give gifts."

"A prutah to one person. A piece of bread to another." Martha huffed, settling her slender fingers against her chin. "Is it enough, Esther?"

"I would say so, yes. You are far more generous than most in Palestine."

"Yet I have wealth that is far more than most in Palestine." Her defined eyebrows slanted in contemplation.

"But you give far more than most aristocratic Jews."

"I do not give, Esther." She raised her hand in frustration. "Not the way Jesus does."

"What are you trying to say, Martha?"

"O Abraham!" Martha slapped her hand on the wooden frame a little too roughly. The loom rattled. "I am saying that I am building a hospice on our property. I am going to personally care for the sick and the poor. The time for me to give of the plethora that I already have is here. I need to physically, tangibly, personally help the ill. Clothe the naked and feed the hungry — the hungry right outside our doorstep. The kingdom of Heaven is at hand, and I am not going to miss it!"

"Do you know how to care for the sick?" I leaned toward her, wondering how her dream would be possible.

"O Abraham, no. But I can learn. And I have several servants and children who can help me with my work. Mary is fully ready to accompany me in this endeavor."

I raised my brows. I was not certain I had ever seen her so enthusiastic.

"And you could help me, too, Esther! These poor people have children who are dying of hunger. There are children without mothers; without fathers."

"If you have not noticed, I am not a mother."

Martha's eyes narrowed. "Then the kingdom that Jesus speaks of is for you as well. If you are childless as you say, if you are so grieved by an empty womb, then the kingdom is yours. You are poor in spirit."

"Poor in spirit?"

"It is what Jesus is saying. Not only is the kingdom for the poor. The kingdom of Heaven is for those who are spiritually poor; without hope or comfort. Even women. Even *rich* women like you and me. You yourself told me what you witnessed at Cana of Galilee. Jesus turned water into *wine*. He took what is plain and made it exquisite!"

"What do you think Jesus is? A prophet of sorts?"

"He could be a prophet." She raised her shoulders. "Certainly not a magician, I will tell you that."

"Jesus would never engage in sorcery or magic." I agreed with her. Magic could easily get one stoned by the Jewish leaders. The law said that anyone who practiced sorcery or divination was an abomination to Adonai.

Midmorning light from a window streamed on our faces.

"He is like John the Baptist," Martha said.

"And now John is imprisoned," I replied sourly.

"May Elohim blast Herod from the earth! Or may Jesus blast him from the kingdom!"

I leaned back.

"I think Jesus *could* be the Messiah," Martha continued, lowering her voice. These were dangerous subjects that could result in blasphemy or scandal or being accused of a crime.

"His disciples think He is the Messiah," I said.

"And men do not give up all that they have just to follow any ordinary man."

I admired her insight.

"Lazarus has criticized men who follow false prophets and false messiahs. There are so many supposed messiahs and revolutionaries." I thought of my father James and Lazarus' late father Syrus. I thought of the Sicarii who once came to me: Elisha, Reuben, and Barabbas. My own brother, Simon the Zealot, was now a disciple of Jesus as well.

"Martha, what does Hezekiah think of this?" I settled my hands in my lap. "Surely the wife of a Pharisee should not be caring for sinners and the unclean."

Martha rolled her eyes. "Hezekiah loathes the idea. He hates the thought of so many sick living in the vicinity of Lazarus' property."

"Then how can you go forward with this plan if your husband is against it?"

"O Abraham, Esther. Listen to me! Hezekiah is never home! Was he with us for Passover the past two years? He is always at some other Pharisee's house in Jerusalem, or hosting prominent men at Lazarus' second home in the city. I do not understand. If he is never in the household, why should he care so much about what happens in his household?"

"Because he is a Pharisee and has a reputation to uphold as a religious leader."

"And it is the duty of religious leaders to be charitable!"

"Why have you come to me, of all people, Martha, with these plans? You know I am not a physician."

"I come because you are like a queen. Like Queen Esther."

I let out a laugh. "Martha?" I was unsure of what to say.

"No, listen to me, Esther! Lazarus is the owner of this house, the property, the business. He is like the king, and as Lazarus' wife, you are the queen."

A queen with no sons to take his father's rightful place as ruler. A queen with no daughters to marry off and make an alliance with other kingdoms.

"And the queen plays a special role in her kingdom. She has the king's ear. Esther was highly favored by the King Ahasuerus of Persia. When she spoke on behalf of the Hebrews, he listened. Therefore, *you* can speak to Lazarus on behalf of Mary and myself. Ask him to allow a portion of our property — perhaps near the family sepulcher — a distance from the house, be used for the building of a hospice; a place for the sick and the dying to stay sheltered and protected. If Lazarus wills it, Hezekiah has no say or choice in the matter!"

I tightly wove my fingers together.

"You surely see, Esther, that this is of goodwill. It is your opportunity to be a mother to desolate Judeans."

"Because *I* am desolate?"

"Because the kingdom of Heaven is at hand and there *is* cause for rejoicing here."

We stared at each other. Her stare was hard. I could not match it.

"I will speak to Lazarus on your behalf," I said. I had tried everything else in my life to be the good wife praised in Proverbs. "I will speak to him when he returns home from Jericho so that you may build this hospice."

She slapped her hands together. "A queenly answer, Esther. O Abraham, a queenly answer."

I still did not know what I thought of all these matters. Only that Martha was well intentioned, and I desired to assist my friend and sister. And I prayed that her marriage to Hezekiah would not be strained by this conflict of interests.

The next morning, I had the opportunity to speak to my husband who had returned from his business travels. I had my maidservant twist my hair in fine braids and lightly cover them with Lazarus' favorite green veil.

But my husband appeared sad.

"Why have you been so frustrated these past months? I can almost feel it steaming off of you. You were jubilant at the wedding feast," I said to Lazarus as he sat in his workroom, counting his prutahs, dinars, and Hebrew shekels.

His frown was too prominent. "Because it was a miracle," he explained. "I cannot deny it." He dropped some silver dinars on the wooden table as if scattering seed for sowing.

"I do not know why I am unhappy," Lazarus said. "Jesus confuses me."

Jesus confused me as well. I fiddled with my veil, released it, and clasped my hands at my waist. "Do you hope He is the Messiah?"

"I do not know," Lazarus exclaimed, thrusting a fist in the air. "Even if He is a bridge to the Messiah, I care not." He settled his fist on the table. Some coins spilled out and sounded against his ring. "Perhaps Jesus knows the Messiah personally? Or spoke to Elohim personally about the Messiah?"

"Perhaps you will follow in your father's footsteps, my husband."

Lazarus gave me a sharp look. "Only if He is the true Messiah. I have resources and networks, still. I could call upon Sicarii to aid in a revolution, but I would only do so with the true Son of David." He rested his elbows on the table. "We could...we *could* start a revolution; make him our king. It is about time! Yet, ..." he said taking a deep breath and staring ahead. "Jesus has done nothing to alert me of His intentions. I *am* His friend — or so I believed...Does He not want me as a partner? Word has it He is in Samaria as we speak. *Samaria*! Meddling with those people will not bring about the kingdom of Elohim that He speaks of."

"Do you know what the kingdom of Elohim is?" I did not.

"The reign of Israel over the world?" He lifted his statement into a question. "Is it the full control of the promised land?" He rubbed his forehead. "The garden of Eden? The restoration of the twelve tribes? When Adonai smites the wicked and rewards the righteous? I do not know, Esther. I do not understand. But Jesus should be speaking to me about this and He is not. I am restless, Esther. I have been waiting and I am yearning for something. The same thing that my father yearned for...just...I do not want to act like foolhardy bandits."

For years, I had looked at Lazarus and seen stiffness, as if he were always bracing himself for a punch.

"You are yearning for children, Lazarus," I reminded him, stepping toward him on the green and white tiled floor. I was not the wife who was like a fruitful vine within his house. He had no children like olive plants around his table. I tired of self-pity and forced myself to stop my usual laments.

"And if you cannot have children, then there must be something else we can do! Something...more. Why are you sad, O my soul?" he slowly whispered the famous psalm. "And why do you disquiet me?"

"Behold the inheritance of Adonai are children. As arrows in the hand of the mighty. Blessed is the man that has filled the desire with them." My eyebrows furrowed, familiar tears welling. I pushed them back. "What could be more than children?"

"Giving your children some*thing*." He raised his right hand, his golden ring which glistened in the room's natural light. Designs from the lattice-covered windows reflected on the floor. "The kingdom promised us by Adonai,"

Lazarus continued. "The fulfillment of the Davidic covenant. Freedom and peace. And that is where I grow wary of Jesus. He preaches a kingdom, but He is spending His time with — with Samaritans and *fishermen*."

"Martha says that the kingdom of Heaven belongs to the poor."

Lazarus eyed me. "It is not so for you and me."

"Martha says that the kingdom of Heaven belongs to the poor in spirit. That is what Jesus preaches in the synagogues. Are you and I not poor in spirit? Desperate for children and fulfillment? You are longing for this *something*."

He crossed his arms, wrapped in the sleeves of his pristine white tunic and leaned back in his scarlet cushioned chair.

"Husband," I said, stepping closer to him. I reached the edge of the table, allowing my thighs to settle against it. "Martha and Mary desire to help the poor. That is, the sick and dying."

"They do so already."

"They wish to build a hospice for the poor and to work at the hospice themselves and assist the needy. Especially the poor of Judea and those in the streets of Jerusalem."

Lazarus raised a brow. "Because?"

"Because they see it as their way of living out the kingdom of Heaven that Jesus preaches."

Lazarus ran his hands through his shiny hair. "On my property?"

"Yes."

He blew out a breath. "Have they any idea what people would think of this? Particularly the scribes and Pharisees in Jerusalem? I cannot see Hezekiah liking this idea."

"They are aware but are adamant that this is what they must do."

"And what are your thoughts on this, Esther? What do you think should happen?"

"I…" I started. I had not truly considered my own thoughts. My life seemed to be going through the motions of keeping the law and trying to please Lazarus. "I think I have not heard Jesus preach. Therefore, how can I believe anything anyone says? Some are calling Him the Messiah, but I have yet to hear it from His own lips. He is a good man. A good man with good intentions." I rested my palms on the polished wood of the table. "I know this as truth: If Martha and Mary wish to devote their time to the poor in Jesus' name, then I think it is appropriate. Martha's husband is hardly here, and Mary is a widow. They must occupy their time with something beneficial. Think of the scriptures, Lazarus. "*If one of your brethren that dwells within the*

gates of the city in the land which Adonai your El will give you, come to poverty,
you shall not harden your heart nor close your hand —"

"*— But shall open it to the poor man, you shall lend him, that which you*
perceived he had need of," Lazarus concluded, folding his arms over his chest
as he leaned farther back. "The law of Moses. I follow it strictly. I let the poor
glean in my fields and pick the olives fallen on the ground after the harvest.
On the seventh year, I release all debts and slaves. Generously."

"I am not saying otherwise. I am saying that Martha and Mary believe
they must take this a step further."

"Because Jesus says to take a step further?"

I shrugged. And my husband relented.

"I will allow it. So long..." He raised a finger. "So long as there is a
mikveh in this hospice. No one is permitted to enter my house without being
ritually clean. Including Martha, Mary, and you.

I felt slightly guilty that I did not expand upon Hezekiah's dislike of the
idea. Yet I told Lazarus, "They will be thrilled."

"And you?"

My insides curled at the thought of ulcers, wounds, fevers and whatever
other illnesses existed. "I am only thrilled if you are thrilled."

"Sadly, then, neither of us are."

"It is better to dwell in a wilderness than with a quarrelsome and passionate
woman!" I heard Hezekiah shout from within his bedchamber.

"You may as well live in a desert. I never see you!" Martha shouted back.
I tried my best not to listen to the argument as I walked down the hall, but I
slowed my pace, knowing that my agreement with Lazarus had contributed
to Hezekiah's anger.

"Rich and poor have a common bond: Adonai is the maker of them all,"
Martha continued.

"This is not a matter of the poor. We know many a poor! Lazarus' wife
is a peasant! This, however, is a matter of cleanliness and uncleanliness! I am
a Pharisee. I am looked upon as an example to Jews of cleanliness before
Adonai. I am an example of prayer; of goodness; of obedience to the Torah!"

"And no unclean person shall enter our house!" Martha firmly replied.
"Lazarus is permitting us to build a mikveh in the hospice."

"Lazarus! Lazarus! Ever since Syrus died — "

"Lazarus cares more for ritual purity than my own father did! You have
no cause for shame."

"Yet I do not see Lazarus standing in the corner of the street praying. He is not in the Temple. Has he stopped all of his studies? He has given no outward sign of generosity to the Temple treasury or to these poor and sick whom you speak of."

"Hezekiah, your own father is one of those sick. Think of this hospice for his sake. So many in our family have died from leprosy."

"Leprosy is contagious. You cannot bring lepers to live with others who are clean from the disease."

"Indeed, Hezekiah, the lepers will stay in the caves outside of Bethany, but I will give them resources. In the hospice, though, we can bring in orphaned children. It will be a place for the blind, mute, deaf, and lame. Those who have diseases or fevers or broken limbs and no one to care for them." I heard Martha give a loud huff. "Why are you so opposed to this?"

"I had no choice in the matter! I was not consulted. I do not have the power that Lazarus has here. But I do have power over my own sons! And they will *not* help you in this endeavor of yours in any way."

"You yourself heard Jesus preach in the Temple! You heard what he said about the kingdom of Heaven. Surely…"

"Surely, that man is one not to listen to. He has no care for the law of Moses. It is not just me who thinks so. The other Pharisees…"

I returned to Lazarus' bedchamber, not wanting to hear any more of the couple's argument or Hezekiah's dislike for Jesus. I bit my lip. This household hierarchy was knotted with tension.

"Adonai," I prayed, walking toward the small eastern window. "Lift up your countenance upon us and give us shalom."

The door banged open, causing me to start. I looked at Lazarus who strode forward, the red-brown acacia wood of the door frame behind him.

"Esther, I am going to Galilee!" he declared, his long vest flowing behind him.

I took in a quick breath. "For business?"

"For Jesus!"

I sputtered. "You believe He is the Messiah?" I touched my hair, feeling the pins that held my locks up. My heart thumped with foreign excitement.

"No." Lazarus narrowed his eyes. "But since Jesus will not come to me and tell me His purpose, I have no other option than to go to Him."

"I thought He was in Samaria," I said. Lazarus would never travel there.

"I spoke with a Greek Phoenician. Jesus is in Capernaum again. And there are several reports of healings."

I put my fingers to my lips. *Jesus. Jesus, my friend. What are You doing? What are You thinking? Why will You not speak to us plainly? What do You hope to achieve?*

"I am leaving in the morning," Lazarus said decisively. My heart raced and something hopeful rose in my chest, feeling light as air.

"Esther, do you wish to stay here and help with this hospice project Martha has begun?" Lazarus asked, stepping closer to me. His eyes were bright and eager. "I am sure the familial tensions will be pleasant here in Bethany," he joked.

"Lazarus," I said. "Are you giving me the choice to come with you?"

"Yes. Yes, I am."

My eyes fixed firmly on him. "Then yes. I am coming with you."

Chapter 17

But a shoot shall sprout from the stump of Jesse,
and from his roots a bud shall blossom.
Isaiah 11:1

It was a brief moment in which my eyes met His. No words were spoken, and no words could have been heard anyway with the noise in the crowded home. But something stopped in me when I met His eyes.

Or something started.

His were pensive with a direct, definite focus on me.

My brows furrowed and I wondered if I had ever exchanged such a glance before with Jesus. It made me pull in my gut and still my breath.

And then a man walked in front of me, breaking our eye contact.

I scratched at my head beneath the green veil. Sweat formed at my brow.

Lazarus and I arrived in Nazareth last night on our camels and began the Sabbath in Uncle Clopas' house, where, by the wonder of Adonai, Jesus and His disciples were staying. Jesus and *several* disciples. About fifteen of them.

I crossed my arms, feeling the sleeves of my tunic. Upon entering Nazareth, after dismounting my camel, my mantle was caught on a thistle and tore in two. I did not bring a spare, though we brought several thick blankets with us. Our manservant offered me his mantle, but I refused. It would be improper to wear a male servant's clothing.

"The wind is blowing from the south. There will be heat today," Peter said, standing next to me in the tightly-packed courtyard.

"I am thankful for it," I said. "We could use a hot day during the rainy season." I was surprised, almost embarrassed that Peter chose to stand beside me; a woman; a *barren* one. Surely it was because there was nowhere else to stand in this cramped space and he did not know of my grievous reputation.

The house was lively and full. I did wonder if James Zebedee, the disciple of Jesus, was *too* lively for this seventh day of rest as he practically danced about the home, speaking loudly to each person.

Each one of us had risen from sleep and were preparing to go to the synagogue for the Sabbath gathering.

Glancing at the man beside me, I observed that this disciple of Jesus was much better groomed than his brother Andrew. They did share the same crooked teeth, but Peter's hair was darker than Andrew's. At least Peter knew how to look a person in the eye. Not that he was obliged to do so for me.

I am compared to dirt and am like embers and ashes. I cry to You, Elohim, and You hear me not. I stand up and You do not regard me. I made my perpetual lament like Job once did. And did not Elohim eventually show Job favor?

"You will return to Bethany after the Sabbath, then?" Peter asked, his eyebrows forcefully slanted in an emotion I could not read.

"Perhaps. It...it depends on my husband." My eyes searched for Lazarus and I found him on the roof, speaking to Jesus and Simon and some other men I did not recognize. Jealousy pricked at me. The glance I had of Jesus' face was not enough. I still had not been able to exchange one word with Jesus, who easily vanished from one room to the roof, to outside, to nowhere to be seen.

Peter coughed into his arm and surveyed the courtyard: The oven in the corner and the brooms, rakes, and rollers leaned against the wall. The heavy smell of hay and animal drifted from the stable. And of course, there was the small carpenter shop under the beaten awning.

"It is good that we are here," Peter said in a mumble. "That we may see the Master's hometown."

Cousin Joses, Cousin Jude, and other relatives jostled past. I would have moved outside to wait to go to synagogue, but the streets were too narrow.

"You are the sister, then, of Simon?" Peter asked in a sort of mutter.

"I am."

"Simon the *Zealot*," Peter said distinctly. He shifted his weight from one bare foot to the other. He was clearly a very conservative Jew. "Who is now Simon the disciple."

My tongue rolled uncomfortably in my mouth as I swatted at a fly near my eyes. "I am surprised. Simon is a proud man and...he is as you say, zealous. I would expect him to follow a son of Judas the Galilean, not his own cousin...a...teacher." I tested out the word "teacher."

"He has gotten along with Thaddeus very well. Thaddeus was a blacksmith and now, is a disciple of the Master."

"Disciples," I murmured to myself, thinking of all these men leaving their lives to follow Jesus. What of their wives and families? What did *they* do? They would have to keep care of the children and house.

"Pardon me?" Peter looked down at me.

I looked up, realizing I spoke aloud. "You are a disciple of Jesus," I tried to explain, but I did not even know what I would reveal.

"I..." Peter gulped. "I am."

"You look fainthearted," I said, instantly regretting my comment.

"Well I did not ask to do this. The Master asked — no — commanded *me. Me!*" Peter put his hands to his head, taking another long breath. "I will admit to you, woman. I am a sinner. That is what I am."

"Sir, do not be afraid or dismayed. I know Jesus well. He is a simple man. Do not be anxious in His presence."

"Jesus is *Kyrios*!" Peter snapped, causing me to jolt with the rare use of Greek.

"Still dealing with that pride, Peter?" Philip came beside us to slap Peter's shoulder. His curly hair bounced as he joined our conversation.

Peter glared at Philip, shrugging off his hand. "What are you talking about pride? I know I am unworthy!"

"I never said otherwise." Philip looked at me with a mischievous smile. "What I mean is that pride can go both ways. From thinking too highly of oneself to thinking one is so low, he does not deserve Elohim's mercy." He flicked an invisible speck of dust from the sleeve of his tunic.

Who were these strange men? Was Philip trying to irritate Peter or help him?

I focused on Peter, whose shoulders were slouched like a little boy denied a sweet.

"Esther, listen. If it were not for Peter, here, I would not be following Jesus," Philip told me, pulling closer to Peter. Peter shoved him away.

"How so?" I asked, leaning backwards.

"I am from Bethsaida. In fact I lived right next to Peter's father's house in Bethsaida before the family moved to Capernaum. I was a vineyard laborer. Peter, Andrew, and I were always good friends. Then one day, Peter and Andrew came to Bethsaida and told me they had found the Messiah."

I winced at that word.

"From that instant, I knew my life would never be the same." Philip smiled to himself. "We are all unworthy, Peter." He nudged his friend with his elbow. "Do not think yourself more terrible than the rest of us."

Peter mumbled to himself as Philip gave a little chuckle.

"Ah!" Philip exclaimed, on seeing Bartholomew. He pulled the man over, causing Bartholomew to almost trip over a rake. "But I am the one who introduced this man to the Master."

Bartholomew blinked as he looked at us. "Never would have guessed He would be a Nazarene." He scratched his long, unruly beard.

"Wha..." I started. "How...eh...why..." I blushed. What was I even trying to ask?

"The kingdom of Heaven…" Bartholomew inclined his head toward me and started rocking back and forth.

I clutched my hands together. There went that radical statement again. And why was I, a woman, conversing with three strange men? I could smell the sweat, fish, and filth steaming off of them.

"You do not yet believe, do you, Esther?" Philip's bright eyes narrowed upon me, but not without a hint of gentleness.

"Do not…I…well…believe what?" I stuttered, heat rising to my cheeks. I was hot enough without feeling flustered!

"That your cousin is the Messiah."

He was my cousin. My cousin! The Messiah could not be my own cousin. Besides, Jesus had yet to claim this messianic title. Perhaps if He did, my view would be different. But I was more educated than these men who were farmers, leatherworkers, and fishermen who put their hope in a good man. But surely Jesus was the wrong man.

"Esther," Aunt Miriam walked over. I looked down at the small woman. "I heard about your mantle. You will have this one." She presented a clean wool mantle, dyed a dark blue.

I looked back at the disciples, then stepped away from them, begging Aunt Miriam to follow me to the corner, near her aloe plant outside of the traklin. She shuffled after me.

"Aunt Miriam." I lowered my voice as we stepped against the wall. "That is kind of you to offer, but I cannot borrow that."

"It is not to borrow, Esther," Aunt Miriam said, pushing the mantle toward me. Her wrinkled wrists stuck out from beneath her cloak. "It is a gift."

"But Aunt Miriam." I looked at the mantle's deep color. "It is blue. It must be a more expensive color and…and it is a color for Palestinian mothers. I am not a mother."

"Silly girl. Take the mantle."

"I have several at home in Bethany. I do not need it. But thank you for your graciousness."

"Esther…" Aunt Miriam's voice shook.

I offended her!

"Thank you." I accepted the cloak. "May Elohim reward you." I liked the feel of the soft wool.

The courtyard began to empty as our brethren and guests headed out toward the synagogue. I adjusted my veil and then settled the new mantle over it, feeling self-conscious. What would people think of me if they saw me in this color? It was like wearing a rich red and not actually being a virgin!

I walked out down the slope of the village. Lazarus had probably already left with the disciples. The sun continued rising in the east, but it was still a way from the noon hour.

Men, women, and children, including many I did not recognize, filed into Nazareth's stone synagogue, near the base of the village. It had one rectangular base layer, with a smaller rectangle on top of that, which was lined with some small windows near the roof. The hill that Nazareth rested on fell toward the Jezreel Valley. Its fields, vineyards, olive groves, shepherds' pens, and watchtowers were visible. Soft green trees contrasted against the brown grass. Purple thistles further accented the landscape.

Thistles! I pulled the disquieting new mantle tighter around me, wishing for my old one.

Pharisees in their strict white and black garb, entered the synagogue with the throng of people. They also must have come from different towns. I too made my way, but as I reached the door, I saw Jesus, facing me, but speaking to Pharisees. I froze as if suddenly struck by lightning. My heart felt odd. Warm and…excited? The kingdom of Heaven?

A body slammed into me from behind.

"Esther…" Uncle Clopas' voice was a growl.

Almost in a daze, I hardly looked back at Uncle Clopas as I mumbled an apology and continued through the wide entrance of the synagogue.

The kingdom of Heaven.

How many times had I heard that response? How many times had that reason been given to me? John the Baptist. Jesus. His disciples. Martha and Mary. But where were they going to end up? In Herod's prison like John the Baptist?

I felt a sense of worry rush through my fingertips and to the edge of my toes. If Jesus preached the way John did, then I feared for His life.

I wove my way through the large hall that was surrounded by stone pillars, and filled by men and women. Men placed tallits over their head for proper prayer. There must have been about three hundred of us.

Some stood, while others sat on stone benches along the sides of the hall. I squeezed beside Aunt Mary, my mantle the same color as hers. Usually, we women stayed near the back and the outer edge of the synagogue as the men gathered closer to the center. It was unlike the Temple, though, where women were forbidden to enter the inner courts.

The stone *chair of Moses* was near to my left, the seat reserved for the rabbi.

I caught another glimpse of Jesus. Our eyes met briefly.

Aliza pushed her way next to me, but I did not acknowledge her. I looked at Jesus, feeling very attentive to His presence. It had been this way since I was a child, but never before had I thought about *why* I was drawn to Him. This was not like the love-sick infatuation I held for Lazarus as a girl. Or the timeless love I had for Lazarus as a mature woman. Or the respect I had for my relatives. Or even the sisterly bond I had with Martha and Mary. It was something entirely different that I could not explain.

In the very center of the building where a wooden dais stood, Jesus talked to Nazareth's rabbi. I looked at the profile of Jesus' freshly shaven face. His pale-colored tallit, lined with blue, served as a canopy over His hair.

The rabbi Jesus spoke with, a Pharisee, was wearing his black and white linen vestments, alerting us of his status. He wore a turban beneath a large head-covering that was near the size of a blanket. I thought this was the rabbi who disliked Jesus. Was he now showing Jesus favor? Did he believe in the miracle at Cana?

The synagogue was filled with chatter.

"They are going to have Jesus read," Aliza muttered in disgust.

I looked from her to Aunt Mary, and back to her again, trying to keep my eyes from rolling behind my lids. Aliza scratched at her freckled nose.

"Mary, you must be proud." Aunt Miriam said as she shuffled on her poor feet to Aunt Mary's other side. "Look how acclaimed your son is!" Aunt Mary acknowledged Aunt Miriam with a soft glance but did not say anything.

Ima joined us as the leading Pharisees raised their arms, milling about the crowds to silence them.

The lot of us quieted quickly at their command, showing our shared respect for the holy, learned sect. A few men and a woman sat on the mats in front of me. As my calves hit the back surface of the stone bench behind me, I too sat down, along with my relatives. Light flowed in from the small windows near the roof of the building.

Nazareth's rosy-cheeked rabbi spoke first. "Today, we have our very own Jesus of Nazareth with us." Rabbi glanced behind him at Jesus, who inclined His head in acknowledgment. "A highly esteemed man, upon whom Adonai seems to have bestowed the wisdom of Solomon." Rabbi lifted a curved hand and pointed his finger upward with excitement.

"Solomon!" Aliza breathed. "That is a lofty comparison."

"He is only a carpenter, you know," one man in front of me whispered to another.

"Oh, I have heard Him speak before," the other responded in an angry tone. "He is just some want-to-be rabbi."

A desire to defend Jesus snatched me, but I squirmed from its grasp. I did not know what I believed myself. How then, could I defend Jesus?

Jesus' eyes met my eyes, and a shock went through me once again. I looked away as a scribe gave Jesus the Torah. I blinked several times as Jesus unrolled the sacred Word on the dais, a pleasant expression on His face.

"In the beginning." Speaking the Hebrew, Jesus' calm yet authoritative voice captured the room. "Elohim created Heaven and earth…"

He read the whole creation narrative, surely having it memorized. I certainly memorized the first several chapters.

"And He said: Let Us make man in Our image and likeness. And let him have dominion over the fishes of the sea and the fowls of the air and the beasts, and the whole earth, and every creature that moves upon the earth…"

My attention did not wane as Jesus spoke the familiar words Adonai spoke to the serpent, punishing the foul creature. "I will put enmity between you and the woman, your seed and her seed. She shall crush your head, and you shall lie in wait for his heel."

Oddly, Jesus stopped there and did not continue with reading about the punishment of man and woman. Instead, He rolled up the Torah and handed it to the scribe. Jesus had spoken of this passage before, even when He was a young man. He was always a firm believer that the Messiah would come to save us. In fact, Jesus' name meant "Elohim saves." But He had never suggested that *He* was that savior.

"Amen, amen, I say to you," Jesus said, in Aramaic. His voice reverberated off the walls. "That he who hears My word and believes Him that sent me, has life everlasting, and comes not into judgment, but is passed from death to life."

Who was it that sent Jesus, then? My lips pressed firmly together.

"Your word?" Rabbi asked.

"And who is the one who sent You?" another Pharisee asked.

"What do You mean by eternal life?"

My eyebrows furrowed. I wondered if Jesus was speaking of the kingdom of Heaven.

"Are you saying that the judgment of Adam and Eve will pass us?"

"The Wisdom of Solomon reads that Elohim created man incorruptible and in the image of His own likeness," Jesus said. "*But by the envy of the devil, death came into the world,*" He continued. "The prophet Daniel said to know and take notice: That from the going forth of the Word, to build up Jerusalem again, unto the anointed one, the prince."

I closed my eyes, trying to breathe. Where He was going with this was all too obvious. But could I admit it to myself?

"Young man," a Pharisee said, his voice ringing as he stepped before the dais. "We know the prophecies of the Messiah. We know we are in the age of the Messiah and we believe that Adonai has indeed promised us a savior."

Men nodded their heads and mumbled agreements.

"What have You to say," the rosy-cheeked rabbi exclaimed, staring at Jesus with hungry anticipation, "about the coming of the Messiah?" The rabbi looked at the crowd. "Why do we continue to be persecuted at the hands of our enemies?"

"Rome holds Israel captive! She must be set free!" A man raised his fist in the air.

The rabbi held up a hand. "You Zealots must let our Jesus speak." He turned to Jesus. "Tell us. When will we be delivered? How?"

"The kingdom of Heaven is at hand," Jesus said to the crowd of listeners.

My heart leaped at His words. I had heard it said so many times. Could it really be here right now? At this time?

Jesus tapped His hand on the dais. "Amen, amen, I say to you, whoever commits sin is the servant of sin. Now the servant abides not in the house forever, but the son abides forever. If therefore, the son shall make you free, you shall be free indeed." Jesus' warm eyes blazed.

I did not know why, but my eyes glazed with tears. Sin. Sin. All I knew was my sin. I could not escape its grasp. Or its consequences.

"My dear man, who is the son? Are You speaking of the Messiah?" Rabbi pulled at his beard.

Jesus turned to the scribe. "Bring Me the writings of the prophet Isaiah." He looked back at the crowd as the scribe pushed his way through the people at Jesus' request.

People spoke in urgent, questioning tones. I glanced at Aunt Mary, who was unmoving, like one of the stone pillars. My heartbeat accelerated; my mind too clouded with confusion for my thoughts to form.

As the scribe returned with the scroll, handing it to Jesus, the Pharisees hushed the crowd.

I sat on the edge of the bench. A couple of men chose to stand in front of me. I raised my chin to get a look, between their shoulders, at Jesus unrolling the scroll.

Finally, the men in front of me sat down, and I saw Jesus examining the readings. He glanced at us, then looked down again, saying in Hebrew, "The Spirit of Adonai is upon Me. Wherefore He has anointed Me to preach the Gospel to the poor." I flinched at "poor," as I thought of being poor in spirit. Jesus paused to look at us. The synagogue was quiet. "He has sent Me to heal the contrite of heart. To preach deliverance to the captives." His words rolled from His tongue. "And sight to the blind, to set at liberty they who are bruised to preach the acceptable year of Adonai and the day of reward."

Something rose in my throat. My entire body was warm. The acceptable year of Adonai was every seventh year, in which all debts were forgotten, and all slaves were freed.

Slowly, Jesus raised His head to us again. Rolling up the scroll, He handed it back to the scribe who was attending to Him.

I could hear my blood drumming in my ears as I stared at Jesus. He did not complete the usual reading where Adonai spoke of His vengeance.

"Let us sit, My friends," Jesus suggested, both hands resting on the dais.

"Rabbi!" The rabbi exclaimed. "Take the chair of Moses. I insist."

My heart galloped as people parted, like the Red Sea had for Moses, to let Jesus make His way to the chair of Moses, near to my left. For the briefest moment, I thought we made eye contact, but perhaps it was my own fond wishing.

Jesus sat down. "This day is the Scripture fulfilled in your ears."

Eager murmurs rippled around me as that strange warmth spread through my chest. He was serious. He claimed to be the Messiah.

"Can it be?"

"Where does He get all these things?"

"I cannot believe my ears!" Cousin Joses' voice caught my attention.

"What is the wisdom given to Him?"

"He speaks of the Messiah!"

"And you know what mighty works are wrought by His hands!"

"Oh, Israel! How I have longed to hear such words!"

"Is not this the carpenter's son?"

"Is not His mother called Mary?"

My mouth parted. I broke my gaze from Jesus and looked at Aunt Mary, whose soft gaze was on her son. Did she believe that her own son was the Messiah?

"He is my cousin. Just a carpenter." Cousin Joses raised his voice in response.

"And His brethren are James and Joses and Simon and Jude!"

"He is just a Nazarene like yourself. How then, can He claim such a thing?"

"And His sisters, are they not all with us?" A man gestured at Aliza and me.

"...Rabbi! If what you say is true, then command me to follow You!"

"Rabbi! Tell us, are You indeed the Holy One of Elohim?"

Rabbi. Rabbi. They were all calling Him. I looked at Jesus in anticipation.

"He turned water into wine at Cana. I am certain of it."

"I heard He cured a woman of a fever in Capernaum."

"He also commanded the fish of the sea in Capernaum. There was a multitude of fish that the fishermen caught, I tell you! Those fishermen in this man's boat caught a surplus of fish!"

"Sir, give us a sign if what You say is true."

"Yes!"

"Perform a miracle as You did in Cana."

"Is not this the son of Joseph?"

"If You did so for the people of Capernaum, then surely You must for us as well."

"Give us a sign so we may believe in You."

Jesus put up a hand to silence the crowd. "Doubtless you will say to Me this proverb: 'Physician, heal yourself, as great things as we have heard done in Capernaum, do also here in your own country.'"

"You will perform a miracle in Capernaum, but not for Your own kinsmen?"

"Do you think us unworthy of a sign?" Cousin Joses' voice was dominated by anger.

"We beg of You, show us a sign."

"We would believe in You if You but performed a wonder."

I continued to stare at Jesus in fearful expectation, growing nervous at the angry tones that began to distinguish themselves in the crowd. The mood of the crowd was shifting from wonder to indignation.

"A sign will not be given but the sign of Jonah the prophet," Jesus said firmly, clasping His hands on the arms of the chair as men rose from their seats. I also stood.

"What is that supposed to mean?"

"You cannot be who You claim!"

"What is it You are claiming?"

Jonah. I thought of the prophet who spent three days in the belly of a whale. And then Adonai saved the evil Ninevites. He overlooked their sin when they came to worship Him as the El of Israel; the one true Elohim.

From what I could see of Jesus, He looked anguished. "Amen, I say to you, that no prophet is accepted in His own country. In truth I say to you, there were many widows in the days of Elijah in Israel, when Heaven was shut up three years and six months, when there was a great famine throughout all the earth."

I knew the story well. The land of Israel was barren. Like myself.

"And to none of them was Elijah sent, but to Zarephath of Sidon, to a widow woman."

Adonai had blessed Sidon; the Gentiles; a woman outside of Israel.

"And there were many lepers in Israel in the time of Elisha the prophet and none of them were cleansed but Naaman the Syrian."

The crowd's mood shifted again, toward anger and violence. Mad voices blared around me like foul trumpets. Soon I was unable to see or hear Jesus as some stood in frustration and others yelled at Him in fury.

"You dare claim yourself a prophet!" Cousin Joses shouted at His cousin. "Blasphemer!"

Despite the people blocking her view, Aunt Mary remained in her seat, continuing to look in her son's direction.

"*You* think *You* are the Messiah?" Rabbi shouted. "But You will not show us a sign? You would rather show your signs to Gentiles instead of Your own people!"

"He never even showed a sign to anyone! He is a false prophet!"

"We are Israel! We are Jacob's offspring! There is no other chosen race!"

"Get out of our synagogue!"

"How dare You!"

"He should be stoned for this!"

"Get out! Take Him out!"

I gasped as I was roughly shoved.

I saw the top of Jesus' dark hair. His tallit had fallen on the ground.

Putting my hands to my cheeks, I prayed they would not harm Him. Peter pushed men away and yelled at them like he was a wild animal. John and Philip shouted, trying to get Jesus' attention, as He made his way toward the exit of the synagogue. James Zebedee, as large of a man as he was, was easy to spot and easy to hear as he bellowed, "...no right! This is indeed...a holy man...open your eyes...fools..."

My brother Simon and Cousin Joses yelled in each other's faces.

"Esther!" Lazarus firmly clamped his hand on my shoulder. "You are to stay in the synagogue. I do not want you getting into this brawl."

I nodded, eyes shot open in horror, as Lazarus left with the angry crowd.

Soon the synagogue was empty save a handful of women. I stood looking at the open door, light streaming in it. I heard the shouts and cries of men condemning Jesus. Cursing Him. Rejecting Him.

Slowly, I turned my head to look at Aunt Mary. Her hands were lightly clasped in her lap.

"I do not like Jesus," Aliza pouted as she too sat back down. "But I do not want Him dead."

I returned my attention to my other female relatives.

"We will pray," Aunt Mary said gently when I reached her side. She picked up Jesus' tallit that had fallen on the ground.

I followed her to a back corner where she fell to her knees. Without any need for prompting, I followed her example. I felt that imitating her was in the best interest of Jesus. Strangely, she was the calmest person there. I sat back on my heels and clasped my hands together, glancing upward. The small windows above me showed hints of the blue sky.

This day is the Scripture fulfilled in your ears. This poor man cried, and Adonai heard him and saved him out of all his troubles. I sought Adonai and He heard me. And He delivered me from all of my troubles.

I placed a hand over my mouth as my body trembled. Adonai. Adonai!

My heart has uttered a good word. I speak my works to the king. My tongue is the pen of a scribe that writes swiftly.

"Give praise, O you barren, that bears not. Sing forth praise and make a joyful noise, you that did not bear a child," I said aloud in a shaky tone. Perhaps the women looked my way. I did not care. "For many are the children of the desolate, more than of her that has a husband says Adonai. For Adonai has called you as woman forsaken and mourning in spirit, and as a wife cast off from her youth, says your El. In a moment of indignation have I hid My face a little while from you, but with everlasting kindness have I had mercy on you, says Adonai, your redeemer."

Different prophecies from Isaiah dashed through my mind and leapt from my tongue. "And you shall be found in justice, depart far from oppression, for you shall not fear. All you who thirst, come to the waters," I wept, tears breezing down my cheeks. "You who have no money make haste, buy, and eat."

The image of Jesus reading the scroll was heavily printed on my closed eyes. I thought of the rest of the passage from Isaiah. "For your double confusion and shame, they will praise their part. Therefore, will they receive double in their land, everlasting joy will be unto them!"

I looked to my side. Through my blurred vision I saw Aunt Mary was gazing at me. Both of us on our knees, I took her hand. It was calloused from years of hard labor. Her fingers were long and, to me, they may as well have had sapphire, diamond, and pearl rings upon them.

I kissed her fingers. For she was the mother of the Messiah.

"I do not want to go home. I want to go with Jesus," I told Lazarus the next morning, tears in my eyes. We stood near the path to the spring. From there issued the stone Roman road that would take us south toward Judea.

There were cacti in clumps, hidden beneath tall trees at our left. A lizard scurried past us on a rock.

"You are not married to Jesus. You are married to me."

"Lazarus! Listen! He is the Messiah! Are we just going to walk away from Him?" I looked up at the birds swirling in the pale blue sky.

"No," Lazarus decided, raising a hand in the air to alert the servants. "We are going to *ride* away from Him."

The servants brought our camels. I looked away from the creatures' large eyes that were surrounded by thick lashes.

"But He said He is the Messiah!"

"I am sure He is," Lazarus breathed, turning his face from me.

"Are you teasing me?"

"I do not know! I do not know what I think, woman! Whatever He may be, He does not want me." He straightened his shoulders.

"He said this?"

He looked back to me, his brown eyes filled with pain. "He said He does not want my money; my connections! He does not want any involvement with Sicarii or...or any of it. All He wants is for me to get rid of it all and follow Him. That is what He said." He started adjusting his head covering for travel.

I clung to the mantle around my shoulders, scrunching my nose as a waft of the camels hit me.

"Then He does want you," I pressed Lazarus, tugging my mantle tighter. A wind rustled the ends of it. My veil was wrapped tightly around my head, unfazed by the breeze. "He wants *you*. Not what you have to offer Him."

The servant tapped Lazarus' camel, so the beast would lie down. Lazarus got onto its back. On its spiny legs the camel rose to its full height, almost twice as tall as me.

"They tried to hurl Him headlong down the hill." Lazarus looked down at me, his covering wrapped fully around his head and neck.

"But He passed through their midst!" I raised my voice.

All of Nazareth was still buzzing about what happened after Jesus left the synagogue, followed by the angry mob.

"We do not even know what direction He went in. He vanished."

"With your resources, we could track Him and follow Him." I looked at the path that led downhill to the cubed homes of Nazareth. "And you saw Aunt Miriam! Jesus healed her lame feet! Truly, she is now the fastest walker in all of Galilee!"

"Get on your camel, wife."

"Lazarus, what if Jesus miraculously healed my barren womb?"

"So this is what all of your dreaming is about, eh?" Lazarus sighed. He looked at me as if I were a fragile, sickly woman, about to fall to the ground in weakness.

Perhaps I was.

"Esther." I knew he was trying to say my name gently. "Let us go back to the comforts of our home."

Tears streaming down my cheeks, I did all that a wife could do. Obey my husband. We set off for Judea. With each step of the camel, rocking me roughly back and forth, I thought of what I was going back to. My life of misery. Farther away from the One who had promised to give me glad tidings and bind up my broken heart. *Adonai, will You not bring again the captivity of Your people Israel and Judah? Or will we continue to be scattered across the nations?*

At least I would remain near Jerusalem. Surely Jesus would return to the Holy City for the pilgrim feasts. *Arise, O Jerusalem and stand on high. Look about towards the east and behold your children gathered together from the rising to the setting sun, by the word of the Holy One rejoicing in the remembrance of Elohim.* All of these prophets like Baruch! Now was the time of their fulfillment! Renewed motivation raced through my veins as dust and wind hit my eyes. The kingdom of Heaven was at hand. Jesus was the Messiah. And I would be right at the center of the world for the collection of Israel from all the nations; those scattered by the exile; those who had inherited Egypt, Assyria, Babylon, Persia, Greece, and Rome. They would all return to Israel. We would all be a united kingdom as we were under David.

The prophet Micah said *for the law shall go forth out of Zion, and the word of Adonai out of Jerusalem.* I smiled to myself, thinking more about the prophet Micah who said that from Bethlehem *shall He come forth unto Me that is to be the ruler in Israel.*

Our family was from the special city foretold by Micah. We traveled there for a census the year I was born. Few knew of this, but I was His kindred.

Jesus was born in Bethlehem.

Chapter 18

*On that day — oracle of the L*ORD *of hosts — I will take you,*
*my servant, Zerubabel, son of Shealtiel — oracle of the L*ORD
— and I will make you like a signet ring, for I have chosen you
*— oracle of the L*ORD *of hosts.*

HAGGAI 2:23

The Feast of Unleavened Bread was here, and as always with the promise of springtime. The first day of the feast, Passover, was behind us and it was now the fifth night of the week-long celebration.

We had an honored guest with us in Bethany.

Our journey home from Nazareth this past winter had been swift. Lazarus immediately resumed his work in Judea but was sour and restless. His temper flared easier than oil and a flame. He vowed that Jesus would not be welcomed under our roof, but later, when Jesus requested to visit for the feast of Unleavened Bread, he obliged without any protest.

I thought he was confused. In turmoil over Jesus' claim as Messiah as opposed to all that Lazarus had been taught since childhood about who the Messiah should be. I never realized quite how much Syrus' viewpoints were engrained in Lazarus. Lazarus swore he would never participate in acts of violence and zealotry as his father had, but if Jesus told him to raise a dagger, then I think Lazarus would have.

I wondered if his anger was greater because he did *not* follow Jesus. When Jesus was rejected at Nazareth, Lazarus could have run after Jesus and followed Him. Yet he chose not to so that he could keep his prestige, run the household, maintain his interpretation of the Torah, and live in comfort.

But he was anything but comfortable.

He still permitted Martha and Mary to build their hospice. Perhaps it was because Lazarus truly did believe in the kingdom of Heaven that Jesus spoke of. Yet Lazarus continued to ask, "*What is the kingdom of Heaven?*"

The hospice was a large structure that was completed just before the feast. Martha and Mary were moving the poor and sick into it. If any died, Martha ensured they were given a proper burial. She hardly spent any time at home anymore. She was at the hospice that very moment, despite Jesus' presence in the house with us.

As for me, I had helped Martha and Mary. Not literally *in* their hospice. I refused to go inside. I could not bear being among the sick. Particularly sick and dying children. I would bake bread for them, and I would weave mantles for them, but I would not hand them to the sick or dying. Martha did not understand me. She said that I should not use my lack of children as an excuse to not be around children. "All the more reason to help," she said.

I felt assailed by it all. I thought that since I was in the presence of Jesus earlier this year, He would heal my infirmity and give me a child. But my womb was still lifeless. Perhaps I was not truly poor in spirit, so the kingdom of Heaven was not mine.

I entered the banquet hall with a pitcher of wine. It paled in comparison to what Jesus made in Cana, but it was the finest wine Judea had to offer.

And there He was, in the seat of honor toward the left as Lazarus was directly beside him. Thirty or so male disciples also reclined at table.

In the light of so many oil lamps, Jesus' hair looked highlighted with auburn. His eyes were even warmer than usual. As I walked toward the men, Jesus looked up at me. He smiled. I smiled back. When our eyes unlocked, I took a deep breath. Being in His presence was so different than it used to be. He still made me feel peaceful and somewhat confused, yet now, I had a certain awe and reverence for Him.

It was the end of the meal. Lazarus chewed pomegranate seeds, one-by-one; slowly. "They are saying you healed a man on the Sabbath," he said, his elbow resting against a cushion as he picked up another seed. "At the pools of Bethesda."

"This is true." Simon spoke for Jesus. My brother wore a band around his head; his meaty hands dug into the meaty fish. "But the Master is Kyrios over the Sabbath. It is fitting to do good on the Sabbath."

I held back a smile for my brother. It was odd to think that this prideful Zealot of a man now called his own younger cousin "Master."

"You hypocrites," Jesus said. Lazarus started to gag and covered his mouth. He took a swig of wine.

I walked between the seated men on the floor, wove myself around them as I headed toward the main table. I glanced at Mary, seated on the inside of the horseshoe-shaped table, directly across from Jesus; the only other woman in the room beside me.

"Lazarus," Jesus said. "Do you not order your servants on the Sabbath to untie your camel or your horse from the manger and lead it away to water it?"

"But, Rabbi," Lazarus said, leaning toward Jesus. "What of the law? Are you casting it aside? Surely Moses and Elijah would not condone this." He squished a pomegranate seed.

"Do not think that I have come to destroy the law or the prophets." Jesus took a sip of wine. "I have not come to destroy, but to fulfill." His goblet clanked as He set it on the table. He tossed a few pomegranate seeds into His mouth.

"Lazarus, please." Mary looked up at Jesus. She was sitting on her heels. "Let us not condemn the Master. He is our guest."

Lazarus put up a hand. "I have one more question for You, *Sir.*"

Mary blew out a breath.

I noticed my hands shaking as I filled Bartholomew's cup. Then Philip's. James Zebedee's. John's.

"Speak plainly to me," my husband asked. "What is the kingdom of Heaven?" He sat up fully.

Jesus' face was long. His hair almost touched His shoulders. His eyes were a swirl of shades of brown. "Lazarus, hand me your ring."

A few men rustled in their seats. Lazarus looked around, then at his signet ring, the one he inherited from his father to use for signing papers. It marked that Lazarus was the master of the house. I wondered for a moment if my husband would refuse Jesus' request.

He did not. Lazarus pulled the golden ring off of his finger and passed it to Jesus. Jesus placed the ring on His ceramic plate. I blew out a breath, thankful Jesus did not throw it out the window. It was a foolish thought, but Jesus was not one to act normal.

Lazarus gaped as he looked at the plate. I backed away from the table and stood in the corner of the hall. I held a fine linen wash towel beneath my pitcher of wine.

Jesus looked like a father, ready to teach his son a lesson. But I dismissed the comparison.

"Lazarus, the kingdom of Heaven is like a treasure hidden in a field, which a man having found, hid it." Jesus took lettuce leaves from a salad to spread over the ring, completely covering it. "And for joy goes and sells all that he has." He pushed a basket of fine fruits, oranges, peaches, and apples, away from Him. "And buys that field."

Now Jesus removed the ring from the lettuce and held it at eye level, its gold sparkling in the lamplight. "Again, the kingdom of Heaven is like a merchant seeking good pearls. Who, when he had found one pearl of great price, went his way, and sold all that he had and bought it." He returned the ring back to Lazarus.

Lazarus' face tensely contorted. He looked at the ring in the same way he looked at the Torah when studying it.

"Mary," Jesus said, looking down. "Where is your sister?"

Mary straightened, obviously pleased that Jesus addressed her. "Master, she is in the hospice we built, working hard. She practically lives there now."

"We will visit her," Jesus decided. His hands spread against the linen tablecloth.

My eyes widened. I kept both hands firmly on the clay pitcher to ensure I did not drop it.

"Will you lead us, Mary?" Jesus asked.

Mary quickly stood up, her cheeks red and her smile luminous. "This way, Kyrios." Jesus rose and the disciples followed. Lazarus stayed seated. I stood with my pitcher of wine in the back of the room.

I could not go *in* the hospice. I had yet to step foot in it.

"Esther," Jesus said as He walked around the table. "Come with us."

My throat went dry as I tried to gulp. Jesus kept walking, out the door, and into the courtyard. Disciples brushed past me. Was that the first time Jesus said my name since He arrived? He did not say it slowly, but distinctly and calmly, like a soft breeze.

"Lazarus." I stepped toward my husband when they all left. "Are you going?"

He slipped the gold back on his ring finger and looked up at me. "Yes," he said. He stood up, looking dizzy.

"Are you well?" I asked him.

"No." He shook his head, walking across the room and out the door, following Jesus. I set the pitcher of wine on the table.

Esther, come with us. Jesus had requested. Surely I had to go because my husband was going. I had to go because I was woman of this household and must visit the poor and ill on my husband's property. I had to go because Jesus was my dear friend and kindred. I had to go because Jesus was the Messiah.

I hurried out of the banquet room and into the courtyard. I went through a hallway that was a part of the servants' quarters. I saw my maidservant and ordered that she grab my mantle, which she did. I passed by the servants' kitchen, work rooms, and sleeping area and reached the back entrance.

I emerged into the night. Torchlight glowed ahead of me. I pulled my mantle around me. It was the one Aunt Miriam gave me. Though I initially disliked her gift and was sure I would trade it for one of the many I had in Bethany, this one smelled like Nazareth. Wood, animal, charcoal, bread, and aloe. Though I had ones of superior material, this one was the perfect balance of weight for warmth and lightness for travel. If only it was not that motherly blue.

I reached the group as they went downhill on the path to the family sepulcher. A palm tree waved in the breeze of the pleasant air. Above, the night was clear, stars embroidering the sky. We passed rocks and boulders and the shadowed stretches of olive groves. I had often walked between these olive trees in despair and guilt as I prayed to bear fruit like them.

Not too long later we reached the hospice, smoke piling out of the limestone structure. Martha was not frugal with the construction of this long, one-story building, about the size of Lazarus' courtyard.

"Do you believe now, Esther?" Philip looked back at me, switching his torch from one hand to the other.

"B-believe what?" I asked. Men did not usually freely address me the way these disciples did.

"That your cousin is the Messiah."

"I believe," I said quietly.

Philip's lips curved into a smile. His curly hair mounded like burning coals in the firelight. "Now then stand and see this great thing which Adonai will do in your sight."

I looked away. My sight? Was he commenting on my green eyes? Or was it my own selfish focus? And when he said "Adonai," was he speaking of Elohim or was he speaking about Jesus?

I looked at the group. My brother Simon was not there and many of the disciples were missing. "Where are the others?" I asked Philip.

"The Master sent them to the lepers' caves, telling them to bring the lepers here to the hospice."

My mouth uncontrollably dropped as we reached the doors of the hospice.

Martha emerged from its door and fell to her knees when she saw Jesus. Her mahogany veil tightly covered all of her head and hair. The sleeves of her tunic, which was covered by a long apron, were rolled up to her elbows. She spoke to Jesus in a hushed but hurried tone. I could not decipher the words.

As she stood, the glow of the inside light shone on her. She almost fell. Jesus touched her arm to steady her. She disappeared into the building and Jesus followed. The couple dozen disciples started to go inside.

I bit my lip. Could I face the sick and ill? Only about half of the disciples seemed able to fit in the building.

Seeing a window, the wooden shutters wide open, I went to it and raised onto the tips of my toes to look in. Before I could see anything, I heard screams and shouts.

A chill washed over me. Those screams sounded joyful and triumphant. More so than at a wedding feast. As if a war had been won.

Summoning my courage, I raised onto my tiptoes again and peered in to see many people.

"I am healed!"

"Blessed by Adonai!"

"He has forgiven me!"

"Jesus! Master."

They were throwing off their mantles and blankets. Removing bandages and tossing aside crutches.

Soon, men, women, and children skipped out the door, their hands raised.

I felt faint. I looked between the inside commotion and those outside.

And then! The sound of even more people. The disciples walking toward us with lepers. Peter and John led the way as cloaked figures followed. Some limped. Some carried others. They all looked shrouded and bound for burial.

I took a quick breath, growing nervous that they might touch me. I had never been this close to lepers. As they came nearer to the light, I saw bandages on their faces, scars, and disfigurement. Their flesh looked like ripped papyrus or bark scratched from a tree.

Before they met the joyous people or entered the hospice, they began throwing off their own bandages.

"I am clean!"

"My wounds have vanished!"

"Look at me!"

"Praise be to Jesus of Nazareth!"

More chills glided over me.

"He has healed every person here!"

"Son of David!"

"Elijah!"

There was a strange chaos and I was too fearful to move. People went in and out of the hospice to see Jesus or to run away in joy. Many sprinted away toward the village. Others, toward the Mount of Olives, near Jerusalem. Others, to the road toward Jericho.

I recognized Simon the Leper's voice. "Not one of us is left with an ailment!" Lazarus' uncle was healed!

My hands rested over my abdomen. Was this then true for me? If Adonai would let it be so!

"As your reward for heeding these ordinances and keeping them carefully, Adonai, your Elohim, will keep with you the covenant of mercy He promised on oath to your ancestors. He will love and bless and multiply you." I whispered the law of Moses; the law that Jesus was fulfilling before my eyes.

"Adonai will remove all sickness from you. You shall consume all the peoples which Adonai, your Elohim, is giving over to you. You will be blessed above all peoples; no man or woman among you shall be childless."

A smile trembled on my face, shook, spread, and then firmly settled.

And as Jesus came out of the hospice, His head turned, looking straight at me.

Jesus departed for Galilee a week ago. He left the day after His rampant round of healings. He seemed intent on leaving Judea before word spread of His miracles.

Ever hopeful, I placed a hand over my womb. I could be pregnant! I could be. Jesus could have healed me. He healed everyone else! I saw the way He looked into my eyes; tender and warm.

I did not have the *knowing* feeling that Mary described, in which a mother could simply tell she was with child. Yet I had deep hope. I had faith in the Messiah who had come to set the captives free and bind up the brokenhearted. Jesus had come for *me*, the afflicted one.

By the end of this month, if my blood did not flow, I would know with certainty that it was so.

Early one morning I was on my knees in Lazarus' bedchamber. I faced west, toward the Temple in Jerusalem. I was trying to pray, but a child was all my mind could think of. I heard the door open and the footsteps of Lazarus coming behind me. He lifted me up from the floor and turned me toward him. He kissed me quickly and firmly.

"Lazarus?"

"Arise, make haste, my love, my dove, my beautiful one, and come!"

"Lazarus!" I laughed at his use of the song of Solomon.

"For winter is now past, the rain is over and gone." He clasped my hand and spun me around. "The flowers have appeared in our land; the time of pruning is come. The voice of the turtledove is heard in our land."

"Lazarus, what are you saying?" I gasped between laughs.

"The fig tree has put forth her green figs. The vines in flower." He took in an exaggerated breath through his nose. "They yield their sweet smell."

He kissed me on the cheek. "Arise, my love, my beautiful one, and come." His earth-brown eyes were spiked with excitement.

I smiled, pleased but totally confounded.

"Take your choice of mantle and most durable sandals. We leave in the hour." He dropped my hand and turned toward the cabinets on the east wall.

My mouth dropped. "Lazarus!" I hurried beside him as he opened a cabinet door. "As in, we are truly going away?"

"Yes." He looked back at me with a laugh. "We are going to Capernaum."

"Capernaum," I whispered. "To—"

"To find Jesus!" He turned around, his arms spread wide open. "And follow Him!"

"Lazarus!"

"Are you not pleased?" He asked, stepping toward me. "You were the one who first wanted to go after Him."

"And you were adamant that we would not. What has done this to you?"

"It is Jesus, Esther. I am — I am going after the treasure buried in a field!" He laughed again. A deep, belly laugh. He turned back to the cabinet. "I am going in search of the pearl of great price! The kingdom of Heaven is at hand!" He pulled a drawer open, filled with a portion of his money. He took a pouch and started counting silver dinars as he placed them in the pouch.

I stared at his fingers. His bare fingers.

"Lazarus…" I started cautiously, stepping toward him. "Where is your signet ring?" My hands twiddled in anxiety.

"I gave it to Martha."

"*Martha*?" My hands fell at my sides.

"All of the property. The business. The money. The title. She is mistress of this household now. She can do with it whatever she wills. Turn the whole place into a hospice if she wants. If there are even any sick left in Bethany," he added, "since Jesus healed them all." I pulled off my veil so that it rested over my shoulders as a shawl. "W-what of Hezekiah? Should not her husband be next in line? Or your uncle Simon, now that he is cleansed from his leprosy?"

Lazarus continued dropping coins into his pouch. "Oh, Hezekiah is furious. Typically, he would be next in line. But he is a Pharisee who can tend to the household we have in Jerusalem. He has no time to run the house in Bethany *and* the business."

"This will cause abnormal marital relations. The wife as head instead of her husband..."

"Think nothing of it. Martha is a strong woman. I trust my sister over Cousin Hezekiah. And Hezekiah still gets *some* inheritance. As for Uncle Simon — Jesus may have healed him, but Uncle Simon is just grateful to be alive. And he adores his daughter-in-law."

Lazarus plopped more coins into his pouch.

I put my hands to my face. "And those coins?"

"Thirty dinars. That is all we shall take with us."

My heart thumped heavily. "Us," I whispered.

"You *are* coming with me? That is what you want, is it not?" He tied the pouch to his belt, beside his sword. He turned to look at me again. His eyes were so hopeful and his shoulders so relaxed.

"Yes, but..." I did want to see Jesus and be near Him. I wanted to inherit this kingdom. But what if the kingdom was inside of me? "What if I am pregnant?"

"If you are, it is still soon enough to be traveling."

"Not if I should be here, preparing a place for our firstborn *son*. The one who would have that signet ring you gave Martha! The one who would take your inheritance!"

"Esther! You have been barren our whole marriage. You truly think you are with child?" He walked toward me, lowering his face to look down at me.

"I can only hope, Lazarus! Jesus healed so many, He must have healed me as well."

"And if He healed you, then should you not go and follow Him? Dedicate this child to Adonai? To the work of the Messiah?"

"I am a woman, Lazarus. It is not that simple. I cannot travel around the regions like cattle in a caravan," I said, waving a hand in the air. I let out a grunt. "With a lot of men. It is unheard of."

"You will be traveling with your husband," he decided as if that was the simple solution to one of his business proposals.

"You think Jesus will accept you as a disciple?" I raised a brow.

"He asked me once before! I would say this is a late acceptance of His offer."

"And if He does not allow this?"

"Then I will still dedicate my life to the kingdom of Heaven. Is that not what you told me you wanted?"

"I did...I just...now...I feel that I must first..."

"Esther." Lazarus put his hands on my shoulders. He looked at me with the forcefulness of the sun. "Listen to me. Jesus says that no one who sets his hand to the plow and looks to what was left behind is fit for the kingdom of Elohim. This is not a matter of first arranging matters before following Jesus. We must leave all that we have. Sell all that we have. And go to Him!"

"You are carrying a pouch of silver on your belt!"

"For our journey to Jesus!" He removed his hands from me and patted the pouch at his side.

"Why have you changed your mind so suddenly? You were as sunken as a ravine just yesterday. Spending nearly the *whole* week in the Temple."

"I was there praying. Praying and studying. Speaking to men of prestige like the Pharisee Nicodemus. I have prayed, repeating Jesus' words to myself and pondering the miracles that my own eyes have seen. I have looked through the Scriptures and I have come to believe that Jesus is indeed the Messiah. Do you believe this?"

"Yes," I said. I did. I truly did.

"Then it is settled. You are coming with me."

Chapter 19

The LORD, your God, shall you follow, and him you shall fear;
his commandments shall you observe, and to his voice shall you
listen; him you shall serve, and to him you shall hold fast.

DEUTERONOMY 13:5

Hundreds walked up a mountain on the coast of the Sea of Galilee. Typically, my eagerness would allow for a quick pace, but the growing number of people slowed down Lazarus and myself.

"His name has spread like wildfire," I exclaimed. Dozens walked with us from Judea all the way to the sea region of Galilee to follow, or at least *see* the acclaimed teacher. Word was that He commanded unclean spirits to come out of both men and women; that a paralytic could now move and walk freely; a leper was cleansed; a man's withered hand was restored; that the power coming out of Jesus could be known just by touching Him. They said any disease or pain could be healed by Jesus.

But of course, I had already witnessed such things for myself.

"In my mind," Lazarus said, "I imagined we would peacefully arrive in Capernaum. We would be welcomed into Peter's house. We would get to speak with Jesus and if Jesus willed, I would follow Him as a disciple! Yet when we arrived this morning, the whole town was empty. Apparently, Capernaum uprooted itself to this mountain."

"After He preaches today, we will see Him," I decided, walking toward the base of the mount.

"Surely every other man has the same intention as us!"

I yearned to see Jesus, but I feared what would come of it. Would Lazarus and I travel together with His disciples? Would Lazarus send me back to Bethany? Would Lazarus return to Bethany with me? Would I stay with Lazarus' relatives in Magdala? Or even return to Nazareth?

"I do not remember the last time I walked for six days straight with only my feet for transportation," Lazarus said. He took in my perturbed expression. "I am not complaining. I am simply stating the truth. Are your feet not sore?"

"Husband, I used to do this all the time. I will get used to it again." I thought of the camels we might never ride again and changed the subject. "I cannot tell if Martha is excited or dismayed as the new mistress of the house."

"Martha will enjoy it, I am sure. She does well with power in her hand. As for Hezekiah, I do not wish to think of it."

"Martha said that Hezekiah plans on living at the house in Jerusalem, so he does not need to enter the disgrace of his own home in Bethany."

Lazarus nudged me to the side, helping me avoid a pile of mule dung swamped by flies.

"I also thought that if we could not find Jesus," he said, "we could at least find one of His disciples who would lead us to Him. Andrew and Peter probably do not even remember us."

"They came to your house. And Simon is my brother," I reminded him. "If we find them, they will lead us to Jesus." I looked at the yellow-green grass at our feet, trying to avoid any more dung.

Lazarus and I spoke with many visitors, listening to their claims of who Jesus was and what they hoped to receive from Him.

"He is a sorcerer!" a man from Tiberias told us. "I want Him to perform His magic for me!"

"He healed a blind man! And hundreds of others!" A Sidonian woman told us. "My child is cross-eyed — Jesus will heal my little girl!"

The variety of visitors was astonishing. There were beggars and poor people in rags. Men carried friends on mats and stretchers. Women clung to their children. Many limped. Pharisees walked like towers amongst them. There were Jewish aristocrats and government officials. There were even tax collectors. Greeks and Romans were present but avoided by most. There were prostitutes, their bells dangling from their ankles. We saw a couple of Samaritans and several Syro-Phoenicians. Among them were ordinary Jews in simple but reverent clothes, be they from Judea, Decapolis, Philistia, or Galilee.

Some passed on donkeys, while others carried baskets, jugs, and satchels on their shoulders. The smell of sweat, animal, dung, grass, and even sickness mixed together. But then the crisp breeze from the sea wafted over us. I saw the sparkling glints of the waters past the trees as I walked upward.

"How many would you say are here?" I asked my husband.

"At least a couple thousand," Lazarus observed, his shoulders pulled back high and straight. His eyes scoured his surroundings like an eagle; his face was firmly shielded by his tallit. He was embarrassed that he had not bathed or washed his hair and would likely not be able to soon now that we left Bethany behind us.

I heard the word "messiah" thrown about by people around me, each time making my heart leap. Pride also touched me when I heard the familiar conversation:

"Where is this Jesus from?"

"Nazareth."

"Nazareth, you cannot be serious."

"Oh, but I am. Jesus of Nazareth, son of Joseph. From the tribe of Judah."

"Was Joseph not a carpenter?"

"He most certainly was a carpenter. But he was a son of David!"

I often chuckled to myself when I heard these words and thought of how unreal it was to be the cousin of, and from the same village as, the popular Jesus. Jesus the Messiah.

I felt the weight of the muscles in my calves as we reached the top. People at my right and left situated themselves on the ground. I took in the landscape, the plain of Gennesaret right below the mountain. There were cypress trees from the top to the bottom of the hill. I could see the sea clearly now, its blue waves a steady motion. The surrounding hills had a variety of textures, created by tall and short grasses, dirt, bushes, pine trees, wildflowers, thistles, fields, and boulders.

"But where is Jesus?" Lazarus mumbled to himself, his chin raised in the air.

"He is not up here! He is at the base of the hill! You see?" I peered downward where the hill met the plain. People stormed toward Him, and I wished I could make out His expression.

We soon discovered that Jesus intended to speak at the top of the mountain. He moved upward so slowly that it looked like He was not moving at all. He reminded me of what Moses must have looked like, walking up Mount Sinai, though I doubted the Israelites bombarded Moses the way these people bombarded Jesus. A few men who I recognized as disciples tried pushing people away from Jesus.

Lazarus took my wrist and guided me down to the cool grass to secure our spot in the crowd. The wealthy had their servants set down their litters and canopies and cushions on the hill.

Lazarus crossed his legs, but sat straight, not supported by his usual cushion. After much fiddling around, he decided to lean his hands behind him on the ground for support. My legs were knotted at my side, one hand on the ground and the other in my lap. There was still no sign of life within me, but that did not mean it was not there.

One man stood directly in front of my view, but when the man sat, I was able to see Jesus for a moment, with his sand-colored tunic. Then my view of Him was again blocked. I had only ears to hear.

A hush slowly made its way through the crowd.

"Blessed are the poor in spirit, for theirs is the kingdom of Heaven..." Jesus began, His gentle voice rippling through the late morning air, surprising me with its clarity and strength. The crowd grew even more silent. Even the babies stopped crying and the children stopped babbling. I listened intently as I wanted to grasp every one of His words. *The poor in spirit.* Just as Martha had said.

"So let your light shine before men, that they may see your good works, and glorify your Father who is in Heaven."

My body vibrated at the mention of "Father." My Father in Heaven.

"Do not think that I have come to destroy the law or the prophets. I have come not to destroy, but to fulfill."

He spoke of anger, adultery, divorce, and oaths in a way I had never heard before. Scribes and Pharisees spoke of the Torah, but they did not teach it with the authority that Jesus had; authority as if He Himself wrote the Torah.

"You have heard that it has been said, 'An eye for an eye, and a tooth for a tooth.'"

Lazarus and I looked at each other.

"But I say to you, to resist evil. If one strikes you on the right cheek, turn to him also the other. And if a man will contend with you in judgment, and take away your coat, let go your cloak also to him..."

My eyebrows furrowed profusely as I listened. Jesus kept mentioning the one name, Father.

"Love your enemies. Do good to them that hate you and pray for them that persecute and calumniate you, that you may be children of your *Father.*"

"Be perfect as also your heavenly *Father* is perfect.

"...and your *Father* who sees in secret will repay you.

"...for your *Father* knows what is needed for you before you ask Him.

"Thus therefore, will you pray: Our *Father* who art in Heaven...

"For if you will forgive men their offences, your heavenly *Father* will forgive you also your offences.

"...and your heavenly *Father* feeds them...

"For your *Father* knows that you have need of all these things.

"How much more will your *Father* who is in Heaven, give good things to them that ask Him?

"Not everyone that says to Me, 'Kyrios, Kyrios,' will enter into the kingdom of Heaven, but he that does the will of My *Father* who is in Heaven, he shall enter into the kingdom of Heaven."

Tears welled in my eyes. Jesus always called Elohim His father. More so than He ever did to Uncle Joseph.

A blurred image of my abba crossed my mind. It had been so long that I hardly remembered his face.

Your heavenly Father. Jesus said. *Your Father. Our Father. Your Father who is in Heaven.*

I inwardly moaned in wonder. I could not see Jesus, but it felt like the very voice of Elohim was speaking to me from above. Or was Elohim here on this earth, speaking to me right now? Jesus was not just saying "my Father in Heaven," but also called Him "your Father." *My Father!*

I pulled the edge of my dark blue mantle to my face and pressed my lips against it. I breathed in the wool fabric, still in fresh condition.

The sun warmed my back.

And Jesus' tone. He shouted but was entirely peaceful.

I felt loved.

I was loved by my Father in Heaven, who provided for me more than an earthly father ever could. He was perfect. He would make me perfect.

Jesus finished speaking and others rose immediately, running up the mountain toward Him.

"Esther..." Lazarus looked at me with the giddiness of a little boy. I turned to him slowly, as if a quick movement would make this feeling of love disappear.

"If I did not previously believe He was the Messiah," Lazarus said, "I am now certain He is." He raised his eyebrows at me. "And if I did not previously wish to be His disciple, I am now certain I do." He pushed himself off the ground with the swiftness of the wind. Lazarus took my hand and pulled me up next to him.

"I will follow Him too." I spoke slowly, relishing the warmth of the sun and the new warmth inside me.

Lazarus and I turned our heads as the volume of the crowd increased. Cries and shouts blended together in a splendid melody of joy.

"Lazarus, what is happening?" I took my husband's arm. Lazarus was at least a head taller than me. "I cannot see!"

He laughed, looking mesmerized by Jesus who was at the top of the hill.

I stood on the tips of my toes, startled by everyone's eagerness and fanatic cries. I gasped in disbelief as an elderly woman pushed me to the side, breaking my hold on Lazarus so she could get a closer look. My eyes narrowed in her direction. I would think after what we just heard, she would not be so rude.

I returned my hold on my husband, who was like an anchor in a ravenous sea. "What do you see, Lazarus? What do you see?" Impatience nestled within me as I awaited his response. "What is it?" I continued to plead.

"I think He just healed a man. The man was missing a leg, but…but now he is throwing his cane in the air." Lazarus did not take his eyes from that direction as amazement waved over his face.

I wished desperately to see, but I could not. All I could do was listen to Lazarus's words and try to stay standing as the crowd pushed forward. "People are yelling praises, questions, and pleas," he said.

"I know it! I can hear! I just cannot see!"

"They grab His cloak, reach out to Him, and try to touch Him, and Jesus is touching and blessing them. He is smiling and talking to them."

I easily imagined Jesus' pensive face, welcoming smile, and tough, firm hands reaching for others.

"What of the miracles?" I prodded.

"I cannot see all of them. A woman who has…I do not know what illness, but He must have healed her. She is ecstatic."

Some people were sobbing while others laughing. Some screamed in a way that I could not tell if they were frightened, shocked, or overwhelmed with joy. I supposed it could have been all three. It was like what I experienced in Bethany, only ten times greater.

"I am healed! I am healed!" I heard a man yelling below us. "I was mute but now I can speak! Hear my cry! Hear my cry that blesses Adonai; that blesses Jesus of Nazareth! Praised be Elohim!"

"Blessed be Adonai," I said quietly to myself. "Blessed be Jesus of Nazareth. Blessed be my Father in Heaven."

That day, my husband's and my hope of speaking to Jesus did not come true. We followed Him all the way from the mountain, across the shoreline, and to Capernaum, with hundreds of others. It felt foolhardy chasing after Him with the rest of the people, like chicks after their mother hen, but we were willing to do anything to see our very own Jesus of Nazareth.

When we reached Capernaum, Lazarus and I found Peter's house, but there were so many people poking their heads through the windows and knocking on the door that they did not answer to anyone. I knew that if my brother Simon or even Peter knew of our arrival, they would let us in immediately. If, in fact, Simon and Peter were still in there. Word was that Jesus and His disciples had vanished.

As it was now late spring, and the weather increasingly warm, Lazarus and I chose to sleep outside under an oak tree in the outskirts of the town. We had no other option for lodging. Thankfully, Lazarus still carried his money with him. We found a woman willing to give us bread and a fresh wineskin for a generous silver dinar.

The mantle Aunt Miriam gave me worked as a fine pillow, though Lazarus and I laughed at how different traveling was without a servant or a camel or a tent.

He and I now stood in Capernaum's synagogue to offer our morning prayer with those gathered; mostly men. At the end of the short service, I nudged Lazarus in the arm.

"It is Peter, Lazarus! Do you see? Jesus' disciple, Peter." Before I lunged after the man, Peter walked past a thick stone pillar toward us. He even raised a hand in recognition.

"Lazarus!" Peter crossed his arms over his chest, jerking his head upward in acknowledgment.

"Peter! My wife and I…we arrived yesterday."

"You heard Him preach, then?" Peter lowered his chin and mumbled, "Went a little better than His sermon in Nazareth's synagogue, no?"

My husband nodded Yes, then nodded No. "As in Nazareth, He has vanished. We attempted to find Him but have failed."

Peter's lips curved slightly, his thick eyebrows raised knowingly. "Come with me." He turned. Lazarus and I exchanged glances and charged after him.

We emerged from the synagogue's stone archway, Lazarus and Peter pulling their tallits from their heads. The bustling scene of Capernaum was before us.

The air was filled with different smells — the smell of fish, fumes from glassmaking and pottery, fresh sea air, and the hot basalt stone that the houses were made of, soaking in the sun.

"That is the house of the synagogue official," Peter told us, pointing to a lofty structure of three stories on his right. "A lot of benefactors helped this synagogue get built. It was finished just a few years ago. Do not ask me why, but a Roman centurion donated most of the funds." Peter shrugged, rubbing his face with his arm.

My nose crinkled at the thought of a Roman being a benefactor of a Jewish synagogue.

Peter moved on, past the carts, women pulling children, men hauling animals or sacks and baskets on their shoulders.

A couple of finely dressed women in silk purple tunics passed leisurely down the street as if they were browsing in a marketplace of fine jewels. Peter scoffed. He looked back at me. "Greeks," he murmured. "They think that since they have money, they have priority to see the Master. But they have His message twisted. They travel here as if they are on vacation, sight-seeing. They do not want to give their lives for the kingdom."

The synagogue was now a stone's throw behind us. I twisted my body to avoid two men carrying a large brass pole down the street.

"And that would be my house," Peter said, motioning to the left. "But we are not going in there." He grunted. "And the roof? Do not ask! I need to have the whole thing replaced. Men were a bit desperate to get into the house, so they decided to dig a hole in the roof." He gave an annoyed sigh. "Desperate, is what my wife says. I say they are mad fanatics. Selfish people who will break others to satisfy their own cravings. There are many of them here."

Neither Lazarus nor I chose to tell him that we were outside his home last night, perhaps with the mad fanatics he spoke of.

We walked down a narrower street. The sun quickly warmed this early morning as the sea breeze did us good. We passed a short, thick palm tree beside a prickly bush. The ground became rockier, with larger stones as we reach the sea. The crowd had thinned.

A storm of excitement gathered within me at the very thought of nearing my cousin, but I also felt like my gut was going to roll out of me from nerves.

Perhaps Jesus would tell me that I was with child.

I averted my eyes from the partially clothed fishermen scattered across the shore, standing in their boats, and arranging their nets. There were at least a dozen boats at sail in the small, calm sea, which was more of a large lake. The opposite shore was clearly visible. The blue of the water perfectly matched the blue of the sky.

I was curious as Peter led us toward an empty fishing boat, tied to a wooden post.

"This one is ours," he said, gesturing toward the empty boat, the sails rolled down.

Lazarus and I looked at Peter quizzically; Jesus was nowhere in sight.

One corner of Peter's lip lifted. He patted a lump of undyed wool blankets bundled in the wooden stern of the boat. Only, it was not a lump of blankets, but Jesus Himself.

I gasped as Jesus sat up, throwing the blankets off. He and Peter laughed loudly.

"That time already, is it?" Jesus sighed as He rubbed His eyes. His hair was in disarray, reminding me of our childhood. His eyes were warmer than the sun as they settled on me.

I steadied myself by gripping the edge of the boat. "Jesus! We did not realize...I did not know we were going to wake You." Why did I sound like such a pathetic fool?

"Nonsense," Jesus said, hopping out of the boat in a swift motion, like the agile young man He was. He dusted off His tunic and smiled at us. "I thank you. I would have slept all day if it was My will."

"Your will should be done, then," Lazarus injected, shifting his weight from one foot to the other. "Only Adonai knows how exhausted You must be. You have been swarmed from all sides." Lazarus glanced over his shoulder to see if anyone noticed Jesus' presence.

"It is not My will that must be done, Lazarus," Jesus said. "It is My Father's will that must be done." He pointed a finger upward.

I took in a breath at the lovely title, "Father."

"Still speaking of your Father, then." My husband spoke up.

I gave Lazarus a scolding look. He could not insult Jesus! Not now!

"He is my Father, Lazarus. Call him our Father in Heaven." Jesus leaned His legs against the boat behind Him. "Hallowed be His name," He added, gazing directly at me.

I smiled timidly.

"Did You sleep here all night?" Lazarus asked.

Jesus looked at Peter. "My disciples and I went onto the sea at dusk. It is good to fish at night. But I let them do most of the fishing. I fell right asleep." He lifted His shoulders slightly. "Human as I am."

"We have not lacked fish as of late," Peter mumbled.

"Lazarus. Esther." Jesus said placed a hand on Lazarus' shoulder, and I blushed as His bronze-brown eyes kindly settled on me. "I have been waiting for you two to come and see Me."

My mouth dropped. I stole a glance at Lazarus whose eyebrows arched in surprise. We saw Jesus just two weeks ago.

"We have been waiting to see You as well," Lazarus admitted. "In truth, we have been following You, but have not been able to reach You, because of the crowds."

With His free hand, Jesus reached for my small hand. His grasp was steady and unflinching. My heart thumped and my whole being felt extremely warm. It was not the sun. It was something about His presence; something hopeful; something promising.

"You wish to follow Me?"

Lazarus and I were silent. Was Jesus speaking literally or figuratively?

I found the words splashing out of my mouth. "Yes! Jesus," I added in a reverent whisper. "I believe You are the Messiah."

"Flesh and blood has not revealed this to you," Jesus said, gently squeezing my hand. "But My Father who is in Heaven."

And now it felt as if I were being adopted into a new family.

"Here am I! Send me." Lazarus repeated what Isaiah said to Adonai when he heard Adonai's voice. I could hear the smile in Lazarus' words as I kept my eyes focused on Jesus and my hand encircled by His.

"That I should do Your will, I have desired it, and Your law in the midst of My heart." I too chose our beloved scriptures to speak. "Father," I added, testing the title. It was time to speak of Elohim the way Jesus did.

"Come after Me," Jesus said simply, relaxed. "You will be My disciples."

Peter patted Lazarus on the back and gave me a sheepish smile. Jesus dropped His hand from Lazarus' shoulder and used it to pat my hand.

"We brought very little with us," Lazarus said as Jesus released my hand. Lazarus removed a pouch from his belt. "I gave my whole inheritance to Martha. But here are a humble 27 dinars for You to do with as you see fit. That is all I have left." He offered the heavy pouch to Jesus.

Peter laughed in short expulsions of air. His chortle turned into a cough. "A *humble* 27 dinars," he snorted. "That is a whole month's worth of wages for me!"

"The kingdom of Heaven is yours, Lazarus." Jesus said. He looked at the pouch Lazarus thrust forth, but did not accept it. "You have relinquished your title and wealth to your sister. Much has been given to you. Much will be required of the person entrusted with much, and still more will be demanded," Jesus continued, looking at the two of us pointedly, "of the person entrusted with more."

Lazarus' outstretched hand became limp as he drew the pouch back. He eyed Jesus, trying to decipher what his new Master wanted.

"Lazarus," Jesus said, "When you give, give generously and not with a stingy heart; for that, Adonai your El, will bless you in all your works and undertakings. Give your money to the poor you meet."

He spoke of Deuteronomy. In the Torah, regarding the Sabbatical Year, the seventh year was one of freedom for all.

"Jesus," I started. "Jesus." I blushed. I had spoken His name so many times as a young girl. Could I regard Him the same way with the knowledge that He was the Messiah? "M-Master. What of me? What do you want me to do for You?"

Jesus' hair was blown by the sea wind. It was longer than I last saw it, reaching His shoulders. The sun revealed hints of red in its burnished brown frizz.

"Esther, you are a good woman; far and from the uttermost coasts is your price. You do Lazarus good, and not evil, all the days of your life."

I blinked back tears. He spoke of the proverb that praised a good wife! The one that I so vigorously tried to model. Would Jesus now make me bear fruit?

"Elohim created man to His own image. To the image of Elohim, He created him. Male and female He created them," Jesus repeated the words of creation from Torah. Yet He made the words much more intimate with His paternal reference.

Jesus looked from Lazarus to me to Lazarus. "It is not good for man to be alone. Let Us make him a help like unto himself." He inclined His head at both of us.

Confidence sprouted within me.

"You will meet Susanna of Magdala, Mary the mother of James Alphaeus, as well as Salome, the mother of James and John."

"*Disciples?*" I asked keenly. My face perked up like a flower finally receiving water.

"Yes."

Excitement danced in my stomach. I could not believe I was doing this! And there would be other *women* disciples!

"My wife was horrified when I first told her I was a disciple of the Master," Peter explained, his bushy eyebrows raising. "She cannot go from town to town with us anyway. She has children and a household to tend to."

"She is blessed *diakonia*." Jesus used the Greek word "to serve." He did not use it as an action but as a state of being.

I quirked a brow, wondering why He used a Gentile tongue.

"We will have to tell you all of the stories about the rest of the disciples leaving their old way of life," Peter said, a one-sided smile behind his beard. "James and John were fishing and immediately left their father in his boat! Then again, I was fishing as well, but Andrew had — "

"Jesus!"

A few people ran toward us.

"Teacher!"

"It is Him!"

"Blessed be Adonai!"

"We better hurry back to the house," Peter suggested, glaring at the small cluster of men and women reaching for Jesus. "And lock the door so no one can get in!"

Jesus started grasping hands. He cupped a woman's cheek and looked back at us. "Learn of Me, because I am meek and humble of heart." He returned His attention to the people, giving His whole attention and consideration to each person, without holding back. He focused on each one as if he or she was the only person in the world.

"Let us return to the house, then. Come." Jesus motioned us to follow Him, raising His voice over the crowd.

Lazarus and I exchanged questioning glances.

Peter mumbled incoherently.

As we reached Peter's large village house, more people were gathered, waiting for Jesus. The one-story house was long and wide, and clearly housed several families. Peter pushed his way toward the door, roughly shoving people aside. "Let me through. Let me through!"

I was jostled. Elbows jabbed my stomach and shoulders scraped mine like sandpaper. I huffed from the effort of trying to stay near my husband.

"Try not to let anyone in the house," Peter called over his shoulder. He banged on the double wooden doors. "Meirav!" He shouted. "It is me! Let me in!" The crowd was louder than his voice.

Eventually, the door opened a bit and Peter slid through. With great effort, Lazarus and I were able to jam ourselves into the house behind Peter, who quickly slammed the door shut once we were inside.

"Come, welcome our newest disciples! Lazarus of Bethany, and his wife, Esther," Peter called out.

My heart picked up at the word "disciple."

Children skipped about the main court and I heard oxen and goats in the stable beside us. On one side, an open oven spewed smoke. A few women left their cooking and grinding grain to come and see. Men within the house emerged from its many rooms, and those working on layering the roof appeared in the courtyard to greet us as they looked at us with friendly smiles. I could smell the mud, ash, and chalk that composed the drying roof.

John, who had almost no facial hair, stepped forward. "Peter, where is the Master?"

Peter huffed, glancing at the door behind him. "He...uh..."

"*You abandoned Him to the crowds?*" James Zebedee raged, stepping beside his brother John, who was at least a head shorter than him.

"I did not abandon Him, James. Jesus insisted that He spend time amongst the people." Peter looked up at the large man.

James Zebedee, John, and a few other men hurried out of the house, most likely to assist Jesus. After putting a hand through his hair and sighing again, Peter muttered to himself and returned back outside.

The noise of the crowd carried into the courtyard. The morning light was harsh.

Beginning to feel self-conscious, I looked to the group of disciples, who stared at Lazarus and myself. Was it Lazarus' rich vest? My fine linen veil? My striking eyes?

Finally, a young woman, who must have been at least a few years past twenty, and whose face seemed to literally shine, came toward us with out-stretched arms. "Welcome! Welcome!" She surprised me with an embrace. My nervousness started to melt away at her warm manner. She pulled away, gripping my arms. I noted her large dimples beneath eyes that shined like crystals. "Esther, is it? My name is Susanna. Susanna of Magdala."

Susanna. Jesus has told us we would meet here, but I was sure I had heard of her sometime past. Perhaps because she was from Magdala. I wondered if she knew Mara or anyone in Lazarus' family.

The other disciples, about a dozen of them, also came toward Lazarus and me. They began to introduce themselves and I did my best to nod in acknowledgment to each. I recognized some of the men, as they had stayed with us for the Feast of Unleavened Bread in Bethany.

"Welcome," they said as they patted Lazarus on the back — some even embraced him or kissed him on the cheek. The men slightly bowed their heads to me and smiled. I did not think I had this much attention on my wedding day.

Susanna laughed, sounding like a merry flute player. Strangely, I did not think she was laughing at anything, except out of pure enjoyment of the moment.

A woman at least a decade older than myself, with very straight posture and sun-brown skin squeezed through the crowd with an even older woman, whose back was sharply arched. The first woman took my hand in her small, dainty hand. "Esther," she said. "You will do well here."

How could she be so sure?

"Esther, dear, I am Mary, wife of my dearly late husband, Alphaeus. May he rest in the bosom of Abraham."

I squeezed her hand and smiled at her. "Ah, you are the mother of James. Jesus mentioned you."

"Yes, yes." Excitement gleamed from her eyes. "We have two James. This is Salome, wife of Zebedee and mother of James and John." Mary Alphaeus introduced us to the old woman. "The younger, smaller James is my son."

"My father's name was James," I told both women.

Salome's neck twisted like a rooster's as she looked at me. She leaned toward me, lowered her voice, and said, "My sons are part of the *Twelve.*"

"As is *my* James!" Mary Alphaeus added, clasping her small hands at her chest.

"The Twelve?"

Glowing with happiness, Susanna touched my shoulder. "The Master has chosen a group of twelve men."

Mary Alphaeus lowered her chin with a proud smile. "They have a special role in the Master's ministry," she explained. Her voice was high-pitched. "The Master said that they are His *chosen* ambassadors. He is calling them *Apostles.* And my son is one of them!"

Apostles. I recognized the Greek word. It meant "to send forth."

"Are Peter and Andrew among the Twelve?"

Both women nodded enthusiastically.

I found that odd. Peter and Andrew looked older than Jesus. How then, could they be sent forth as successors? Usually, men young enough to be Jesus' sons, like John, would succeed a great teacher.

"My James was a farmer." Mary Alphaeus said proudly, folding her hands in front of her. "Before he was called by the Master."

"When was he called?"

"Only a few days ago."

"My sons were the first to be called," Salome interjected, a wrinkled hand resting between her hip and back.

These were two rightly proud mothers.

"Esther!" I recognized Simon's voice immediately and turned.

"Excuse me," I said to the women, then cast my mantle tighter over my shoulder and stepped quickly toward my brother.

"Simon!"

His large arms engulfed me. When he kissed me on the cheek I could smell wood and mortar. "Esther. I hoped Lazarus would be close behind us. I knew Jesus was working on him. If he had come sooner, the Master could have made Lazarus one of the Twelve."

"Are you a part of the Twelve?"

Simon smiled proudly, his fierce eyes glinting. "You would not believe our very different jobs. Carpenters obviously. And fishermen. But we have a farmer, a leatherworker, a merchant, a potter, a blacksmith, a tax collector — "

"*Tax* collector?"

Simon crossed his arms over his chest. "Matthew. I know you will like him. Master would have had scribes and Pharisees, but, if one is a scribe or Pharisee, or a wealthy Jew — "

"As Lazarus and I are," I continued for him. "Then they are to sell all that they own and give it to the poor."

"The poor will have a festival with all that Lazarus has."

"Well, Lazarus did not give all to the poor. He gave his wealth to his sister."

Why did I feel guilty? "But he relinquished his title," I added.

Simon sniffed, rubbing his chin with the back of his hand. His eyes looked down at me disapprovingly. "He will need to give it to the poor."

My lips pressed into a thin line. I did not want to try and explain to him that Martha now owned the property. Nor did I want to exhaust a defense for Lazarus, who had 27 dinars in his pouch to spend on the poor.

"I take it you are no longer a Zealot." I was quick to change the subject.

"No." Simon stuck his pinky in his ear and twisted. He shook his head. "No. I am to *love* my enemies. Love Rome." He chuckled. "Jesus — the Master — says that zeal is good. Unless it pushes out love."

I studied his tan face. Did Simon, a man filled with anger, rage, and even violence, now show *love* to the Rome he once hated?

"How do you feel as a disciple of your own brother?" I changed the subject once again.

Simon pulled at his eyebrows. "I say the rest of the family is next."

"I cannot see Joses or Aliza following Jesus. James and Jude, yes, I can. But certainly not Ima."

"Clopas has softened. He was more than willing to take Mary into his care, now that…well now that half the men in our family have left." Again he crossed his stocky, hairy arms over his broad chest. "Or died."

My mood changed as I recollected memories of our abba. Would he have dropped all things to follow Jesus? Would Zealots turn to follow the Messiah, or would they continue their own pursuits? Or would Jesus create a new form of zealotry that peacefully established the kingdom of Israel?

"Esther, you are shaking." Simon put a meaty hand on my shoulder. "Are you well?"

"Yes. Yes, I am fine." I clasped my hands, not realizing they were trembling.

"I…this is exhilarating…yet…I am overwhelmed — there are so many changes. I…I do not know…"

I had no more time to think about how dramatic my life had been of late, for Susanna joyously linked her arm with mine and pulled me toward the center of the courtyard. Though it was morning, a man pulled out a flute and began playing.

"That is Thomas," Susanna explained inclining her head toward the flute player. "He is one of the Twelve as well."

"Why is he playing his flute?"

"You are now a disciple! A follower of Jesus. This is indeed something to celebrate."

Chapter 20

But the Lord Almighty thwarted them,
by the hand of a female!
JUDITH 16:5

"How did you become a disciple?" I asked Salome as we left the synagogue in Magdala. My sandaled feet moved from the mosaic tiles out to the dusty streets. I put a hand on Salome's back to steady her.

"James and John are my only sons," Salome croaked the explanation. "They left my husband Zebedee in his fishing boat when the Master called them. I was a mother whose children had left her. We had cousins and other relatives in the household still. But then, Jesus called me to be a disciple. And Zebedee gave me permission to follow the Kyrios. I tell you, my husband is a righteous man."

She breathed fiercely, likely struggling in the crowd. She must have been at least 60 years old.

I looked back at all the people buzzing with excitement after listening to Jesus teach. The rust-colored tiles of the synagogue's roof were bright compared to the clay roofs of the houses.

Salome shrugged my hand off. She was an independent woman who clearly did not want to be coddled because of her age.

I tapped my fingers to my lips. They smelled like sweat and sickness. Walking so much, totally surrounded by sick people seemed to leave a permanent odor. I had not bathed since I left Bethany.

I witnessed many miracles these first few days as a disciple. The most extraordinary was Jesus healing a centurion's servant. Jesus treated the Roman as He would any other man and even claimed that the centurion had greater faith than anyone in Israel. Then again, Jesus was always one to find the Samaritan or the Gentile or the unclean and treat them as courteously as if they were law-abiding Jews.

"And Zebedee? Does he still have a fishing business?" I wondered.

"He does." Salome drifted from one side to the other as she walked. "He is still partnering with Andrew and Peter's father. And of course, the cousins and other relatives in both families help out." Salome's hands curled in loose fists as she stepped forward.

Still, it astounded me that Jesus had called such an older woman to be a disciple.

"How many children do you have?" Salome asked. She looked at the dark blue mantle wrapped around my shoulders.

I tightened it around myself. "I have none. Do not pay attention to the color of the mantle. It was just a gift from my Aunt Miriam," I said through gritted teeth.

"Oh, a barren one, are you?"

"Yes." I almost whispered. What was it that Jesus had said? That each tree is known by its own fruit. What if I bore no fruit at all?

I thought of Aunt Mary who wore the same dark blue mantle.

Ima always said that Aunt Mary conceived Jesus in sin. But maybe Adonai was simply making good things come from an unchaste woman. Tamar had dressed as a prostitute to seduce Judah, so she might have an heir of Jacob. Rahab *was* a prostitute and she, a Gentile, became the mother of Boaz. Even Ruth, who married Boaz, was not an Israelite. And Bathsheba? She produced a king for David, and she was another man's wife! Would Adonai's own Messiah come from a woman who sinned? Still, I did not understand Aunt Mary. She was quiet, passive, and hardly ever spoke, yet she was the mother of our Messiah.

We were a large group following Jesus through the large fishing town of Magdala. We passed several dye works and simple textile factories as well, the industrial fumes scenting the town. On one side of this village of many palm trees, I could see the pale blue sea when I looked through the pattern of houses like a lattice. On the other, I could see green hills layered with plants and the scattered openings of caves by the cliffs.

We arrived in Magdala last night. Susanna hosted us in her home which was like a castle. The daughter of a wealthy Jewish merchant who had done business with Lazarus, Susanna was the most joyful person in our group. She giggled randomly. I thought she did so because she purely enjoyed being a disciple.

"Now, Esther," Salome said, interrupting my thoughts. Her raspy voice was loud and purposeful. "I must know. Your husband was a joyful man your first two days with us, but today, he looks as if he were walking through the Valley of Death."

I kept my voice low. "We are in Magdala." I tried to find the words to explain. "Lazarus' sister lives here." Understanding immediately dawned on Salome's textured face.

"I see. I see." She forcefully swayed her arms as she walked. "You mean the Magdalene. Who has not heard of her? Then again, we cannot believe every tale we hear, can we? We must test them and see if they are of Elohim, hmm?"

I twisted my lips, slowing my pace as the crowd bundled near Susanna's manor house. "These tales you can probably believe. What have you heard?"

Salome cleared her throat. A man shoved her to the side, eager to get a glimpse of Jesus.

"Young man!" she called after him. "You must not be rude here!" Salome gave me a perturbed glance as the man obviously did not hear her. "Esther, I am not a gossip. I hear the gossip, but I am not much of a gossip. Our Master says to not judge so we will not be judged. But I will tell you, girl, I will tell you. They say Mary Magdalene had relations with her husband before she was married. And then she committed adultery and married the adulterer while her first husband was still alive. And *now*, she is a widow to both dead husbands. Rich husbands, they say."

"This is true."

"And worst of it all: Magdalene is a demoniac."

I sighed, pushing a loose strand of hair under my veil. "Yes, they say she is possessed by seven demons. I can only pray that *those* tales have been exaggerated."

"Well, we have yet to see her here." Salome surveyed the wealthy town as if we would spot her. Houses here were tall, some built with limestone. The synagogue was close to the front gate, and the homes stretched in back of it, all the way to the shore of the sea by the port docks.

"No, and it would be best if we did not run into her." It would bring shame and embarrassment to Lazarus. He *never* mentioned Mara.

"She may be just the woman who our Messiah can help."

"She has never wanted anyone's help," I said stiffly, remembering what she was like as a child. Probably committed adultery in her heart, as well as physically. Neither of which were good, according to Jesus.

Salome grunted. "I know Gentiles more civilized than these people!" She looked at the crowd trying to enter Susanna's house and shrugged off her mantle. "Take this." She handed it to me. She pushed ahead with more strength than I would have expected and disappeared into the thickness of the crowd, heading toward the cedar wood entrance.

Eventually I too made it to the door. Salome and Mary Alphaeus stood outside of it, granting some permission to enter and rejecting others.

Salome gave me a cross look. "Get inside, now, Esther," she commanded. "We are going to barricade this door today if we have to. Disciples only!"

I glanced hesitantly at the two women. Salome and Mary Alphaeus were the eldest among us. Mary Alphaeus was as dainty as a lily, but Salome had a certain roughness. She put up a hand to a stranger. "Young man, you may not enter," she said sharply. The man glared but turned away.

"Esther, dear, get inside, now. Come along." Mary Alphaeus looked at me.

"Perhaps if James Zebedee or Simon took this task — " I began.

"No. No, dear one. They must tend to the Master," Mary Alphaeus insisted as she motioned a group of strangers away with the light flutter of her fingers.

I decided not to push the stubborn women, and entered the house, Salome's mantle bundled in my arms.

The courtyard was packed with our lot of disciples, at least 40 of us. I was still learning everyone's names.

A flash of heat came over me as a small pain hit my lower stomach. I bit my lip. A cramp that warned me of my monthly menstruation. Unless it was a cramp from a child!

I folded Salome's mantle and set it on a stone table against a courtyard wall. Jasmine bushes lined the court, giving a pleasant smell to the warm, damp air. The small white flowers on top of the green bushes added a stunning display to the limestone walls.

"Esther!" Susanna exclaimed upon seeing me. She warmly touched my arm. "I want to ask if you will help me in the kitchen."

I obliged, wanting to love and serve the way Jesus told us to in His sermons.

Thomas walked over, hands clasped behind his head. "The Master should stop collecting so many disciples. We have too many to count!"

Judas the Apostle stepped beside Thomas. With a smooth voice he said, "Thomas. Thomas. On the contrary. Should we not want more disciples? More people to believe in Jesus and to find the kingdom of Heaven!" He fiddled with his collar, tight around his thick neck.

Thomas looked at Judas with narrowed eyes. He lowered his hands. "That is not what I mean. I am just concerned we will have too many mouths to feed. There are more technicalities than simply *proclaiming the kingdom*. We have monetary needs, physical demands, logistics, and such."

"Fear not, sir," Susanna interjected, but her laugh was nervous. "Adonai has blessed me with many provisions." Her voice wavered, but she kept on. "We have enough room to lodge all of us and enough food to go around."

"But think of when we leave for the Feast of Tabernacles in autumn! Any pilgrim feast will be at least a 2-week journey."

"I will send enough provisions with you." Susanna took a step back, toward the stone table.

"And I am certain my sisters-in-law in Bethany will host us for the feasts," I added, looking at Susanna, whose bright smile suddenly faltered.

"The Master has appointed me as treasurer," Judas said confidently. "I will make certain our finances are dealt with wisely."

"Listen! Listen!" Mary Alphaeus' high-pitched voice carried as she ran about the courtyard — though she looked more like a sheep trotting than a fast horse. "A centurion and his soldiers are here!"

My eyes darted to the closed door, hoping that it would remain that way. Then chaos erupted in the courtyard.

This must not have been the centurion whose servant Jesus healed.

"What do they want?"

"I tell you, they will likely take all of our provisions."

"We have nothing to fear! We have done nothing wrong!"

"What if they are looking for trouble?"

"Esther!" Lazarus stood at my side. "You and Susanna should go to an upper room and wait." He took my arm and looked at Susanna, his face contorting.

Susanna was trembling. Any happiness that exuded from her disappeared.

"Silence." Jesus quieted our shouts. He stood in the center of the courtyard. Everyone stared at the Master in anxious desperation. We could hear the pound of horses' hooves outside and the shouts of Magdalene men and women.

"Be not afraid," Jesus said calmly. "You have nothing to fear from them."

"Rabbi!" Simon called as he reached Jesus' side. "Some are saying that You are a revolutionary. You are proclaiming a kingdom. Some of us should leave — by way of the sea if we must!"

"There is no time for that, Simon." Peter stepped forward.

"We will not leave," Jesus said firmly. "Nor hide."

"What of our women?" Lazarus glanced at me and then at Jesus. I touched his hand on my arm, but he did not relax his grip.

"And Rabbi," Simon insisted. "I am — was a Zealot — what if — You forget my past!"

"You forget your faith," Jesus rebuked him with a steady tone. He placed a confident, comforting hand on Simon's shoulder.

There was pounding on the door.

The courtyard filled with gasps as the disciples' heads swung in the direction of the knocking. It had become more urgent.

"Andrew, open the door," Jesus quietly commanded.

Andrew obeyed, eyes cast on the ground as he pushed through fellow followers to get to the entrance. As soon as he unbolted the door, it swung open and at least five Roman soldiers marched in.

We stepped back as the soldiers explored.

A fire raged through me. Hate. Was it as much hate as the Sicarii had?

"What is it you wish from us?" Jesus asked in Greek with His usual collected tone. Unlike His disciples, He stepped forward.

A centurion with a vine staff came face to face with Him. Men in his position used the staff to discipline both soldiers and citizens. He spoke our native Aramaic tongue instead of Greek.

"You must be Jesus of Nazareth. The lunatic who thinks He is some el."

"He is a teacher and a rabbi!" James Zebedee belted. "And a man of shalom."

"Are you a man of shalom, *Jew*?" The centurion gave Jesus a hard stare. "You have brought a violent storm of crowds to Galilee."

"*You* probably scared them all away — " James Zebedee started.

"Silence, James," Jesus said without looking behind Him.

Lazarus tightened his grip on my arm. I looked at Susanna, her lips quivering. Pity wrung my heart. I reached for her hand, but she pulled away. She glanced at me nervously.

"They say you have dagger-men among you, Jew." The centurion looked at the lot of us, tapping his reed staff on the palm of his hand. "Sicarii. Is this true?"

"All who take the sword will perish with the sword," Jesus replied, as if He were still preaching in the synagogue to Jews as opposed to Roman soldiers. "My disciples are to keep away from worldly desires that wage war against the soul. They are of shalom."

"Shalom," The centurion said. "You Hebrews. That is all that Caesar asks for. Shalom. You follow this, Jew, and You will see no harm."

Jesus did not respond, but kept His eyes firmly on the centurion.

"That is a fine cloak you have there, Jew." The centurion looked at the auburn mantle Jesus had slung over His shoulder. I remembered Aunt Mary weaving the mantle for Jesus when we were about 15.

The centurion stepped close to Jesus, so that their noses nearly touched. Jesus kept His ground. I shuddered, looking at the wooden rod at the centurion's side.

The centurion quickly pulled the mantle from Jesus' shoulder. I flinched. Jesus did not. I felt a rush of heat on my face as I watched the centurion fling the mantle over his own metal-armored shoulder. "Remember who is Caesar, Jew. That is what all of you rabbis must remember."

All Jesus did in return was look at him. Jesus' warm, gold and brown eyes looked at him the same way those eyes looked at me.

Then Jesus took off His belt, tossed it on the ground, and pulled His outer tunic over His head in a quick motion. He offered the linen garment to the Roman.

"Take this as well," He said.

The centurion stared. A couple of soldiers behind him snickered. Surely, the centurion wondered if he should laugh at the poor tunic or at such an ungrudging offering.

"Thank you, Jew," the centurion said. "I will put it on my *pig* to keep it warm before I feast on it." The centurion took the tunic.

My eyes narrowed. Gentiles thought we were foolish not to eat swine, but it was unlawful. *They* were the pigs!

The centurion turned around, raised a quick hand in the air, and the soldiers straightened and followed their leader out of the courtyard, leaving the door open behind them.

Everyone sighed with relief. Lazarus let go of my arm. Excited conversation erupted over our brief interaction with Rome.

I tried to calm my raging feelings which subsided into worry when I turned to Susanna.

"Are — are you well?" I decided not to reach for her again.

She gave me a faulty smile. "Yes. Yes, I am."

I took another deep breath, again trying to calm my nerves. "Shall we go to the kitchen, then?"

Susanna nodded, offering a firmer smile this time.

We proceeded across the courtyard.

"Master, take my cloak!" I heard a disciple say.

"To him that strikes you on the one cheek, offer also the other. Give to everyone that asks you and of him that takes away your goods, ask them not again."

Jesus' voice carried with me as we passed through a hallway lit by several lamps hanging from the ceiling. How could Jesus ask such things of us for our enemies?

After taking the long hallway, Susanna and I entered the banquet room, which was empty, save two servants cleaning the walls, floor, and tables.

"Susanna?"

She looked at me, rolling her sleeves to her elbows. "Yes?" She asked with enthusiasm. Too much enthusiasm.

"What is it? Something is disturbing you greatly. Is it the Roman parade?" I asked.

"I…Esther…you do know my past, do you not?"

I was unsure of her meaning.

"I am trying to forget it. Forgive and forget it." Susanna released a chuckle.

"Did one of the men hurt you?"

"Esther." Susanna sounded both forceful and calm. "Many men have hurt me." She smiled. "But here I am." She lifted her shoulders. "The Master has given me a new life. A new purpose."

"You do not need to tell me, Susanna, but…if you want to, I will hear what you have to say."

She smiled, linking her arm through mine. "I will explain why I am so apprehensive." She faintly giggled, then led me toward a corner of the banquet hall, near the kitchen. "I am the woman of this household. My father's only child — who lived past the age of 4, that is. The last child took my mother's life at his birth, poor one. And my father, may he rest in the bosom of Abraham, died about a year ago." She motioned for me to sit on a scarlet sofa.

"When I was 14," Susanna said, "I was betrothed to a man here in Magdala. A relative, actually, of your husband Lazarus." She tilted her head.

"About a month before my wedding day, I was in the back of the house — by the back entrance that leads to the Sea of Galilee. I took it to get a breath of the sea air, as I like to do. It is a beautiful sea. I enjoy watching the fishermen in their boats going about. I would count the number of boats I saw and how many men were in each boat." Susanna settled her hands in her lap, laughing softly.

"But that one day, as I was on the shore in the privacy of my father's backland, a Roman soldier came and called out to me. 'Woman, woman.' I tried to get away from him but then…well, he assaulted me."

My mouth dropped. "Susanna…" I began. Then it dawned on me. Lazarus had told me of a woman raped by a Roman on her own property.

"Susanna, I…I am so sorry. I did not realize…"

"Be not dismayed, Esther." She chuckled softly. "It *was* terrible, I admit it was. My betrothed left me and no man has wanted me since. I am…unclean. Defiled." She raised her shoulders again. "My father was heartbroken, and I was as well. Not to mention I could not even stand in the presence of a man after that. I was too scared. Sometimes, even now, I still am afraid. But Romans. Especially Roman soldiers. They terrify me. They terrify everyone, but for me — "

"For you, they must be like bears lying in wait," I said, thinking of the lamentations of Jeremiah when Jerusalem was destroyed. Anger racketed my bones. Righteous anger.

"Well, yes," Susanna said. "They are. Were. Are. I am trying to forgive them, and my father and my betrothed and every other man."

"You want to be merciful to them." As Jesus demanded.

"A couple months ago, when Jesus first came to Magdala, He found me in the marketplace. He was the first man I looked at who did not strike fear in me. His eyes were warm and kind and tender. He walked over and He said…." Susanna gulped, tears glazing her eyes. "He said, 'Woman, do not be afraid.' He did not call me 'woman' the way my attacker did. He did not say it as an insult or a belittling of me. He did not call me 'woman' as if He wanted to purchase a she-goat at market. He called me 'woman' as my title. As who I am and I did not need to fear who I am and what I am. Speaking the words of the prophet Isaiah, He healed ten years of feelings of hurt and worthlessness. Feelings of being abandoned. He said, 'You shall no more be called Forsaken and your land called Desolate. But you shall be called My pleasure in her and your land inhabited.'" A lone tear slid down her cheek "'For the young man marries a virgin, so I will marry you. As a bridegroom rejoices in his bride, so will I rejoice in you.'

"Esther, I knew my life would never be the same and could never be the same. Elohim was indeed pleased with me and healed my brokenness. He sent His Messiah to me and the Master knew everything about me." She laughed, showing her fine white teeth. "He knows everything. And still our Father loves me."

I looked at her, taking in her beauty, her smooth skin, brightened by her light-colored clothing. I never would guess that this was a woman who was raped and used. Her chin dipped into her neck, as if a lover was lavishing her with gifts.

"That is why I tremble, Esther. In front of Romans and even some Jewish men. I wish I did not, but I do. I cannot help it. Jesus has healed me; He has. But though He healed my wounds, I still have the scars." She closed her mouth, her lips still curved. "I am so pleased to be a disciple. I offered my hospitality to Him and told Him I would give Him anything He wished. He smiled and told me that He wanted me as a disciple; that He was going to Judea but that I should stay with Meirav, Peter's wife, in Capernaum, until He returned. He told me to keep my household and servants, but to free my slaves. The rest of my ownings would be for His ministry, He said."

A distant shriek sounded outside, causing both of us to start. A woman's scream. It was unnerving to hear a scream like that after the story I just heard. We hurried out of the banquet hall, down the hallway and into the brightness of the court.

The shrieking got louder. A hunched figure entered the house, still screaming. All of the disciples looked at her.

The woman's long brown hair was in tangles and knots. Her face was ashen, and her eyes glazed. I took a step forward. Her hair was the color of Mary's, my sister-in-law, and of my husband. She had the same sharp features as Martha. Beautiful, but hers were evil.

Mara.

"Mary Magdalene!"

"Adonai, bless us!"

I shivered and the hairs on my arms stood straight up. The evil that entered the house was real enough to touch.

"He has cured demoniacs before, has He not?" Mary Alphaeus asked. Her tone was high-pitched.

"Not one with *seven* demons." Peter focused on Magdalene with horror.

Men and women backed away from her as she walked to the center of the courtyard.

"Jesus!" she cried. "Jesus of Nazareth! Son of the Most High! Where are You now?" Jesus walked toward her, still in His inner tunic.

"You!" Magdalene cried, pulling at her eyes. I worried she would tear them out.

Suddenly, Lazarus jumped out and grabbed her arms. In return, she tried to scratch him.

"Mara!" he yelled. "Mary! Mary, Come to your senses!"

"Lazarus," Jesus commanded. "Step away from your sister."

Lazarus' face was almost purple, and knotted with frustration. He released the struggling woman and stepped away.

"You!" Magdalene pointed at Jesus. Her hair was in disarray around her head. "Dare I call out to You! Oh omnipotent Jesus of Nazareth! Dare I?" She spat in His direction as Jesus continued to calmly approach her. "Son of the Creator! Who made a horrible reality! Your horrid world! Your horrid people! You horrid — "

"Silence!" Jesus raised His hand sternly as drool fell from Mara's lips. "Leave her, and never return! All of you!"

Magdalene began to sob, almost to the point of choking. Her breathing sounded like wind hitting the waves of the sea. She crumpled to the floor.

Townspeople outside of the house, gathered with awed expressions. Lazarus stepped backwards.

My sense of shock dissipated. I heard birds chirping, but did not realize that they had been silent.

Mary Magdalene put her face to the floor as her breathing began to slow down. She continued to weep, but more quietly.

Jesus walked to her with His hand outstretched. He was about to put it on her head, but she jolted.

"Do not touch me!" she hissed, scrambling to her feet. Her eyes dashed around at the disciples. She looked behind her to the crowd of villagers. "Do not touch me," she repeated in a moan. She quickly turned and ran, pushing her way through.

Her weeping was still audible as she ran into the maze of houses in the town.

My shoulders sagged. Clearly, the demons had left her, but Mara's old personality had not.

The others stood in confused silence in the courtyard. I thought to go to Lazarus and comfort him, but he walked toward an inner room. I suspected he wanted to be alone with his anger, an anger and shame he had carried with him since childhood.

Even with all of Jesus' words of love and mercy, I could not blame Lazarus.

Chapter 21
32nd Year of Our Lord

[He] Gives the childless wife a home,
the joyful mother of children. Hallelujah!
PSALMS 113:9

I spun the grain mill in Peter's courtyard, feeling the stone crush the grain, pounding it into flour. I had been a disciple for several months now, and was still getting used to hard work. My hands were red and the callouses I had when living in Nazareth returned.

Meirav, Peter's wife, was a healthy-looking woman with black hair and a constantly flushed face. She had a constantly bold and unflinching personality as well.

"When you are done with the grinding, Esther, feed some grains to the chickens, will you?" Meirav looked at me pointedly as she walked across the court and into the kitchen. She was running in and out of rooms, ever busy, ever serving.

I did as she asked.

The men would return any day from their pilgrimage to Jerusalem for the autumn Feast of Tabernacles. Salome, Mary Alphaeus, Susanna, and I stayed at Susanna's home, as both Susanna and I were bleeding and unclean.

"I am past the time of such worries," old Salome told us, smiling mischievously at us as she helped wash and change our necessary linens.

I ground the grain harder, thinking of those wretched cycles. It was my fourth cycle since becoming a disciple. My fifth since Jesus healed all of the people in Bethany. My eighth since I went to Nazareth and believed that the Messiah would heal me.

And now my only friend was darkness. Every person around me was healed by the Master; a Master whom most were calling the Son of Elohim; Messiah *and* Kyrios.

"Peter calls Him Kyrios," Meirav grunted later that day. "As does Andrew, not to my surprise." We women sat in the traklin of Peter's house for a light midday meal with the children. It was a crowded room, each of us brushing elbows.

"But you do not think so," Meirav's mother Adina stated — as opposed to questioned. I noticed she seemed to enjoy stirring Meriav's pot in regard to Jesus — particularly *hosting* Jesus in her home.

"It does not matter what I think," Meirav said, raising a calloused hand in the air. "I stand by my husband in all things. What he wants, I want. What he believes, I believe." Her tone was fierce. Plopping a chunk of cheese in her mouth, she shrugged.

"It is good to be like Ruth, Meirav. So long, as I am your Naomi. My El is your El." Adina spread butter on her sesame-seasoned bread.

"You are my mother, not my mother-in-law."

"All the more reason to follow me."

"I follow my husband," Meirav said. "Wipe your face, Lydia," she said to her youngest daughter. The child rubbed her sleeve against the honey sticking to her mouth. Meirav turned back to us. "If my husband follows Jesus, then I follow Jesus."

"But you do not think He is the Son of Elohim?" I asked, still trying to sort such matters out for myself. I ate a dried date.

"I think He is a Son of Man. Adonai called Ezekiel a Son of Man."

"But Jesus calls Himself *the* Son of Man. And all are calling Him the Son of Elohim as well. Even the demons that He calls forth from man." I crossed my legs in front of me. In my frustration I felt like a rock was sitting on my head; as if a corridor of my heart was in turmoil.

"That is true." Salome raised a finger, glossed with goat's butter. "And the Master is forgiving sins, which only Elohim can do. That as well as healing."

"He healed a centurion's servant," Adina said, leaning toward Salome. "Did I tell you that when you arrived yesterday?"

"Yes, dear. We saw the centurion our very selves." Mary Alphaeus smiled, wiping the corner of her mouth. Her eyes looked as fragile as glass. "Before we went to Magdala," she added, her voice high and dainty.

"I want to go to Magdala!" Lydia cried. She licked honey from her dirt-covered fingertips.

"You will get to eventually," Meirav said as she chewed in the corner of her mouth.

"But I want to go now!" Lydia's voice was fresh; she was a sweet girl and I would want to grant any of her requests. Of course, a mother like Meirav knew better.

"And you heard that in Nain He raised a widow's son from the dead?" Adina tested another bit of information on Salome. The old women's wrinkled faces were a matched pair.

"We heard that as well," Salome said dryly, cracking her neck. Adina leaned away at the unpleasant sound. "Apparently on their road to Jerusalem for the feast."

"Which surely only the Son of Elohim can do," Mary Alphaeus added, a soft lift to her shoulders. She nibbled on her bread.

"I want to go to Nain!" Lydia repeated. Honey dripped from a piece of bread onto her lap. "I want to see Jesus! I miss Him."

My heart twisted, looking at the child's soft features. "But Jesus has told men and women He heals, not to say He is the Son of Elohim," I said, ignoring my feelings for that little voice, little hands, and angelic face. "Why would He not want people to proclaim that He is the Son of Elohim if He is not?"

"The Pharisees say He is — " Mary Alphaeus stopped mid-sentence.

"The Pharisees say everyone is unrighteous." Salome cut her off. "Except, of course, they themselves."

"A Pharisee came to the door yesterday, asking for Jesus. Like all the others, I turned him away." Meirav shifted her broad shoulders. "My question is, why was that Pharisee not in Judea for the feast?"

"I am trying to think what verses in our Scriptures speak of the Son of Elohim coming to us," I whispered to Susanna at my side, ignoring talk of Pharisees.

I knew that Susanna was more learned than the rest of the women. "Jesus cannot be the Son of Elohim if He is the son of Mary," I continued.

"The Messiah is supposed to be the son of Elohim." Susanna smiled, her dimples fully visible. "The second psalm says of David, 'You are My son, this day have I begotten you.'" Hope sprung from her crystal-like eyes.

"But David was not Elohim."

"Neither was King Cyrus the Great. But both were messiahs who did the work of Adonai." She smiled brightly, her teeth a pristine white behind her polished pink lips. "We are speaking now of the final age of the Messiah. The one who is to come after Cyrus." She laughed, so confident and sure of the promise. "The one foretold by David who will establish the everlasting kingdom."

"I know this. I believe Jesus is the Messiah. But I do not know if I believe He is the Son of Elohim."

"He calls Adonai His Father," Salome said from across the table, raising her eyebrows at the two of us. I leaned away from Susanna, annoyed that Salome joined our conversation.

"And He tells us to call Him *our* Father, yet we are not sons of the Father," I explained.

"No, we are daughters," Salome said.

My eyes narrowed. "How can we be daughters of the Father? We are not Elohim. There is only one Elohim. Adonai, whose name we dare not even speak."

"You think, Esther, that fatherhood and sonship are — are so much like flesh and blood! Because you have no children, are you then not a woman and not a mother?" Salome patted one of Meirav's sons on the head, her eyes focused on mine.

I was neither a woman nor a mother. My eyes blurred with tears as I saw the innocent faces of children looking at me or playing with their food.

"Esther, dear," Mary Alphaeus said. "Salome does not mean offense, do you, Salome?"

Salome licked her fingers. "Never."

She could be far too blunt of a woman.

"I do...oh,...I need to go get something." I stood up, forcing a smile. I blinked rapidly, knowing I gave a pitiful excuse.

"Esther?" Susanna called after me, but I clutched my mantle and left. Unfortunately, right when I entered the courtyard, I slammed into returning disciples. I forced a smile, my face aching.

"Welcome." I pushed down my feelings.

Lazarus saw me and ran to me on his long legs. "Esther!" His hair was cut shorter than it had ever been. Above his ears. It made him look younger and a simpler man. He embraced me.

"It is a new year," I said to him routinely. "How was the feast?"

"On our way to the feast, we stopped in Nain! Jesus raised a widow's son back to life!"

"I heard."

"I wish you could have seen it for yourself, Esther! I have no doubt that He is the Son of Elohim."

My smile fell flat as more men and a couple of women piled through the door. "Are there more disciples?"

"About sixty, now," Lazarus said, adding a laugh. I was envious of his carefree joy. "We have the wife of Herod's own steward with us! Jesus healed her sickness when we stopped in Sepphoris on our way back up here. We had a crowd of at least a hundred others just following our steps as well!"

As more people entered the house my head felt light and overwhelmed. I barely saw Jesus go to the court and Lazarus was soon caught up talking excitedly to others.

The wife of Herod's steward. My nose crinkled at the thought.

I decided to squeeze out of the house and into the streets. Yet there were even more people there. A foolish thing to do.

Until I saw my mother.

"Esther!" She cried as a man roughly pushed her aside.

"Ima? Aunt Mary! Aunt Miriam. Uncle *Clopas*!" I stared at them, pleasantly surprised. "Here! Against this wall." I pulled them toward the side of Peter's basalt stone house, away from the door. "James and Jude." I smiled at my cousins as they formed a huddle around me. I began kissing each of them on the cheek.

"We thought we would not know which one was Peter's house, but when we saw the crowds, we were certain," Ima told me, her face looking fresh, despite the crinkles at the corners of her eyes. Her wide forehead was slickened with sweat.

"Ima, you look well."

"Because I am, Esther." Ima took my hand and squeezed it. I stared at her in shock. I could not remember the last time she showed me such affection.

"D-did you see Simon?" I felt the roughness but also the warmth of her skin.

"No. I have not seen anyone we know. Until now." She started caressing my hand. It took all of my strength not to pull it away in bewilderment and weep at her tenderness toward me.

I cleared my throat, the heat of at least a hundred bodies wafting around me. "Surely, when they hear that you all have arrived, you will be let into the house," I told them.

"I *am* Jesus' aunt," Ima said with a free smile.

"As am I!" Aunt Miriam added, raising onto her toes, trying to reach our height. She gawked at the surrounding crowds as if she were examining each person individually.

"Mary," Uncle Clopas said in his usual rough voice. But his tone just an increment lighter. "Are you well? You have been quiet this whole journey here."

"Clopas," Aunt Miriam said softly, tilting her head. She did not look at her husband but continued examining the crowds. "She is always quiet. You are well, are you not, Mary?"

"Yes." Aunt Mary's eyes were clear and defined; warm like her son's. Like her *son*. Her dark blue mantle framed her face, one corner swung over her shoulder. Beneath it was her black widow's tunic, her tan hands sticking out from underneath. Dust from her couple days' walk coated her. "I am eager to see my son," she said.

"Jesus is speaking!"

"The prophet preaches!"

"Listen!"

We turned toward the house, which was bursting like wheat from its shares. Above us, the autumn sun was bordered with wisps of clouds.

"We will never get in there with the crowd." Uncle Clopas looked at the rectangular structure of the house. Men, women, and children piled up on the new, spacious roof, peering into the courtyard.

"We could always dig through the roof," Ima teased, adding a laugh.

I looked back at her. "Please do not dare." I looked back at the people.

Ima never teased!

One man had a boy sit on his shoulders and the boy was looking through a square window into the house.

I heard the muffled sound of a man speaking. It must have been Jesus.

We pressed ourselves against the people outside of the doorway. They smelled like sheep and mule; fish and sweat.

I stood next to a woman who looked ragged and poor. She turned her face to me, and I stepped back. She was terribly disfigured, one eye almost entirely hidden by the mounds and scars on her face. I gulped, trying not to show my nervousness at being near her.

"...you do not light a lamp...may shine to all that are in the house...." I heard Jesus' voice, a master of gentle authority. "Not anything secret that shall not be made manifest...that also which he thinks he has, will be taken away from him..."

I twisted my lips, overtly conscious of the woman beside me. Would Jesus heal her?

I then noted Aunt Miriam pressing her tiny hands against people's backs. One woman, about Aunt Miriam's height, turned to her.

"I am the aunt of Jesus!" Aunt Miriam said simply. I looked away, embarrassed by her forward declaration. "And I am here with Jesus' mother and His brethren! We wish to see our Jesus of Nazareth."

The short woman took Aunt Miriam's hand and kissed it reverently. Instead of annoyance at her pushy declaration, more people turned around and parted their lips in awe of us. They began whispering eagerly to each other. Murmurs waved across the crowd. Someone breathed hard right into my face. I turned my head away.

Uncle Clopas, Aunt Miriam, Cousin James, Cousin Jude, and Ima looked impressed and pleased with the crowd's reaction. Their chins were raised, eyes bright, and lips curved upward.

Soon I heard a man shout, "Master! Your mother and Your brethren stand outside, desiring to see You."

Excitement and pride rippled through me. But then, every person in the crowd turned to look at us. I blushed as they took in our image.

Surprisingly, as Ima stood beside me, she put her hand gently on my arm. I looked to her hopeful expression, surprised by her uncharacteristically gracious demeanor.

"Who is My mother and who are My brethren?" I heard Jesus' voice, much louder than it previously had been. "Here! Behold, My mother and My brethren. For whoever will do the will of My Father that is in Heaven, he is My brother, and sister, and mother."

Gasps emerged from the crowd. Ima gave a grunt-like sound. Aunt Miriam's mouth was hanging wide open and Uncle Clopas' thick arms crossed over his chest. Cousin James and Cousin Jude spoke quietly to each other.

And Aunt Mary. She appeared calm and unfazed as she looked forward at the double door entrance.

"Shows what little we are worth," Ima muttered. "I only raised Him all His thirty years of life."

I narrowed my eyes. Ima hardly did one thing to help raise Jesus. As for me, I did not know what to think or what to feel or what to make of Jesus' words.

Tears welled up in my eyes and my vision blurred. I tried to hold them back, but I could not. And the whole crowd seemed to be staring at me!

I pulled from Ima's grasp and pushed away from the crowd, hardly able to see anything with my blurred vision. I backed up, just needing to breathe. I needed relief. I just needed to get away from all of these people. From Jesus' rejection of me.

I walked between the empty houses and let out a breath when I saw a flash of the sea between the homes. Moving toward it, I pulled at the collar of my tunic, feeling warm.

A sad calm passed over me as I reached the sea, large pebbles planted on the shore. I forgot my feet were still bare from being about the house. Quickly, I stepped forward into the water, pleased with its coolness.

I took in the scene. Boats, piled with fishermen were in the middle of the sea, and I saw the silhouette of buildings from different towns on the opposite side. The waves were small and light, the water a glossy mix of blues, matching the sky.

My toes curled over the pebbles in the water as I gazed ahead at the land on the opposite side.

"You have healed many a man of his affliction," I breathed as if Jesus could hear me. "And many a woman." More tears. "Was I not Your friend, Jesus? According to You, I am not even Your brethren. I am not Your sister. My only friend is darkness." I repeated the psalm I knew too well.

I started when I heard someone approach.

Turning, I saw it was Aunt Mary.

My lips balanced into a straight line as she walked toward me, her sandals lightly crunching on the ground.

"Shalom," I said, wiping a tear from beneath my eye.

"Shalom, Esther."

I turned back toward the sea, disturbing the water with my movement. "Your journey…" I began. "Your journey here was pleasant?" I felt the damp hem of my tunic tugging downward.

"Yes," Aunt Mary said gently. She took off her sandals. I looked at her peaceful profile as she stepped into the water beside me.

"Dearest and littlest of my daughters," Aunt Mary said. "What are you doing?"

I tightened my blue mantle around me. "Aunt…I am not your daughter." I looked down at the ripples.

"No?"

"Are you insulted by the words of your son Jesus? That He did not wish to see you, His own mother?" I sneaked a glance her way.

"No."

My shoulders slouched. She always chose the opposite of what anyone would naturally suspect. I tightened my mantle even more. It had served me well these past months. It blocked the cool at night but was still light enough to not burden me during the day.

"Aunt Mary, you came this whole way to see Jesus. And in return, He said we are not His brethren!" I sounded bitter as pepper.

"What is it He said about His brethren?"

Surely, she already knew. Was she humoring me by making me repeat it? I obliged her, nonetheless, a sharp, dark edge to my voice. "Who is my mother and who are my brethren?" For whoever will do the will of my Father that is in Heaven, he is my brother, and sister, and mother."

"If I do the will of Elohim, then I am indeed His true mother."

"Mother, mother," I mumbled. "You think even *I* could be His mother?" I tried to say it lightly, but my frown was too prominent. "I am no one's mother, Aunt. Unless your meaning of motherhood is entirely different than mine."

"I think it is." Aunt Mary tightened her own blue mantle around her.

"It looks like we have the same mantle," I noted, changing the subject. "Both are blue. Did Aunt Miriam copy yours to make the one she gave me?"

"No, I made the mantle I wear as well as the one gifted to you."

I looked at mine. "Then why did Aunt Miriam have it?"

"I have made several of the same types. I instructed Miriam to give it to any woman she sees fit."

"Sees fit for what?"

"Motherhood."

"But I am not a mother!" I let out an exasperated sigh.

She looked serenely at the water as I mentally picked apart different memories of Aunt Mary. I always found her to be a passive woman, but without my knowing it, she was as active as the sea and as forthcoming as the dawn.

My eyebrows furrowed. *Joseph, Jesus, and I. I asked them to pray with me for you.*

You are in the hollow of my mantle. You, Esther, are in the crossing of my arms.

Look, Esther, you are a mother. She would say such things whenever I held a child. *You are a natural mother.*

Whatever He says to you, do it. So she said to the servants at the wedding at Cana.

We will pray. She decided when Jesus was rejected at Nazareth those long months ago.

And now, with this dark blue mantle wrapped around me, clothing me as a mother.

For whoever will do the will of My Father that is in Heaven, he is my brother, and sister, and mother.

"Are you saying the will of Elohim is for me to be a mother?" I asked quickly, stopping my running thoughts. "Or..." I mused, "That I am a mother if I do the will of Elohim?" My fingers glided over the edge of my dark mantle. I looked at the pattern of cypress and palm trees that textured the opposite shore. "I do not know if I want the type of motherhood you speak of."

"And why is that?"

"Because I do not do the will of Elohim. Jesus has made it clear that we must be perfect if our heavenly Father is perfect, and I am not. I thought that when I followed all of the commandments, Adonai would give me a child. Then, I thought that if I followed Jesus, He would heal me of my affliction, but He has not. I am still barren." I started to weep again. I pulled the edge of my mantle to my face and pressed my lips upon it.

"I should be a star," I gasped, looking up. "Ima always said I was her star. That is why she named me 'Esther.' It means 'star' in Persian." I looked at Aunt Mary. She did not say anything, but her expression was soft as rose petals. "I was supposed to shine; she would tell me. Like the great Queen Esther of Persia. And it seemed like I did when I married Lazarus. *Queen Esther* who was a poor Jew, *chosen among all the women*, was made *queen*. So, *I*, Esther, a poor Jew, was chosen among women for Lazarus of Bethany, son of Syrus. But now," I said, looking down at my water encircled feet. "Now I am closer to a speck of sand, covered by heaps of camel dung in the desert. I am no star. Even Jesus says to let our light shine before men, but I am a dark cave, far under the earth." I breathed deeply. "I am a fierce complainer, Aunt. I know it. But it is the truth!"

"What is a star, Esther?" Aunt Mary asked after I was silent for a moment.

I looked up at her clear eyes and then at the blue sky. "A bright light. It draws attention to itself." I sighed. "I know what you must be thinking. That we are all stars, no? We are descendants of Abraham — as numerous as the stars in the sky." I raised a hand in defeat, then let it fall to my side.

"If you are at sea, Esther, and you are lost, how do you know what direction to go in?"

My eyebrows descended toward my nose. "If you are skilled at reading the stars, or at least fishing, I suppose you could look to the stars for help. Everyone knows that if you see the morning star before sunrise, that direction is the east."

"Does that mean you attempt to travel *to* the morning star?"

I let out a hard laugh. "Well, no. I would not travel *to* the morning star. I would travel to what the star is pointing to. The star would guide me to my home destination."

"Then what is a star?"

"A guide," I said slowly, my eyes taking in her figure. Her mantle thickly covered her head and shoulders, down to her calves, just missing the water. Every line of her garments was a blend of soft curves and waves. "To a destination." My eyebrows relaxed slightly. "You mean to say that a star does not draw attention to itself. It points the way to safety. It points the right way home." I cleared my throat, understanding her. "Then it is not a matter of me shining brightly for people to look at me — if I have wealth or status or good deeds. If they look to me, it is only so I can point them to their destination." My words hung in the air as I contemplated them.

Aunt Mary did not need to show any expression or make any sound to show she agreed with my reasoning.

"Is this my role as a woman?" I asked. "Pointing others the right way?"

"The role of a mother is to point her children to the right way. Where will you point your children to, Esther?"

More tears glistened in my eyes. No one had ever told me that I had children before. "A star must guide the sailor to the *right* place. I...I want to guide my children the right way. We..." I smiled, lowering my chin. "We do not want them running their boat into a cliff."

Aunt Mary's chapped lips settled into a smile at that.

"If I am a mother — a star, as you say — who points the way for my children — the right way — what then, is the right way?"

Her smile broadened.

"My son."

Chapter 22

In their distress they cried to the LORD,
who brought them out of their peril;
He hushed the storm to silence,
the waves of the sea were stilled.

PSALMS 107:28-29

For a few days, Jesus did get to visit with His mother and brethren. Uncle Clopas and Aunt Miriam left with my cousins and Aunt Mary early this morning. I was sad to see Aunt Mary leave. She had given me so much hope and inspiration these past days, encouraging me to love all people the way a mother loves her child.

Ima stayed with us as a disciple.

She was the last person I would have guessed to follow Jesus. And ironically, Ima was the first person I tried to be a mother to.

I had also gotten to know Joanna a little better. Another new woman disciple who was the wife of Herod's steward. She was beautiful and a little prim, but clearly adored Jesus who had healed her of some malady of the spine. I had only seen her stand straight and proper with no sign of illness.

Currently, I was holding tight to Ima's hand. She did not like crowds, and I promised I would not abandon her to them. I was trying to forgive her for any hostility she had ever shown me, as Jesus said to do. I put it upon myself to make my mother feel welcomed and loved as a disciple. Thankfully, Salome and she got along remarkably well.

"Son of David, save me!"

"Good Kyrios, heal my brother!"

"It is the Messiah!"

"I am cured!"

It became harder and harder to walk in the streets with so many people crushing against us. All sorts of sick and diseased people stuck out their hands. Mothers held their children asking for a blessing. Everyone was yelling at Jesus and following Him — not following His teachings — but literally following Him everywhere we went.

"I tell you, He is Elijah!"

"Jesus!"

"Master!"

"Praise be to You, the Son of Elohim!"

I looked over my shoulder at the calm and composed Jesus. If I were Him, I would either run away from all of these people or faint from the intensity. Instead, Jesus was gracious, treating each person as if they were His closest companion.

"This is appalling!" Ima cried. "Esther, let us return to the house." I pulled at her hand as a woman shoved her.

By mistake, I roughly ran into someone. "Forgive me," I gasped in surprise, looking up at the man. He pushed me aside, looking eagerly ahead at Jesus.

A woman beside me sneezed — right in my face. Disgust rippled through me as sweat slid down my back. I wanted to wipe the wetness from my face, but my arms felt strapped low.

"Where did Jesus go?" I looked to my mother and then back at the thickening crowd.

"Hiding would be wise."

I wondered where all the disciples had gone.

We tried to move but were unable. I squeezed Ima's hand far too tightly, but I had little other option. We were in the center of a mob. For several moments, Ima and I tried catching our breaths and, simply, not to lose one another. I wondered if the crowds were even this heavy in Jerusalem for Passover. The putrid smell of grime, fish, disease, and dung collided with my nostrils.

"Esther," a man called to me. I looked over my shoulder. It was Matthew the Apostle.

I yanked Ima along with me as I hurried toward him.

"Esther!" Ima complained about my roughness.

I bit my lip, pulling her with me, anyway.

"Matthew," I shouted when I reached him. His hand tapped his bearded chin, showing off his long fingernails. Had he not trimmed them since following Jesus? "Where have our lot gone?"

"You had better come with me now!" he said.

"Where?"

"Cannot say lest we are overheard."

"You are going to follow a strange man?" Ima cried, pressing her free hand to her wide forehead.

"He is an Apostle, Ima. We can trust him."

I pulled at her sweaty hand as I concentrated on following Matthew. Soon I recognized the street we took as one that led to the sea. The crowd lessened, and we met the shore. A chill swept over me.

The weather was on the threshold of the winter rainy season.

Matthew led us to a port where I recognized Andrew, standing at the back of a wooden boat, helping some women disciples in. He motioned us over. "Come on! The other boats have already set sail. Not you!" Andrew glared at a stranger, shooing him away. "Matthew! Quickly!"

"I have never been in a boat," Ima said in a breathless whisper.

I looked back at her, patting her sticky hand. "We are with experienced fishermen," I told her with a reassuring smile. "There is no reason to fear."

"Lazarus!" Philip called from the boat. I turned to see my husband running toward us. "We found your wife. And mother-in-law."

Lazarus sprinted toward us, heaving. He put his hands on his thighs. "Where did you go?" He looked at me, scratching his neck.

"We were carried off by the crowds, that is what. Now it looks like it will be the sea," Ima said stiffly, staring wide-eyed at the water in front of us.

"Fear not, Mother," Lazarus said with a smile. Perhaps she gave him confidence, but I doubted it. Lazarus hated the water.

"Come on, now." Matthew reached the boat, making a *tsk-ing* sound.

I guided Ima toward the ridge of the cedar wood structure. Andrew assisted Ima in.

"Good evening, Hannah." Philip looked back at Ima from the front of the boat, oars firmly gripped in his hands.

Ima nodded her head in acknowledgment. "You are experienced at sea?"

"Oh no." He shrugged with his playful smile. "I am a vineyard worker. Peter and Andrew took me out fishing a few times, though." His fingers danced on the handles of the oars. "I suggest you hold on tight."

I boarded behind her, feeling the boat sink as I set my weight on it. "Ima, he is teasing you. All shall be well," I whispered. She settled down on the oak planks.

Lazarus hopped in beside me and I gave him a smile of sympathy as I too sat down.

"Lazarus, we need four oarsmen," Andrew said, still on land. He untied ropes at the skinny tail of the boat. "Care to be one?"

"I will," he said warily. There were about fifteen disciples on board.

"That is everyone," I heard Andrew say to himself. "I hope." He adjusted the rudder, then put both hands on the stern. "Start us up, Philip."

Philip, Matthew, and another disciple — Matthias, I thought — began rowing as Andrew pushed the boat from behind. Once it set off, Andrew ran calf-deep in the water and jumped on. He pushed his way to the center of the boat where the sail was tied up. He adjusted the ropes for the white sail to his liking.

I leaned over to dip my hand in the water once we were a little way from shore. In the early evening sun, the sea was a dark green, and molded into blue further out. It looked like melted crystal. The ripples refreshed me as I stared at the suds and bubbles collecting at the sides of the boat.

Behind me, the crowds stood at the shoreline, still shouting, waving, and praising Jesus; their voices but a distant echo now.

Almost half a dozen other boats, holding the rest of the disciples, were scattered upon the sea.

I removed my hand from the water and glanced behind me at Lazarus who was already looking pale, as he forcefully rowed the oars.

"I am the tiller," Andrew said, instructing Lazarus. "Someone has to steer in the back. The most experienced…if we were not traveling to the other side, I would say we should fish. Good variety we have out here. Mostly sardines. Good salted, smoked, or pickled. Tilapia plankton are easy netted… Peter's favorite. Hardly any bones so they are easy to eat."

Lazarus did not seem to pay much attention as he puffed his cheeks and rowed.

"Are you feeling well, Ima?" I turned to my mother. Greying hair fell from beneath her veil.

"Yes. Yes, I am," she said softly, looking ahead, past the sail, and toward the water. "It is peaceful out here. Quiet. I like it."

Praise be to Adonai! My shoulders lowered.

Already low in the sky, the sun hid behind the clouds. I could see the crevices of caves and such in the hills around us and smoke from a fire on an opposite shore. My mantle flapped in the wind and I pulled it as tight around me as possible.

"Looks like a storm could be coming," Andrew observed from behind me. I turned to him. Lazarus looked like he was going to faint.

"Lazarus! You are sick!" His face had a green tone.

"I know." He breathed deeply.

"I will row for you, husband." I rose, unsteady.

"Esther," he protested, tilting his head to look at me.

"Swallow your pride, man," Andrew laughed behind him. I had never seen this Apostle so carefree. It must have been his love for the sea. "Let your wife row. I want to see this."

"Do not get a splinter, Esther!" Ima called.

I pulled off my mantle. "Please, take this, Lazarus. But if you must spit up, do it in the sea." He was too sick to even be annoyed with me. He thumped down beside Ima on a plank.

I tightened my green veil as I walked toward the oars, but another disciple beat me to it and began the task. Stephen, his name might have been. Allowing him, I headed back to sit with Lazarus and Ima. Lazarus moved aside so I could sit between the two of them.

I put a hand on Lazarus' back and he returned my mantle to me.

"Still think there is a storm coming?" One young man asked. His name was John Mark.

"It is the rainy season. Always a chance," Andrew reported, unfazed. I looked up at the sky, leaning my elbow on the edge behind me. We headed southeast; the other side clearly visible. "But this one will not come till early morning."

"I would not listen to him," Lazarus huffed beside me. "Storms come suddenly out here."

"Do not frighten anyone," I whispered. "What town are we headed for?"

"Gergesa," Matthew responded, appearing to row at a slower pace than the others. He was a frailer man. Tax collecting probably did not involve leaving his cushion. "The Master wants to go to Decapolis. I know He eventually wants to return to Samaria."

"Samaria," Ima said, brushing down her tunic. "I have *never* been to Samaria, hear me."

"The people there are very welcoming — at least in Sychar." Matthew made his *tsk-ing* sound and then huffed from his physical effort. "Tirathana and Shiloh and some other towns refused us during our first visit. But I did enjoy my time with those who accepted us."

I gulped. It was one thing to be a mother to my mother and the disciples. But to Samaritans?

Soon, the boat was rocking much faster. I gripped the edge as Lazarus leaned against me. In the dim light, I could see that we were close to land, but the waters were growing rough. Little splashes plopped into our boat here and there.

Andrew did not say anything, but when I looked back at him, I could tell he was getting quite anxious. Or was it that he always was looking downward? How could he even see if he was staring at his lap?

The wind rustled my garments. I patted my veil.

I looked over at the boat next to us and spotted Peter, James, John, and some others. I looked more closely, assuming Jesus must be with them, but I did not see my cousin.

"Faster, Andrew," Peter yelled over the wind. "Philip! We need to make it over before the storm gets too rough."

"We are trying!" Andrew yelled in return. "The wind is going the opposite way."

The blasting air howled in my ears, and the waves started to reach the level of the boat as my veil fell from my head and my hair whipped my face.

I could tell Lazarus was still feeling awful, but instead of half-closed eyes, they were now wide with fright.

"Hold onto to something," he told us. "We do not want any of you going overboard!"

"Dearest Elohim! Be my surety!" Ima cried.

I grabbed hold of the edge of the boat as my body flew up and then came down with a hard plop, forcing an improper grunt to emerge from me. My backside started to sting.

Our boat filled with voices of panic along with distant cries from those in the other boats. "Fear not," I decided to shout. Surely that is what Aunt Mary would say to us children. "We are with the Master — 'When you pass through the waters, I will be with you and the rivers will not cover you.'"

"One would think so…" Philip cried out from the front of the boat as a wave crashed over my shoulders, "…but the Master is asleep!"

Rain began to pour — not softly — but in hard pellets, stinging every part of me. The sea roared and another wave blasted over the boat. I let out a squeal, blending in with the other cries of fear.

"We are taking in water," Matthias hollered.

I looked around frantically. "What do we do?"

"Get the water overboard," Andrew bellowed. "Use anything — even your hands if you have to — ." A wave splashed in the boat, drowning out Andrew's voice.

Lazarus grabbed a bucket and started filling it up and throwing the water over the boat as I helplessly used my cupped hands to do the same.

"This is not helping," I yelped. "We are taking on more than we lose!" The boat tipped roughly over to one side, and the whole left side of my body went into the sea. Lazarus pulled me out. I looked in the direction of Jesus' boat, but a sheet of rain blocked my view.

"Oh!" Ima cried, and then hunched over the boat, vomiting.

She pulled back, wiping her mouth with her arm.

"Uh…" Lazarus heaved as Ima had. My face tightened in disgust as I returned my attention to Jesus' boat. Was He actually asleep in such a storm?

My body was flung upward once again and fell back on the wood.

I tried to look across the high waves and blinding rain but was unable.

The waters saw You, O Elohim. The waters saw You, and they were not afraid, and the depths were troubled.

"Quiet!" I heard Jesus' voice, as loud as thunder. "Be still!" It was as if His voice were inside of me as much as it was outside.

Immediately, the waves dropped and the rain ceased. The wind stilled and all was peaceful and silent. My eyes searched for Jesus who I found standing tall in the middle of Peter's boat. My mouth was agape; wet hair stuck to my face. The night was now calm as if a storm had never occurred.

We disciples were as quiet as the sea had become, and stared wide-eyed. My heart still beat fast as a sort of fear boiled in the pit of my stomach. Even the wind and sea obeyed Him! I had seen Jesus perform many miracles, but never command nature.

"Why are you fearful?" Jesus looked around at all of us in the boats surrounding Him. "Have you not faith yet?"

Like Adonai who flooded the earth and saved righteous Noah and his ark.

Like Adonai who split the Red Sea so that we might escape from Egypt.

Like Adonai who split the Jordan River so we might pass into the promised land at Jericho.

Like Adonai who hurled a great wind upon the sea at the disobedience of the prophet Jonah.

Like the song of Solomon that exclaims that many waters cannot quench love, nor rivers sweep it away.

I put my hands over my mouth. "You are Adonai," I whispered in shock. But belief. Belief as well. "You are the Son of Elohim.

I shivered in my wet mantle, tunic, and veil as we walked up a steep hill. We had only a few torches for light for all sixty disciples as we trod the outskirts of the town of Gergesa.

"You do not think there are many scorpions in those caves, do you?" I questioned Lazarus. My eyes felt heavy with exhaustion as if bricks were on my eyelids.

"Not if James Zebedee is there," Lazarus teased, obviously feeling he was over his seasickness. "His loud voice will scare them away."

"Lazarus, I am serious," I insisted as we trudged up the incline. Dry thistles scraped my legs. We passed silhouettes of monstrous bushes and the occasional cypress tree.

"I would not worry about scorpions, Esther," Judas assured me as he held Salome's arm to help her up the steep incline. "But I *would* worry about the bats."

Lazarus and several other men laughed.

"I heard you screaming like a young girl on that boat, Judas." Salome gently slapped him on the shoulder.

"It was more like a seagull," Philip laughed, making an imitating sound.

"Hush, now!"

"Philip, I tell you, we cannot let anyone know we are here!" Bartholomew stated rapidly.

"Not until we all retreat and get a restful night's sleep. Especially the Master."

"Who even winds and seas obey," Ima murmured.

"Kyrios," I said to Ima, smiling. I spoke quickly. "I do not understand it, but I cannot deny what my own eyes have seen. Truly, Jesus is the Son of Elohim."

"You are in better spirits, Esther." Susanna stepped beside me and gave me a quick rub on my back.

It felt as if I was in a new family. One of sisters and brothers; mothers and children. And of course, our Father; and our Father's Son.

"He calms a storm for His disciples. Will He dry the clothes of His aunt?" Ima continued her murmuring.

Jesus walked with us and was offered many a mantle for His warmth. He accepted one damp one from Thaddeus.

"One would expect there to be more rain, but the night is clear. Look at those stars," Susanna exclaimed. I too looked up, taking in the sky, bedecked with sparkling jewels.

I smiled fondly to myself. *What is a star, Esther?* Aunt Mary asked when I spoke to her that day by the sea. She made it seem as if I answered the question, but she had set me up for each response.

Crickets, owls, and other animals I could not name sang fiercely. The hill was slippery from the rain, causing us to each climb unsteadily.

We reached a cave but I was the last one to enter. I wanted to ensure I was not stung by scorpions. There was a wide, short entrance to the cave. I was not sure how deep this expansive cave was, and I did not want to know. I made sure I stayed close to the opening.

My stomach growled. Peter, Andrew, James, and John were still at sea, about a mile back, fishing for food.

Soon our little camp was covered in a soft buzz of discussions. Our voices echoed against the walls of the cave about the size of Uncle Clopas' home in Nazareth.

I fed the fire, trying to make it as big yet safe as possible. Looking upward, I was relieved to find no bats. Looking down, I was relieved to find no sign of scorpions.

There was no sign of Jesus either. Was He praying outside somewhere?

I stoked the fire and saw we would need more dry wood. Taking a thick stick that served as one of our torches, I smothered the cloth around it with more oil and then lit it with the fire. There were few trees around here so I would need to use sticks fallen from bushes to feed the fire. Even grass and thistles. I walked away from the flames to the cave entrance.

"Esther, where are you going?" I heard Lazarus ask from behind me. I turned back. My torchlight revealed his face. It looked like most of his clothes were dry.

"To get food for the fire."

"You cannot go wandering about at night. I do not even know this terrain."

"Jesus is out there. You can trust Him." I raised my eyebrows with a slight smile.

"I trust the Master. It is you I do not trust." He straightened his shoulders, returning the smile. He pulled his tallit over his head. "Let us go. I am coming with you."

"So be it." I smiled, pleased I would get a moment alone with my husband. We had few hours to ourselves since we became disciples.

He took the torch from me and we carefully walked down the muddy hill, grasses and bushes brushing against our calves.

The crisp evening air snaked toward us. I shivered but did not want to go back to fetch my mantle which dried by the fire. I could see lights from the windows of houses in the city of Gergesa below. Behind it, the Sea of Galilee glittered against the shine of the moon.

"Who is…do you see that?" Lazarus looked to his right.

I turned with him to see a faint light about a stone's throw away.

"It is Jesus," Lazarus observed. "With some woman. I cannot tell who."

We took a few steps closer. I tried to make out her features. Jesus' figure was easy to recognize with His average but confident build, and authoritative figure. He looked down at the woman, kneeling at His feet, as He held a torch of His own.

It was odd for a woman to be alone with Jesus, even if they were just outside of the campsite. Her hair was in disarray.

"She resembles…" Lazarus started, and I heard him give a shaky breath.

"Magdalene," I whispered. I quickly looked at Lazarus, studying his shocked reaction, and then back at the scene.

The wise and holy Messiah…and a woman who was known only for her sin.

I saw that Jesus was calmly talking to her. I could hear the sound of their voices drifting toward us but could not make out the words. Magdalene clutched the ends of Jesus' cloak. She was shaking. Jesus placed His hand on her head and continued speaking.

Magdalene's body finally relaxed. She looked up at Jesus who helped her up; they looked at each other. Magdalene said something. Perhaps words of thanks.

I looked back at Lazarus, not sure what to say. He was probably still embarrassed by what happened at the exorcism in Magdala. And of course, Mara's actions from all of the years before when they lived as brother and sister.

"Perhaps she has come to ask forgiveness and…and perhaps Jesus has forgiven her…"

"…forgiven her…" Lazarus whispered shaking his head.

I raised my eyebrows, concerned with Lazarus' expression changing from shock, to sadness, to…wrath.

I touched his hand, but he snapped it away. Without a word, he turned around and stomped back in the direction of the camp, taking the light with him. He stopped in his tracks and turned around.

"Let us get what you need," he said. "Quickly."

I sighed in frustration and headed in the opposite direction of Jesus and Magdalene, picking up random sticks and pieces of branches that had fallen on the ground. They were a bit damp but would do. I collected reeds and tall grasses and stored them in my mantle. Lazarus grabbed one large stick and started breaking it with his feet.

Jesus must have forgiven Magdalene. What else could that scene have been? My thoughts wandered to the young Mara. Disobedient. Fitful rages. Promiscuity. And actions Lazarus did not dare mention. Not that he or anyone else in his household ever spoke of her. It was as if she were a sister who died, and her memory was too painful to arouse.

But she was a wicked girl. No one could deny it.

"You are finished, then?" Lazarus looked at me stiffly, the torch in one hand and a collection of sticks bundled under his other arm.

I nodded. Words would be too dangerous. As we walked back I almost slipped on some mud. Lazarus looked at me and I adjusted myself quickly to show I was fine.

We walked through the rounded entrance of the cave and my eyes widened when I saw Magdalene, sitting on the hard ground, warming herself by the fire. Men and women glanced her way but did not go near her. Many rested their backs against the curved cave wall. Simon and Thaddeus looked away, obviously ignoring her.

Surely Susanna would sit with Magdalene, but I found her busy helping Salome and Ima — massaging their old feet. Mary Alphaeus stood to the side with Joanna, who was beautiful as always, with flowery features even after the storm.

It was then that I realized this was my opportunity and my duty. My opportunity to be the mother of a child, a sinful child, but a child, nonetheless. Was she not a lost sheep of the house of Israel, which Jesus spoke of?

I made my way toward the fire. Magdalene looked uncomfortable as she continually changed her position from sitting on her heels, to her bottom, to her side. She could not find a place to settle her hands.

I knelt next to her and released the supplies from my mantle onto the dirt ground. I fed the fire, stoked it with a stick, then situated myself more comfortably on the ground. I glanced at Magdalene whose gaze skimmed mine, then immediately returned to the fire. Now that I was closer, I saw her hair frizzing around her like a wild bush. Her eyes that once must have been lined with kohl, now had black streaks running under them. The woman had a robust figure and striking features.

"Shalom," I finally had courage to say. I tried for a smile. There was a fresh mark on her cheek, as if she scratched against some thorns. She had no veil and her fine rose tunic was tattered and stained with mud.

She looked up at me. Her eyes were dark compared to her light-colored hair.

"You may not remember me, but um…my name is Esther. I am the daughter of James of Nazareth…"

Magdalene's mouth opened slowly. "I…remember you, Esther. My sisters were good friends with you."

I nodded. "They still are…Lazarus actually…he is, um…"

"Your husband," Magdalene finished.

"Oh," I said, surprised. "You know!"

"Word still spreads to Magdala. Even if I have not seen my brethren in years." She twisted her hands uncomfortably. "I remember hearing my older brother took you as his wife. As I am sure you have heard many things about me as well." She rolled her shoulders back.

I nodded, not sure what to say. Lazarus stood with Simon and Thaddeus, arms over his chest.

Magdalene glanced over her shoulder at Lazarus in the recesses of the cave.

I wanted to call to him. Would he not greet his own sister?

"He is avoiding me," Magdalene said. "I cast no blame on him." She sighed. When she turned back to look at the fire, our eyes met. Hers looked nearly black in this faint light. "You are the first person to look me in the eye. Besides *Rabboni,* that is."

There was an uncomfortable silence. Magdalene shivered. I quickly rose and picked up my mantle that was drying by the fire.

She shuddered, looking up at me.

Too unsure of what to say, I simply wrapped the mantle around her. She was stiff and so was I. I looked over my shoulder, wondering if I should be doing this — what the others would think of me. But my eyes met Jesus', whose eyes glowed like the fire. That was all I needed. This was my opportunity to act as a mother.

"What brings you to Gergesa?" I asked settling myself beside her. I cast my straight black hair behind my shoulders.

Magdalene took a deep breath. "I had some trouble, as you probably know. You saw the exorcism a few weeks ago, I assume?" She tapped her fingers against her knees.

I frowned and nodded slowly, pulling my knees to my chest.

"You see, I could not bear such a holy man even looking at a sinner like me. Therefore, I ran." She spoke so simply and bluntly. "I ran. Not even thanking Him." She looked down at the blue mantle that engulfed her. "I was soon to regret it, though. I had wanted Elohim's forgiveness and came searching for Rabboni to heal my soul — not just cast out the demons. I heard He returned to Galilee, so I came to see for myself. Today, with the enormous crowds in Capernaum, I could barely see Him, let alone reach Him. Then you all boarded boats and left." She pulled the mantle tighter, her thin fingers poking out. "So I ran along the shore of the sea, in hopes to see Him on the other side."

"You *ran* from Capernaum to Gergesa?"

"I was desperate!" She looked at me fiercely and then gentled. "I am very good at running. First, I got wet when wading across the Jordan River. And then, after I passed the shore near Bethsaida, there was this horrible..." She shuddered.

"Storm," I assumed, looking at her condition.

She nodded, looking down. She attempted to brush her hair behind her ear, but instead her finger got caught in the snarls.

I tilted my head to the side.

"I thought I was going to die. I thought it was the hand of Elohim striking vengeance upon me, casting me into Gehenna. I do deserve it. I was running through thistles and bushes, tripping over rocks and slipping on the mud. I could not see; the rain was like a wall." Her thick lips thinned under her sharp nose. "But then it stopped suddenly. And the night was clearer than the day. I continued forward, but realizing that Rabboni could be anywhere from Tiberias to Hippos to out at sea I came to my senses. And moped on this hillside." She said it as if it was the most common activity in the world. "I tend to mope. Run and mope. When I came across Rabboni Himself. He called out to me and I felt all of my heavy sins drain from me. He said I was forgiven." She looked at me, hope lightening her eyes. "Then He asked me to follow Him." Her mouth hinted at a smile.

I smiled at her, trying my hardest not to judge her or condemn her. I looked around at the disciples again. Usually when Jesus asked someone to follow Him, we at least played a bit of music. Thomas would pull out his flute and maybe the women danced. Instead, they gave Magdalene a cold shoulder.

She bit her lip. "The others, of course, are repulsed by me." She read my thoughts.

"Give them some time." I said. "You must...I will help you." I put a hesitant hand on her shoulder. She flinched. "The disciples truly are kind people. We may...we all may be a bit judgmental at times, but...we all have a past. We are all...sinners. I am — I am just a lowly barren woman. Even," I lowered my tone, "Even Lazarus sins. We all do."

"No one has sinned as I have sinned," Magdalene said plainly. "You could not even guess all that I have done."

"But Mary," I said, lifting my hand from her shoulder. "There is something I see in you. Something Jesus must have seen when He told you to follow Him."

Magdalene opened her mouth, but no words came out.

"Faith," I said, smiling. "Jesus cast out the demons. And later, you searched for Him. You searched for the Kyrios, for it is Adonai whom your soul loves. You sought Him but you could not find Him. But then, scarcely had you passed the storm when you found Him. You found Him and you must hold Him. Hold Him and do not let Him go."

"You have a way with words." She raised a brow, sharp like Martha's.

I laughed. "In truth, they are Solomon's words, not mine. I have heard Jesus tell those He heals, 'Your sins are forgiven. Your faith has saved you.'"

"He said that to me."

"You see? You bring our lot of disciples the gift of faith. Believe me, we could use some more of it. Jesus chides us sometimes, calling us, 'you of little faith.'" I thought back to the calming of the storm.

Magdalene's eyes narrowed thoughtfully.

"Besides," I said, leaning toward her. "I think you and I will make good friends."

Her eyes snapped to mine.

I gave a little chuckle. "It is like reuniting with my long, lost sister."

She broke into a smile.

A woman cleared her throat behind me, humming like a bird. Mary Alphaeus. Magdalene and I turned and saw Ima, Joanna, Susanna, and Salome standing with her. We rose and looked at them expectantly. And nervously. Joanna looked at Magdalene tenderly as Susanna beamed, letting out a light giggle. Salome held a hand to her hip and Mary Alphaeus clasped her hands at her chest. Ima's face was stern but not condemning.

"Welcome, dear." Mary Alphaeus was the first to speak.

Magdalene nodded her head in acknowledgment.

"I am the grandmother of the disciples," Salome stated proudly. The rest began introducing themselves.

"As am I, I would say," Ima said, glancing at Salome with warning in her eyes.

"My dear ones. As am I," Mary Alphaeus added.

I bit my lip, hoping they would not break into an argument.

"We all help with the cooking." Salome, thankfully, changed the subject.

"I can help you mend your hair if you would like." Joanna touched her own hair, which she had pinned back as if she was joining a banquet in Herod's court. Of course, she used to be in Herod's court.

"Though, often we have no need to cook," Salome interjected. "For we have many providers. Susanna is one of them."

"We are from the same town." Susanna smiled. "You and me. Is that not right, Magdalene? I do not think we have met before, but my father did business with your father."

"Dear, do you know how to sew?" Mary Alphaeus asked, taking a small step toward Magdalene.

Magdalene leaned backward. "I…uh…"

"Ah yes," Salome said, "Mary Alphaeus is an expert seamstress. Careful." She looked pointedly at Magdalene. "She will likely bore you to death discussing it."

I put a finger to my lip, watching all the women talk to Magdalene at once. Their excitement and friendliness was commendable, but I wondered if they were overwhelming her.

"My son is one of the Twelve," Mary Alphaeus informed Magdalene.

"*Two* of my sons are a part of the Twelve." Salome grinned.

"The Twelve?" Magdalene started.

"Has no one explained it to you?" Joanna stepped toward her as Magdalene took a step back.

"We have supper," Peter announced. I sighed in relief. A good interruption from this conversation.

The disciples had returned with a basket filled with fish.

"Come, Magdalene," I took her hand, pulling her away. "You can help us prepare the fish."

She nodded as we walked to Peter and the rest of the men. Oddly, she took off my mantle and, handed it back to me. She tried to tame her hair by tying it into a thick knot, then wiped her hands on her soiled tunic.

A few of the women traded quizzical looks.

"I can cook that for you," Magdalene said, impressing me with her bravery and straightforwardness. She confidently held her hands out to Peter to receive the basket of fish.

"No," Peter said, his face white.

My eyes widened. He could not refuse her help. That would do none of us any good.

Magdalene glared at Peter.

I bit my lip.

"I uh…" Peter continued, "the…other women can take care of…it…do not…trouble yourself."

"Peter," I said with a forced smile. "Magdalene is our newest disciple."

If it was possible, his face turned a paler shade. I grabbed the basket from him.

"Come, Magdalene," I said, gesturing her to follow me.

Magdalene just glared at Peter and I wondered if she was contemplating punching him. But she turned around in a jerked motion and followed me.

I looked at her and leaned in to whisper, lest she was embarrassed. "Perhaps we can clean you up a bit and dress your wounds. I need to do that as well. That storm got the best of all of us."

As we reached the fire, I shrieked. I dropped the basket of fish and jumped away from the fire. "Something touched my foot!"

"That…was me," Magdalene said loudly. All of the disciples looked our way.

"No! There is a scorpion right there!" Judas pointed in front of me.

I shrieked again, moving further backward as Judas started laughing with a couple of the other disciples.

"That," Mary Alphaeus said, "was unkind."

Unkind, indeed! I resisted the urge to swat Judas' arm. "Adonai, deliver my soul from lying lips, from a treacherous tongue."

"You are right, forgive me, Esther." Judas leaned down to pick up the spilled fish from the ground. He looked up at me with sincerity. "Please relax."

"It will take me some time to relax, but yes, I forgive you, Judas," I said, taking pride in the fact that I could forgive in a small way as Jesus commanded. Perhaps not yet a Samaritan or a Roman, but I showed mercy to an adulterer and some rambunctious disciples.

"Fear not," I said to Magdalene. "They will not dare play any tricks on you. I will make sure of it."

Hungry as wild dogs, we all worked together to cook the fish and then we ate with the ferocity of dogs.

After we were cleaned up, Jesus led us in our nighttime prayers.

I joined Lazarus near the back of the cave. The blackness of the cave wall that he stared at was depressing, but I followed suit, staring into the darkness. His presence distracted me from my fear of scorpions.

"You have not said a word all night," I said. I was about to touch his shoulder but thought better of it.

"What is there to say, Esther?" he let out a rough sigh. "My youngest sister who *hated* me, threw bricks at me when I was a boy, insulted me every time she saw me, *stole* any treasures our father gave *me*, snuck out at night to be with men, constantly stained her breath with wine, had relations with my cousin, committed adultery on that cousin, filed a divorce, likely killed any children she conceived, allowed Satan to enter her, disregards the whole law of Moses and, on top of that, ignores and disgraces my entire family! Now, twenty years after she left our household, she is back all of a sudden, following the same rabbi as me!"

I had never heard such a detailed depiction of Mara. Nevertheless. "Jesus is the Messiah. Is not everyone welcomed to follow Him?"

"She cannot follow Him as if nothing ever happened!" he seethed.

"But something did happen, Lazarus! Did you not see? Jesus healed her — rid her of the demons."

"Demons! She was possessed by seven demons!"

He raised his hands in the air in frustration. "She is an adulteress; a sinner; a slave to the devil!"

"Thus says Adonai: 'He gives power to the faint, and to him who has no might he increases strength.'"

Lazarus looked at me with a dark expression.

"My husband," I pleaded earnestly. "Was not Matthew a tax collector?" He turned out to be more pleasant than I expected. Joanna, the wife of Herod's steward was a bit annoying with her primness, but she was a good woman who I was trying to love as a mother would.

"I tell you, woman, do not tell me what to do! My father disowned her! As my father's heir, I am obligated to treat her as if she is dead."

He did not look my way, but I looked at him. I knew what Jesus and Aunt Mary would say. "Lazarus," I said, taking in his strained features and short hair. "You are no longer your father's heir. You have relinquished your title and inheritance. You now inherit the kingdom of Heaven."

Chapter 23

Who is a God like you, who removes guilt
and pardons sin for the remnant of his inheritance;
Who does not persist in anger forever,
but instead delights in mercy...?
MICAH 7:18

Trudging through the crowded streets, Jesus led us to Capernaum's synagogue. The fishing village was filled with the smell of salt from merchants, net flax from farmers, and boat lumber from woodsmen.

Behind us was the sea. The hills surrounding the village looked like extensions of the waves of water. Dark trees spotted the yellow-brown earth; pale rocks spilled from the burnt grass.

Clouds served to warn of rain. I could smell and feel the dampness and chill of the air around us.

"I found that recent parable rather amusing, the one about the man building his house on sand." Ima laughed. "Who would ever do such a foolish thing?"

"What did you say, dear?" Mary Alphaeus asked Ima in her high-pitched voice. It was a wonder the crowds did not crush that frail woman.

"Who would ever do such a foolish thing?" Ima pronounced her Aramaic words distinctly, air blowing from between her clamped teeth.

"What was it?" Mary Alphaeus cupped her ears and tilted her head toward Ima, who sighed in annoyance. We had all learned that Mary Alphaeus was a bit hard of hearing.

"*Who would ever do such a foolish thing?*" Ima said so loudly, it was clear over the noise of people.

"What foolish thing, dear?" Mary Alphaeus crinkled her brows in concern.

"Never mind, *dear*." Ima gave up, looking ahead. About a stone's throw ahead of us was Jesus with people standing on the flat roofs of their houses to see Him. It felt like we moved forward only a *cubit* every quarter of an hour.

"We were just talking about Jesus' parables," I explained to Mary Alphaeus, talking into her ear.

"Oh!" She clasped her dainty hands together at her chest. "I very much enjoyed the one about the man building his house on sand. It was humorous." Her hands fell to her sides.

Ima's eyes turned to mine, hoping to exchange a perturbed glance but I simply smiled in return. The disciples of Jesus were not to be exclusive to another.

"Herod's birthday is this week," Salome's old voice groaned behind me. Her voice croaked like a toad.

"Did Pilate give him a birthday present?" Philip chuckled at his own humor.

"Do not be ridiculous," James Zebedee said in his loud, barking voice. "The men hate each other."

I glanced behind at the lot of them. The crowd pressed onward. Lazarus stood with them, staring at Magdalene intently. I could not tell if he was looking at her with frustration or contemplation.

"Why do Pilate and Herod hate each other?" Susanna asked. We adjusted positions as we passed through a narrow street — we could only fit through with three abreast.

"Pilate attacked some Galileans during Passover this year," Joanna explained. The information was what you would expect the wife of Herod's steward to know. "They have been enemies ever since."

I looked over my shoulder at Joanna. James and Philip stared at her. I had noticed that men tended to gawk at Joanna. She was a very beautiful woman who carried herself with great poise and dignity. She admitted to me, though, that she was frazzled when so many men, Jew and Gentile, leered at her.

"Even Herod did," she told me, clearly disturbed.

I turned my attention to Magdalene, on my left. Her shoulder brushed against a basalt stone wall. I wondered if the inner fire and annoyance on her face was from people stepping on our feet, or her struggle with being a new disciple.

It must have been the latter. This was her first week as a follower of Jesus, and from what I could tell, it was not going well. She had not complained or said she was struggling, but she must have been. Most of the disciples would not even glance her way. Even as we walked in such a compact group, people avoided Magdalene, keeping their distance. Some of the women were kind to her, but I wondered if it was enough for her to feel a part of our caravan and family.

The tension amongst our followers was evident. The hushed voices started the night Magdalene arrived. "Magdalene...demoniac...disciple... Lazarus..."

If I could hear these bits of conversation, surely Magdalene could as well. Magdalene looked my way. She was freshened up since the night she arrived. Her face was clean and the scratch on her cheek was now a thin pink scar. Her eyes were sunken as if date halves were beneath them. She was the tallest of all the women. She wore my mantle as a veil and cloak until we would return to Magdala where Susanna would give her a new veil. In truth, I was cold without it, but I was trying to do it for the sake of my child; for the sake of love. *Hatred stirs up strife, and charity covers all sins.* So the proverb said.

I smiled at her.

Magdalene's thick lips frowned at me in return.

What could I say to such a face? Could I find any words that would assure her? *Be not provoked by evildoers, nor envy them that work iniquity. For they shall shortly wither away as grass, and as the green herbs shall quickly fall.* As the other proverbs said, I could not consider any of the disciples as evildoers. It was for Jesus, the Son of Elohim to call out wickedness and righteousness.

I exhaled forcefully as I was pushed forward. With the speed of snails, we slid closer to the synagogue, at last coming to a wider street.

As I looked at Magdalene again, she appeared as if ready to explode with rage. She looked high above her. I too looked upward and saw nothing but graying clouds and a swallow flying.

"Magdalene?" I put my hand on the woman's shoulder.

She surprised me by roughly shrugging off my hand. Her narrowed, dark eyes fell on mine.

"*I cannot do this,*" she muttered, angry tears streaming down her face.

"Mary," Lazarus pushed from behind us. "Are you well?"

My eyes widened in surprise. This was the first time he had spoken to her since her arrival.

"Mary," Lazarus repeated, putting a hand to her shoulder.

"*I cannot do this,*" she yelled, pushing away from Lazarus, but unable to go far with the thickness of the crowd.

"Calm yourself, Mary, what is wrong?" Lazarus reached for her again.

"Oh, you finally talk to me, brother!" Magdalene snapped. Lazarus' eyes widened in dismay. "You heard me! I cannot do this! I cannot! I cannot! I know what you are all thinking. I thought I could ignore it, but I cannot. I cannot follow Rabboni. I cannot be forgiven. How can I pretend that I am *righteous* and *clean* like all of you?" She sobbed hysterically. Revealing her long brown locks, she pulled my mantle off and thrust it into my arms.

With the force of the sea, she pushed through the crowd until I could no longer see her.

Nearby disciples looked in her direction with bewilderment. Magdalene was gone as quickly as she came. It was they who pushed her away, including my husband. Lazarus' face was afflicted with tension and stiffness.

What have you done? The voice of your sister's blood cries to me from the earth! I bit my lip, knowing my thoughts were extreme and foolish — they were the words Adonai said to Cain after Cain killed his brother Abel.

I craned my head to see Jesus ahead of us. Further out was the synagogue, shadowing the other buildings. Did Jesus notice Magdalene's departure? If so, He did not show any sign of it.

Rage and embitterment wormed their way through me. I squirmed, my skin prickling as I listened to Peter, Bartholomew, and Matthew in front of me.

"She is an adulteress..." Bartholomew said.

"As I was a tax collector..." Matthew responded with a *tsk-ing* sound. "You were there when the Master ate at my home. Adulterers were there."

"But the adulterers did not become actual disciples!" Peter said, seething. "What would people think if we had her parading around with us?"

"They would assume the worse," Bartholomew concluded. "Thinking that all of us would...you know...have a turn with her. Even the Master! They would accuse us of many things."

"They already do accuse us of many things." Matthew *tsk-ed*. "They call us lunatics, rebels, blasphemers, liars. Unclean. And we already have a variety of women in our company."

"In truth, our reputation would not worsen," Bartholomew stated.

"Look around you," Peter exclaimed. "People are *flocking* to the Master." He raised his hands above the heads of the people. "It is only some Pharisees and priests who label us as liars and blasphemers. They are nothing other than jealous. Most people believe that Jesus is Kyrios — or at least that He comes from Elohim."

"It does not matter now, anyway." Matthew sighed. "She is gone. You scared her away."

"What do you mean, 'you,'" Bartholomew protested. "I did not see *you* welcoming her."

"I did not glare at her, like some. I just thought it would be best to give her some space. I did not want to frighten her."

"Frighten her? You did not want *her* to frighten *you*..." Matthew and Bartholomew continued their bickering. I tried to drown their voices from my hearing.

At last, we reached the synagogue. Jesus, at the head of the assembly, made His way up the few steps to the porch and then through the wide entrance, framed with neatly packed stones.

The multitude followed closely behind Him. I stayed toward the back of the congregation with the women as we entered the large court, framed with at least a dozen pillars. Stone benches lined the walls, and mats were scattered across the floor. In the center of the court was the typical dais that held the Torah.

Jesus did not go there, but settled down on the stone chair of Moses, blessing little children who were shoved in His arms.

In all truth, I was in no mood to hear Jesus preach. My agitation and irritability made me not want to hear another word. What type of mother was I? How could I let this happen to Magdalene?

I smiled bitterly at how foolish my thoughts were. Yet I truly was worrying like a mother for her children. I worried for Magdalene, but I also worried for Lazarus and all of the disciples. *The ox knows his owner and the ass his master's crib, but Israel has not known Me and My people have not understood.*

I knew that even if I failed Magdalene, our Father in Heaven would not.

Thus says Adonai, can a woman forget her infant, so as not to have pity on the son of her womb? And if she should forget yet will not I forget you.

As people began to sit, I leaned up against a pillar, the cool stone refreshing my back. Lazarus chose a spot beside me. I decided not to say anything to him, feeling disgruntled with his actions. *Woe to the sinful nation, a people laden with iniquity!*

Around me, there were numerous tax collectors. At least, I assumed that what they were due to their wealthy rings and long, groomed hair as well as the occasional whisper of their title. There were even a few prostitutes; bells jingling from their ankles and wrists. Their kohl-lined eyes stared eagerly at Jesus. Many Gentiles were gathered as well — be they Greek or Roman or Germanic. They were clearly not Jewish as they did not cover their heads for prayer and had lighter complexions.

I raised my eyebrows curiously. It was unusual to see any sinners in the synagogues. Though Jesus seemed to accept their presence, it did not stop the fact that various people were glaring daggers at known sinners, keeping as far from them as possible.

A couple of Pharisees with scribes behind them pounded through the crowd, marching toward Jesus, their chins raised.

Jesus returned a little boy to his mother. I wondered what it would be like to have children and then have them blessed by the Master. I shook off the thought and looked at the lot of people.

These are my children.

But my stomach boiled in disgust at the sinners and Gentiles around me.

The short, stout Pharisee spoke loudly, in a shrieking tone. "This man receives sinners and eats with them!"

I sighed, my thoughts unable to stop drifting to Magdalene.

"Look at the sinners here!" the small Pharisee squeaked, pointing at the tax collectors and prostitutes. "He actually lets them sit in His presence!"

Small gasps and shouts arose.

"Teacher, why do You allow this?"

"Do not let them defile us!"

"Rabbi, tell them to leave. We do not want them here!"

"And He heals on the Sabbath! The Sabbath! In violation of the law of Moses!"

Jesus raised His hands. "Silence!" He spoke calmly, yet strongly, immediately drawing my attention like a shofar blaring in the night.

Once everyone was quiet and settled, Jesus began His teachings with two parables. All He spoke of was in parables. He told one about a lost sheep, and the other, a lost coin.

So He had come for the lost sheep of Israel. Like Magdalene.

"A certain man had two sons." Jesus began a new parable, and I sighed, trying not to be annoyed with the length that the preaching might take. "And the younger of them said to his father, 'Father, give me the portion of substance that falls to me.' And he divided to him his substance. And not many days after, the younger son, gathering all together, went abroad into a far country and there wasted his substance, living riotously."

I wondered how long Jesus was going to preach today. It was already late in the afternoon, so He should not be too long. Still, it would take a while to get Him out of these crowds again. I crossed my arms over my waist, tapping my fingers on my elbows. I looked down at my nails. Dirty and chipped.

"And after he had spent all, there came a mighty famine in that country, and he began to be in want. And he went and cleaved to one of the citizens of that country. And he sent him into his farm to feed swine. And he would have filled his belly with the husks the swine did eat, and no man gave it to him."

My stomach twirled with disgust and restlessness. The son was like a foreign exile. Now tending *unclean* animals. That was odd to think about since just yesterday, Jesus drove demons out of a man and into a herd of swine. The swine ran into the sea and drowned themselves. The Gentile people had begged us to leave them. Still, many travelers came to Gergesa to see the famous Jesus.

"And returning to himself, he said, 'How many hired servants in my father's house abound with bread, and I here perish with hunger? I will arise and go to my father and say to him: Father, I have sinned against Heaven, and before you. I am not worthy to be called your son. Make me as one of your hired servants…'"

If the father would even acknowledge his son. He should not have given his son his inheritance in the first place. The son practically had wished his father dead. I interpreted the parable for myself, continuing to tap on my arms.

"And rising up he came to his father. And when he was yet a great way off, his father saw him, and was moved with compassion, and running to him fell upon his neck, and kissed him."

I stared at Jesus, a brow raised. He sat on the very edge of the stone chair as if He were about to jump off of it.

I released a quick, deep breath as I continued to listen. The father hardly let his son speak but ordered his servant to put the best robe — traditionally reserved for the eldest son — on the returned son and a signet ring on his finger. The father ordered the fattened calf to be killed. A celebration began. A full calf would have fed the entire village. The father celebrated then, with the village that this son who was lost was now found. The son was dead but was now alive.

I thought of Magdalene. A small smile of satisfaction touched my lips. I let her use my mantle as the father gave the son his robe. She was like the son who squandered his father's inheritance. She returned and repented. Jesus embraced her and welcomed her, but the disciples did not. Perhaps this parable would enlighten them.

Jesus was here for the lost sheep of Israel. He had made that clear. But I came to realize that there were more than just Israelites. The children I was to inherit were not only righteous, ordinary Jews. Indeed, I was trying to mother the sinful, foolish, squandering, poor, sick, disowned, adulterers, tax collectors, and prostitutes.

Yet this sinking feeling remained in my gut. It warned me that there were still others Jesus had come for. Others I did not want to think of who were worse off than Jewish fools and sinners. Samaritans and Gentiles.

"The fault is mine," Lazarus told me for at least the third time since Magdalene's departure. Tonight, after supper, we sat in the courtyard of Peter's house, around a fire. "Elohim have mercy on me."

I gave Lazarus my usual reassurance. "Stop cursing yourself," I told him dryly. "Multiple disciples would not speak to Magdalene. All grumbled like our ancestors in the wilderness." I touched my dry lips, poking at the wrinkles.

Ima and Salome were already sleeping. Susanna, Mary Alphaeus, and Joanna sat opposite us. I could see their laughing selves between the stretch of flames. Susanna's face glowed even more in the firelight and the womanly laughter sounded like a chorus of pipes and flutes.

Between them and Lazarus and myself, sat most of the Twelve and a few other male disciples. Others were on the rooftop or inner rooms of Peter's house. A few men spoke to each other in a corner of the court behind us. My mantle was wrapped tightly around me in the cold chill of that winter night. I stretched my bare, blistered feet as close to the fire as I dared, in order to warm them.

"Imagine if one more person spoke to her," Lazarus said. "If one more person acknowledged her; welcomed her. She might have stayed. I, of all people, should have welcomed her." His pace increased as he spoke. "I cannot stop thinking of that parable of the prodigal son…and of the signet ring… it was simple for me to give my ring to Martha, but to Mara? I never even considered that sister. I counted her as dead!"

Lazarus looked at his hands, motioning with them as he spoke. His cloak hooded his head for warmth. "I was speaking with Matthew about this. The Master, or Adonai Himself, is the father in the parable. As Adonai forgave our people numerous times in the desert, so is our Father's relationship with us. My sister Mara is like the prodigal son. I, on the other hand, am like the older brother. I am a son of our Father, and when my sister returns, I am jealous and angered that she has been forgiven and *I* ignored."

"I do not recall hearing what happened to the older brother in the parable…" I mused, trying to recollect Jesus' words. Perhaps my mind had wandered by the end of His sermon.

"There was more to the story, wife," Lazarus told me, the fire bringing out an eager glint in his brown eyes. "The elder son was in the field, and when he came and drew near to the house, he heard music and dancing. And he called one of the servants and asked what these things meant. And he said to him, 'Your brother is come, and your father has killed the fatted calf because he has received him safe.'" Lazarus spoke at an even quicker pace. I could hear the excitement rising in his voice and I saw it in the way he lifted his hands.

"And he was angry, and would not go in. His father therefore coming out began to entreat him. And answering, he said to his father, 'Behold for so many years do I serve you, and I have never transgressed your command-ment, and yet you have never given me a kid to make merry with my friends. But as soon as this son is come, who has devoured his substance with harlots, you have killed for him the fatted calf.'

"That is when the father told him, 'Son, you are always with me, and all I have is yours. But it was fit that we should make merry and be glad, for this your brother was dead and is come to life again. He was lost and is found.'"

My mouth parted, regretting that I truly did not pay attention to that part of the parable. "I will admit that I would be angry as well…if I were the elder son, that is."

"Exactly," Lazarus pronounced. "I think the elder brother represents you and me. Esther, I should have rejoiced when Mara returned! Not ignore her and refuse to speak to her. I should have embraced her and introduced her to all of the disciples." He waved a hand at those sitting around us. "She was lost, but Jesus found her."

"We, the devout Jews. We are the older brother," I agreed, staring at the rising flames in front of us. I relished the hard warmth that wafted over me. "Magdalene and every sick person. Gentiles and heathens. Jesus wants me to adopt even *them* as my children."

"Children?" Lazarus looked at me.

"I am not with child, husband," I assured him. "Perhaps like all of these parables, I am seeing myself as a mother to the lost children of Israel."

Lazarus fingered the edge of his cloak that surrounded his face. "Are you satisfied with this type of children?"

"No," I said truthfully, my eyes drifting to the side. "I will never be satisfied. But Adonai said to Isaiah, 'as one whom His mother comforts, so I will comfort you.'" I raised my shoulders. A shiver passed through me. "As a woman disciple of Jesus and as the niece of my aunt Mary. It is my duty as a woman to act as mother."

All of a sudden, James Zebedee's voice carried clearly into the court-yard from outside. "John the Baptist is dead! John the Baptist is dead!" He pounded on the wooden doors. Peter rose from his spot by the fire, stumbled, and opened the left side door.

We all turned our heads to watch a heaving James bound into the dim light of the court. "John the Baptist!" The burly man stretched out his arms. "He has been beheaded! By Herod! He is dead, I tell you!"

Each disciple burst upward like the fire with shouts and questions.

I remained seated, glancing warily at them.

"This was the man who prepared the way for the Master. Yet John was killed?" Andrew stepped forward, his old tunic sagging over his shoulders. He reached James Zebedee but did not look at him. Andrew kept his eyes focused on the compacted ground.

"The Baptist should not have suffered," Judas said, scratching his thick neck as he too walked toward the cluster of disciples. "Adonai's messenger should prosper in glory as the Master will prosper in glory."

"The kingdom of Heaven is already at hand! Our salvation is here!" Peter said firmly, his large eyebrows incredibly visible in the dark night. "John cannot *die*. None of us can die!"

"I tell you, he did!" James Zebedee bellowed, lowering his head near Peter's face.

"Hush, man!" Meirav called from one of the inner rooms. "You will wake up the children!"

"This is the end of the age where the sick and the forgotten and the scorned will reign with the Master as our Elohim and Messiah." Thomas put his hands behind his head, pacing back and forth along the length of the long courtyard.

My eyes searched for Jesus, but I did not see Him. He was likely in some hidden place praying.

"Will we flee somewhere? What if they are after the Master next?" Bartholomew rocked back and forth, looking at Peter expectantly.

"We will remain in Galilee," Peter said, slurring his words. "Until the Feast of Unleavened Bread. I suggest you all go to bed," Peter said, crossing his arms over his chest. "We have another demanding day tomorrow."

"Of course, *Mother*," Philip said in a high-pitched voice of sarcasm. I looked upward. I could not see Philip but perhaps he was already lying atop the refurbished rooftop. "Whatever you say, *Ima!*" He mocked.

Chapter 24

He has rejected your calf, Samaria! My wrath is kindled
against them; How long will they be incapable of
innocence in Israel?

HOSEA 8:5

There were three ways to get from Judea to Galilee. The first and easiest was to go straight through Samaria on the low ground of the Jordan River Valley. Jews avoided this easy route, however, so they would not come in contact with Samaritans.

The second was a harder path of heavy mountains close to the eastern side of the Jordan River; it did not cross any part of Samaria. Most Jews traveled this second route to avoid Samaritans.

The third route was the Via Maris, a Roman highway on the coast of the Great Sea — another route that Jews avoided as it was crawling with Samaritans *and* Gentiles.

For the first time in my life, I traveled by the first and easiest path. On the one hand, our journey was remarkably direct and smooth. On the other hand, it was disturbing as we passed plenty of Samaritan towns. Many villages gave us no sign of welcome, but kicked dust at us and shouted curses and insults.

I did not think the Samaritans hated us because we proclaimed the kingdom of Heaven. They hated us because we were Jews coming back from Jerusalem. We worshiped Elohim on Mount Moriah in Jerusalem — not Mount Gerizim in Samaria. That was at the heart of our conflicting views.

Jerusalem. The city which Adonai chose for all the tribes of Israel.

As we traveled through the Samaritan district, I was particularly unnerved that the Twelve were not among us. Typically, they played the role as Jesus' protectors — not that Jesus intended for them to be bodyguards — but they themselves acted as such.

But Jesus sent the Twelve on mission ahead of Him to Galilee, Perea, Decapolis, and Phoenicia. He put them in pairs, telling them to visit all the towns that He was traveling to. They were to take nothing with them for the journey and they were to proclaim the kingdom, cast out demons, raise the dead, cleanse lepers, anoint the sick with oil, and heal them.

Meanwhile, to my dismay, Jesus wished to visit Samaria with the remaining disciples before making His next round of travels.

We had just finished the Feast of Unleavened Bread in Judea, staying with Lazarus' sisters, Martha and Mary. They were all too glad to host us, with their uncle Simon the Leper. The tall Hezekiah was nowhere to be seen.

I learned that with her wealth, Martha kept Lazarus' manor house and a few servants, but also built another level to her hospice. Surely, every poor person in Judea now had at least some wealth because of her.

Even as she helped the needy, Martha was also hard at work keeping house, promising that anytime Jesus was in Judea, she would have a plethora of supplies for Him as well as lodging.

"That is Jacob's well," Salome told me as I walked beside her, grasping her bony arm. I slowed my pace, noting my strides were difficult for her to keep up with.

In front of us, Ima walked easily. She had been particularly quiet this journey. I could not blame her. It was unnatural for all of us; for any Jew, frankly.

I narrowed my eyes to focus on the small outline of the well. "Our father, Jacob? Jacob as in Israel?"

"The very same," Salome said with her croaking voice. "The town of Sychar is but a mile from it. See the field to our left? Same one that Jacob gave to his son Joseph."

Then this was the well where Jacob first saw Rachel. He fell in love immediately upon seeing her.

I come here like Jacob, Esther. That was what Lazarus said to me the day he came to Nazareth to ask Uncle Clopas for my hand in marriage.

"Have you been here before?" I asked Salome. She acted as if she had.

Dirt crumbled in my sandals, coating my feet. The dry brown grass irritated my ankles. Around us, mountains shot up like great palaces. I saw shepherds on the hills with goats and sheep eating from the ground. Clouds rested low in the blue sky.

Salome said she had not been to Jacob's well. "But James and John told me of their first visit here. That was when there were only half a dozen or so disciples. But look at us now." She gestured over her shoulder at the surrounding multitude. Seventy of us. And we did not even have the Twelve among us.

"Do you think *these* Samaritans will welcome us?" I wondered as we neared the well. The last town we went to was Tirathana. Salome was certain they would not welcome us because when James and John first went, men hurled stones at them from their watchtowers, giving John a gash in the head. This time, Tirathana did not throw stones at us, but many shouted, demanding that we leave.

They were a hopeless cause.

"I am surprised the Master would return to those who reject Him," I said. My nerves swelled. Part of me wished this next town would *not* accept us so I would not have to converse with Samaritans.

"He is giving them another chance, I suppose. They are lost sheep, no?"

"Truly," I said. They were not exactly Gentiles. They were unfaithful Jews who *married* Gentiles. Half-breeds.

...Just as bad, if not worse. I separated my opinion from my thoughts. *"Blessed are the merciful, for they shall obtain mercy,"* Jesus said.

"I hear they buried the Baptist in Sebastia. Hmmm." Salome coughed into her arm as she swayed with her walking. I tightened my grip on her other elbow. "If we stop there, we could visit the tomb."

"Why did they bury him in Samaria?" I asked.

"Many of his disciples were Samaritans," Salome said. "My son John was not, of course, but the Samaritans had permission from Herod, blasted man that he is, to bury the Baptist there. His body at least..."

"His body?" Ima looked back at us, showing the first sign that she was listening to our conversation.

"They beheaded him, Ima," I told her quietly, watching her face contort in disgust. Sweat dripped down her wide forehead.

"Herodias probably buried John's head in a pile of dung," Salome muttered. I flinched at the repulsive image.

We reached Jacob's well, its cracks attesting to its ancient origin. We could not draw water from it as we had no jugs or buckets to draw from such a deep cistern. Yet we discussed the story of Jacob and his twelve sons, who became the twelve tribes of Israel. We remembered that hundreds of years after Jacob and his sons, the tribe of Judah and tribe of Benjamin split apart from the other ten tribes. Only Judah and Benjamin were faithful to the house of David. The other ten were lost, and married idolaters, eventually becoming the Samaritans they were today. Now, most of the tribe of Benjamin resided in Galilee while the tribe of Judah obviously resided in Judea.

We continued to the village of Sychar, surrounded by steep mountains. As the town and terraces came into view, a woman who must have spotted us, came running in our direction. Jesus, as usual, was at the head of the disciples. He picked up His pace.

I watched as the Samaritan woman came closer, and was surprised when she fell on her knees before Jesus and hugged His legs, causing all of us to halt.

Jesus put a hand on her veil-covered head. "Photina." I heard Him say her name.

"Kyrios." She looked up at Him, steadying the dark brown veil on her head. "You have returned to us. Much has changed since You first visited."

Jesus helped the woman rise. She beamed at Him.

"A Samaritan woman," Salome breathed beside me. "Remarkable."

"Will you welcome us into your home?" Jesus asked.

"Oh, Kyrios! You need not ask. But You must know, I no longer live with the man with whom I had lived in sin. I now live with a friend and her family. She will surely rejoice at the news of Your arrival, for she has come to believe in You because of my testimony."

"Let us go," Jesus said, and we started up again toward the village.

As we reached the closely packed mudbrick houses of Sychar, more people came to greet us. A usual occurrence when Jesus arrived somewhere. An *unusual* occurrence when a Jew arrived in a Samaritan town.

We dispersed into different houses that welcomed us to stay with them. About a dozen disciples were placed in each of five homes. Lazarus and I, along with Susanna, were included in Photina's house.

"Esther," Jesus said quickly as He passed me. "You can help Photina."

The blood drained from my face. I tried to stuff down any anxiety or revulsion.

Jesus, the villagers, and the disciples walked toward the center of the village, beneath a large olive tree. Still, from afar, I caught another quick look from the eyes of Jesus.

With that, I reluctantly decided to skip Jesus' preaching for the day in order to help Photina prepare supper, as she was one of our hostesses. I did not know how to act around a Samaritan. Would Aunt Mary tell me to act as a mother toward this woman and those of the village? It unnerved me to see that a Samaritan woman came to know Jesus at such a friendly level.

I stood in the courtyard.

"I hope we will have enough food," Photina called from inside. She came out with a large jar and set it on the ground of the court. She cast her veil aside, revealing her black hair in a long braid. "Thankfully," she said, looking at me with a huff, "we have an abundance of lentils. What do you say to some lentil soup?"

"Anything you provide us with will be sufficient," I said stiffly, trying to remind myself that Jesus came for her sake as well as mine. "Do not fear. Jesus will always perform a miracle. If needed," I added, clearing my throat. I sounded so strange! "We have become so accustomed to miracles; they have become the object of humor."

"Miracles such as...?" Photina drawled.

"Well, Jesus raised a little girl from the dead in Capernaum." I gulped. "And stopped a woman's blood hemorrhaging — all the woman did was touch Jesus' cloak."

"Raised from the..." she stopped speaking to give me a pointed look. "You will need to tell me everything you know about the Kyrios. Including this raising from the dead."

"I will," I said unwillingly. It was my duty as a follower of Jesus to speak of His deeds. I inwardly groaned. Did it have to be to a Samaritan? I tried not to think of any impurity or unlawfulness she may have committed.

"You are the woman of the household?" I asked, looking over my shoulder. Not another soul was in the building.

"Oh no. No. A friend of mine. Wife to a blacksmith. My friend and her husband are listening to the Kyrios as we speak. Someone has to make supper, though." Photina turned to the stove in the corner of the court. "There is a basket of dry grass and twigs in the room over there, if you would kindly feed the fire."

I set out on my task looking at the room that served as a bedroom and traklin. Finding a basket of grass and such on a shelf, I grabbed it and reentered the courtyard. Photina had grabbed a large iron pot and set it on the curved stove; the fire kindled beneath it.

"Esther, you said your name was?"

"Yes. Wife to Lazarus of Bethany." I bent down to throw a handful of grass into the stone opening of the stove.

"Bethany, eh? A small village, is it not?"

I smiled sheepishly. "Yes, but we lived in a countryside manor home, just outside of the village. Lazarus was an olive grove owner before he became a disciple of Jesus. Now his sisters keep house." I straightened my back.

"I have got some water in the corner there. It will be enough for the soup, but I will need to get more from the well before we lay down for the night."

I walked to the jugs on the other side of the court. Picking up the largest one, I strained my back. I shuffled toward the stove and Photina grabbed the other side of the jug to help me pour the water into the pot. I did my best to not touch her skin or garments.

Silence.

"Upon entering your town, I was told that the well was the famous Jacob's well," I said to Photina to fill the quiet. I took the emptied pot back to the other side of the court.

"Yes. That well is where my life changed."

My green eyes opened wider as I walked back to the stove. Photina handed me an apron and I nodded my thanks as she put on one, herself. Curiosity overrode my hate.

"You must tell me."

"Oh, I will, Esther. Remember, though, that you must then tell me everything you know of the Kyrios."

I gave a shaky laugh, tying the apron strings behind my back. "We have a bargain, then."

Photina set me to work cutting onions, carrots, leeks, and celery as she prepared the red lentils, ground cumin, salt and freshly ground black pepper, both of us kneeling on a mat on the floor.

"Several months ago — well, maybe it was over a year ago now," Photina started. "Time has gone by swiftly. I was…well…let me put this simply: I was an adulteress."

I almost sliced off my thumb as my gaze shot to Photina. Her brown eyes had hints of blue in them.

"I know. I am a sinner." She looked away, flushing.

"I know a woman; my sister-in-law, actually." My eyes softened. "She has a past…similar to your own."

"Well, I have had five husbands. And the man who I was living with… was not my husband." Photina patted down her hair with the back of her wet hand. "I was scorned by every person in Sychar — every person in Samaria. The first person who showed a sign of compassion to me was the Kyrios."

"How did you come to meet Him?"

"I would go to the well every day at noon."

"Noon? Why at such a hot time of day?"

"It was to avoid the other women. Being the sinner of the village is no merry title. I would rather brave the heat than the condemning stares of my fellow villagers."

"I see," I said, sliding the cut pieces of celery across the wooden cutting board on the ground.

"One day, as I went to the well, Kyrios was there. He asked me for a drink. I was surprised, as you can imagine, for He was a Jew, and I a Samaritan *woman*. But then..." Photina got up to open a jar of lentils with the work of her thumb. "Then He offered me living water. Water that would not leave me thirsting again." Tears glossed over her eyes. "He then told me to call my husband. I told Him I had no husband. He knew. He told me that I had had five husbands, and the man with whom I had been living was not my husband. I tell you, the Kyrios knew everything about me. I thought He was some sort of prophet, but then He told me that He was the Messiah. He was the Kyrios."

A smile touched my lips as I recalled the day that Jesus was rejected at Nazareth. That was the day when I became confident He was the Messiah.

"From that hour, my life was changed. I started telling the villagers of the Kyrios' arrival. I left the man with whom I had been living with in sin. I took my son and we moved into this home."

"Ah, you have a son?" A son conceived in sin?

"Yes. Victor. He is listening to the Kyrios right now. You will meet him at supper." She went inside to fetch a bowl and stick to grind pepper. Returning, she settled on the floor beside me. "Now I have spoken enough. Tell me about the Kyrios!"

The Samaritan men set to work the next day, whether they were blacksmiths, carpenters, farmers, or potters, or worked in some sort of olive, date, or wine factory. Lazarus and the other male disciples went out to assist them in their work. Meanwhile, we women disciples were helping clean up the house from the midday meal.

"It is story time," Photina exclaimed, as we finished washing the dishes in the tin tub. Later we would have to take the dishes to the mikveh to ritually cleanse them. That is what a Jew would do. I was not certain if a Samaritan followed the purity laws.

"Storytime?" I gave a respectable, soft laugh. I had been slowly warming up to Photina.

"Yes. Every day, after the midday meal is finished and before we begin preparations for supper, we gather the children beneath the large olive tree in the center of the village and tell them a story."

I sighed, thinking of all the darling children, including Photina's son, Victor. He was a charming little boy — about age 8 —with big brown eyes that seemed to hold the sun within them. He was like any other child, despite his mother's sin and his being Samaritan.

"Esther, you can tell the children the story for the day." Photina put a finger to her square chin.

I coughed. "Me? Surely they would rather hear a story from Jesus Himself."

"The Kyrios is far too busy." She stepped close to me. "Tell them the story you told me about Jesus last night. They would like to hear what the Kyrios was like when He was their age."

I looked down at my hands. The story I told her was about Jesus loving His enemies, even at an early age. I was not qualified to teach such a lesson. I was a woman who held grudges and anger in her heart. "I...I..."

"Come, Esther." Susanna put a hand to my elbow. She gave a laugh.

I met Susanna's perfectly shaped almond eyes. "Susanna," I whispered, "I do not have children," I told her. I knew I was to be a mother to all, but to *Samaritan* children? I could not be *their* teacher and educator! They held blasphemous beliefs, having drifted from the promised house of Israel.

"All the more reason for you to take a turn," Photina cut in, putting a hand to my other elbow to lead me outside. "Victor," she called to her son, who was with a couple of other children, grinding grain on the roof of the house. "It is story time."

The children gazed down with bright eyes and hurried down the ladder to follow Photina, Susanna, and me to the olive tree.

I surrendered to my fate as children hurried from their homes at Photina's call. Soon I had close to two dozen children gazing up at me with expectant eyes.

The olive tree provided good shade but sweat beaded at my hands and neck.

I cleared my throat. "Shalom, children." I smiled. "My name is Esther, and...I am a disciple of Jesus."

"I like Him," Victor said, his hands clasped in between his knees.

"Me too!"

"I like Him too."

"Yes." I chuckled. "I like Him very much as well."

I looked at Photina who nodded rapidly, encouraging me.

I gulped and turned my attention to the children. "Well, Jesus happens to be my cousin." I leaned against the knotted bark of the tree. "As children, we lived in a small village called Nazareth. Have you ever heard of it?" The children shook their heads.

"Yes, well…Nazareth is a very small village in Galilee. One morning, when Jesus and I were about Victor's age," I said, watching Victor's eyes perk in interest, "our mothers gave us permission to play. That was when Jesus had the idea that we pretend to be dancers in a king's wedding."

"A king's wedding?" A child laughed.

"Yes. So we began twirling, spinning, and leaping."

The children stared at me with parted lips.

"This was just outside of the village, by the way, and suddenly," I paused for effect, "Roman soldiers came riding toward us on their horses."

One of the children gasped.

"We immediately stopped dancing, and the leading Roman, who was a centurion, glared at us from atop his big black horse." I looked slowly at the different expressions on the youthful faces. "The centurion started yelling at us. 'You foolish children!' he said. 'I could run you right over if I wanted to.'" I raised my hands. "Jesus and I stepped back in fear, but then Jesus' father, Joseph, came from his workshop. He stepped in front of us to protect us. The Romans rode on, into our village and started attacking different houses."

"Why did they attack?" Victor asked, his big eyes filled with worry.

"They said that they were heading back to Jerusalem from a journey, and they needed food. So, they started taking our provisions. Our bread, cheese, corn, vegetables, and chickens. "Jesus' father told Jesus and me to stay hidden behind the houses. That is what we did, *until*…we saw the mean centurion fall off of his black horse."

"He fell?" a child wondered.

"Yes. He lost control of his horse and he fell right off and *hard* onto the dusty, rocky ground." I slapped my hands on my lap when I said the word 'hard.'

"He deserved it for stealing your food!"

"Did you laugh at him?"

"Listen well, children," I said, leaning toward them. "Jesus did not laugh at the centurion. I told Jesus that the Roman deserved it, but Jesus went to the centurion and helped him up from the ground. Jesus brushed the dirt from the centurion's clothes and smiled gently at him. And guess what the centurion did?"

The children waited silently for me to answer.

"The centurion started weeping!"

"He wept?"

"He was a baby."

"I have never seen a Roman cry."

"Neither had I," I said, shaking my head slightly.

"Then what happened?"

"Oh," I said, giving a light shrug. "The centurion got back on his horse and just rode away."

"*He did not even say 'thank you,'*" Victor grumbled.

"He did not. But what do you think the lesson of this story is?" I asked them.

"Do not weep like the weak centurion!"

"Jesus should not have helped the Roman?"

"No. I told Jesus He should not have helped the centurion, just like you suggest." I sighed. "But Jesus teaches us to *love* our enemies."

"*Love?*"

"I know it is difficult, no? I do not think I have been able to do so, quite yet. But Jesus encourages all of us to try our very hardest to love. We should love our parents. We should love our brothers and sisters. We should love our villagers; our priests and rabbis. *And* we should love our enemies."

"Even the Romans?"

"Yes." My lips thinned. "Even the Romans."

"What about the Jews?"

"Listen here," I said gently. "*I* am a Jew." A couple of the children gasped.

"And you are Samaritans," I said. "Though the Jews and Samaritans are enemies, I must say that I...I love you."

Did I totally mean those words?

"I love you too, Esther!" Victor said to me. He scooched closer and rested his head on my lap. My heart caught in my throat.

"What is our Esther teaching you little ones?" Jesus came walking toward us. I started.

"She is teaching us to love our enemies!"

I blushed, refusing to meet Jesus' eyes. "Just as You love Your enemies."

Victor jumped away from me toward Jesus.

"Even the Romans."

"Good. Good." Jesus bent down as the children rose, surrounding him. "A good lesson." Jesus' eyes met mine.

I looked away, biting my lip. We had not spoken much since I began following Him. And now, of all times, He came when I was speaking like a hypocrite!

Supporting myself with the trunk of the tree, I stood up.

"Children," Photina called. "Give the Kyrios some space."

"No," Jesus said. "Let the children come to Me." He picked up a little one, and with a grunt, settled her on His hip. He patted Victor's head. The young boy looked up at Him with adoring eyes.

"Photina." Jesus looked at the woman. "What do you say to a feast tonight?"

"A feast?" Her eyes widened. "I...well, we do not have much."

"It will be sufficient." Jesus smiled.

"We can all put our provisions together, Photina." A Samaritan woman touched Photina's arm. "If every household contributes, we will have a splendid feast. I will even contribute a chicken."

"A chicken!" the children yelled in excitement.

"What are we celebrating?" Photina asked, her cheeks reddening.

"Life," Jesus exclaimed, giving the child in His arms a little bounce. "The kingdom of Heaven. The blessings Adonai has bestowed on us. Thanksgiving for you generous women."

And so we women set to work on the feast. Chicken as the main course, dressed with hot mint sauce. Artichoke and chard made into a salad. Leftover lentil soup was put to use, and of course, wine.

We ate near the large olive tree in the center of the village. And it was indeed a feast. When we all had eaten our fill, a few Samaritans pulled out their musical instruments and began to play, shaking tambourines and gliding over the strings of a lute. Thomas played his flute. The young people and children danced as a fire was built, its smoke drifting in the air.

I held a cup of sweet wine as I watched the dancing.

Ima stood next to me. "Our Jesus sure enjoys feasting."

"Even when He was a child, He knew how to enjoy Himself."

"I suppose this is true." She looked down at her wine. "I think His joy always made me envious. His and Mary's. Do you know why I was so cruel to them, Esther?"

"Because of Mary's sin," I said plainly.

"Yes, well... This is true. A woman's sins are never forgotten. In time though, the anger can abate. A wise decision, Joseph made, to move. Do not know why he chose Egypt, of all places. He should have stayed in Judea — perhaps Emmaus, with Miriam's relatives."

I did not know, and felt unsettled.

"People wanted to stone Mary!"

"Stone her?" I gasped, clenching my clay cup. "When she was pregnant with Jesus?"

"*I* did," Ima said, a world of regret, shame, and defiance in her eyes.

"Why? Tell me!"

"Joseph. Joseph defended her and took his betrothed as his wife," she sighed.

"Ima, I do not understand. You are...you always hated Aunt Mary. But now you no longer condemn her?"

"I..." Ima started. "I do not know. I...you must understand Esther... and please, do not tell this tale to anyone." I assured her I would not. "You see." Ima took a deep breath. "Mary claimed that she was with child by the Holy Spirit."

My eyebrows furrowed. "The Spirit — "

"Listen, girl. She said that an angel told her that she would carry the Son of the Most High Elohim."

If therefore the son will make you free, you will be free indeed. Jesus had once said.

"The Son of Elohim," I whispered.

"But Mary claimed that she did not know man. Not as a woman knows a man and then is with child. Rather, she conceived by the power of the Spirit."

The Spirit of Adonai is upon me. Wherefore he has anointed me to preach the gospel to the poor.

"I laughed at her!" Ima snapped. "I hated Mary for that. Always acting like a pure, innocent woman who did no wrong. I saw her as Bathsheba, alluring King David so that her son Solomon would one day be crowned king of Israel."

"You *saw* her this way. But you no longer do?" I asked, heart drumming.

"Her claim was ridiculous! Blasphemous. So blasphemous. Blasphemous unless..."

"Unless it is true," I finished for her.

"Yes, well, here I am. With *Jesus*. In *Samaria*. And...I think *it is* true."

I took a deep breath. Conceived by the power of the Spirit.

I looked at the children dancing freely, bubbling with laughter.

She swung her arm around me. "I hear you were the storyteller today." I blinked several times, not accustomed to such tenderness. From my *mother*.

"I was. The reluctant storyteller."

"I am sure it was splendid, Esther. My star." She leaned her head next to mine, her breath spiced with wine.

Tears beaded in my eyes. "It...felt wonderful. Like they were all *my* children — my very own. I do not want to leave them." I twirled the clay cup of wine in my hand. "Still, I am not sure if they truly took a liking to me."

"Hush, now," Ima said, holding me closer. "You *are* a mother, Esther. I regret that I was not much of one to you."

A lone tear slid down her crinkled cheek.

"You are my mother." I leaned over to kiss her soft cheek.

Just then Victor ran up to me, a couple of children behind him. "Will you show us how you and Jesus danced, Esther!? When you were my age?"

"Yes!" Another child exclaimed. "Let us pretend we are dancers at a king's wedding!"

I glanced at Ima. She pulled my wine cup from my hand. "It is true, Esther," she called out as Victor took my hand, pulling me toward the dancing crowd. "They did not take much of a liking to you."

Chapter 25

For I will re-establish my covenant with you,
that you may know that I am the LORD,
that you may remember and be ashamed,
and never again open your mouth because of your disgrace,
when I pardon you for all you have done —
oracle of the Lord GOD.
EZEKIEL 16:62-63

"The door!" Susanna exclaimed at the loud knocking. She coaxed the fire in the outdoor oven of Peter's courtyard.

Most of the Twelve had returned from their mission and were reclining at table in the back room for supper. Some disciples were on the roof, already eating their fill of fish.

"I will answer it," I said, wiping my hands on a spare cloth. I walked to the wooden double-door entrance, unlocked it and peeked around the right door to see if there were any miracle-seekers. I recognized the two men with smiles as wide as a child's.

"Simon!" I looked up at my brother. "Thaddeus." I nodded toward the other disciple.

"We have returned," Simon announced, happily walking into Peter's house. Thaddeus followed. There was dirt on their skin and tunics and their feet were in even worse condition. It made their giant smiles look all the more peculiar.

"It is about time, my brothers." I smiled, closing the door behind them. "You are the last of the Twelve to arrive. Judas and Peter returned two days ago. The others returned this past week." I kissed Simon's scruffy cheek. "John and Philip had me choking with laughter with their story-telling."

The two Apostles looked at each other with knowing smiles. "We had a delay," Thaddeus drawled in his deep voice.

"How so?" I laughed, noticing their strained expressions.

"A lot of little happenings that made our journey home to Capernaum all the longer," Simon explained, a bit mysteriously, scratching the back of his neck. He pulled off his brick-colored headband soaked with sweat.

"Such as Simon getting pulled into a lake." Thaddeus bellowed in laughter. "By a *woman*."

I raised a quizzical brow.

Simon scowled as Thaddeus explained. "We were casting an evil spirit out of a man, and a woman watching us was so frightened, she jumped back towards the water. She grabbed Simon's tunic, so she would not fall in, but ended up falling and taking Simon with her."

My laughter harmonized with Thaddeus'.

"It is not so humorous when you are the one getting drenched," Simon growled.

"*Anyway*, we ended up spending the night with the woman's family and did some preaching there. I cannot quite explain it. The Spirit simply led us to stay out a little longer," Thaddeus continued.

"Alright, now." I spread out my hands. "Several others are just beginning their meal in the back room. Once your feet have been washed, please join them." I pointed toward the left of the court where we had a jar for ritual purification and a pitcher and bowl for practical foot washing. "Everyone will be glad to see you."

Some men and women on the roof of Peter's house called out greeting to the two disciples.

I returned to Susanna, who was still by the oven. "I have the next load of fish." She smiled brightly as if handing me a block of gold. "Nicely smoked," she added.

I carried the food into the dimly lit dining room where at least thirty disciples were crammed. My eyes focused on Jesus, as usual, at the typical left-hand seat of honor at the horseshoe shaped table. He smiled, leaning against the wall behind Him, His legs crossed beneath the low table. He took a sip of wine.

"...she believed in a split-second," James Zebedee said, snapping his fingers. "And she started telling that to everyone, right and left — the most energetic person I have met by far."

I set the steaming fish between James Alphaeus and Judas, then took off my apron. Before I could put it away, Ima beckoned for me to sit by her.

Mary Alphaeus did her best to make room for me as I squeezed between her and Ima.

"...and people followed us *everywhere!*" Bartholomew's voice carried through the room. "We could not escape from the crowds. We even had to sneak out at night to get away, as we usually do when we are with You, Master."

"The scribes and Pharisees are getting riled at how excited the people are," Judas cut in with his smooth voice. "I hear that Caiaphas and the high priests in Jerusalem feel the same way. We were driven out of some synagogues because of our preaching." His lip twitched beneath his dark mustache.

Peter put a hand on his shoulder. "Yet the Spirit of Elohim led us forward. We were denied by some but accepted by many others."

Ima affectionately rubbed my shoulder. Mary Alphaeus handed me a greased fish of my own, which I immediately tore apart and ate. I listened to the stories of the Apostles with as much energy as I gave to my eating.

Susanna tried to exchange a few quiet words with Jesus, who rose and carefully stepped between the guests. He put a hand on John's head to steady Himself, then pointed at Lazarus and then me, beckoning us to follow Him.

Surprised, I stood, my muscles complaining from all the walking I was doing these days. Lazarus and I exchanged questioning glances as we did our best to navigate through the maze of bodies on the floor. Finally, just behind Jesus, we made it to the courtyard. The evening rays of sun made softly draped shadows.

Several disciples gazed down at us from the rooftop.

When Jesus took a few steps forward I saw who everyone was looking at. Magdalene.

The woman came to Jesus and kneeled before Him to kiss His feet.

I looked at Lazarus, unsure of what my husband would do, then returned my attention to Magdalene, who Jesus helped up. Her face glistened with tears. Thick, light-brown locks of hair escaped from her veil, and a small, hesitant smile touched her heavy lips.

Magdalene's focus shifted to Lazarus. I looked back and forth between the pair's anxious expressions. Brother and sister each had their eyebrows tightly scrunched together in the same incline. Lazarus took a slow step forward as Magdalene did the same. They kept taking tentative steps toward each other.

"Mary...I," Lazarus started in a croaking whisper.

"Forgive me," she said quickly. "Forgive me for all that I have done! For my anger, for my cruelty, for disconnecting myself from you, and for — "

"I have already forgiven you," Lazarus cut in plainly.

Her mouth fell open, although no words escaped.

"You must forgive me also," Lazarus continued. "I should have welcomed you when you first returned! I am following the Messiah, and I acted in complete opposition to what Jesus preaches. Forgive *me*, Mary, for how I have treated you."

After a quick moment of silence, they threw their arms around each other. A small tear escaped my eye. I quickly brushed it away as my gaze met Jesus', and as it did, a sense of guilt pinched me. I still felt the anger and hate that boiled in my heart for Rome who occupied us; an anger and hate that was close to what the Sicarii had. And now these hypocritical Pharisees and rich Sadducees! My eyes flicked away from Jesus'.

He opened His arms. "Come, Magdalene."

People came out to greet her. Indeed, they began shouting praises to Adonai for her return. I rushed to Magdalene's side and linked my arm around hers. The disciples rejoiced, and we laughed, which reminded me of the parable of the prodigal son, when the younger son returned and the father called for a celebration.

Thomas pulled out his flute and played a lively melody. Philp began beating on a drum in an unusual rhythm.

Grabbing Magdalene's hands, I pulled her toward the center of the courtyard and leaned back, supporting myself with her weight, as she followed, and we spun.

She laughed — nervously at first, then full and spirited. Mary Alphaeus handed me a tambourine which I began rattling to the odd beats of the disciples' music.

We skipped and turned; shouted and belted; sang traditional Hebrew hymns.

> *Adonai is my light and my salvation,*
> *Whom shall I fear?*
> *Adonai is the protector of my life.*
> *Of whom shall I be afraid?*

Jesus clapped almost as loudly as the drums until He tripped, and Thaddeus and Judas caught Him. Then James and John joined them, lifting Jesus in the air.

I laughed at Jesus' startled expression as His Apostles began bouncing Him up and down. Once they set Him back on His feet, Jesus nudged Peter with a brother-like playfulness.

My heart beat with happiness, and I sang, not caring how I sounded. Sweat dripped down my tunic, but it did not bother me in the least.

Ima brought out more wine, as Lazarus pathetically attempted to leap in the air. Magdalene and I looked at each other and burst into giggles as we followed him, trying to jump as high as possible.

"Oh," I squealed. My feet burned when they hit the floor. "I am getting too old for this."

"Esther, you have nothing to complain about," Salome pointed out, putting her hand on her apparently aching back. "I have not danced in twenty years, and fear my heart is going to fail."

"Fear not," Joanna said, turning slowly. She raised her chin. "If it does, Jesus will set it to beating again, just as He did to the hearts of that man from Nain *and* Jairus' daughter."

"Were they dead?" Magdalene shouted over the noise.

"Yes," Lazarus said. "But Jesus has power even over life and death."

Magdalene's smile broadened, revealing large teeth. "I am not in the least surprised."

Chapter 26

Then the LORD *said to Moses: I am going to rain down bread*
from heaven for you. Each day the people are to go out and
gather their daily portion; thus will I test them, to see whether
they follow my instructions or not.

EXODUS 16:4

Below me, metal helmets glinted in the sun. Red robes taunted as they flapped in the wind. Voices cold as stone caused my stomach to turn. Fierce horses stood ready to trample anything in their path. The Roman soldiers were prepared to stifle the crowd in case of a riot.

I stood on the roof of Peter's house next to my mother, marveling at the vast numbers below.

"It is time!" Magdalene shouted, almost as loudly as James Zebedee. She moved about the house like a dignified noble on his chariot. "Calling all to the synagogue." She cupped her hands around her mouth. "The Master is going to preach! Synagogue time!"

I examined the woman. Her tan veil was tied with an interesting knot behind her, almost appearing like a tail. Her sharp features were confident and steady. One would never guess that she had become a disciple but a week ago. All manner of shyness and timidity had dissolved, and she was now a figure of sociable, collective authority.

"She is too bold," Ima said securing her maroon veil. "A woman should not tell a man what to do. Especially the chosen Twelve of the Master. She speaks to Peter as if she were his equal!"

"She is an aristocrat," I said. "She is used to a status of jurisdiction. Perhaps Adonai is using her skills to accomplish His Son's work." It is what Adonai was doing for me. He was using my lack of children to make me the mother of many children. The freedom Lazarus and I had allowed us to travel closely beside Jesus. "Think how Jesus still uses fishermen to catch fish for us to eat," I continued.

Ima gave me a mischievous smile. "It would seem that is no longer necessary." She scratched her wide forehead; hints of grey hair lined her veil.

I smiled back, knowing what she meant. "How many baskets were left over?"

"Twelve, they say. Filled to the brim with the leftover barley loaves. Could be more," she said.

"It may be His greatest miracle yet," I said. "Matthew calculated there were five thousand men — not even including all of the women and children!"

"I think His calming of the storm at sea was the greatest miracle."

I shook my head, marveling at it all. "They are all great, no? But this one makes me think of the manna and the quail that Adonai provided for our ancestors in the desert. And think of the miracle at Cana. Again, He has given us a surplus of nourishment."

"Rumor has it," Ima interjected, "that Jesus walked on the water last night."

"So I heard. For once, Lazarus was upset he did not ride in the boats. He could have witnessed it. We will have to trust the word of the Twelve."

"Well, my star, let us go. Let us hear our teacher teach." Ima linked arms with me. I smiled, enjoying her scent of sweat mixed with bread.

Immediately, we hit the crowd.

It looked like everyone followed Jesus from the other side of the sea, here to Capernaum after yesterday's miracle. Out of all the crowds Jesus attracted this past year, this one was by far the largest.

I saw disciples here and there, scattered like spring flowers about the landscape. I did not know how we would enter the synagogue. There was not nearly enough room.

"Our Father, help me," I heard Ima say.

I strengthened my hold on her. "Fear not. I will help us navigate." She did not seem to hear me over the noise. All I saw was her sharp frown. I pushed forward, but when we neared the synagogue, everybody was trying to get in.

My shoulder rubbed against a large man as I attempted to enter. I was shoved forward from behind, and then backward. A Pharisee in front motioned for me to move back. "Out of the way! Get back, woman."

As I was pulled backward, I saw Joanna and Susanna up ahead. "I am with them!" I told the Pharisee, pushing forward to reach my friends and, at the same time, not upset the Pharisee. I pulled Ima along.

"I said get back! We have no room for you here." The Pharisee pushed my shoulder. I clung to Ima, trying to move forward but it was like swimming against a current.

"Please! I am a disciple of Jesus!" I cried.

"I am sure you are. We are not allowing any more in the synagogue, lest the building burst from the lot of you."

I stumbled back against the crowd. Ima looked like she was going to be sick.

I heard my name called ahead of me. "Esther." I searched frantically until my eyes fell upon John with his hand outstretched. "She is with me," he yelled to the Pharisee.

I darted my free hand outward until it grasped John's and we held firmly to each other. With Ima attached to my other arm, I allowed John to drag me forward, breaking through the wall of bodies.

Finally, we were flung into the synagogue, which was only three-quarters full and almost calm. Most of the chaos was outside.

"Esther, dear, are you alright?" Mary Alphaeus lightly touched my arm. "Dear Hannah, you look ill."

I stared at Mary Alphaeus, unsure how a frail woman like her made it inside the synagogue ahead of me.

"My son helped them," Salome stated proudly, putting a hand on Mary Alphaeus' sticklike shoulder.

"Someone could get trampled and die from this crowd," Ima said testily. She took deep breaths to calm herself. Misery was carved in every angle of Ima's face, but there was nothing I could do about it. We were trapped inside the synagogue — the crowds serving as lock and bolt.

My eyes scanned for Jesus, and when I found Him, He was already speaking, though I could not hear what He was saying.

He sat in the chair of Moses as men questioned Him.

I was not sure how long it took for the crowd to quiet down, but when it did, I finally heard the conversation between Jesus and His fellow Jews.

"Rabbi, when did You come here?" An average-sized man asked, his beard hiding his neck. "We were searching for you yesterday in Bethsaida, but you managed to cross the sea to Capernaum?"

"Amen, Amen I say to you," Jesus said. "You seek Me, not because you have seen miracles, but because you did eat of the loaves, and were filled."

I raised my eyebrows, agreeing. Every person in or out of the synagogue desired a sign. Even *I*, after all I had seen, still longed for more.

"Labor not for the meat which perishes, but for that which endures to everlasting life, which the Son of Man will give you. For He has Elohim, the Father, sealed."

Isaiah. *Why do you spend money for that which is not bread and your labor for that which does not satisfy you? Listen diligently to Me, and eat that which is good, and your soul shall be delighted in fatness.*

"What will we do, that we may work the works of Elohim?" a Pharisee asked.

"This is the work of Elohim," Jesus said. "That you believe in Him whom He has sent."

"What sign therefore do You show that we may see and believe You?"

"What can You work?" A woman shouted.

Did they not just witness the multiplication of the fish and loaves? Yet they sought more. The people of Nazareth had requested the same thing, and Jesus did not give it to them. I groaned.

"Our fathers ate manna in the desert," a Pharisee said. "As it is written, 'He gave them bread from Heaven to eat.'"

"Amen, amen, I say to you," Jesus said firmly, raising a finger in the air. "Moses gave you not bread from Heaven, but My Father gives you the true bread from Heaven. For the bread of Elohim is that which comes down from Heaven and gives life to the world."

"Kyrios, give us always this bread," The Pharisee exclaimed.

"*I* am the bread of life," Jesus said, slowly turning His head from side to side. "He that comes to Me shall not hunger and he that believes in Me shall never thirst. But I said to you that you also have seen Me and you believe not. All that the Father gives to Me shall come to Me, and him that comes to Me, I will not cast out."

I thought of the life-giving water that Photina told me about in Samaria.

Because I came down from Heaven, not to do My own will, but the will of Him that sent Me. Now this is the will of the Father who sent Me: That of all that He has given Me, I should lose nothing, but should raise it up again in the last day.

The men and women muttered to each other. Most of them had fiery tones. I wondered if the last day was going to be here and now. I looked around, but no one seemed excited by this prospect.

"And this is the will of My Father that sent Me: That everyone who sees the Son and believes in Him may have life everlasting and I will raise him up in the last day."

My heart swelled as it did in the synagogue at Nazareth. Jesus spoke of the fulfillment of the kingdom. *We would live forever with Jesus as our eternal king?*

"Is not this Jesus, the son of Joseph, whose father and mother we know?" Someone whispered close to me.

"He is the son of Mary of Nazareth!" Ima said.

"Then can He say, 'I came down from Heaven?'"

"Murmur not among yourselves." Jesus spoke louder, leaning His head back. "No man can come to Me except the Father who has sent Me, draw Him. And I will raise him up in the last day."

Hosea. *I will draw them with the cords of Adam, with the bands of love, and I will be to them as one that takes off the yoke on their jaws and I put his meat to him that he might eat.*

"It is written in the prophets, 'And they shall all be taught by Elohim.' Everyone that has heard of the Father and has learned, comes to Me." Jesus tapped His fingers on the stone arm of the chair.

I searched my mind for the prophecies I had studied so diligently. I thought of Isaiah — the same passage that I repeated in Nazareth. *Give praise, O you barren that bears not. All your children shall be taught of Adonai and great shall be the shalom of your children.* Indeed, Adonai was to teach the children of Israel at the coming of the Messiah. Was this not what Jesus was doing?

Jeremiah. *They will teach no more every man his neighbor and every man his brother, saying, "Know Adonai." For all will know Me from the least of them to the greatest, says Adonai. For I will forgive their iniquity and I will remember their sin no more.* That was the new covenant that Adonai spoke to Jeremiah. A covenant that would be written on our hearts!

"Not that any man has seen the Father, but He who is of God, He has seen the Father," Jesus continued.

Had Jesus then, seen the Father? I put a hand to my chin. If Jesus was the Son of Elohim, then He must have seen Elohim. He was Elohim.

"Amen, amen, I say to you, he that believes in Me has everlasting life."

My heart fluttered with joy.

"I am the bread of life. Your fathers did eat manna in the desert and are dead. This is the bread which comes down from Heaven that if any man *trogo* of it, he may not die."

If Jesus was the one who truly came down from Heaven, then that meant that —

"I am the living bread which came down from Heaven. If any man trogo of this bread, he shall live forever; and the bread that I will give is My flesh for the life of the world."

My jaw dropped.

"His flesh!"

"Disgusting!" Ima muttered beside me.

"This must be a parable."

"Look at Him, He is serious!"

"How can this man give us His flesh to eat?"

"Amen, amen, I say to you, except you trogo the flesh of the Son of Man, and drink His blood, you shall not have life in you."

Fear raced through me. He could not mean this. Drinking blood happened in war. *I will make my arrows drunk with blood, and my sword shall devour flesh.* That was in the Torah. And we were not to drink the blood of animals. It was unlawful. But the actual *blood* of Jesus?

"He that trogo My flesh and drink My blood has everlasting life. And I will raise him up in the last day. For My flesh is meat indeed and My blood is drink indeed. He that trogo My flesh and drink My blood abides in Me and I in him."

I grimaced at His use of the Greek word "trogo." Jesus was never this graphic. To chew and gnaw on his *flesh*?

I was not the only one disturbed. Men and women stood and shouted at Him.

"As the living Father has sent Me and I live by the Father, so he that trogo Me, the same also shall live by Me. This is the bread that came down from Heaven. Not as your fathers did eat manna and are dead. He that trogo this bread shall live forever…" Jesus yelled over the murmuring crowds, His hands firmly gripping the arms of the stone chair.

"How can He give us His flesh to eat?"

"This saying is hard."

"Who can listen to it?"

"The man is a lunatic!"

"He speaks of cannibalism!"

"How can such a thing be of Adonai?"

"Who can accept it?"

Men started filing out of the synagogue.

People roughly bumped me as they passed. I looked back at Ima and the other women. We joined together and walked toward the stone chair of Moses. Jesus was standing. Lazarus and the Twelve were with Him.

"It is mainly the disciples who are left," Ima said.

"Are all hundred of them in here?"

"So it would seem. Esther." Ima said my name sharply. I looked at her with full attention. "This saying is hard," she said quietly.

I could not wrap my head around it. My thoughts turned dark.

"Who can accept it?" My mother asked raising her hands in the air.

"Does this shock you?" Jesus spoke loudly.

Ima and I jumped and looked at Him.

"What if you were to see the Son of Man ascending to where He was before?" He continued.

The prophet Daniel. *I beheld therefore in the vision of the night, and lo, one like the son of man came with the clouds of Heaven.*

"It is the spirit that gives life, while the flesh is of no avail. The words I have spoken to you are spirit and life."

My eyebrows furrowed.

"But there are some of you who do not believe. For this reason, I have told you that no one can come to Me unless it is granted him by My Father."

Our disciples continued to murmur. Some filed out of the synagogue with the crowds. It was difficult to enter the building, but now, it was all too simple to walk out.

"Esther." Ima looked at me. "Come."

"Where are you going? Back to Peter's house?"

"No. I am going home."

"*Ima?*"

"You and your husband will leave too if you know what is good for you."

"Ima! How can you say this? We cannot leave Jesus now! I believe! *You* believe!"

"I do not believe in the trogo of my nephew's flesh. It is cannibalism, Esther, and you know it. You are an intelligent girl."

"I do not see someone trying to take a bite from Him right now, do you?"

Ima's eyes narrowed. "Stop being a foolish little girl, Esther. Whatever He means, it is not the truth. *He* thinks *He is some new manna.*"

"You cannot leave with the crowds, Ima. They are mistaken."

"Obviously, the faithful Jews and the Pharisees and scribes know that Jesus is speaking as a false Messiah. Else they would not leave the synagogue like this. Will you be faithful like them? Or will you partake in a cultish practice?"

"There is no cultish practice. You *saw* Jesus multiply bread Himself."

"That is one thing. It is another for Him to think the bread is His own *body.*"

"He speaks of the spirit."

"This is dangerous, Esther."

"Ima please." I gently touched her arm.

She looked at me intensely with her pretty brown eyes; cupped my cheek with her dry hand. "Esther. If Lazarus is a fool and remains a disciple, you can come live with me in Nazareth. Would you like that, my star?"

"What of your son Simon? Do you not want to remain with your *son* here in Capernaum?"

"Men will grow and lead where their wills take them. There is no one like a daughter. A daughter who stays faithful to her mother." She caressed my cheek as tears burned my eyes.

Not now, Father in Heaven! Not when she just began to show me love!

"Ima," I croaked. "I believe Jesus is the divine Son of Elohim." I sniffled as the tears cascaded down my cheeks. We stared at each other, her image blurred by my tears. "I cannot go in your direction."

Thirty. That was how many remained. Before Jesus' discourse in the synagogue in Capernaum, we had about one hundred disciples.

Now, the Twelve remained. And only eighteen others. Surprisingly, many Greek Jews remained. Stephen, Nicanor, Timon of Cyprus, and Matthias. John Mark. Barnabas, Silas, Nicolas of Antioch, Philip of Caesarea, Prochorus, and Parmenas. Thanks to our Father in Heaven, Lazarus remained, and I stood by my husband's side. Magdalene stood with us this time and was adamant about it. Most of the other women were still here. Joanna, Susanna, Salome, Mary Alphaeus.

Not Ima, though.

Jesus' sermon on Him being the bread of life reached the ears of all, causing them to leave. Ima left with the crowds traveling to southern Galilee. Thousands of people walked back to wherever they came from because: "This man is not the Messiah."

We, however, travelled to Tyre and Sidon. Many people come to Jesus from the Gentile territory. He performed another miracle and fed four thousand Gentiles. My stomach twisted at the thought of miracles for Gentiles. *Gentiles!* I supposed if His own people rejected Him in Capernaum, Jesus should go to the Gentiles who would receive Him.

Magdalene at my side, I now sat stiffly around the fire in the outskirts of Caesarea Philippi with the remaining followers. The disciples murmured to themselves. Jesus was off with the Twelve, praying.

Aunt Mary said that I should point the way to her son. But what if everyone was pointing in the opposite direction? What would Aunt Mary make of her own son's words now? Could this virginal conception that Ima spoke of be true? If so, why would Ima leave us?

What if Ima was right and I should have left with her? My husband and the closest of my friends here were staying. Was that the only reason why I too stayed?

"Can I believe something if I do not understand what it means?" I asked Magdalene.

Her hair was done up in a unique knot. Her lips thinned as she looked into the fire. The light danced on her skin like the reflection of water from the sun. She threaded her fingers together. "Adonai promised us a Messiah," she said. "I believe it. But I still do not understand what it means."

As the sun dropped below the mountains, the blue sky turned into a blend of orange and peach.

I fiddled with my hair beneath the loose covering of my veil. I pressed the tips of my fingers to my lips. "I believe Jesus is the bread of life," I said. "But I do not understand it."

"Likewise." She looked at me with composed agreement. She scratched the back of her neck. "You said to me, Esther, many months ago — when I first came to Rabboni — that you saw something in me."

I thought back.

She gave a little laugh, her voice deep and smooth. "It may not have clung to you the way it clung to me. But you said you saw that I had faith."

"I remember. Yes."

Magdalene slapped her hands together, gently swaying. "You of little faith," she murmured. "You of little faith, Rabboni says to us." She stopped moving. "I remember hearing about Rabboni's miracles when I was…hmm… when I was troubled by unclean spirits. I did not see the miracles with my own eyes, but I believed that they were true. I heard that He could even cast out demons. Even the demons in me could not prevent me from searching for Him. It was simple to find Him because…well…when one is so filled with evil, any hint of good can be blinding. Rabboni blinded me."

She inhaled deeply. "That is what I have been thinking about, Esther. Faith. Rabboni says that if I have faith the size of a mustard seed, I can move mountains."

I looked to the hills that surrounded us and give a one-sided smile. "Would you care to test that out now?"

We laughed.

Magdalene sobered. "That is just it, though, is it not? What are we searching for with wonders and signs? Do we want to watch a mountain shift just to see it for our delight? Or do we want to know the one whose power moves mountains? Jesus says that my belief in Him is something the Father has given me and not of my will. Faith. I am convicted, Esther. I believe. I cannot explain much right now. I hope that later I will. If," she said, raising a finger. "If Rabboni permits me to."

"I admit; my faith was shaken with what happened in Capernaum."

Magdalene nodded slowly, still focusing on the fire. "Yet here you are."

"In truth, I am uncertain how or why. It is something out of my own power and understanding. Yes, I am here, believing and following Jesus, believing that He is the Messiah and the Son of Elohim — of my Father in Heaven. And I believe Jesus is this bread of life. I do not know what it is, but will remain here, and I will follow Jesus anywhere."

"I know what it is." Magdalene leaned slightly toward me. "Faith," she said, her sharp eyebrows raised.

Salome called out. "They are coming back!"

Magdalene and I looked up. Jesus was walking toward us, the Twelve behind Him. He walked with purpose, as He always did.

When He reached us, Jesus looked around, His face was golden in the firelight. "If anyone wishes to come after Me, he must deny himself and take up his cross daily and follow Me," Jesus said.

I straightened my shoulders.

"For whoever will save his life, shall lose it. But he that will lose his life for My sake, shall save it." He gazed at the lot of us, arms settled at His sides. "For what is a man advantaged if he gain the whole world and lose himself and cast away himself. For he that will be ashamed of Me and of My words, of him the Son of man will be ashamed when He will come in His majesty and that of His Father and of the holy angels."

I wondered if I really understood His words.

"But I tell you of a truth: There are some standing here that shall not taste death till they see the kingdom of Elohim."

Did He mean that He was ready to establish His everlasting kingdom? But doing that should not end in loss of life. Or in crosses! I thought of the wretched beams that rebels carried on their shoulders to their execution. A terrible burden; a terrible suffering.

Did following the Messiah mean that I must die? Was He not the bread of *life*?

Chapter 27
33rd Year of Our Lord

Then the LORD *said to Moses: Assemble for me seventy of the elders of Israel, whom you know to be elders and authorities among the people, and bring them to the tent of meeting.*

NUMBERS 11:16

The men were in Jerusalem for the Feast of Tabernacles. The *Day of Atonement* behind us, we were in the new year. We women were lodging with Photina in Samaria. The men had left for Judea some weeks ago and would return soon.

I held young Victor's hand as we played in the center of the village. A few younger children, perhaps of 5 or 6 years, skipped around us.

"I am going to climb the tree!" Victor exclaimed, looking at the giant olive tree, thick with twisted knots.

"You will not be able to reach its branches," I told him, looking up at the canopy of soft green leaves. An autumn breeze rustled those leaves and my garments.

"I can if you lift me up!" Victor exclaimed, his eyes pleading.

I looked behind us. Men and women were at work. There were fumes from furnaces and the blacksmith's shop. Older children were on the roofs grinding grain. Men pushed carts down toward the fields. Some women were just back from Jacob's well with water vessels on their heads.

"Please, Esther! Ima would let me if she were here."

His mother was in the house as I watched the children.

"May I climb it, too, Esther?" One child asked.

"I will allow Victor to climb it," I decided. "Because he is old enough."

"Yes!" Victor screeched.

"Hush. We do not want to disturb anyone."

Casting my mantle on the dusty ground I lifted the child by his legs. He squirmed as he reached for a branch.

"You have it?" I grunted beneath his weight. He was heavier than I imagined.

He secured his hold, clinging to it like a leech. He twisted around and I released him.

"I am up!"

My hands were a bit shaky. Should I have allowed him to climb the tree? But then Jesus and I climbed many a tree and many a steep hill when we were younger.

The children cheered as Victor slowly slid his body upward on the branch. "Uh!" Victor started nervously. "E-Esther. I am scared. I am scared. I do not like it up here."

Pushing beyond my sense of panic I reached out and said, "Stay calm, Victor." I craned my head for a look. "You are alright. You will be fine."

And a mother's worst fear occurred.

He fell and I did not catch him.

His scream startled me and the cries of the other children pierced my heart. In horror, I rushed over and saw Victor in twisted agony. I wished I could feel his pain for him.

"*Jesus*," I said to myself. If He were here, He would help Victor.

Some of the women, including Photina, ran to us.

I bent over the boy. "Victor," I gasped. "Your arm." I gently touched his bony shoulder.

"It hurts," he wept. "It hurts!"

"What happened?" Photina cried out.

I looked back at her, my face flaming. "He fell off the tree. I tried to catch him, I did. I think he has broken his arm." Blood trickled down his leg and arm. He was dusty from the fall.

"Victor!" Photina reached for her boy. "I am here!"

My hands raised to my cheeks. What should I do?

"Ima! Ima," Victor sobbed. "Ima." His soft face was covered with messy tears.

"Be not afraid." Magdalene was beside me. She crouched down next to Victor.

"Let them be." I heard Salome's sharp croaking voice. "They need space."

Susanna raced to get bandages.

"We should take him into the house and cleanse him and bind his arm."

"Should we send for a physician?"

Magdalene moved closer to Victor who clutched his broken arm, bent like a twig. Photina held her boy from behind, supporting his back.

Magdalene placed her hand on the boy's head. "In the name of Jesus the Kyrios, Son of Elohim, be healed."

Victor's arm began to wiggle until it was straight and functioning. He looked at his healed arm with amazement.

"It is a miracle!" Photina exclaimed, hugging her son. "A miracle!"

I still felt rigid and tense. I never should have let him climb that tree — but women and children had started dancing in celebration.

"Magdalene! Thank you."

"I have done nothing, Photina," she responded. "It is the power of Jesus. Adonai is at work. The kingdom of Elohim has come near to you." She stood up in one swift motion.

Women flocked to her, but she walked away from them.

"We still need to clean his cuts and bruises," I said in a shaky voice, looking at his more minor wounds.

"No! I am healed!" Victor pushed from his mother's arms, stood up, and raised his perfect arms in the air.

As Victor celebrated, a Samaritan woman cried out, "Jesus has returned! The Master is here!"

I turned. My eyebrows furrowed. When they left for Jerusalem, there were forty disciples, Jesus having gained a few more in Tyre and Sidon.

Now there were at least sixty walking toward us, Jesus at the front of the crowd.

We had a short time to reunite, during which I greeted my husband. I still felt shaken. Lazarus introduced me to some of the new disciples, who I greeted, although I was in a sort of fog, occupied by Victor's fall.

Jesus gathered all of us together, Samaritans and Jews. He stood under the large olive tree in the center of the village as we crowded around Him in a circle.

"The harvest indeed is great, but the laborers are few," He said. "Pray therefore the master of the harvest, that He send laborers into His harvest."

Isaiah. *Adonai will strike from the channel of the river even to the torrent of Egypt, and you shall be gathered together one by one, O children of Israel.*

"Go: Behold I send you as lambs among wolves."

I flinched.

"Carry neither purse nor scrip nor shoes and salute no man by the way. Into whatever house you enter, first say, 'Shalom be to this house.'"

King David sent ten men ahead of him to tell Nabal of his coming. *And you shall say, "Shalom be to my brethren, and to you, and shalom to your house, and shalom to all that you have."*

"And if a son of shalom be there, your shalom shall rest upon him; but if not, it shall return to you. And in the same house, remain, eating and drinking such things as they have, for the laborer is worthy of his hire. Remove not from house to house. And into what city soever you enter, and they receive you, eat such things as are set before you. And heal the sick that are therein and say to them, 'The kingdom of Elohim has come unto you.'"

I looked around for Magdalene, who had said the exact same phrase to Photina and her son. When I found her, I saw the sharp line of her profile gazing at Jesus with avid excitement. It was then I realized that Jesus was speaking to *me* as well as her.

"But into whatever city you enter and they receive you not, going forth into the streets thereof say, 'Even the very dust of your city that cleaves to us, we wipe off against you. Yet know this, that the kingdom of Elohim is at hand.' I say to you; it will be more tolerable at that day for Sodom than for that city."

Jesus expected us to be rejected? Yet those who rejected us would have it worse than the condemned of Sodom and Gomorrah.

"Woe to you Chorazin, woe to you Bethsaida. For if in Tyre and Sidon had been wrought the mighty works that have been wrought in you, they would have done penance long ago, sitting in sackcloth and ashes. But it shall be more tolerable for Tyre and Sidon at the judgment than for you. And you, Capernaum, which is exalted unto Heaven, you shall be thrust down to the netherworld." He used the Greek word for Sheol. The netherworld was the place of the dead.

"He that hears you, hears Me, and he that despises you, despises Me and he that despises Me, despises Him that sent Me."

I put my hand to my chin.

"Are you speaking to all of us, Master?" Lazarus asked.

"Yes. I previously sent the Twelve, but now I send the others."

Ever close to Jesus' side, Peter asked, "Does that mean the Twelve are to go out again?"

Jesus shook His head. "I am sending out the other seventy. The Twelve shall stay with Me."

"Master," Stephen called out. "Where? What cities do you wish us to enter?"

"I am going to Galilee, Phoenicia, Gaulanitis, Decapolis, and Perea. You will go in pairs of two."

"What of the women?" Salome asked, her voice raspy.

"The women are my disciples, too, and shall go in pairs."

Magdalene settled beside me, clearly eager for this journey. "Esther, may I accompany you?"

"Me?" I looked around. Should I not go with my husband?

"You and I shall be paired together." Apparently, she had thought this through. "Joanna and Susanna will go together. And then, Salome and Mary Alphaeus will be a pair."

I was skeptical. "Salome and Mary Alphaeus?" They were the two frailest and oldest women in our group. Physically — not intellectually.

"Mary Alphaeus complements Salome, since Salome has a strong will and Mary Alphaeus has a gracious, kindly manner. And both women know how to get done what must be done. Mary Alphaeus is more than capable of assisting Salome as she walks."

"We are two women, Magdalene," I said. "We cannot go about a road by ourselves."

"Most of the men will head north toward Galilee. They will go even farther north toward Phonicia. We can travel with them and split ways when we are safe to walk from town to town. Others will probably travel east toward Decapolis or south toward Perea.

I sought permission from Lazarus, who obliged, as he was going out with Stephen. I touched my veil and looked down at my sandals. That was all I would be taking with me. These and my motherly mantle.

"You think we are to go to Galilee, then?" I asked Magdalene.

"We will make a place ready for the Master in Sepphoris," she said.

"Sepphoris? That is by Nazareth." I brightened.

Magdalene also beamed. "Then perhaps we will visit Rabboni's brethren."

"That is the town of Joppa." I pointed to the watchtowers at our left for Magdalene's benefit. The other disciples, including Lazarus and Stephen, split off, northeast toward the Sea of Galilee. "Many of our farmers have fields there," I continued.

And many a Sicarii came from Joppa. I thought of Barabbas, Reuben, and Elisha.

Magdalene smiled. "Strange. I went to Nazareth several times as a young girl to visit your family, but I was so wrapped up in my own head that I did not pay attention to any of my surroundings. You are from a beautiful land, Esther."

We passed by grazing cows. "Winter is coming. And this area is so rich with travelers. But yes, I would say it is beautiful." I looked at the terraces of olive groves and fig trees. The golden fields were empty now that the harvest was over.

Men on horses passed us. Ahead, a man on a wooden cart urged a donkey to haul him and his load. Far behind was a slave wearing her bands, a large basket in her hands.

"I have not seen my mother since she left us in Capernaum," I said. "I pray she is well." I bit my lip. "And that she receives us."

"Rabboni says that He has come to set a man against his father and a daughter against her mother. Whoever loves father or mother..."

"...more than Me is not worthy of Me," I finished for her. "I remember that saying very well because I did not understand it. I also do not understand why Jesus speaks more and more of suffering when He insists we are sent out to heal and give life. Did you hear what He told us before the Feast of Tabernacles? When we were rejected by a Samaritan village, Jesus said He must go to Jerusalem and suffer many things. Well, now He is back out of Judea and I have not heard of any elders and chief priests trying to kill Him as He says."

"It must have been an interior suffering. His heart is moved with pity when He recognizes the scribes and Pharisees whose ears are closed to His words." Magdalene's hands swayed as she walked.

"Yet we have seen many an angry Pharisee. Rome, on the other hand, has thankfully not struck in anger. Jesus is shalom."

"Yet He has come, not to bring shalom but the sword," she said.

"Yet He wishes for us to bring shalom to the houses that receive Him!"

"And unrest to those who do not."

"Logically," I interjected, "it is some double-edged sword. If He is to bring shalom, then He must also bring unrest. I was going to say violence, but I am not sure that is what He means."

"It fits well with Adonai in the scriptures," Magdalene said.

"You mean to say that when Adonai gives shalom to Israel, then the nations around them are struck down?"

"Yes. And I think that the people who accept Jesus' word as being from Adonai, those are the ones who will be given shalom. If you reject Adonai, then how can you have shalom? For Adonai *is* shalom."

"I am happy to have someone to talk with about such deep things," I said. "Even if it makes my head turn."

"Mine too. I get dizzy," she agreed. "Yet our Heavenly Father seems keen on us contemplating Him and marveling."

"Thus says Adonai, 'Here is the covenant I will make. Before all our people I will perform marvels never before done in any nation anywhere on earth.'" I sucked in a deep breath. "Now He wants *us* disciples to do these marvelous works?"

"So that all the people among whom you live may see the work of Adonai!" Magdalene continued the passage from the Torah, excitement rising with each syllable.

Two Roman soldiers on their horses rode toward us. I gripped Magdalene's arm. How I hated them as they strutted like peacocks and surveyed their surroundings like prowling lions. It surprised me that they did not leer at us as so many had. Just as they passed, Magdalene pulled my hands from her arm and smiled politely at the two Romans.

I held in my breath. Did a smile such as Magdalene's encourage a man to attack a woman? Or did it simply baffle the Romans that her smile was courageous, serene, and loving?

I sighed in relief after they rode past us as if we were invisible.

"There is Nazareth!" I pointed at the hill above us. We could see the watchtowers, vineyards, terraces, shepherds' caves, and farmers' fields. I looked warily at the farmers plowing their fields, made easy by the rain as of late. Some had begun their barley sowing. "Magdalene, I must admit to you." I unburdened myself. "I do not think I can heal a person the way you healed little Victor. I do not think Adonai has given me that gift. I have never done such a thing. I pray for healing, but I never actually *heal* anyone."

"But you do not heal, Esther. Jesus is the one who heals."

"And I believe it," I said. "But what if...what if I see a person who is lame who could use the healing of Jesus. What if I go to him, say, 'in the name of Jesus, the Messiah, be healed,' and the Father does not heal him? That is what I fear. How will they believe in Jesus? They will think we are false."

"Has Jesus healed you of your affliction?" Magdalene looked at me sharply.

I knew instantly what she was referring to. "No. Not exactly. He has not given me children."

"Do you believe that He can?"

"Yes. He can do whatever He wills. But He has taken this weakness of mine and used it for good. My heart is so much more open. To you, my brethren, and even my enemies. *Samaritans* even." Though not murderous Rome.

"Then there are more wonders coming from your affliction than there would be if you were healed."

"Are there?"

"Only Elohim knows. What I find most important is love."

"Love," I repeated.

"When we pray for the sick, we are not healing because we want to see how many wonders Jesus will perform for us. If we first love them and not the curing of illness or other wonders, then we need not fear the outcome. They must be loved, for they are sheep without a shepherd, as I once was. Rabboni cast the demons from me and I was healed of my affliction. But what truly healed was my heart. I was forgiven and I was loved by Rabboni. The spirits of fear, destruction, and anger dissolved when I approached Him. He replaced those spirits with trust, healing, and joy. So now, I bless the name of Jesus. I bless it, and I cannot wait to share it!" Magdalene spread her hands out and ran over to a farmer. I put my hands to my lips unsure of what to do.

The farmer saw this exuberant woman running to him and left his plow and ox in the field. I walked a little closer, but with great hesitancy.

"Shalom." Magdalene's voice was like music. "Do you know Jesus of Nazareth?"

"Unfortunately."

"He is the Messiah, I tell you. The kingdom is at hand. Jesus is the Son of Elohim."

I gasped as the man slapped Magdalene on her cheek. I ran to her. She stood her ground, shooing me away as the farmer spoke.

"*Woman*. No one talks about Him around here, and we are trying our best to forget Him. You understand these claims will get *Him* killed *and* you? I suggest you leave."

Other farmers stopped their work to gawk.

"Nevertheless," Magdalene calmly said. "Know this, the kingdom of Elohim *has* come near." She straightened her shoulders. "Come, Esther. We will go into the houses in the village."

"Esther!" The man peered at me. "Esther, daughter of James the Zealot?"

I took a short breath. "Yes, Sir."

"Be careful here, Esther. Your cousin is not well-favored."

I took a step back.

"May Elohim reward you for your kind warning," Magdalene said, taking my arm and pulling me away.

"*Kind!*" I said as we walked up the steep hill to the village. "He slapped you on the cheek!"

"If only I had offered my other as well."

I took a breath, trying to calm myself. I did not know if I had ever been as terrified as I was right then. How did they treat Aunt Mary if they so hated her son?

And it was her we saw upon entering the village. By the synagogue.

"Aunt Mary!" I exclaimed, running to her. She held a heavy sack on her shoulder. "I will take this burden from you." I pulled the sack from her.

She smiled, gently touching my arm. "Esther."

My fears started to dissipate from being in her presence.

"The sack you have is not clean, daughter," she told me. "They are bandages and medical instruments that must be washed."

I surprised myself when I did not flinch. "Then I will help you wash them. Are you going to Uncle Clopas' house?"

"Yes, we will wash them in the courtyard."

"Let us go," I decided. I looked up to see Aliza standing in the doorway of her husband's house. Instead of coming out to greet me, she ran back inside. Perhaps to get something before greeting me? We did not get along well as children, but not to the level of never speaking to each other.

I made introductions. "Aunt Mary, this is Magdalene. Another Mary. She is sister to my husband Lazarus."

"Magdalene," Aunt Mary said warmly. "I remember you, my child."

Magdalene slowly approached Aunt Mary, her lips slightly parted. Instead of saying anything, she threw herself onto the ground, then looked up, tears in her eyes. "The Mother of the Kyrios. You are most blessed, dear lady."

A child leading a goat by a rope stopped to stare.

"Get up, my daughter," Aunt Mary said, gently tapping Magdalene's head. "Rise." Magdalene did so. Aunt Mary took her arm. "Will you lead the way, Esther?"

I nodded and began up the hill, through the narrow street toward home. I saw women on their roofs staring down at us, their faces unwelcoming. When a man with an ax swung over his shoulder peered at me, I wondered if he wished to murder me. I walked quickly, glancing behind me a few times to ensure Aunt Mary and Magdalene followed, already deep in whispered discussion.

I entered the familiar small courtyard, breathing in the scent of home. Aunt Miriam was there, looking over the outdoor oven.

"Esther! Esther! Welcome!"

My cousins' wives and children came out to see us as well.

Aunt Miriam reached me with ease, her feet now assets as opposed to obstacles. I kissed her cheek. "Shalom."

She looked at the sack over my shoulder. "You have the remnants, then. Come, I have begun a fire." She took me to the corner of the court.

"Where are these from?" I plopped the sack on the floor.

"Mary has been tending to a woman with a hemorrhage down the way. Messy work."

"The poor woman," I said.

"Her or Mary?" Aunt Miriam chuckled. "Set it down here, now."

I picked the sack up again and set it down where she'd asked. "Where is Ima?"

Aunt Miriam frowned. "She no longer lives with us, Esther."

"No longer..."

"She is now with Aliza and her family down the street."

"Did Clopas throw her out?"

"No. Clopas bid her to stay, but she does not want to be associated with us. Rather like the rest of Nazareth."

I frowned, wondering if Ima would even come to greet me. Perhaps Aliza was running into the house to tell her I was here and that she should stay put.

"Your brothers and uncle are in Sepphoris right now," she said.

"Magdalene and I cannot stay long. Since we are also rejected here, we are going to Sepphoris."

"Magdalene?" Aunt Miriam looked at the woman dressed in a rose tunic and tan-brown veil. "*The* Magdalene?"

"Yes," I said, hoping Aunt Miriam would not embarrass my friend or herself.

"What brings you here? Two women traveling alone? Is Lazarus here as well?"

"Jesus has sent us on mission to all the towns He will visit."

"My Jesus is coming here?" Aunt Miriam said, putting a hand to her chest.

"I...I do not think so, Aunt. He has already been rejected."

"But not by us!" she exclaimed. "Or by all of us," she added. "We are a divided household."

"Yet the kingdom of Elohim has come near to you." I took her hand and patted it.

Aunt Miriam rolled up her sleeves. "Now, now. We have much to discuss. Did you bring anything with you, Esther?"

"No." I smiled knowingly. "Jesus told us to take nothing for our journey."

"Are you hungry?"

"Very."

"Then let us eat." She slapped her hands together. "We will wash the bandages later." She called out to a child to help her and hurried into the stable with one of her grandchildren, probably going to the storage caves. We ritually purified our hands.

Soon we women were seated in the traklin. Aunt Mary was weaving another of her dark blue mantles while Aunt Miriam expertly mended a tunic. Magdalene and I devoured our food, enjoying the rare treat of a leftover fattened sheep with some wheat bread, figs, and dates.

"Is life…is it hard here?" I asked Aunt Mary. "To have your son so famous? Does anyone visit you just to see the mother of the Kyrios?"

"I do not get many visitors," she replied. "Tell me, how is my son?"

Of course, I had forgotten that was what would be on a mother's mind. "Your son is…" Confusing? Melancholic? Not well-loved? Controversial? Hard to follow? Busy?

"Your son is tired," Magdalene said for me. "He has few places to lay His head. But I think He is eager to return to Galilee. Jerusalem is a tense place for any person, let alone a Jewish rabbi with disciples. A Jewish rabbi who is Kyrios," she added.

"I plan to see Him in the early spring," Aunt Mary said. "For Passover, as usual. He invited me to stay with you in Jerusalem."

"A wondrous idea!" I said. "Jesus has gained many more disciples, and they will all wish to meet you."

"I plan to see Him then as well," Aunt Miriam stated proudly. She had poked her finger with her needle, but because her skin was so calloused, it did not affect her.

"You look troubled, Esther." Aunt Mary reached out a hand for mine and rested her other on the loom.

I wondered how much I should tell her. I did not want to worry Jesus' mother. But it seemed I was the one who was worried and not her. "The children of Israel are still suffering," I held her soft but calloused hand. "Even with the Messiah among us. I just…I am eager for it to all end."

Magdalene turned toward me sharply. "The end in which we are raised up?"

"Yes," I said, releasing Aunt Mary's hand so I could return to my meal. "I am trying to be content, but in truth, I am ready for the kingdom to be *here*, and not simply near. I am experiencing rejection. *You* are experiencing rejection and…and disdain. Jesus is receiving it. I cannot wait for this pain to end and for Jesus to be crowned Prince of Shalom. Everlasting shalom."

"Are you willing to offer yourselves to Elohim and bear all the sufferings He wills to send you, as an act of reparation for the conversion of sinners?" Aunt Mary said.

I paused from placing a piece of salted lamb in my mouth.

"Yes!" Magdalene exclaimed.

I did not say anything.

"Then you are going to have much to suffer," Aunt Mary told her. "But the grace of Elohim will be your comfort."

"If a mother sees her son reaching for a scorpion, will she not pull her son away from the scorpion?" I asked quickly, eyebrows furrowed as I looked at Aunt Mary. As if she were swimming at sea, she was surrounded by the blue of her mantle and the blue of the mantle she worked on.

"Naturally," Aunt Mary said. "But if her son is reaching for a scorpion, to protect the other children the scorpion is about to attack, what will she do?"

"She will crush the scorpion herself."

"And if the son is a good, grown man, what will the mother then do?"

I thought for a moment. That was not the point I was trying to make. "She will let her son crush the scorpion for the other children," I finally said.

Aunt Mary's sweet face was strong and composed. "Yes," she said. "The mother will."

Chapter 28

*The counsel of the L*ORD *belongs to those who fear him;*
and his covenant instructs them.

PSALMS 25:14

Our mission in Galilee went surprisingly well. Though Magdalene and I only lodged in Nazareth for one night, we were pleased. Uncle Clopas and most of my cousins were pleased to see us as well, but my mother and sister never approached.

Before we set off, Aunt Mary gave Magdalene one of her blue mantles, for which Magdalene was grateful. Magdalene and I then left for the giant city of Sepphoris. It was strange. Although I lived by it all my life and my brethren traveled there nearly every day, I had never been there myself.

There was a rich variety of peoples, religions, trades, and tongues, which produced a variety of reactions to our message. It was mostly a Jewish city, but I thought most of them were only Jewish by name.

Magdalene and I were well-received by the women we met. One was sister to our own disciple, Joanna. Prostitutes came to her door to see us and we had a gathering in which we told them what Jesus had done for us. I let Magdalene do all of the healing. I prayed beside her each time.

I discovered that the women were particularly interested in *my* story. Especially on finding that Jesus was my cousin. I told them story upon story about Him, Nazareth, Aunt Mary, and Uncle Joseph. They were in wonder when I spoke of my conversion in the synagogue at Nazareth. They rejoiced with me when I told them my husband and I chose to leave Bethany and follow Jesus as His disciples.

And we listened to *their* stories. One girl, Kezia, was a prostitute. Rebecca was a Jewish adulterer like Magdalene. Another, Damaris, was a Greek slave to Herod Antipas. Mahalah was a Jew, yet her brother, a good standing Pharisee, abused her sexually when she was a young girl.

Each woman had found freedom and forgiveness in our message and witness. Through us, they encountered Jesus. I prayed with them and spoke kind words to them, as a mother would to her child.

My own, dear children.

"I did not want to leave Sepphoris," I told Magdalene as we approached Bethany with Jesus and His disciples. I felt that they needed me! Was a mother to leave her children? "The women I met there are desperate for love and attention, and I could only care so much for them. I am only one person."

"Who they need is Jesus," Magdalene told me as we walked with a cluster of disciples. "You prepared the way for Him to come there, and He came."

Jesus had finished His latest rounds from Galilee to Phoenicia, to the Decapolis, to Perea, and so forth where the seventy prepared a place for Him. Now that this missionary journey was over, Jesus wanted to visit Bethany.

We passed a row of smaller houses and turned toward the hilly path that led to Martha's manor house.

Magdalene said she was heading for the market.

"Now? We are about to see your sisters."

"And I think it wise that I go to market in Jerusalem. Perhaps Judas needs help buying supplies."

"You have not seen Martha and Mary since your conversion, Magdalene. They will forgive you as Lazarus forgave you."

"Yes, Lazarus forgave me, and they will in time. But I am going to market now. I am sure I will be with you at the house by nightfall. Maybe Joanna will come with me." She stepped back into the crowd of disciples and disappeared from my sight.

"Esther," Lazarus said. "Come. Let us run ahead! I want to be the first to see Martha and Mary. I did not even see them when I was last in Judea for the Feast of Tabernacles."

"Run like children?" I looked up at him.

"Yes, for the kingdom of Heaven belongs to such as these."

I smiled at that. Together, we took the familiar path between two hills, running ahead of the disciples. We passed through several olive groves and down a dirt path, until the large manor house, three stories high, loomed.

As we neared the double doors, Mary breezed out of the house like the wind on the sea.

She beamed. Her thin eyebrows were raised in exclamation.

"Mary!" Lazarus engulfed his sister in an embrace.

"Oh Lazarus! I have missed you! Ah, and Esther! Welcome, welcome!" Mary embraced me.

"Mary, my sister," I said, moving away from her embrace. "Where is Martha?"

"In the house," Mary said. "She is worried. I do not see why. The Kyrios has visited us on several occasions."

"But is this the first time you have had Jesus and all eighty-two of His disciples?"

"Yes," she admitted, leaning her head to the side.

"And now we *know* Jesus is *Kyrios*. Which changes everything!"

Mary waved a nonchalant hand. "Where is the Kyrios, then?"

"He and the others are right behind us. Lazarus and I were just so excited to see you — "

"I see them!" Mary called. I followed her gaze to the disciples walking up the path.

"Martha!" Mary called over her shoulder.

"I am *busy*," Martha yelled.

"Martha, stop hiding from us," Lazarus teased. He hurried inside. "Seeing you has become a rare occasion, Martha!" he called.

I followed him. As I entered the courtyard, the sun was shining above us and casting shadows. Potted plants lined the court — bay laurel shrubs, roundly trimmed and little bursts of feathery juniper.

I looked around for my sister-in-law.

"Found her," Lazarus shouted.

"Lazarus, be careful!" Martha scolded. He was lifting Martha off of her feet in a giant embrace.

"Really, is that the way to greet your only brother?" He set his squiggling sister down.

"I *have* missed you, Lazarus." She gave him a serious look and then a swift embrace. "I am just filled with anxiety! There is so much to do, and I am not even close to being prepared. Thank goodness the Kyrios is not here yet. Perhaps you can help me. Where is Esther?"

"Here." I rushed up to her and laughed as I give her a tight embrace. "Martha, it is good to see you!"

"I have missed you both! Oh, and welcome. When do you suppose the Kyrios will arrive? By sundown? We have much to do!"

I bit my lip as Lazarus and I exchanged glances.

"The Master has already arrived," Lazarus murmured.

Martha's eyes widened. For a moment, she was speechless. "Where is Mary? I need her assistance! I cannot count on Uncle Simon to make a meal! Lazarus, call the servants. Tell them to wash our guests' feet!" Martha ran out to the courtyard.

If this set her off, what would happen when she saw Magdalene's return from market?

I followed her. "Martha, fear not. Jesus and His disciples are a loving bunch and easily pleased. We are used to sleeping under the stars and eating simply bread and cheese. Whatever you have planned will be sufficient."

"But Jesus is Kyrios! This is not a time to grow lax." She entered the workroom, directly across from the kitchen.

"All shall be well, Martha."

Martha replied with a deep sigh.

"Do you not have more servants?" I was about to peer into the servant quarters.

"Only two remain. I chose to spend my money on the poor instead. I could use ten servants, though, for a night like tonight. You must understand! Even Hezekiah is coming!"

"Your husband?" I leaned toward her in shock.

"No, the late Hezekiah King of Judah! Of course, my husband!"

"Tell me what to do, and I will help."

She didn't hesitate. "Move all the extra cushions and mats into the banquet room." Martha left with the rustle of her tunic.

"Lazarus," she commanded from the courtyard, as I set to work. "Make sure everyone is comfortable! And tell Mary she needs to actually *help* when the Kyrios visits." I shook my head. She was a volcano waiting to explode. Perhaps she already had.

When Jesus and the other disciples arrived I moved into the courtyard with a bundle of green-toned cushions in my arms.

Susanna asked if my sisters-in-law could use assistance.

"Probably," I responded. "Come, follow me." I led her into the banquet hall and began arranging the cushions. She followed my example.

"Which one is the older sister?"

"Martha is older than Mary. Lazarus, Martha, Mary, and then Magdalene. That is the order. All relatively close in age."

"I am jealous of you, sometimes. All of you. To have known the Kyrios when He was a child. To grow up with Him as His friends!" She laughed at the thought.

My eyes snapped to hers. "I am surprised you are even capable of jealousy."

She laughed. "I have no ill will or envy toward you. I simply want to know the Kyrios more fully."

I smiled at the woman's tender heart.

Like a bee flying from flower to flower, Martha moved from one spot to another. Her voice carried as she assigned me, Lazarus, servants, and of course, Mary, with different tasks.

Susanna and I were in the kitchen, where she put us to work preparing supper. I arranged dates, figs, raisins, and other dried fruit on a platter, all the while wondering when and if Magdalene would arrive with Judas and Joanna.

Not only Magdalene but when would Hezekiah arrive? Since Lazarus gave his signet ring to Martha, Hezekiah hardly entered this home. If anyone could crack a Pharisee's stone heart, it was Jesus. I simply hoped that this Pharisee was not intending to trap or trick Jesus as many had attempted before. It was not that Jesus' preaching was incorrect. It was that Jesus stressed His coming for the poor — not the wealthy and learned.

Disciples filled the courtyard. Fruit platter in hand, I passed by on my way to the banquet hall, but Mary Alphaeus, the dear, frail lady, took the platter from me.

Back in the kitchen, Martha was so involved in her work she did not notice I had left. She prepared a bowl of olives and baked onions as a dip for the bread. Beside it she set olive oil flavored with rosemary and a bowl of olive relish, complete with coriander seeds, mint, rosemary, rue leaves, and red wine vinegar.

"Where is she now?" Martha muttered under her breath.

I glanced at her as I grabbed the olive dips to bring out for supper. I was unsure if she was speaking to me or not.

"She is getting careless and lazy," she continued. "*Selfish*. Very *selfish* of her."

Eager to get away from her complaints, I returned to the banquet hall where more people were gathering. The normal stench of sweat was in the air, but also the delightful fresh smell of bread, fruit, and eggs, poached fish, fava bean salad, and meatballs.

Jesus was seated on a large cushion at table, His legs crossed, His hands settled in His lap as He looked at Mary on the opposite side of the table. She smiled up at Him and listened intensely.

I placed the olive dips on the table. Lazarus sat nearby and shared a smile with me.

Next to Lazarus was Hezekiah. I hid my surprise at his appearance in the house. His beard and mustache were longer and grayer than I remembered and covered his lips. It appeared he did not say a word to anyone but observed with eyes hard as rocks.

"Kyrios," I heard Martha say behind me. I turned around to see her standing with one hand on her hip and the other holding her honeyed yogurt. "Have you no care that my sister has left me alone to serve? Speak to her that she may help me."

Mary looked at her hands as Jesus said, "Martha, Martha, you are anxious and troubled about many things." He tilted his head as He looked at Martha. "But one thing is necessary. Mary has chosen the best part which will not be taken away from her."

I was embarrassed for Martha's sake. She stood with her mouth agape and then quickly turned away, leaving the mass of people. I followed her back to the kitchen where she hovered over loaves of bread. Her shoulders were hunched. I slowly approached her and quietly stood by her side, unsure of what to say.

"He is right, after all." Martha sighed, not looking at me. "I am...I am a foolish woman...whenever I am nervous about something, my thoughts feel jumbled, and I say all sorts of things...things I do not really mean." She rubbed her nose with her sleeve. "He must think me a terrible sinner. He must despise me."

"*Martha*." I put an arm around her shoulder. "You know Jesus better than that. He does not despise you, He loves you." I squeezed her shoulder. "Trust me, that He has met far worse people," I added. "I have an idea. Go sit with Mary and Him, and I will finish up with the preparations."

"I just..." Martha put up a hand. "I just want to be alone for a moment!" I could tell she was holding in tears.

"I will bring the loaves out and then all the supper preparations will be finished. You go take the time you need while I finish serving."

Martha turned her back to me and her shoulders trembled, "If you are sure..."

"I am certain. I used to live here, remember? And do not forget, there are other women helping us."

I was not sure where Martha went. Perhaps to her chambers. But by the end of supper she appeared, and cautiously sat next to Mary at Jesus' feet.

Jesus smiled warmly at her and reached over the table for her hand, which she tentatively gave to Jesus. And smiled.

I sighed in relief.

Now we just needed to pray all worked well when Magdalene arrived.

It was late evening and most of the disciples were preparing for bed. Martha was still happily sitting at the feet of Jesus. It was now Mary who helped clean up from supper.

I noticed Lazarus pacing back and forth, past the main door. I went out into the courtyard, now filled with the shadows of night.

"Magdalene is probably stalling," I told him, knowing the source of his worry.

"They should be back by now. How long does it take to go to market?" He slapped his hands on his thighs.

"Fear not, beloved. I heard that Judas and Joanna went with her. I am sure they are fine."

"And Martha and Mary are not expecting them," he continued. "In their minds, all of the disciples are safe in our home. Perhaps we should have told them that Magdalene was among us."

"Perhaps," I said, leaning against the doorframe. "But what if they became upset and angry?"

"Either way. They might be upset and angry because we did not tell them."

Magdalene did not want to overwhelm them with such a crowd *in addition* to the prodigal daughter's return. Which Lazarus knew but he said he would go looking for them if they did not arrive by the time the moon was a quarter-rise.

"Pardon me," Mary said from behind me. I moved from the doorway. Mary walked toward the entrance.

"Where are *you* going?" Lazarus asked, putting a flustered hand to his wavy hair. He was far too concerned with the matters of us women.

"I just need to shake out the tablecloth." She looked at the bundle in her arms, opened the wooden door, and disappeared into the darkness.

Lazarus sighed. I heard a squeal of excitement from outside.

"Martha! Come quickly!" Mary shouted.

Martha ran to the courtyard, passing Lazarus and myself, and bolted out the door. Laughs, squeals, and cries mixed together in a joyous melody.

I smiled at Lazarus. "Magdalene has arrived."

"Thanks be to Adonai!" he said, heading toward the open door as Judas and Joanna walked in, bundles of supplies in their arms.

"Praise be to Elohim, they have rejoiced at her return," Joanna said, adjusting her bundle at her hip.

"Magdalene was immensely anxious," Judas said.

"As were all of us." I gave a relieved laugh.

I peeked outside the double doors. A smile flared on my face at the touching scene of three sisters in a joyous embrace, the stars and moon as their lanterns.

Mary looked up with a tear-stained face. "Lazarus! Come." She extended her hand and Lazarus joined his sisters, engulfing them in a large embrace. The siblings were together for the first time in almost twenty years.

"You as well, Esther." Martha motioned for me to come, and pulled me into their affectionate grasp. My laughter joined theirs.

This was my true family.

The realization pierced me. Here, with the disciples of Jesus — they were my family. People from my hometown had rejected us; my mother disapproved of us; yet here I was with a loving family under our heavenly Father.

Once we finished with the joyous embraces and chatter, we went inside. Martha linked arms with Magdalene.

"Come on," Martha said, leading her through the courtyard, Lazarus behind them.

"We were anxious about Magdalene's arrival," I told Mary. "Lazarus and I worried you might be angry we did not tell you she was a disciple."

"Perhaps I would have been," Mary mused. "But the Kyrios spoke to both Martha and me. It was His words that led us to open our hearts to forgiveness. We were so eager for Magdalene to arrive. I could barely keep in the excitement!"

My shoulders sagged in relief. "Blessed be our Father. This reunion reminds me of the parable of the prodigal son."

"The who?"

"I will need to tell you the story later." I patted her arm. "Jesus told the parable a while ago."

"And you must tell me more parables and stories! We only hear so much about Jesus' teachings, and some of the rumors we cannot trust." Mary looked ahead of her, likely for Magdalene.

"Later. Go talk with Magdalene," I said. "You deserve to make up for lost time."

Mary smiled thanks and hurried across the courtyard to the banquet hall.

I thought of the hospice and those suffering so near to me. I had still not set foot in the building. Yet Jesus seemed to be beckoning me to take a step further than being a mother to my relatives or my husband's relatives. I still had not set foot in Martha's hospice. Who was there? Was I to be mother-like to the sick and diseased? The perpetually unclean? The physically repulsive?

I went out a back door and down the moonlit path toward the hospice and family sepulcher, as if I were being pulled.

Laughter was in the air as I stood in the hospice's open doorway to survey a comely scene of mats, blankets, pillows, and cushions for supreme rest. The sick and young rested or paid attention to someone.

"Esther," Jesus exclaimed, His eyes lighting up. "Come." Several children in ragged tunics sat around Him. "You are just in time. Listen, children, Esther and I are going to tell you a story."

Heat rushed to my cheeks. A couple of women and an old man sat by the back wall, gazing lovingly at the children sitting next to Jesus. "You will tell them a parable?"

"No. This will be a true story," Jesus said. "Come sit, my friend. Children, introduce yourselves."

"Shalom, my name is Zattu."

"And I am Pilha."

"Harim."

"I am Tamar!"

I bent toward Jesus. "Kyrios, I am not worthy," I said to Him. This would have been acceptable if He was just my childhood friend from Nazareth. But now He was the Son of Elohim; my Messiah and Kyrios.

"Dear one, sit with Me."

I blinked several times, then did as He asked, crossing my legs beneath me.

"It is better that two should be together, than one," Jesus said, quoting Ecclesiastes. "They have the advantage of their society. If one fall he shall be supported by the other."

I pulled my blue mantle tight around me. As a mother, this hospice was my place. I looked at the poor and sick children, finding compassion for them. They looked so eager and hungry. Hungry for love. I looked at Jesus expectantly. He had to begin this. I did not know the story He wished to tell.

A faint smile touched His lips as He looked at the children. His burnished brown hair had a red tint in the dim lamplight. "Tonight," Jesus said, "Esther and I will give you a combination of stories. They will merge into one lesson."

Jesus looked at me, as if for permission to continue. I nodded my head at our audience, feigning confidence.

"Esther and I were five years old when we first met," Jesus said. "We are cousins. My family lived in Egypt for a time, until we returned to our hometown, Nazareth, where Esther and the rest of our brethren lived. We were good friends, were we not, Esther?"

Heat crept to my face. "Yes," I rasped and cleared my throat. "I do not even remember the first day we met. Only that Jesus was always there; always dear to me."

"Nazareth is a very small village. We had a spring, shepherds, houses, a synagogue, fields, and terraces. Tell them what we would do Esther." Jesus looked at me expectantly. "As children."

"During work time," I found myself saying, "we always waved enthusiastically at each other when we passed." I demonstrated, rapidly waving my own hand in the air. "Nazareth is so small, though, that if I stood on the roof of my uncle's home, and Jesus was on the other end of the village by the synagogue, we could see each other clearly. We would wave and jump and sometimes try shouting at each other from the distance. That is, until our mothers told us to stop making so much noise."

"Along with the other children, we enjoyed running around in the dark, when we were permitted." Jesus folded His hands pleasantly in His lap. "We had a joyful time, frightening each other as we crept between the houses."

"Sometimes, we would go visit the shepherds in their caves," I said, my shoulders lowering as I began to relax. "Of all the animals, sheep are Jesus' favorite. Once, a shepherd lost one of his sheep, and we went searching for it. Jesus was the one who rescued the little lamb."

Jesus and I exchanged glances again. His warm eyes made my heart melt and filled me with awe.

"Esther had quite an arm when it came to splashing" Jesus continued. "She would flick water at Me when she was supposed to be doing laundry."

I laughed. "Jesus always had ridiculously messy hair."

He let out a light-hearted grunt.

"He did!" I said. "It is much tamer now, but it used to always be in disarray, spiking in all directions."

"How old would you say I was, when My hair started to flatten?"

I tapped a finger to my chin. "I would say...fourteen. Perhaps fifteen. Your frizz is still there..." I looked at His hair, down to his shoulders now, with fluffs and waves.

"We had a joyous time visiting friends and family. We would travel to Bethany for the pilgrim feasts. As we walked amidst our caravan, Esther and I would try counting the number of birds we saw."

"Ah, yes. The birds." I leaned forward. "Jesus and I always enjoyed birds."

"We would try singing with them, too," Jesus said. "But I think the birds had much better voices." The children laughed at that, as well as the adults.

311

I too laughed freely, surprised at how simply the words kept coming. "We once tried counting the stars, as Adonai told Abraham he would have so many descendants. As you can imagine, we were unable."

"Once Esther was married to my good friend, Lazarus," Jesus said, "we were saddened to part from each other. She left Nazareth to live with her husband here in Bethany."

"We missed each other greatly," I said. "But Jesus told me that whenever I prayed to Adonai, He too, would be there with me." Jesus and I exchanged smiles, my heart very warm.

"And I was. Many years later, I started my ministry."

"When He became famous," I added light-heartedly.

Jesus gave a sarcastic shake of the head. "I asked Esther and her husband to follow Me as My disciples."

"We said, 'Yes.'" I said. "Eventually."

"And we are still good friends."

The two of us were silent for a moment. I felt loved by Jesus.

Unsure if I should or not, I finally spoke. "Our friendship seemed to change, at least to me. He was still the same Jesus...but He is a teacher. A rabbi. My master! He was...He is the Messiah. The Son of Elohim!" I blew out a breath. "You must imagine how embarrassing it is to think — I *teased* the Messiah! I splashed Him with water and sometimes even *scolded* Him as a child. I acted the way I would act around any friend. Not the way I would act around *the Kyrios.*

"*That,*" Jesus said, "is where the lesson from our multitude of stories comes in."

I slanted my head.

"I want Esther to act the way she would act around any friend, because I *am* her friend." Jesus' brown eyes met mine. "You are My friends if you do what I command you. I call you friends. Whoever has seen Me has seen the Father."

My heart beat fast at that amazing glint in His eye. The sincerity of His expression. He put it so simply for the children; that He was one with Adonai. It was curious that I was invited to be a daughter of the Father, sister to Jesus, and mother to the children.

"As the Father loves Me," Jesus said. "So I also love you. Remain in My love."

Love. As Magdalene said when the seventy of us were sent out. Love.

After a while, Jesus decided that it was time for the children to go to bed. I helped tuck them under blankets of wool. Most of them had no mother or father. I kissed each on the cheek — even the dirty cheeks.

"I am glad Martha and Mary are here to be mothers to these children. And that I came tonight." I walked toward Him.

"You, a mother." The lamplight behind Him was like a crown around His head.

"Your mother has taught me this."

Jesus smiled. His beard had gotten longer. "Blessed among women. Do you understand the story we told tonight, Esther?"

"Yes. That you are my friend. Still. Even as Elohim's Son."

"I am friend and I am Father. Believe Me that I am in the Father and the Father is in Me."

I continued to look at Him. All these months I had traveled with Him, I was focused on being a spiritual mother.

"There is no mother without the Father, Esther. As My Father in Heaven loves all His children, so too a mother loves all children of the Father."

"So, since all people are children of the Father, then you are asking me to even love my worst enemies," I said, my chest tightening. "Jesus…I do not know if I understand Your free forgiveness and selfless love."

"I have much more to tell you and show you, but you cannot bear it now."

"Will I bear it later?" I asked.

"You will."

Chapter 29

Do not envy the violent and choose none of their ways...

PROVERBS 3:31

The next morning, I was outside with Jesus, Lazarus, Mary, and Magdalene, walking in the olive groves. Most of the disciples were inside, eating breakfast and preparing for today's short walk from Bethany to Jerusalem.

"Master," we heard Martha faintly call.

The olive trees lined up neatly across the hills. We walked between the trees, on dark, tilled soil which massaged the soles of our bare feet.

"Master," Martha repeated, hiking toward us. "There are men who have arrived at the house and are asking for you. They are...they are Zealots, I believe. Sicarii," she said.

Mary gasped. I had forgotten Mary did not know of her father's secret dealings with rebels.

"Sicarii!" Lazarus' voice rattled. "I told them not to return to my property!"

Martha gave Mary a weary glance, then looked pointedly at Lazarus. "It is my property now, brother." She returned her focus to Jesus. "Kyrios, should I send them away?"

"No," Jesus said calmly. He took Mary's hand and patted it. "I will see them. Will you lead me, Martha?"

Martha's head jerked in agreement. The two of them walked away. I could see the red-tiled tip of the house striking out from above the soft green olive trees.

"Well, I have no doubt what they will be wanting." Lazarus slouched his shoulders like a little boy.

"Which is?" Mary started nervously.

"To join forces with Jesus and bring about the kingdom of Heaven," Lazarus said through gritted teeth.

"This cannot be. The kingdom of Heaven brings shalom," Magdalene reasoned, rolling her shoulders backward. She stood tall — almost at Lazarus' height.

"We can trust Jesus to deal with them civilly," I said as we made our way back to the house.

Upon entering the courtyard, we saw Jesus and the Twelve standing in front of a group of a dozen or so foreign men. I recognized one of the men immediately.

"Barabbas," Lazarus growled. The Sicarii who was a partner with my late father-in-law.

"You are a passive man, then," Barabbas said loudly as he looked daringly at Jesus.

Lazarus was quick to step forward. "I will not have you disrespect my honored guest in my own home."

"*Your* home?" Barabbas muttered. "Does not your little sister now own the premises? What a demeaning action for yourself *Lazarus* of Bethany."

"As it is my home," Martha said, stepping forward, ever brave. "I ask that you leave. The Kyrios has clearly stated that He wants no involvement with your weapons and violence."

Lazarus turned to me in a swift motion and whispered in my ear. "When I handed my inheritance to Martha, she got rid of all the guards so she could focus on the hospice! Except for one male servant who can hardly be considered a bodyguard," he hissed between his clenched teeth. He lowered his voice even more. "These men could take over the house as easy as the Babylonians took over Jerusalem!"

I pulled at the ends of my veil.

Jesus spoke loud and clearly. "From the days of John the Baptist until now the kingdom of Heaven suffers violence, and the violent bare it away. It shall continue this way. So also will the Son of Man suffer at their hands." He stepped closer to the dozen men.

"Barabbas, to you, I say, love your enemies," Jesus said. "And pray for them that persecute and calumniate you, that you may be the children of your Father in Heaven, who makes His sun to rise upon the good, and bad, and rain upon the just and the unjust."

Many of the Sicarii looked down or shook their heads. They all wore wide cloaks, and I knew that their curved daggers were hidden beneath their garments.

Barabbas shook his head. "You are just another false prophet. And a cowardly one," Barabbas rubbed his chin on his shoulder.

"You have what you came for," Martha said boldly, her spine straight. "You have heard the Kyrios' answer. You may now leave in shalom."

"And take these dates stuffed with honey, dears!" Mary Alphaeus eagerly ran toward the group of men, offering them a basket of the fine food. Her incredible kindness was nearly comical.

"Sweet," Barabbas said mockingly, grasping the basket from old Mary Alphaeus. "Dear woman. Another mistress of this *feathered* house built on a rainbow, eh?" Barabbas teased, looking back at his own followers.

I put an arm around Mary Alphaeus. Lazarus was fuming with anger and obviously trying not to burst.

Barabbas turned toward him. "You are nothing like your father, you *pig*!"

"Pig! Pig!" my brother Simon yelled stepping forward, looking like he would punch Barabbas. "It is *you* who are the swine. And we will not cast our pearls before swine like you." Jesus put a hand to Simon's chest.

"Shalom! Shalom!" Magdalene shouted.

"And we heard you travel with prostitutes," one of the Sicarii yelled, pointing at Magdalene.

"*Sha-lom*," Magdalene fiercely repeated.

"You think that I have come to give shalom on earth?" Jesus stepped between His disciples and the Sicarii. "I tell you, no; but separation. For there shall be from henceforth five in one house divided, three against two, and two against three. The father will be divided against the son and the son against his father. The mother against the daughter and the daughter against the mother. The mother-in-law against her daughter-in-law and the daughter-in-law against her mother-in-law."

Ima.

Jesus had said such things before.

"We do not need a pathetic bunch of lambs like yourselves," Barabbas decided. "We will select our own leader who will not squirm at the sight of blood. But these pearls you speak of..." he continued. "It would be wise of you to keep your purse close to your body." He tapped a finger to his black-bearded chin then clutched the hilt of his dagger. "Or even...your body close to a guard."

"I will stay here," Lazarus decided later that morning. "That is my only option, Jesus. Tell me You agree! Barabbas is threatening us! I am not leaving my sisters here with these dagger men running rampant in Judea." He paced back and forth, arms over his chest.

"You will stay here," Jesus agreed. We looked at Him in surprise. "Esther, you will stay with your husband."

"But Jesus! Master..." I started.

"Esther, what king, about to make war against another king, does not first sit down and think whether he be able with ten thousand to meet him that with twenty thousand comes against him? Or else, while the other is yet afar off, sending an embassy, he desires conditions of peace. So likewise every one of you that does not renounce all that he possesses cannot be my disciple."

I straightened. I thought I already was a disciple. Was there still more I did not know?

Could my renouncing Jesus' command keep me from being a true disciple?

"And me, Rabboni?" Magdalene looked head on at Jesus.

"You will continue travels with Me and the Twelve," Jesus decided.

Envy pinched my heart, but I remained obedient.

"So now, you come back to rule the house," Hezekiah shouted at Lazarus, marching down the stairs toward us. His black tallit was thick upon his head. He was taller even than Lazarus. "First, you give the ring to my woman and run off after a lunatic and now you think you can just come back?"

"I know you do not want me back in this house," Lazarus said darkly.

"I no longer live here!" Hezekiah shouted back.

"Hezekiah, please!" Martha pleaded, grasping her husband's arm.

Hezekiah shoved her away. "Step away from me *woman! Woman. Woman!*"

"Listen here, Hezekiah," Lazarus said. "Martha had every right to take my place, especially since you were living in Jerusalem."

"I would have lived here if I were master of the house. But I will not be controlled by my wife!"

"You are — " Martha started.

"Silence, Martha," Lazarus ordered his sister.

To Hezekiah, Lazarus said, "Yet you come to see Jesus when your wife hosts Him in her home. There is something that beckons you here. Is it the hope and promise that Jesus brings as our Messiah — "

"The Messiah would not insult the leaders of Israel! *I* am a Pharisee. And this Jesus would rather kiss a leper on the cheek than cordially speak to me."

Martha pulled me close. "He is going to report everything he sees and hears to the chief priests. I am certain," she whispered.

"Hezekiah, my brother," Lazarus started, stepping toward his cousin. "As I return here, I...I humbly ask for your forgiveness and acceptance." Lazarus slowly fell to his knees. He gazed upward at the fuming Pharisee.

I held in a gasp at the humble act, for Lazarus was a prideful man. Yet the kingdom of Heaven belonged to those who are like children.

"I mean you no harm and I ask that there be shalom between us," Lazarus continued. "May we live together as we once did. Your father Simon is healed from his leprosy, and Magdalene has repented. This should be a time of our rejoicing — not fighting for power."

Hezekiah crossed his arms and looked down at Lazarus. "It is a simple thing for you to say, but *my wife* is the one who holds all the power. You have humiliated me."

"Hezekiah — "

"No!" Hezekiah held up a hand. "I will hear no more from you. I am going back to the Jerusalem house!"

Lazarus and I returned to his old bedchamber that night.

"I think Hezekiah harbors hate for Jesus just because he harbors hate for you," I suggested as I crawled into bed, into sweet softness and luxury I had almost forgotten existed since following Jesus.

"He is like most of the Pharisees," Lazarus replied, sitting down on the mattress with a *thump*. "Many Jews harbor hate for Jesus."

"Rumor has it, the chief priests are plotting to kill Jesus."

"They have been plotting for a couple of years now." Lazarus fell back onto the bed with a groan.

"And our Jesus remains unharmed." I turned to Lazarus. There had been few moments alone as traveling disciples. "The priests have no power to carry out such a task."

"Anyone can throw a stone," Lazarus said, "but legally, they would have to bring him to Pilate or Herod for an execution. And even then he would have had to have threatened Caesar." Lazarus shuddered. "But the only people Jesus threatens are the prideful and self-righteous, the Sadducees and Pharisees."

I blew out the clay oil lamp.

Darkness settled.

"And I admit that I was prideful and self-righteous," Lazarus said.

"But you do not wish to *kill* Jesus!"

"Of course not. I would never wish that. Esther, for every adversary the Master has, the Master has a faithful follower." I felt my husband's breath on my cheek. "Which means it must be time."

"Time?"

"The Master said, 'Yet a little while I am with you, and then I go to Him that sent me. You shall seek Me, and shall not find Me, and where I am, there you cannot come.' I think Jesus may go to Greece from Alexandria to Rome! Since the Assyrian exile our tribes have been dispersed. He must go to *all* of the lost sheep of Israel. Even those at the ends of the earth, no?"

Greeks were loathsome to certain traditional Jews, although there were many Jews who adopted Greek thoughts and practices. They would worship in a synagogue, perhaps, but they did not follow the law. Most did not go to the Temple for pilgrimage as decreed by the law of Moses.

"As Jesus went to the Samaritan people, perhaps He will go to the rest of the unfaithful world," I said slowly.

"And He will be king of the world. Of every nation." There was a scratch in Lazarus' voice.

"How can this be?" I said. "In what way can He do this? He does not have the support of the Temple leaders."

"He will take the place of the chief priests," Lazarus suggested. "Then Israel can rise up to claim the world."

"With shalom?" I asked. "Or this violence and suffering He now speaks of?"

"I do not know *how* He will do this, but He will do it!" Lazarus said, totally convinced. "He is the Son of Elohim. Wind and sea obey Him. Life and death are in His hands. The end of this age is upon us."

"Since I was a girl," I said, "I always thought that the Messiah would come as a warrior and overthrow the Romans. Lead the Zealots and anyone else who would join Him. Like Barabbas."

"And like our fathers."

"Yes."

We were both quiet for a moment. "Do you think in the end, Jesus will at last give us the bread of life? And the everlasting water?"

"He *is* the bread. The bread is with us, come down from Heaven," Lazarus said.

"We have yet to trogo His flesh," I said dryly.

"Yet we have partaken much of the kingdom with Him."

I twisted my lips, not satisfied with that answer.

"Enough of this, wife. My eyes are heavy, and I have no energy to uncover the secrets of the world tonight."

I felt for his face in the dark and kissed him on the cheek. I then settled against my pillow and I drifted immediately to sleep.

Chapter 30

He has made me eat gravel, trampled me into the dust;
My life is deprived of peace, I have forgotten what happiness is…
LAMENTATIONS 3:16-17

Hear, O Israel, Adonai is our Elohim. Adonai alone. I gave my first prayer of the day. Opening my eyes, I saw the dim light of the rising sun through the square window on the east wall.

Lazarus breathed more heavily than usual. He must have been in a deep sleep which he needed, considering the continued stress of Sicarii and his cousin Hezekiah. Even if his encounter with them was a full two months ago.

It had been that long since we last saw Jesus, as well. In many ways it felt like we were living our old life. While we were in the same bedchamber, when we left the room, our lives were very different than they used to be. Lazarus now focused the full of his time on speaking to different leaders and travelers regarding Sicarii. I spent my time in the hospice with Martha and Mary, caring for the poor and sick. Through the power of Jesus, Martha healed a woman whose neck had a painful inflammation. It was a miracle.

I heard the cock crow. I slid out of bed and looked out the window that was hardly larger than my own face. The yellow-browned hills looked gold as the sun rose.

"The sky was red last evening," I said to the still sleeping Lazarus, "And so today is indeed a fair day." Spring was clearly upon us. Passover would come in a month's time!

"Do you think Jesus will go to Jerusalem for the feast after what happened at the last feast?" I wondered aloud. The Feast of Dedication was a couple of months past and I had not seen Jesus since. Word was He was now in Jericho. "It would be unwise," I continued, "but Jesus does not tend to heed our warnings. Even though they had stones ready in their hands. If it were not for all of the disciples, Jesus would not have passed through unharmed.

"I suppose that if our Father wills for Jesus to remain unharmed, then it will be so," I said. Lazarus didn't respond.

"Nevertheless." I turned back to our wide bed. "It is good that He and the disciples withdrew from Jerusalem after that. Blasphemy is a serious crime. Of course, Jesus did not commit a crime, but Hezekiah and the other

Pharisees and Sadducees would say otherwise — and it is they who make up the Sanhedrin."

I went back to our bed. "Lazarus. I know I am being very talkative this morning. Forgive me. But should you not rise as well?"

He did not answer. He was breathing more deeply than usual. A strange heat came off him and he was shivering. His legs curled as he clutched the blanket to his chest as if trying to stay warm. He appeared to be freezing. I shakily put my hand to his forehead. He felt like fire.

I quickly stood but clumsily fell. My arm flailing backward, I stood again and ran out of the bedroom.

"Martha!" I cried. "Mary!" I ran across the second floor of the house.

A servant appeared, hurrying toward me. "Mistress?"

"Go find Martha and Mary," I pleaded. "They are probably in the hospice. Tell them this is an emergency."

With that, I returned to Lazarus' bedchamber, but was unsure what to do. I arranged the blankets so he was tucked in and warm. He was shaking.

"Esther," I heard Martha's voice and sighed with relief.

"Martha! Mary!" Both women had entered the room. "It is Lazarus!" My voice cracked. "He...he has a fever! An awfully high fever!"

Martha ran back out of the room and I heard her calling out the names of her children.

"I will fetch more blankets," Mary said.

The early morning light revealed Lazarus' uncomfortable hunched position.

Martha returned. "Call a servant to bring some water," she demanded of her daughter-in-law.

Dear Adonai! Our Father in Heaven! You are our light and salvation! Whom shall I fear? You are our protector.

I fell to my knees, clutching my hands together, unsure of what I could do to help. Martha's daughter-in-law came, holding a bowl of water and cloth. Mary knelt next to me and dipped the cloth in the water and dabbed at Lazarus' sweating forehead.

"Lazarus?" I whispered. "Lazarus."

Anyone could die of a fever.

He turned my way and grumbled. I grabbed his hand, staring desperately at him.

My head jerked. I frantically looked around me, then remembered where I was and what had happened. Lazarus was still breathing heavily and laying still. I rubbed my face with my left hand as my right held Lazarus' hand. I was not sure how long I had slept, but light was streaming through the window on the eastern wall. It must have been late morning. I had been in this position since last night.

The orange and red frescos in our room served as colors of sunrise.

"Esther," Mary said as she touched my shoulder. I gave her a small smile. "Martha is with a servant at the market in Jerusalem. They are buying food and herbs and anything that might help Lazarus. They should be back soon."

I nodded and touched Lazarus' forehead. Still warm but not as hot as last night.

"We have seen many fevers before, Esther," Mary said. "And we have seen many recover. At our hospice."

"Yes. Your house for the sick and destitute. Should you not be seeing to them?"

"Lazarus is our brother. One of the servants and my son's wife as well are with the sick. Anyway, Lazarus may still have a fever," she said, "but I think the worst is over." She asked if I wanted something to eat.

"Please." I lifted the cloth from the bowl of water beside Lazarus and squeezed it, then brushed it against his face. His handsome features glistened with sweat.

"Wha--where arrrrre," Lazarus heaved.

"All is well," I said. "We are at home." I stroked the cloth against his cheek. "All is well." He turned on to his side and I placed the cloth back into the ceramic bowl. *Jeremiah.* "For I will close up your scar, and will heal all of your wounds, says Adonai."

The day went by in a dreadful blur. All we could think of was trying to make Lazarus comfortable. He did not stop shivering, but Martha insisted that we not overheat him with too many layers of blankets. We called for a physician, but it could take days for him to arrive, even if he was in Jerusalem, for a doctor had many patients.

"I will sit with him," Mary said. "You should stretch your legs. Go down to the kitchen and you will find food on the main table."

"Thank you." I smiled weakly at her as I stood up. My muscles were cramped from being in such a position for so long. I stretched. "I am glad he has stopped shaking, at least."

"Me as well. He gave us a fright."

"The just cried and Adonai heard them, and delivered them out of all their troubles," I mumbled as I trotted downstairs. "Adonai is near to them that are of a contrite heart and he will save the humble of spirit." The psalms kept rolling from my lips. I walked into the kitchen and upon the counter was grape juice, fine bread, butter, goat's cheese, and eggs. I immediately started eating, realizing how hungry I was.

Where was Jesus? Was He still in Jericho? When was He planning on joining us? I hoped it would be soon.

I heard Martha in the courtyard, and I turned around to see her and a servant walk in, baskets in hand. "How is he?" she asked as they set the baskets on the floor.

"Better," I said taking a sip from my drink.

"He may not want to, but Lazarus *must* eat." Martha took pieces of a yellow flowered plant from the basket. "I purchased some yarrow," she said. "It helped improve a man's condition just last week."

I nodded as I plopped a piece of bread in my mouth.

"He does not want to drink." I heard Mary's faint voice call from outside. Martha leaned out the kitchen door, peeking into the courtyard and craning her head upward.

"He must!" She shouted at Mary. "Or he will be dehydrated." She looked back at me. "He is not a camel or a cactus. He needs continuous liquid."

I bit my lip, hoping Mary would not accidentally drown Lazarus. I grabbed what was left of my bread and hurried back upstairs. Mary was holding Lazarus' head up as she put a polished wooden cup to his lips.

Lazarus tilted his head, avoiding the cup. Mary gave a frustrated sigh.

"Come now, Lazarus." I knelt next to Mary and touched my husband's arm. "Drink."

He lifted his head more to sip from the cup then immediately put his head back in Mary's hands, exhausted from the effort.

I ran a hand through my unkempt hair.

"All shall be well." Mary put a hand on my back. "We have prayed to the Father. All shall be well."

I laid down next to him to watch him sleep soundly. I smiled, seeing his even breathing. With one hand on his arm, I too drifted into sleep.

"Esther!" Martha shook my shoulders. "Esther! Wake up!"

My eyes popped open. Martha was hovering above me, her face lit with fright. Lazarus was shivering and thrashing his arm, which landed on my face.

"His fever! It is worse," Mary gasped.

"How can we help him?" I begged.

"We have been doing everything we can..." Martha replied. "O Abraham...I do not know..."

No one said it, but I knew we were all thinking the same thing, that Lazarus was dying. "I know what to do," Mary said. She stepped forward, drying her eyes. "We will send word to Jesus. The man who opened the eyes of the blind will surely heal His own disciple from this illness, whatever it may be."

"There have been many a time when the disciples could not heal but Jesus could," I said, jumping toward Mary. "Please! Do send word." I fell back beside Lazarus. "Beloved." I wiped a strand of hair from his face. "Beloved, do not fear. Jesus is coming. He will heal you," I told him. "He will heal you."

"I will see to it." Mary quickly walked from the room.

A few neighbors visited throughout the past day or so, many who had been healed by Jesus or cared for at the hospice. They were kind, but I tired of everyone telling me, "It will be all right. He will be fine. Lazarus is a strong man. Do not fear."

"If Jesus comes, he will be healed," they also said.

But they did not understand that we sent word to Jesus over two days ago. They did not realize that Jesus never sent word back to us; that He should be here in Bethany by now, and He was not.

The physician, who was a Pharisee, visited. He had visited the day before, a quick visit. "Tell me, woman. What sins have you and your husband committed?"

My skin prickled. "You think he is possessed by a demon?"

"It is a possibility." The Pharisee walked closer to me, past the bed. "I anointed him with the prescribed oil yesterday, and there has been no change in his condition. It is a logical conclusion that demons may be the cause of this illness."

Mary stepped beside me. "Sir. I assure you, my brother is not possessed by a demon. Esther, here..." She looked at me. "Has seen many who are tormented by demons, and she agrees that this is simply not the case."

"Are you not the Esther who is a barren woman? The green-eyed one?" The Pharisee scratched his beard.

I looked down, shamed. "Yes, Sir. I am."

The Pharisee made a ticking sound. "I fear this will only make demons an even more likely cause of this illness."

I shook my head. "Our Master, Jesus of Nazareth, has told me that my barrenness is no curse from Elohim. Besides, if I had children, I never would have been privileged to follow Jesus the way I did." I raised my face and looked him in the eye.

He shook his head, frowning.

I turned away, trying not to show my hurt. Why did we summon a physician in the first place?

"If you will allow me," the Pharisee said. "I will attempt to cast out the demon and heal him."

I paused, then said a forceful, "No. Please! Leave me! Let me be alone with my husband if there is nothing else you can do." My voice cracked as my throat filled with sorrow.

"I will escort you out, Sir," Mary said, before the Pharisee could give any objections. I heard him muttering curses at Jesus and His "blasted disciples."

I worried that Jesus might not come because of what happened in Jerusalem earlier this year. It would not be safe for Him to travel to Bethany with Jerusalem just over the Mount of Olives. What if Jesus stayed in Jericho and kept preaching throughout the desert region and Perea? I pitifully tried to ignore my fears. Jesus was my cousin who loved me. He raised men from the dead. Lazarus was a dear friend of His. He would not simply ignore His beloved follower. Jesus was my last and only hope of saving Lazarus.

"How is he, Esther?" Martha gave me a cup of water to drink.

"He is sleeping."

"Perhaps the worst is over," she said.

I did not say anything in return at first. I was not willing to get my hopes up on his recovery. "I would feel much better if Jesus was with us." I turned to look at her.

Martha walked closer and smiled. "You know Jesus. He always has a plan, even if we do not know or understand it."

I gave a slight nod and moved toward the bed. Lazarus was sleeping. I raised my eyebrows, confusion lurking inside of me. He was very still — too still. Fear gripped my heart and I immediately examined him closely, and could not see him breathing.

"*Martha*," I cried.

Mary also ran up behind her sister. "What is it, Esther?"

"Please! Please! Please! Do not! Do not let...please! No! No, no, no! Please! Lazarus." I could not make out a pulse.

"Esther..."

"No..."

"O Abraham!"

I covered my face as if I could hide from that terror, falling backward. I looked upward, to my Father in Heaven. This did not happen! "No! No! No!" I could not bear it! Lazarus! Lazarus! Lazarus!

Why? Why my good husband?

My sisters-in-law were wrapped in their own grief. My sobbing increased.

Jesus. What of Your faithful servant? A devout Jewish man who has done no wrong! Where are You? I thought You would come to us! Have You forgotten us? Ignored me? Will You heal centurions and the worst of sinners, but not my husband?

I should have taken him to one of the springs in Galilee or the pool of Bethesda in Jerusalem. We never should have stayed in Bethany. If we had stayed with Jesus, Lazarus would have been in perfect health.

"I should have done something," I moaned, Martha wrapped her firm arms around me as our tears fell.

I could not help him! I could not help him! Why could I not help him?

PART 3

ETERNAL
LIFE

Chapter 31

With mourning and lament I sent you away, but God will give
you back to me with gladness and joy forever.
BARUCH 4:23

It was evening. The first of seven days of mourning. According to the law of Moses, Lazarus had to be buried within the first day.

I stood in an olive grove. The trees lined up around me. Within their thickness, I felt hidden. Isolated. Somehow, the twisted branches were appealing to me, the way they stretched toward me as if to swallow me into a tomb. My sandaled feet rolled over the hard pits of olives fallen on the rooted ground.

Directly to my right was the hospice. Further northwest was the family sepulcher. Lazarus' body was being cleansed and anointed as preparation for the sepulcher.

My need to step outside of the house was strong. Every time I looked at his body I felt fear and disbelief.

"I am a widow," I whispered. A familiar tear fell down my face.

Despite our tensions and disagreements, I would take comfort if Ima came to offer her condolences. I would take solace in Aunt Mary's presence as well, but I could not expect her or anyone from Nazareth to travel here to Judea. By the time word would reach them, Lazarus will have been dead for several days.

And Jesus? The one who just told me that He wished to remain my friend, despite His divine nature? Where was that friend now? I knew He was not a long distance away. He was still near Jericho, so I heard.

I counted my losses. My father. My mother now hated me. I had no children. Jesus had forgotten me. I had no husband.

And this strange motherhood that Aunt Mary spoke of? Was I also to live like a wife even though I had no husband?

"Esther." Martha's voice wavered, unlike her usual firm and authoritative tone.

I did not answer but waited for her to find me amidst the maze of olive trees. At last, she spotted me, and sighed. I looked at her with a plain face.

"Esther." Martha sniffed as she neared me. She rubbed her red eyes. "They are wrapping him."

Once again, I did not answer. I did not want to see all of the people who came to show us pity.

But I did want to see *him* one last time.

Making up my mind, I forced myself to stroll between the trees, south toward the manor house. Martha followed me silently.

Upon entering the courtyard, I saw many people; all of whom I had originally been hiding from. They were quiet and still for such a large group.

Contrary to the loud crowds who came to see Jesus.

Jesus!

Again, I ignored the name. Where were He and His disciples now? Where were our true friends — our true family? What about our Father in Heaven? Susanna, Joanna, Salome, Mary Alphaeus? Peter, James, and John? My own brother Simon? What of Magdalene, Lazarus' own sister? We sent word to them when Lazarus was sick, but they never came.

Those who did come to pay their respects were mostly residents of Bethany. Hezekiah actually showed his face, standing tall compared to a handful of other Pharisees he was with. They hardly spoke but stared at Mary of Bethany as she anointed her brother's body in the center of the courtyard. Simon the Leper was there, observing but not doing anything. And there was a crowd of poor and recovered victims of sickness whom Martha and Mary cared for and Jesus had healed.

I tried not to look at anyone directly. Here came their looks of pity for the barren woman with strange green eyes; the barren widow with no sons; the disciple with no Master.

I stepped forward. They each spoke softly to me and offered their condolences. I nodded and tried to smile. My head was full of painful pressure as I mouthed words of thanks.

The women embraced me — some rather stiffly, and others as if their goal was to strangle me. They kissed me on the cheek. The men bowed their heads in solemn sadness. The children clung to their mothers' garments, quietly asking questions. They were silenced.

I gave a sad smile to a little girl and my eyes glossed with tears as I made my way on the baked clay tiles toward the center of the court.

Where Lazarus laid.

Though his face was a bit pale, he looked like the handsome man I knew. Unfortunately, his unmoving body was far too evident.

Lazarus was wrapped in the customary linen cloths and bands, except for his head. I could clearly smell the spices and oils he was anointed with. Myrrh. Poignant and sickening. My stomach tumbled with nausea.

Mary was beside me as I stopped to stare at my dead husband. I did not look at her while she handed me the burial cloth for his face. I knelt next to my husband with fresh tears. I gave him a last kiss on the forehead. One tear landed on his cheek. I had no concern that I continued to touch the dead. I was already ceremonially unclean and would perform ritual purifications tonight.

With shaky hands, I covered Lazarus' head with the burial cloth.

Martha helped me stand up as four men set the bier — wooden sticks twined together — next to Lazarus. They gently lifted his body and placed him on the bier, which they lifted up taking Lazarus out of the house. We all followed with Martha, Mary and I directly behind his body. Hezekiah and Simon the Leper followed after us.

"Elohim will not abandon you, Esther," Martha whispered to me. "And neither shall I."

A hint of warmth opened in my heart. Her loving words touched me much deeper than the ones of others I knew. I nodded my head, unable to speak, and Martha, Mary and I linked arms as we followed the men to the tomb.

We processed toward the family sepulcher; where Syrus, Eucharia, and the rest of the dead relatives lay in the white limestone structure. Along the way, we passed mostly olive trees, but a couple fig trees, palms, and cacti. A white donkey grazed in the distance. A worker's wheelbarrow was near the back of the tomb.

It felt like a long walk, although it was close to the house. The stone in front of the tomb had already been rolled away from the short, rectangular door. I could smell the damp, moist air swirling from the tomb opening.

A piece of me went with Lazarus as the men carried him down the steps and into the chambers of the sepulcher. My stomach filled with dread.

How I had to now live without him!

I sobbed as they sealed the entrance to the tomb.

I had a sudden urge to see Jesus; to feel the comfort of being in His presence; to be near to His goodness and hear His loving words; to see the compassion in His eyes.

My mind drifted through sweet memories of Lazarus.

Rise up. Lazarus would say. *To battle against it.*

The day he asked Uncle Clopas for my hand. *I come here like Jacob, Esther.*

You have wounded my heart, my sister, my spouse, you have wounded my heart with one of your eyes.

I want you to read from the prophet Ezekiel, Esther. I think you would like his imagery and metaphors. He is very dramatic, like you. And I want you to tell me what you think of him; his thoughts on death and dying. You will be awed that all that you think you know is but a drop in the ocean compared to what you can learn. I did read Ezekiel. And found that Adonai took dry bones and brought them to life. Would he not do the same for Lazarus?

And when we went after Jesus together! *Arise, my friend, my beautiful one, and come. Take your choice of mantle and most durable sandals. We leave in the hour.*

Here am I. Send me. Lazarus had told Jesus.

Why then, did Jesus send him to Sheol?

The fourth day.

Like my sisters-in-law, I had a dry face, stinging chapped lips, heavy heart, and eyes drooped with exhaustion.

No one from Nazareth had come. Not one of Jesus' disciples had come.

I sat on a cushion in the banquet hall of Martha's house. I tried to think bravely and hopefully, but could not. This was my family here. Martha and Mary. Hezekiah had not been seen since the day of Lazarus' burial and Simon the Leper was present but wordless to us women. Mary's son and Martha's sons and daughters were with us, but they paid comfort to their mothers, not to me.

I hardly knew the others. Some rich relatives from Magdala had come; some wealthy and some poor who I somewhat recognized. Workers and businessmen who Syrus and Lazarus had partnered with.

Except the Sicarii. Word was that a group of Sicarii, led by Barabbas, attacked Roman soldiers in Jerusalem yesterday, trying to start a rebellion. Apparently, Barabbas murdered two soldiers, but the rest of his compatriots were unsuccessful. All men involved were imprisoned at the Antonia Fortress in Jerusalem — Rome's headquarters.

Not able to move my lips and speak to anyone, I spoke to my Heavenly Father. *I will not lose faith! I will not lose faith! If armies in camp should stand together against me, my heart shall not fear. Oh Abba, Father! If a battle should rise up against me, in this will I be confident. Father, where is my comfort?*

I thought of the rest of the twenty-seventh Psalm. *One thing I have asked of Adonai; this will I seek after; that I may dwell in the house of Adonai all the days of my life. That I may see the delight of Adonai and may visit His Temple.*

But one thing is necessary. Jesus had said to Martha and Mary when Mary sat at His feet. *Mary has chosen the best part which will not be taken away from her.*

Has this better portion not been taken away from all of us? Where was the Kyrios, that we might sit at our dear master's feet? Even more than Master, where was my dearest friend? And should not Magdalene have at least come in representation of our family of disciples?

I grabbed the empty dishes of food on the table and stood up to put them away.

"I can take those for you, dear," a woman said, her smile sympathetic.

"No. No thank you. I can do it," I replied. I was still a woman who was able. I could clean and care for a house with or without the loss of a husband. And the two servants knew well that they were not to stop me from doing menial tasks.

As I walked out into the courtyard, heading for the kitchen area, I heard two women whispering. I stopped next to the door of their small guest room.

"...Lazarus and Esther..."

I did not recognize either voice.

"Pity...they gave up everything...for a false prophet..."

"...that Jesus did not even come to the burial..."

"They sent word to Him...never came..."

"So much for their miracle-worker...now His disciple is dead!"

"And this Esther is a barren woman as well. Probably cursed."

I took in a quick suck of air and continued to the kitchen, my eyes stinging with tears. *I will not lose faith. I will not lose faith.* They did not know Jesus like I did. If they did, they would not say such things. Jesus loved Lazarus — like His own brother. *I will not lose faith. I will not lose faith!*

I stifled a sob as the all too familiar grief washed over me. I set the dishes with a clank on the kitchen counter, beside the basin of water.

"*Esther*," Magdalene's voice called. I turned to see her run into the kitchen and embrace me, grasping me firmly.

"Magdalene! Oh, Magdalene!" Fresh tears rained on my face. "You came!"

"And I am not alone. Rabboni is here with all the others as well!"

A burst of light sparked in me. "All of you? Here in Bethany?"

"Yes!" Magdalene gasped. "At last! I have been waiting with great anxiety to come, but Rabboni had us wait." Magdalene looked at me with sympathy. Her face was flushed. Her hair was knotted tightly beneath her veil.

"Where is Jesus?"

"He is just outside of town. Martha went out to greet Him."

I put a hand to my chest as I comprehended the news. "Jesus is here…" I whispered to myself. I raised my eyes to Magdalene. "I was starting to think you all would never come! Magdalene! I have nothing to prepare for their arrival."

"Esther, my brother and your husband is dead. That is why they come. Not for hospitality. Rabboni comes to console you and expects no lavishness." Magdalene pressed her hands on her thighs. "Martha will lead them here — it will be any time now. Let us not tell any of your guests, lest we make a commotion."

I nodded in agreement, processing this surprise. "Are *all* of the disciples with Him?"

"Yes! Everyone! I came ahead with Andrew and Judas to announce our arrival."

"Andrew and Judas? Praise to Elohim in the highest. You did not tell me they were already here!" I grabbed her arm and pulled her into the courtyard.

There they were. The shaggy, overgrown sheep that I knew. Andrew in his rugged tunic, still avoiding eye contact. Judas playing with the collar of his tunic around his thick neck.

I smiled one of my first real smiles in days. They *were* here. And the rest of the Apostles, the women, and all the disciples were on their way. My true family was coming at last!

"Welcome, brothers," I said.

"Esther," Judas said in his smooth voice as Andrew clasped his hands in front of himself awkwardly. They glanced at each other. "We are so very — "

"No!" I stepped toward them, raising my hands. "Please." I lowered them. "There is no need to say anything. Your presence speaks clearer than any words could."

Judas's shoulders sagged as Andrew sighed with relief.

"Where do you come from?"

"Jericho," Andrew said. "The Master healed a blind man there."

I frowned. Instead of healing my husband, he healed a stranger?

Andrew cleared his throat. "He…knew of your husband's passing before the news even reached us."

I bit my lip, holding back tears. If He knew, then why did He not come? As Elohim's Son, He knew all things!

"I…thought you may not come. Not with the Jews in Jerusalem seeking to kill Him."

"This did not deter Him. He loved Lazarus," Judas said. He cleared his throat. "We all loved him," he added, hardly loud enough to be a whisper.

"Come inside," Magdalene said from behind me.

She patted my arm as we walked into the courtyard. "Where is Mary?" she asked.

"Still in the banquet hall," I replied. "Stay here and I will return with her."

I hurried, and spotted Mary sitting with her somber expression. A woman was speaking to her, but she did not seem to be listening.

I sat next to her and smiled. "He is here," I whispered.

She looked at me, tears winking in her eyes. "If He had come sooner, Lazarus would not have died."

I frowned and forced my tears back. "But He is here now." I patted her knee. Martha, Mary, and I went through a sort of cycle of comfort. When one sister was especially sad, I comforted her. When I was filled with extreme grief, they comforted me. Then, when I had cried all my tears and the next sister was very pained, and it was her turn to be comforted.

"Mary!" Martha surprised me by entering the room, walking past the people with hushed whispers. She crouched down near Mary, whispering to the two of us.

"The Master has come and calls for you."

Mary straightened her veil, immediately rising. She squeezed through the crowd and disappeared.

Magdalene approached Martha and me, a smile above her pointed chin. "Let us go too." Magdalene's grief was not as dramatic as I thought it would be. She did not beat her breasts and wail. Her smile was small and sad, but she looked ever hopeful and confident.

"Where has Mary gone? Is she going to weep at the tomb?" The woman who was previously speaking to Mary asked me.

"No," I said. "No. Jesus is here. She is going to greet the Master."

I too stood up and walked outside with Martha and Magdalene. Passing Andrew and Judas, they and the other mourners followed us. Their voices increased in excitement as Jesus' name waved over them.

I walked swiftly down the eastern path to the main village, doing my best to smile like Magdalene at the staring villagers and their consoling looks as I passed by.

Mary was a little way in front of us when she thrust herself onto the ground. Jesus stood in front of her, and the disciples were behind Him.

My heart cried out at the sight of Him and I picked up my pace so that soon we were standing before Jesus and the disciples. Each Apostle was solemn. Salome and some of the other women cried.

A thought pressed on me. Would I continue as a disciple like the other widows in our group?

Despair tugged at my heart.

Should I continue to follow Jesus despite the fact that He did not heal my husband? Besides the fact that He did not come when we sent word to Him?

My eyes pricked with tears as I looked at Jesus, who Himself looked troubled. The grief I had grown accustomed to rippled through me. Fresh tears fell from my face — this time it was not just the thought of my dead husband, but all the people here: The disciples; the ones Lazarus and I lived and traveled with. And here was Jesus, finally coming to His dear disciple.

The love and care that Jesus and His band showed comforted me. Any anger I may have had for them disappeared.

I wiped my eyes. Jesus looked as if a sword had pierced His belly or a swarm of bees stung Him.

Mary, at the feet of the Master, gazed upward. "Kyrios," she said. "If... if You had been here...my brother would not have died."

I smudged the tears on my face and hurried over to the weeping Mary. I put my arm around her and pulled her upward. My eyes fixed on Jesus'. The compassion and sadness that filled His face caused me to moan.

He had warm eyes, swirling like a gentle flame, colored like cinnamon. His hair rested on His shoulders, His beard full.

"Where have you laid him?" Jesus shakily asked.

"Kyrios," I said, my face gleaming with tears. My insides felt like melting wax as I looked at my dear old friend. "Come and see."

I held on to Mary as we led the way to the tomb, past the olive groves. Jesus was beside us. To my surprise, He was weeping! I had not seen Him cry since He was a little child. Now, He wept for Lazarus. How could I also not shed more tears?

I did not ask Him what took Him so long. Nor did I ask why He did not heal my husband. I simply relished the fact that He was here, at last. Here to mourn with us.

People from the village began to follow us and one woman stood next to me. She motioned toward Jesus. "See how He loved him."

"Yes." I smiled through my tears. "Yes, He loved Lazarus very much."

As we walked, more Jews from the village joined us. I was touched by their procession to the family sepulcher.

I heard a man say, "Could not He that opened the eyes of the man born blind, have caused that this man should not die?"

"That is what I thought," a woman replied.

I bit my lip and looked back to my beloved Jesus. Magdalene offered Jesus her handkerchief to dry His eyes. He gave a somber smile to Magdalene who bowed her head as she took back the handkerchief as if she had just served a king His supper.

We were now beyond Martha's home, the olive groves to our far right. A servant stood in the doorway of the hospice, to watch us pass by.

The tomb came into view near the northwest. A large, round stone covered the entrance. Limestone hewed out of bedrock. We stopped. I glanced back at all the people, each looking sad.

All were silent, gazing at the tomb. I could not stop sniffling and I heard whimpers, groans, and coughs from those behind me. I felt Mary squeezing my hand. Ours were both clammy and shaky as we gripped each other. After a respectful wait, Jesus spoke.

"Take away the stone." He stepped in front of us, moving closer to the sepulcher.

His sudden movement startled me. I glanced between Jesus and the blocked tomb entrance.

Martha ran up behind Jesus and touched His arm. "Kyrios, by this time he will stink," she said. "He has been dead for *four* days!"

Jesus looked at all of us. "Did I not say to you that if you believe, you will see the glory of Elohim?"

Martha stepped back. My brother Simon and the Apostles Thaddeus, James, and Philip walked to the stone and rolled it away. They grunted as the opening was slowly revealed. It was a narrow, rectangular entrance. Anyone would need to bend low to get through.

"What do you suppose He is doing?" I whispered to Mary, leaning my shoulder against hers.

Mary shrugged. "He wants to see the body? Or honor Lazarus in some way? I do not know."

I sniffled and rubbed my nose with my arm.

Now I expected Jesus to walk into the tomb…or something of the like… but He simply stood outside it and looked at the sky. A few more tears wet my face as I stared at the back of His head. His dark brown fluffy hair fell behind His shoulders.

"Lazarus, come out!"

I jumped, hearing Jesus' booming voice. Not to mention, His ridiculous words.

Everything was terribly silent. Even the birds stopped chirping and the wind was still. My eyes were fixed on the tomb and the darkness inside.

A shadow moved within the sepulcher. My heart felt as if it was about to burst from my chest.

The light from the sun shone down on the figure of a man wrapped in burial cloths. He was hobbling out of the tomb. His hands and feet were wrapped in bands, and a cloth covered his face.

I felt weak as my mind raced.

"Lazarus," I whispered, stunned. "Lazarus!"

I let go of the paralyzed Mary and sprinted toward my husband.

"Loose him and let him go," Jesus said.

I stopped abruptly. After a moment of fear and uncertainty, I hesitantly reached out to touch the thin burial linen covering a face. I removed it and screamed.

My husband was looking at me. He appeared to be in perfect health. His earth-brown eyes were brighter than I had ever seen them. His skin was smooth, and his face was slightly flushed. His hair and beard were oiled back and he smelled of aloes and myrrh.

He appeared to be in shock as he surveyed the people watching him.

"Lazarus," I whispered.

He looked at me but did not smile.

Tears welled up in my eyes. "You are alive! You are alive." I raised my hands in the air, then looked at his body wrapped in cloths. I began to untie them.

People shouted and gasped and cried. Martha, Mary, and Magdalene ran to us and helped me untie the bands. My hands shook like an old woman's as I undid the wrappings around his hands.

I heard Magdalene laughing with joy and praising Elohim.

I pulled the last of the cloths from around Lazarus' feet, then flung my arms around my husband. I started sobbing from pure shock. Lazarus caressed my sweaty back.

"He is alive," I kept saying. I looked up at him. "You are alive!" He held me but did not say anything. I felt the arms of Martha, Mary and then Magdalene wrap around us and they laughed and wept as well.

Smelling the strong ointment and spices on Lazarus, I blinked. Then let out a joyous giggle. "You are alive!" I pressed my face against his chest, taking in that scent of myrrh.

I too took a step back while each sister took a turn embracing him. "He is alive," I repeated, the words not sounding real; the meaning behind them sounding ludicrous.

I looked over my shoulder to see Jesus smiling at me. I ran to Him and fell at His feet. Grass and dirt stained the palms of my hands. I tilted my head backward then finally found myself bold enough to look Him in the eye.

"Jesus," I said. "Oh, Master!" I cried. "*Jesus.*" His name sounded so sweet on my lips. "I...I thought...I thought You would not come...and then...I thought You...just...I do not know what...just...I...then You...he is alive!"

I put my hands over my mouth as I sobbed more. "You were gone... You had left me...I wanted to see You...and then...this is greater than I ever could imagine."

Jesus placed His warm hand on my veiled head. "Esther." He said my name and it was as if spirited energy shot up from the soles of my feet to the top of my head. I almost gasped as I took in His precious, loving face.

"Esther," Jesus said again. "I am the resurrection and the life. He that believes in Me, although he be dead, will live."

I stared at Him, in awe of His words. "Yes, Kyrios! I know You are the resurrection and the life!" I bowed. "My Kyrios! O my Kyrios! If I but realized that those who sow in tears will reap with cries of joy! When I had a little passed by them, I found him whom my soul loves!" I spoke of the Song of Solomon in which the woman spoke of her beloved.

Jesus placed His hand under my elbow and helped me rise. Part of me wished to withdraw from His hold as my insides coiled with the shame of unworthiness.

He spoke more quietly. "Life will not be the same as it was for you and Lazarus. You *must* place your full trust in Me."

"Yes, Kyrios," I immediately said with a bright and grateful smile. I did not know exactly what He meant but I did know that my trust rested in Him.

I looked back at Lazarus. He was surrounded by all of the Jews. They were touching him and staring at him and laughing and weeping. Lazarus tried making his way toward Jesus and myself, though it was hard to move with the crowd pressing on him. Some of the disciples gave him brotherly embraces and I heard a mix of praises and questions.

My mind formed questions for Lazarus.

When I looked around at the great happiness, awe, fear, and faith of all the people, I beamed. This was a faith they did not have until they witnessed such a miracle!

"Kyrios, this will bring many people to believe in You," I said in delight as Lazarus pushed closer toward us. Lazarus and Jesus were staring at each other.

Once Lazarus was next to Jesus, Jesus put His arm around his shoulder and led him away from the crowd. The crowd, in turn, respected Jesus' and Lazarus' distance. But only after James Zebedee pushed people away and shouted, "Get away you fanatics! Can you not give the Kyrios some space?"

I watched my cousin and husband with intense curiosity. As Jesus spoke, Lazarus kept nodding. Finally, Lazarus said his first words since his return to life. If only I could hear what they were!

Magdalene grabbed my arms and almost leaped in the air with excitement. "How wondrous He is!"

I laughed. "Praise Adonai! Praise Adonai, my soul! I will praise Adonai all my life! I do not think I could be happier!" I longed to speak with Lazarus, though — and leave all the people.

"Look at them." Magdalene surveyed the crowd. "Many appear terrified."

"I myself am filled with fear," I said. "This is His greatest miracle yet! We have seen His power over illness; His power of words; and His power over nature; even His power over life and death, for we have seen Him raise others from the grave. I just never thought He would do so with *Lazarus!* A man dead for *four* days!"

Susanna, Joanna, Mary Alphaeus, and Salome walked toward us.

"I knew this was going to happen, my dear," Mary Alphaeus stated proudly once she reached us.

"Did you?" Salome asked suspiciously.

"Esther. We have missed your presence among us!" Joanna embraced me.

"Blessed be Adonai!" Susanna laughed freely.

"I knew it the moment the dear Master said that this sickness is not unto death, but for the glory of Elohim, that the Son of Elohim may be glorified by it," Mary Alphaeus said.

"Jesus *said* that?" I asked.

"And He purposely stayed two days longer in Jericho when we heard that Lazarus was ill." Salome set a hand on her hip.

"I was thinking the reason He did not come was fear of the proximity to Jerusalem," I told them. "Or discontentment with me."

"The Master seems to have His face set on Jerusalem," Salome said, both hands on her hips. "We will see if they will be throwing stones or palm branches at His arrival."

Chapter 32

...and they anointed David king over Israel, in accordance with
the word of the LORD given through Samuel.

1 CHRONICLES 11:3

My eyes immediately turned to Lazarus' side of the bed. The spot where he should be sleeping, but was not.

I threw aside the silk blankets, and looked around his bedchamber. I tossed on my blue mantle, and walked to the lofted hallway of the second floor.

The house was dimly lit with natural light but no one was awake.

Where was Lazarus?

I searched the house as quietly as possible so I would not wake anyone, but he was nowhere to be seen!

In my bed at night I sought him whom my soul loves — I sought him and found him not. I called, and he did not answer me.

I walked down the stairs and into the courtyard. I peered into different rooms, packed with guests. The servants were awake and moving. I even looked in their chambers, then walked all the way to the third floor, and he was still nowhere to be seen.

The only other place Lazarus could be was outside.

Not bothering to put on my sandals, I emerged from the double doors in the back of the house. Insects buzzed. The air was chilly. I wrapped my head and shoulders with my mantle.

The bottom of the sky was light blue.

I could have searched for Lazarus amidst the olive groves, but something told me he was by the tomb.

Walking the dirt path in the back of the home, I passed the hospice where I made a point to peek into a small window to gaze at curled up bodies on the floor. I then continued toward the family sepulcher, biting my lip.

Where are you? Have you seen him whom my soul loves? I continued walking. Finally, I saw his silhouette on a rock, a little away from the tomb.

I hurried toward him. "Thanks be to our Father in Heaven! Lazarus! Hardly had I left them when I found him whom my soul loves. I held him and would not let him go! I thought I would never find you!"

Lazarus slowly turned to me, his face painted with shadows. He was clean and freshly shaven. His eyes appeared bigger than they used to, and he appeared younger.

"I kept waking up in the middle of the night to make sure you were still beside me," I told him. "Then I woke up and you were gone!"

He took a moment to respond. "I did not mean to worry you."

Such few words. I could count how many he had spoken to me since his return to life. Was that why I drew back from holding him?

"What are you doing?" I touched the cool surface of the rock he rested on.

"Thinking."

"Oh," was all I said. I drank in his serious expression. His wavy hair sailed over his ears.

"Is everything well?" I sat next to him on the rock. "We did not get to talk much yesterday. We were so busy and the numbers of people were great...I was desperate to speak more with you in private but by the end of the night, you looked so tired...I thought you might fall ill again from the exhaustion."

"I am well," Lazarus said. "You are right though, I was tired. There were so many questions and people. It...was overwhelming...coming out of that tomb and seeing the shocked faces."

I nodded, thinking how my reaction must have seemed. Once the linen was taken from his face, I fell into his arms, hysterical.

"You were dead." I said the strange words. "Then, you were alive again."

"I can barely grasp it myself," Lazarus whispered as a breeze rustled his hair.

Would he not tell me more? Was he thinking about his illness? Of what happened once he died? Was he confused when he awoke? Frightened? Happy? I had not seen him smile yet. Was he disappointed he was alive?

"What happened?" The vague question streamed from my lips. "When you died...what do you remember? Do you remember anything?"

"I knew you were going to ask that."

I frowned at his melancholic expression. I had annoyed him.

"I remember enough. I remember you and my sisters' worried expressions, I remember feeling terrible, I remember being confused, and I remember hearing you weep."

My eyes stung with tears. I started to ask him what happened once he was dead, but he spoke first.

"When I died, I went somewhere."

My stomach clenched. I wanted to push him to speak more but forced myself to wait for his own timing.

"There are people — souls…so many who go to Gehenna."

Gehenna. Jesus had spoken of the place. Not of the valley near Jerusalem that bore the name, but the place that was fiery and where there was wailing and grinding of teeth. A place of punishment after death.

"You went to Gehenna," I whispered, trying to imagine such a thing.

"No," Lazarus said firmly. "I did not go. But I saw souls go there. It is terrifying, Esther. Terrifying." He looked at his hands in his lap.

"Where were you, then? If not in Gehenna?"

"The gates to the kingdom were not open to me or to anyone. I…I saw your uncle."

"Uncle Joseph? Where?"

"I do not know what to call it. It is a place where he and the righteous await their entrance into the kingdom. A place for the dead. Sheol, perhaps."

"But you were near a kingdom! Was my father there?"

"There were many, many souls there. I came in contact with only a few."

"What did you speak of?"

Lazarus' lips pressed together in a thin line.

I waited as patiently as possible. "Will you tell me?" I finally asked.

"There was much we spoke of, Esther." Lazarus tapped his fingers against his knee. Quietly, he added, "I cannot tell you every word."

My shoulders slouched in disappointment. "Did Jesus command this of you?"

"I discussed it with Him, yes. Many things were revealed to me during that time of death. Things I cannot yet share with you. Do you understand?"

"You remember I am your wife," I sulked, jealous of what was revealed to him.

Lazarus slowly turned to me. Leaning forward, he pressed a soft kiss on my forehead. "My beloved."

I forced patience upon myself. His show of affection did much to aid me. "Forgive me, Lazarus." I scooted closer to him. "Tell me what you will. I am simply overjoyed that you are alive."

Lazarus put his arm around me and pulled me closer. "I as well. And I am glad to see you glad."

But something about him did not seem glad — his happiness was only at a superficial level.

I spoke. "Those four days, I started to think that all that I had come to know was gone and false. My identity as a woman and a mother; as a disciple of Jesus; as your wife." I pressed my head between his shoulder and neck. "I want to be your wife, Lazarus. Not just some mother to motherless children, but a woman who has a husband."

"You are."

"I want to *be* it!"

"We will be husband and wife more so than before, Esther. We are rising from the grave. Our lives will not be the same as they were."

"That is what Jesus said. Maybe because the kingdom is coming, as you saw it."

"The kingdom is near, Esther. But we may only enter it if we die."

"But Jesus is the resurrection and the life," I told him. "All of our suffering and pain, He takes away. Look at what He has done for us."

"So that we may believe," Lazarus said. "And now we must follow His example."

I did not respond. We simply sat on the cool rock, silent in each other's company.

The sun peeked up from the hills. The sky was a splendid blend of yellow, orange, and pink.

"The others will rise soon," I said. "Your sisters will need help in the kitchen."

Lazarus pulled his arm from around me and we stood up. We peacefully walked back on the dirt path. As we passed the hospice, we saw Martha carrying a large water jug at her hip.

She smiled at the sight of us.

"I see you have set right back to work," I observed.

"The poor are always with us. Even when we lose our loved ones," she said. "And even when our loved ones return."

"Have you many sick persons now?" Lazarus asked.

Martha shook her head as she fell into step beside us. "No. Mostly poor. The Kyrios has healed nearly every ailment. Lazarus, I thought you would be sleeping."

"I was asleep for four days."

Martha chuckled as we approached the manor house. We entered through the back door and into the servant quarters.

We passed the well in the center of the courtyard and headed to the kitchen, drawn by the smell of freshly made bread.

Mary, Magdalene, and several other women were spinning about, preparing what appeared to be an extravagant meal to break our fast. Susanna and Joanna sat on the floor, each with their own stone grain mill. With the flour the women ground, Magdalene made leavened bread, baking it in the domed oven in the corner. As she waited for the leavened bread to rise, she made unleavened loaves that baked in hardly any time at all.

Mary arranged fruit. She opened up a flask of honey to flavor the Jericho dates with. "We were wondering where you were, Lazarus," she said.

"And it is remarkably good to see you looking this well, Lazarus," Magdalene added with a smile that displayed all of her fine teeth. She hunched over the oven, using her sense of smell to determine if her bread was ready.

"What can I help with?" I asked.

"Could you get out the almonds?" Martha took charge, setting her water jug on the wooden counter.

I did so. I did use to live here and knew the house well. The almonds looked and smelled fresh and must have just been plucked from the tree this early spring. I set them in a bowl of white glass.

Judas walked in, flipping a bag of coins. "It smells good in here." He grabbed a fistful of the almonds I just placed in the bowl and plopped them in his mouth.

I bit my lip, holding back the urge to tell him that it was not yet time to eat.

Love. Forgiveness. That was no easy task!

"It will be a busy day," Magdalene said.

"Why today out of all days?" Mary asked, slicing open a pomegranate.

"With the recent excitement of Lazarus *and* Jesus being here." Magdalene pulled circular loaves of bread from the oven and toppled them onto a wooden tray. "We are already stuffed with visitors, and word gets around quickly. I would not be surprised if more people come today to see Rabboni and Lazarus."

"Lazarus, you are going to be famous," Mary teased, nudging him with her elbow and wiggling her thin eyebrows.

Lazarus frowned in response. "Are you going to the market, Judas?"

Judas nodded, ripping a piece of bread off a freshly baked flat loaf. "Jesus does not plan to stay in Bethany long. We are going to Ephraim next, and then, we will be heading to Jerusalem for the feast of Passover. I need to make some preparations," he said in his honeyed voice.

Judas grabbed another handful of almonds. He then plucked a date from the center of the counter. "I will be back later," is all he said as he walked out.

"That will taste better with honey," Martha murmured at Judas' stolen date.

"Preparations for what?" Mary asked, adding her pomegranate seeds to her fruit bowl display.

"Probably with Nicodemus in Jerusalem to discuss the feast. There are so many of us disciples this year. Our numbers will be increasing due to the miracle," Magdalene concluded, plopping flat circles of dough in the oven.

"Passover!" Mary exclaimed, her shoulders raised in excitement. "It is my favorite feast of the year."

I heard the light chatter of other disciples, who were waking up in the neighboring rooms. I put the almond jar back on the shelf and spotted an alabaster jar. It was small but had vibrant rose-colored swirls painted on it. I did not recognize it.

"What is this?" I asked aloud of no one in particular. I felt the movement of liquid inside of it. It must have been finely priced.

"It is nothing!" Mary ran over, grabbed the jar, and hurried out of the kitchen.

I watched her, wondering. Then I realized Lazarus was no longer in the room.

"He disappeared on me again! Where has my husband gone?"

"The hospice," Martha said. "There is a part of the roof that needs finishing. We have only one manservant now and he needs the help."

"Finishing the roof!" I spat. "Lazarus cannot! He just…he just rose from the dead! Of all things he should be resting right now."

My brother Simon glided into the kitchen with Philip, Thaddeus, and James Zebedee. "Do not fret, Esther, we are going to help him."

"What are all you men doing in my kitchen?" Martha demanded but her voice was drowned by those male voices.

"And we will keep an eye on him for you, Esther," Philip said with a one-sided smile.

"We will be done in an hour with all of us working at it," Simon calculated.

I nodded in approval and relief.

"Oh," James Zebedee said as he stuffed almonds into his mouth. "Bartholomew finished making sandals for James Alphaeus. Did you not also need a new pair, Magdalene?"

"Yes. Mine are practically falling off of my feet," she said, her gaze steady as she lifted more bread loaves from the oven.

"You should have told me," Martha scolded. "I have several spare pair of sandals."

Magdalene lifted her shoulders in dismissal.

346

"Where is Judas?" Matthew walked into the kitchen, which was becoming more crowded.

"Making preparations," I told him.

"Making preparations…that is rather vague. "*Tsktsktsk*. Did he say what he meant by that?"

I shook my head.

"He has been doing that a lot lately." Bartholomew now entered the kitchen, pulling at his long beard. "Leaving to go do his *duties*. I do not think he is even asking the Master for permission."

"James Zebedee." Thomas put his hands behind his head and cracked his neck to the side. "Your mother is feeling more back pain. She was just complaining to me about it, but I think she does not want to admit it to you and John. Perhaps she should stay with Martha and Mary. I think traveling might be getting too much for her."

"She will hear nothing of that," John said as he slid into the room, beside Thomas. "She said she is continuing to follow Jesus, even if we have to carry her every step." The Apostles laughed.

"Alright, alright." Martha put her hands on her hips. "Get out of my kitchen. We will bring the food to you," she commanded, waving her hand. "You are making a ruckus! All of you men!"

As the disciples filed out, Jesus watched from the threshold.

"Except for You, Master," Martha was quick to add. "Of course, You can be in the kitchen."

He gave an enormous smile as He joined us. Martha dipped a slice of bread in oil and gave it to Jesus.

"Great is Adonai! Praise to Elohim forever. Our Father in Heaven, hallowed be Your name. Give us this day our daily bread," Jesus exclaimed as He blessed the fruits, nuts, and breads on the table.

"You are especially joyful today, Jesus," I noted. "Master," I added for propriety.

Jesus took a bite from His bread. "That is because My dear friend Lazarus is alive and well."

My heart sang. "Please, tell us, what were You doing when You were near Jericho while Lazarus was ill?"

"I taught the people in nearby towns. I saw great faith there."

"How so?" Mary asked, moving closer. We all left our work to be near Him.

"There was a blind beggar, with great humility and persistent faith. I also came across a tax collector. Matthew, as you can imagine, was quite pleased —

a short man — sought me in Jericho. He got My attention when I saw him sitting up in a sycamore tree as I was passing."

I giggled, imagining what it must have looked like. "Does he believe in the kingdom now?"

Jesus nodded. "He has given half his goods to the poor and is restoring fourfold to anyone he defrauded."

I raised my eyebrows, impressed with such a conversion.

"Do you think it will be safe for You to be near Jerusalem now, Rabboni?" Magdalene asked. "Perhaps the Pharisees and chief priests just needed some time to get over that little…trouble we came across this past winter."

"The chief priests will be only more angered when they hear of Lazarus' return to life," Jesus stated plainly.

"You are afraid, Kyrios?" Martha asked, a hand at her hip.

Jesus turned to her. "Yes, Martha, I am. And until the time has come, I will no longer go about openly among the Jews."

"That is why You are going to Ephraim," I concluded. Ephraim was a small town near the wilderness. It was an ideal destination for Jesus to go unnoticed — if such a place ever existed. "When do we depart?"

"We depart today," Jesus said, nodding. "But you, Esther, will stay here."

My mouth opened in protest, but Jesus held up His hand. "Esther and Lazarus. I wish for you to stay with your sisters-in-law, so that when Judeans come to see Lazarus, they may believe."

I nodded, disappointed that I must be separated from Him again.

Mary smiled. "Lazarus used to love attention as a young man, but I do not think this was ever what he had in mind."

"He will need to be meek," Martha said, her sharp features solemn.

"He will be," I said. Surely death could injure one's pride. "And he will inherit the earth."

"Master!" Peter poked his head in the kitchen. "You may wish to break Your fast with haste. There are travelers at the door who wish to see You. I sent them to the hospice to see Lazarus first, but You know they will want to see You next. Shall I keep everyone out of the house so You can be left alone?"

"No." Jesus looked at Peter. "But prepare to leave within the hour. I will meet with people until then."

Peter gave a curt nod, disappeared, but quickly returned.

"Ah, and Esther," Peter said. "They wish to see you too. And your sisters." He left and I stared at the now-empty entranceway.

I looked at Jesus. All of the time, the crowds yearned for Him, and now I certainly understood why they wanted to see Lazarus. But me?

"Our Father, grant *me* meekness," I whispered to Jesus.

"You have asked; therefore, you shall receive." Jesus touched my shoulder lightly. "Go forth then, Esther. I am behind and before you."

Behold, O Adonai, You have known all things, the last and those of old, You have formed me and have laid Your hand upon me. Where can I go from Your spirit? The Psalms played in my mind like the constant ripple in a river.

Martha announced, "Well, I am not leaving until our meal is served to everyone."

"Esther, you and Magdalene should go," Mary said. "I will help Martha."

I walked out of the kitchen and into the vast courtyard that was alit with its morning hue, and already held many people. Most of them ran past me to Jesus, but a couple of women approached me.

"It is Esther!"

"Lazarus' wife!"

"How do you know me?" I had never seen them before.

"Your eyes. They are strikingly green. If anyone wishes to find the risen man, they simply need to search for his wife's eyes," the shorter of the women said.

I looked down, embarrassed. So, that was how I was known. Better to be the risen man's wife than the barren woman.

Someone touched my arm and I looked up to see Magdalene smiling at me. I was thankful for her support. She was much better at witnessing to Jesus than I was.

"Was he really dead?" the taller of the two women asked.

"I am certain of it. For four days," I told them. "I was by him when he died and throughout the whole burial."

"And then? What happened once Jesus came?" the shorter woman questioned.

"He told us to remove the stone, and He called to Lazarus, who came out," I said simply.

"It is hard to believe." The taller of the women looked at me suspiciously.

"I saw it through my eyes," I said, touching my fingers just below my eyes. "I saw my husband die. I saw my husband rise. The kingdom of Heaven is indeed at hand! Jesus has power over life and death."

Both women tilted their heads, quietly examining me.

"Lazarus is just outside," Magdalene said, putting a hand to the short woman's shoulder. "Come and see for yourself."

Only a couple of weeks later, Jesus and His disciples were back in Martha's house, packed like a herd in a pen. That night, Simon the Leper ordered a *todah* sacrifice in the Temple. It was a thanksgiving offering for Lazarus' resurrection which included the thanksgiving sacrifice of a lamb, the consecration of bread, and the singing of thanksgiving songs.

After our day in the Temple, we journeyed back to Bethany to celebrate and give thanks to Adonai who healed all our wounds and brought the dead to life.

Only Hezekiah did not show his face.

Martha stuck up her sharp chin and carried on with an air of authority. She was still mistress of the household.

In the banquet hall, Simon the Leper sat at the right side of Jesus, laughing and telling stories. Lazarus, who was a few seats away from them, glanced my way. Sadness filled his eyes.

I wondered what had happened to my husband. Why was he so sad? Jesus said we were to be husband and wife at a greater level than before. I took that to mean we would confide in one another more, be more prayerful together.

As the prophet Ezekiel spoke of the dry bones taking on flesh and life, so Jesus took this dead man and gave him new flesh and new life.

But had He given me a totally new husband?

It had been only a couple of weeks since his return to life, but Lazarus would not laugh or smile. I sensed a change in his disposition. He seemed so serious and in constant contemplation. His usual pride, always visible with his square shoulders and head held high, had changed to solemnness. I supposed he was thinking about life and death. But if he was promised eternal life and saw the gates of the kingdom that Jesus was bringing, why would he be somber?

I smiled at him, hoping he would return my smile, but to my disappointment, he did not. I lowered my head, rubbing my arms.

Many had been visiting Bethany, especially those on their way to Jerusalem for Passover. Caravans of people were streaming through the town.

While Jesus and the disciples were in Ephraim, dear Lazarus was touched and poked and asked a wide range of questions. He did not once show anger or annoyance, but he had shown exhaustion.

He told the people practically everything he told me. He remembered being sick with fever. He was very vague about his visit to the afterlife, and told the people that it was difficult waking up in the tomb, bound with burial cloths, and hobbling his way out at Jesus' command.

"I am afraid it may be my fault that the Twelve are indignant toward one another." Salome interrupted my thoughts. She frowned as she adjusted her position on the floor cushion beside me.

"How so?" I asked, pulling my knees to my chest. I rested my chin upon my hand, elbow leaning against my knee. "Though I noticed that several of the Apostles were in a sour mood on returning to Bethany today."

Salome shook her head. "It is my two sons against the rest of the Apostles. I…" she turned her wrinkled face away, as if embarrassed. "I beseeched the Master and asked that James and John be at His right and left hand in the kingdom." She motioned to me, at her right side and to Mary Alphaeus, at her left. "I suppose I did not know what I was asking. I *was* simply trying to look out for my sons — mind you — it is a mother's duty."

I nodded in understanding. "And this request caused the others of the Twelve to be resentful toward your sons?"

"You know how it is when the Twelve argue — and this was about who was the greatest. I tell you, a storm struck." Salome leaned against the wall behind us.

"Dear Salome." Mary Alphaeus' high-pitched voice was faint in the loud room. "Do not forget to tell Esther about what the Master said to them about their dispute."

"I was getting there." Salome pointed a sharp finger at Mary Alphaeus. "Yes, well," she said, smacking her lips together. "The Master said that whoever will be the greater among you, let him be your servant. And he that will be first among you will be your slave."

"Even so as the Son of Man is not come to be served to but to serve," Mary Alphaeus added quickly, in response to a little glare from Salome.

I looked at the two women as I considered what they had said. This was not the first time Jesus told us that we must become the least in order to be the greatest. It was the poor in spirit who possessed the kingdom of Heaven.

"Becoming a slave…" I tested the word *slave*. "All I think of is suffering when He speaks of such things. He seems to want us to suffer." I was troubled by His implications. "Yet He heals all of our wounds."

I put a hand over my stomach. Most of our wounds.

Salome nodded. "You missed His many mentions of suffering these past months while you have been here in Bethany. He continues to mention Jerusalem as well. He says that is where His suffering will be. If that is so, I do not see why we are going there for Passover. Would it not be wiser to celebrate the feast somewhere else?"

"What was that?" asked Mary Alphaeus, cupping her ear.

Salome sighed and practically yelled in Mary Alphaeus' ear, "Would it not be wiser to celebrate the feast somewhere else!"

"Dear, where else can we celebrate the feast beside the Holy City?" Mary Alphaeus was clearly dismayed. "It *must* be in Jerusalem."

Salome gave a huff of annoyance. "Then I say we stay in Bethany, at the very least. The more distance between us and the chief priests, the better."

"You do not think they would actually sentence Him to death?" I leaned toward Salome, lowering my voice. "With what could they charge Him?"

"They could think of something. The Master refers to the Pharisees and priests far too often, calling them hypocrites and the like." Salome rubbed her thighs, then rested her hands atop her knees.

"Lazarus' uncle, Simon the Leper is a Pharisee. And he is here with us, enjoying the feast."

"One of the few."

"We still have a week or so before Passover begins," I said. "Perhaps we can persuade Jesus to stay out of the city, for His safety."

"Dear, He has rebuked us whenever someone suggests that." Mary Alphaeus' voice was like a bird's chirping.

I shook my head and looked about the room, which did little to distract me from my growing worry for Jesus. *Father, help us. Bless us. Protect Your Son!*

Susanna briskly approached, passing those sitting on the floor. She wiped her hands on her apron. She, Martha, and Mary insisted that they continue waiting upon us, with the servants, until the meal was completed.

Susanna asked if we had seen Mary.

"Not as of late," I said. "Was she not with you in the kitchen?"

"She was." Susanna sighed. "Martha sent me out looking for her. Mary's been in a very strange mood tonight. Have you noticed?" Susanna gave a rare frown.

I shook my head, feeling guilty that I had not noticed. I was not as sensitive and motherly as Susanna. "Is she well?"

"I am not sure. She seems distant — lost in thought. She is clearly preoccupied with something."

Salome nudged me with her elbow. "I would not be surprised if it was your husband's return to life. That is enough to stir anyone's emotions."

"Any sign of her?" Martha came in, a dessert dish of dried apples mixed with toasted sesame, in her arms.

Susanna lightly touched her forehead. "No."

"I am worried about her. Do you think she is at the hospice? If she is, she should at least tell me." Martha's lips formed a thin line as she and Susanna continued serving.

"I will help them," Mary Alphaeus said, and the delicate lady left for the room.

I too was about to assist, but Salome trapped me with her running tongue. "They say Herod wishes to see the Master."

"That would be an interesting encounter, indeed." I looked her way, slightly agitated.

"All he wants is to see Jesus perform a miracle," Salome said, shaking her head. "I sure hope the Master does not give him one. All that man wants is entertainment."

"Herod should come see Lazarus for himself, then. I do wonder what would happen if Herod came to believe that Jesus is the Messiah, the Son of Elohim." I leaned my head against the stone wall, the smell of toasted sesame entering my nostrils.

Salome laughed bitterly. "I doubt it. More likely for Herod to think he is Elohim himself. That man's only pursuit is his own."

"The Romans are the ones who think they are Elohim," I pointed out. "Herod is a Jew."

Salome huffed. "So he claims…he is just like his father who massacred those infants in Bethlehem all those years ago in fear of the Messiah." She tilted her head in Jesus' direction. "Well, it looks like he did not succeed."

I nodded. The story had gone around the disciples about Jesus' birth in Bethlehem.

My gaze followed hers to Jesus, seated on the opposite side of the room. He looked His usual calm self as He spoke to Simon the Leper, although He waved His hands as He talked.

Jesus disappeared from my view as a few people walked in front of me. When they left, a woman was seated at Jesus' feet.

I straightened to get a better view and identified the woman's soft pink veil as belonging to Mary.

The noise lowered as heads turned to watch the strange act.

The smell of nard overcame the smell of lamb. The strong scent reminded me of Lazarus' death. Was it not within the past month that we anointed my husband's body?

I resisted the urge to stand and walk over to them. I did see Mary place a little jar on the floor beside her — the same small jar I saw her with in the kitchen a couple of weeks ago, with rose swirls encasing it.

She poured the dripping nard over Jesus' bare feet.

Salome and I exchanged glances.

Now Mary gingerly removed her veil so she could wipe Jesus' feet with her hair, which she did with grace and delicacy, as if pressing too hard would damage His skin.

Simon the Leper leaned back, clearly uncomfortable with what he saw his niece doing. The disciples began to murmur, as they often did, many of them showing obvious signs of disapproval.

"Why is she doing this?"

"It is Mary, the sister of Lazarus."

"Untimely...Could she not do this in private?"

Judas's voice penetrated the room, above all the others. It was a smooth voice, like freshly pressed oil. "Why was this ointment not sold for three hundred dinars and given to the poor?" He reclined at the far end of the table, and fiddled with his collar. "Is this not a waste?"

Mary looked up at him, her face unreadable.

"Let her alone," Jesus said, looking down at Mary. "That she may keep it for the day of My burial."

The murmuring only increased.

"There He goes, speaking about death again," Salome whispered. I quite agreed.

Mary resumed wiping His feet as Jesus said, "The poor you always have with you, but Me, you will not always have."

Suffering and burial. Death. Slave. I reflected on his words, unsure. Jesus was the light of the world. The good shepherd. The gate, the resurrection and the life. The bread of life. If we ate of His bread, we would never die, but would have eternal life. Surely, it was time for Him to *give* us this bread, so we could all partake of it.

Chapter 33

Exult greatly, O daughter Zion!
Shout for joy, O daughter Jerusalem!
Behold: your king is coming to you, a just savior is he,
Humble, and riding on a donkey, on a colt, the foal of a donkey.
ZECHARIAH 9:9

Bethpage was behind us, nestled on the opposite side of the Mount of Olives where we could see stone terraces topped with olive trees. We dipped into the Kidron Valley, its grass burnt from the touch of endless sun. The Holy City's crowded architecture rose mightily above us like a king on his throne. The flat, golden-tipped roof sheltering the Holy of Holies in the Temple was like its crown.

It was a short walk from Bethany to Jerusalem, an hour or two at most. More people joined our assembly with each downward step we took — not only those from Bethany, Bethpage, and Jericho — but Jews from all across Palestine. Idumea to Phoenicia. Then, there were Greek Jews who travelled from Ethiopia to Rome herself, all on pilgrimage for Passover. Thousands, their shoulders constantly brushing against mine.

How lovely are Your tabernacles, O Adonai of hosts!

It was not only the great Temple the people wished to see, but Jesus.

A fly batted at my cheek. Swiping it away, I let my eyes fall on the Master. People shouted praises at Him like never before. They craved even the slightest contact with Him and hailed Him as king.

I smiled. Ironically, our great king sat upon a white donkey. I saw Jesus' head of dark hair, the center of all the attention. Jesus had requested that Andrew and James Zebedee retrieve the humble animal for Him. If He were not riding it, I feared He would literally be trampled on by the people. The Twelve stayed especially close to Jesus, as usual, to keep people from getting too close. A few people waved palm branches as they shouted to Jesus.

"The Kyrios will not be celebrating Passover in our home," Martha told me as we walked, disappointment etched on her defined face.

"It cannot be celebrated in Bethany. The law of Moses says it must be in Jerusalem," I replied.

"You know what I mean! In the house we own in Jerusalem. Where Hezekiah always is."

Since Jesus began His ministry, we had been hosted at the house of Nicodemus for the night of Passover. I had assumed that was where we would feast this year.

"You will still have plenty of people to serve at your home," Magdalene assured Martha. "Some of the disciples, our relatives, the caravan from Nazareth and Cana…"

I frowned at the word "Nazareth." My mother would be coming and likely staying with Martha and Mary. Would Aunt Mary, Uncle Clopas, and Aunt Miriam be with them as well? Or would they stay with Jesus?

Martha heaved a heavy sigh. "I am most pleased when I am serving the Kyrios."

I did not know where my sister-in-law Mary was, but she was likely finding another way to remain close to Jesus' side.

"Do not fret, Martha," Magdalene said, gently touching her sister's shoulder. "You can still come into the city, as you are now, to hear Rabboni preach in the Temple."

"Count yourself blessed," I said. "Jesus is staying under your roof in Bethany until Passover begins."

"He seems to prefer our Garden of Gethsemane," Martha pointed out.

"He goes there to pray. Not to sleep." I thought of the canopy of olive trees behind us, their leaves rustling in the breezes, and smiled fondly. At night, I could look down from Gethsemane and see the lights of the Holy City. I took Martha's hand and patted it with as much love as I could muster. "He needs the garden. It is a quiet place for Him to retreat. Look at these many people." I gestured ahead of me.

The multitude, my friends included, walked with light steps and an eager pace — almost as if we were dancing. Though I was one with the peoples' excitement over our Kyrios entering Jerusalem, I could not help the small snake of anxiety coiled in the pit of my stomach. It was no secret that the chief priests as well as other Pharisees were planning to arrest Jesus for the stir He was causing.

It was exactly as Jesus said. He had come to cause division. Thousands upon thousands believed in Him, praising Him with all that they were, yet there were the thousands who hated Him with all that they were.

More people grabbed branches from palm trees and waved them about.

"O Abraham," Martha gasped.

"They are proclaiming Him savior and king!" I declared. Palm branches were not simply a means of celebration. They were a political statement.

"They will be wanting a revolution," Magdalene grumbled. "Can they not see that Jesus is no Zealot? Let them put the branches down. He is no political leader."

Years ago, before the Romans inhabited our land, the great Judas Maccabeus victoriously freed Israel by defeating the Greeks. The people praised his victory with palm branches. Was this now the time for Jesus to defeat the Romans in the same way the Maccabees defeated the Greeks? How could this be, if Jesus refused the people any sort of violence or rebellion?

As we sloped upward toward the Temple mount, masses of people streamed from the Temple, running toward us.

"Hosanna!"

"Son of David!"

"King of Israel!"

"Blessed is He who comes in the name of Adonai!"

Joining the people, the disciples, too, shouted praises.

"Hosanna! Hosanna!"

"Shalom in Heaven!"

"Blessed is the King!"

"Glory in the highest," I shouted with them, beaming.

I glanced at Magdalene, her teeth pressing against her bottom lip. Was she *that* nervous that a revolution was going to begin right now?

We came closer to the East Gate of the Temple.

"Enjoy the acclamations, Magdalene," I told her. "They believe Jesus is the Messiah. Be content with that." I giggled with enjoyment as I watched ecstatic people rushing by. Some with dark skin tones in pale tunics. Others with golden hair. Some with rich, vibrant clothing.

I ran a few strides ahead toward my husband. "Look how many believe in Jesus, Lazarus! Surely it is because of your miracle," I shouted at him.

Lazarus looked at me grimly, for at my words, a burly looking man ran toward him and slammed his hands upon his shoulders, yelling, "You are Lazarus! Are you not?"

"Yes..." Lazarus said slowly.

"Praise Elohim." The man patted Lazarus cheeks. "You are alive! Tell me, how did it feel...once you were alive again?"

"I was thankful to Adonai." Lazarus answered the familiar question with his familiar answer. "After the initial shock, of course..."

More people drew closer to Lazarus, realizing that he was indeed the man whom Jesus made rise from the dead.

They began reaching for and yelling at him. I was jostled aside and tried to return to my husband's side, but it was useless. He was shoved ahead of me.

I stood on my tiptoes to see Jesus. Peter and John were assisting Him dismount the mule so they could walk up the steps to the East Gate.

"Lazarus!" A woman screamed in my ear, far too loudly in comparison to the others shouting my husband's name.

Magdalene linked her arm through mine.

"Hosanna," the people chanted.

Magdalene said nothing.

We slowly progressed up the steps to the East Gate. The Pharisees and Temple guards were distraught, not knowing how to control the masses.

Lazarus was still some distance ahead of me as we piled into the southern portion of the Court of Gentiles where we found even more people shouting praises to Jesus.

Moneychangers were lined up along the pillars that separated the court from Solomon's Porch.

The putrid smell of animals readied for sacrifice, birds, cattle, and sheep, was overwhelming.

The horns of the Levite choir echoed faintly from within the inner courts.

The Temple guards, with their shiny cone-shaped hats and tall spears, pushed through the crowds. They listened intently to the orders of the chief priests and Pharisees, in their long-tasseled cloaks and thick turbans. For a moment, I saw Martha's husband, the tall Hezekiah, among them. Many of the Temple guards plunged into the crowd.

I had lost sight of Jesus, but Lazarus was still near, besieged by people.

"Esther!" Magdalene cried, tightening her hold on my arm. I looked at her wide eyes, then followed her line of vision.

"What frightens you?" I asked, taking in her sharp anxiety.

"The guards," she said. "They are nearing Lazarus."

A handful of guards pushed their way toward Lazarus, the center of a storm of people.

"They will not do him any harm," I said, assuring both myself and her.

"I cannot see!" She strained her neck for a better view.

"Here." I pulled her through the crowd to the staircase that led to the Court of Women. We climbed the first few stairs then stopped to look at the crowd. I gasped.

A Temple guard held Lazarus by the arm.

"For the love of Israel!" I put my hand to my mouth.

When a second guard grabbed Lazarus' other arm, a sort of riot erupted. As the guards attempted to seize Lazarus, the people started pushing them away.

"Lazarus!"

"Leave him be!"

"You cannot arrest him!"

"Get off of him!"

"Lazarus," I cried with the people.

The guards struggled but were continually pushed back until a crowd surrounded my husband.

I was so relieved. They could not seize him — not if it was against the will of the people. And it looked like the people were in our favor.

Four days had passed since Jesus entered triumphantly into Jerusalem. No one had tried to lay a hand on Lazarus since he entered the Temple despite the guards' attempt to stop him.

Yet tensions were evident.

I did not know what Jesus was doing. In a rage, He overturned the tables of the money changers, proclaiming the Temple to be a house of prayer, and not a den of thieves. He healed the blind. He healed the lame. He told parables. He answered the tricky questions of the chief priests and elders with both calm and never-before heard wisdom. He denounced the scribes and the Pharisees. He said the Temple would be destroyed. He spoke of the end times, and what to expect. He told more parables.

Vendors in the marketplace outside of the Temple usually hawked their produce, cakes, tools, spices, jewelry, and crafts but their calls were muted by the overwhelming noise of pilgrims in Jerusalem for the eve of Passover.

Peter, John, the women, and myself walked through the crowded streets. We followed one of Nicodemus' servants, Nebo, who carried a large jar of water.

"Those blasted Pharisees!" I mumbled quietly, so no one could hear me. "They question Jesus as if He were on trial."

At every corner, we encountered more people coming from all directions. As we passed houses, we saw bodies crammed into every corner. The floors and roofs were carpeted with people.

"The kingdom of Heaven will not belong to those Pharisees and chief priests." I continued my mutterings.

Sweat made its way down my forehead as I did my best to get through the maze. The size of the homes increased as we made our way through the upper city. The affluent limestone structures of the rich were as closely packed as the feeble homes of the poor.

"Nicodemus has a marvelous view of the Temple," Joanna recalled, holding on to Salome's elbow. "From the roof of his house."

Salome shook her head slightly. "It is not *his* house we stay in, but his *guest* house. The man is a *secret* disciple. Nicodemus will not bring the Master into his own house, but rather keeps the Kyrios next door, to ensure his own safety!"

"I give thanks that we have a member of the Sanhedrin who is a disciple," Susanna said hopefully.

"He seems to be the only one," I pointed out, quickly nudging Susanna out of the way of a man running with a basket of fruit on his head.

"Is not Martha's husband Hezekiah a part of the Sanhedrin?" Joanna asked. Her spine remained straight despite the weight of Salome leaning on her.

"No. He is indeed a Pharisee, but not one of the chief priests," I said. "He shows his distaste for Jesus by silence and absence. But Nicodemus can only be an asset to us, even if he is a fearful man."

"Let us take what we receive," Magdalene said. She apologized to a woman she bumped into. "It is good that we are in the Essene quarter with some distance between us and Caiaphas' palace."

Salome stopped. "There it is," she said, pointing out Nicodemus' two-story mansion. "I remember it well." Beside the mansion was the guest house. Large, but simpler in architecture, it had many more windows than the mansion, which had little need for windows with its large courtyard in the center.

A woman servant who must have been anticipating our arrival greeted us. We filed into a spacious room with a red-toned mosaic decorating the center of the floor.

"The feast will be in the upper room," Peter called behind him. He and John set up the stairs, which lined the back wall. "If we have an overflow, we can seat them downstairs."

"You have Candence and me to assist you." Nebo carried his jar of water into the kitchen area. "With whatever you need for your preparations." The woman beside him must have been Candence. Nebo looked directly at Magdalene as if she were the mistress of us all. Perhaps she was, as she stood confidently at the front of our lot. "We should have all the furnishings you need. Our master says that if you need anything else, to simply ask, and we will purchase it for you from the market. The house was cleared of all leaven last night."

Magdalene clasped her hands in front of her. "Then let us waste no time." She began speaking about the preparations with the two servants.

I smiled as Magdalene took charge. She was the mistress of a wealthy household when her husbands were alive in Magdala. As were Susanna and Joanna, but theirs was a passive joy that allowed Magdalene to lead.

After speaking with the servants, Magdalene turned to us, anticipation glinting in her eyes. "Nebo, you and Candence can bring more cushions and pillows to the upper room, as you mentioned. Oh, and do not forget the candles." She gave instructions to each of us. "Joanna and Susanna will work on the *matzah*. Salome — you begin setting the table with the ritual cups. Mary Alphaeus, you shall help Salome — especially with walking upstairs." She examined us with eagerness and then ran to the stairs, shouting up at the Apostles. "Peter and John! Prepare for the arrival of the Passover lamb — get a fire started in the courtyard next door!"

Nearly out of breath, Magdalene ran back to me as the other women dispersed, setting out on their tasks.

"Esther, you and I will prepare the fruit and nut paste, and the bitter herbs."

"What can I help with?" A dear, familiar voice called from behind us.

I turned, my garments whipping around with me. The light from the open doorway poured gently upon my mother.

Not my mother by blood. My true mother.

"Aunt Mary," I gasped and embraced her sweetly. The warmth from her gentle hands and soft mantle seeped into me.

"Esther, I have missed you." She sighed and pulled away to look at me. "I have waited for this time with great anticipation."

"Dear Mary." Magdalene swept in beside me, taking her turn to embrace my aunt. "Your son will be pleased to see you when He arrives. He and the rest of the disciples are in the Temple as we speak. The men will be purchasing our Passover lamb."

"How have Uncle Clopas and Aunt Miriam been taking care of you?" I asked, eager for my aunt's attention.

"They spoil me." She waved her hand light-heartedly. "They went to the Temple and will join us tonight."

I examined my aunt, her dark black veil wrapped tightly around her head, framing her face which was glistening with sweat from her journey. Yet her soft eyes glistened more. Her eyebrows crinkled in concern; she always did listen with attentiveness. Her shoulders were rolled back with their usual straightness. The dark blue of her mantle draped around her shoulders. The sleeves of her tunic hung down her wrists. I noticed that her hands were shaking.

"My dear aunt." I took her hands. "Whatever is the matter? Are you frightened?"

Aunt Mary smiled, carefully pulling back from my grasp. "I am well, Esther. Passover fills me with many emotions."

She clearly was worried. Her son, no doubt, was the reason for that. If we, the disciples, were fearful for Him, how much more was His own mother?

"Come," Magdalene said. "Let us prepare for the feast as we talk." Her eyes sparkled as she led us to the kitchen area.

We were met with the smell of flour mixing with the oil and salt. During the first Passover, our ancestors had no time to let the bread rise. In their memory, we ate this unleavened bread, matzah.

Joanna and Susanna stopped working with the dough in order to greet the mother of our Kyrios.

"Will you begin cutting the apples?" Magdalene looked to me as she surveyed the table filled with provisions for the meal. She put a finger to her pointed chin. "I am going to ask Nebo for a good bowl for the paste. One that will keep it ritually clean." She left the kitchen.

I brought a basket filled with apples to a back counter, by wooden cutting boards. I searched through a few cupboards until I found a good knife and then set to work peeling the apples.

Aunt Mary appeared at my right, her mantle off her shoulders, and the sleeves of her tunic rolled up, ready for work.

"Shall I core them as you peel?" She looked at me.

I nodded. "That will work well." I went back to the cupboards to search for another good knife, happily finding a thicker one with a wooden handle. I gave it to my aunt.

"Tell me of Nazareth," I said as I ran the sharp knife over the skin of a red apple.

"Jude has another two grandchildren," Aunt Mary said.

My heart ached, not only because Lazarus and I were of the age of grandparents — if we had had children — but for the brethren I could not see. Particularly Ima.

"Abijam passed from this life." Aunt Mary glanced at me.

"Abijam." I had almost forgotten that man. The farmer who I almost was betrothed to as a girl. "Thank goodness Lazarus came when he did."

"I am sorry?" Aunt Mary pushed the juicy apples farther back on the cutting board.

"I was thinking of Lazarus." I picked up a golden apple — my favorite variety, as it had the sweetest taste.

"How does your husband fare?"

"He is rather solemn. I do not blame him, though. Since his return to life — I assume you heard about it?" I looked to her and she nodded with a smile. "Since then, people have been flocking to him. As if he were second to your son. They are eager to touch him and speak with him. I worry greatly, Aunt Mary. Just earlier this week, the chief priests tried to have him arrested. I cannot believe the ridiculousness of our leaders! If it were not against the will of the people, I fear they would have taken Lazarus and killed him."

"But they have no reason to kill him," Magdalene said, entering the room and setting a large white glass bowl, accented with blue, on the center table. She grabbed a large jar and a bowl.

"Other than Lazarus is living proof that Jesus is the Son of Elohim?" I set the knife and apple against the table to watch Magdalene as she transferred handfuls of walnuts from the jar to the bowl. "They hold such anger in their hearts. Such rage over your son's influence over the people," I said, looking back at my aunt. And I had rage in my heart for them. "Magdalene is right, though," I continued. "They may wish to arrest your son, as well as Lazarus." I picked up the apple and continued to peel it. "But our leaders have no law they can use to condemn Jesus and Lazarus and therefore cannot cause them harm."

"We have been on turbulent waters all week," Magdalene explained to my aunt. Finding a satisfactory amount of walnuts in the bowl, she closed the lid to the jar and set it on the center table. She returned, wiping her hands against each other. "Rabboni drove the moneychangers out of the Temple this past Sabbath day. He disrupted the shouts of 'hosannas' and palm waving from the people, but they still hang upon His every word."

"I will admit, I have never seen Jesus so angry before," I told Aunt Mary.

"I am sure I have," Aunt Mary said, expertly slicing apples. "Many men in this world afflict the Kyrios. It pains Jesus greatly." She looked at us pointedly. "You must console my son in order to soften the anger of the heavenly Father."

I thought of the wrath of Adonai. It was frightening to ponder. Surely our heavenly Father was angered by the chief priests and Pharisees. What would Elohim do to those who were against His own Son?

I shuddered. Our leaders repulsed me as much as the Romans.

"Chop up the walnuts when you are done with the apples," Magdalene said. I nodded as I picked up the final golden apple to peel.

Aunt Mary chopped the cored apples as Magdalene left in search of other ingredients.

"We are being very selective this year for who partakes in the Passover meal," I told Aunt Mary. "Though we lost many disciples since Jesus' sermon in Capernaum, we have a new bunch with us. We will spread out amongst the houses. Jesus wants only the closest disciples here. That would be the Twelve and all of us women and a few others. The rest of the disciples will have Passover at Hezekiah's — well, Martha's house in Jerusalem."

I looked to Aunt Mary, who was concentrating on her chopping.

"That day in Capernaum was most peculiar," I mused. "Jesus called Himself the bread of life. He said that we had to trogo His body and drink His blood." I blew out a sigh and set down the final apple.

"And what did He promise if you partook of Him?" Aunt Mary's eyes filled with hopeful anticipation.

"Eternal life."

Chapter 34

Food from heaven you gave them in their hunger, water from a
rock you sent them in their thirst. You told them to enter and
occupy the land which you had sworn to give them.

NEHEMIAH 9:15

Evening came swiftly. The house was filled with the smell of fresh matzah, fruit and nut paste, bitter herbs, wine, and of course, the Passover lamb.

Jesus and the rest of the Twelve had arrived with the slaughtered lamb from the Temple a few hours previous. Lazarus and the rest of the disciples arrived soon after they had finished several ritualized prayers in the House of Elohim.

A pleasant feeling of importance and purpose stirred within me as I mixed the fruit and nut paste. It was far past the need for stirring, but I could not help it. I was eager for this meal, which we prepared only once a year, and wished everything to be perfect for it.

The fragrance of cinnamon and apple pleased my nostrils.

"Esther, stop dreaming. We need to make haste. Salome has already lit the candles," Magdalene said.

I blinked, scooping the delightful olive wood bowl of the nut paste into my arms. As I walked into the main room, I saw Joanna carrying flasks of wine upstairs. She disappeared into the upper room. The voices of the disciples carried down to me.

I began my ascent as well, slightly nervous about such a large celebration.

The upper room was as full of people as the serving dishes were full of food. Weaving between the guests, I walked across the room to place the bowl on the decorative stone table, parallel to the entranceway and nearest to the head table. The fragrant Passover lamb, which the Apostles baked to a dark brown this afternoon in Nicodemus' courtyard, rested in the center of the stone table. The rue that served as our bitter herbs and the salt water we dipped it in was already set at each person's place. And of course, each seat had a cup for wine.

I glanced behind me. The women and servants were scattered about, pointedly seeing to the final touches of the meal as carefully as when they added the last bits of seasoning to the food.

Seated at the head table, on the other side of me, Jesus and the Twelve were laughing, though there was a certain tension in the room. The table was low to the ground and in the common horseshoe shape. Jesus rested at the customary seat of honor on the left-hand bar of the table while the Apostles reclined on either side. They lay on fine cushions of red, maroon, and bronze. John sat close to Jesus' right and Judas sat in the seat of honor on Jesus' left.

A white linen tablecloth with scarlet embroidery covered the head table. Wooden plates held the bitter herbs; cutleries and napkins were set before each Apostle. Candles and several oil lamps illuminated the dishes around them.

The rest of the disciples were scattered about the room. Their table was the rug-covered floor and they sat on a variety of mats and pillows. Nebo and Candence stood dutifully near the door, ready to serve.

I smiled at Aunt Mary, who humbly sat in a corner to the right of the table with Uncle Clopas and Aunt Miriam.

For a brief moment, I envisioned Ima sitting beside Aunt Mary, but I shook the fanciful notion from my mind.

A door behind my aunt and uncle led to the balcony. As for the walls, they were covered with drapery and curtains of maroon and scarlet. All an obvious sign of Nicodemus' wealth, although Nicodemus, himself was not there. Likely he was celebrating the feast in his own home or with other Pharisees. Many would say that it was because of his fear of being seen with Jesus.

Someone poked me. I turned to see Mary Alphaeus. "Sit down, dear Esther," she said in her sing-song voice. "All is prepared."

I smiled and obeyed, choosing to crouch down beside my husband, across from the gap in the horseshoe-shaped table. The table with the bowls and platters of food was close to our left. I adjusted the large bronze-colored pillow behind me so I could lean against it.

"You have been busy," Lazarus observed.

"It is fitting to be busy for a feast, but Magdalene is the truly busy one. She has filled the role of hostess more than any other," I said, as Magdalene knelt beside me on cue. She let out a relieved sigh as she reclined. "More so than the servants," I added, patting her arm.

"I have greatly..." My eyes bolted toward Jesus as I heard His voice. "I have greatly desired to eat this Passover with you." He lowered His tone. "Before I suffer."

Hearing His words, the jubilant disciples silenced. Jesus rested on His side. His face was near the table and His legs were sprawled behind Him.

I was filled with confusion and bewilderment. Suffer? Was He not just smiling with joy a moment earlier? Why did He continue to speak about suffering? He already was suffering as He dealt with the angry chief priests and ecstatic crowds.

"Now," Jesus continued, all of His weight falling on His left arm. "Let us begin our Passover meal." He smiled as if dismissing His previous comment.

I exchanged a glance with Magdalene. Her nose crinkled as if hit by a putrid smell.

The Passover was very much like the todah sacrifice we had a week earlier in Bethany to thank Adonai for Lazarus' return to life.

Jesus held the cup of the first wine in front of Him. With a wave of the hand, He summoned Nebo. The rather frail servant gave Jesus a small pitcher of water. Jesus adjusted His position on the cushions so that He might sit upon His heels. He accepted the water and dripped it into the first cup of wine.

"Blessed are You, Adonai our El, King of the Universe, who creates the fruit of the vine." Jesus murmured the blessing over the cup.

This was the Cup of Sanctification. It reminded us of the promise Elohim made to our ancestors to bring us out of Egypt.

"Blessed are You, Adonai our El, King of the Universe, who has kept us in life, sustained us, and enabled us to reach this season." Jesus drank and the disciples followed.

I sipped the undiluted red wine.

As each of us drank from our cup, Jesus stood and gingerly stepped over the cushions as well as bodies reclining on the floor. John offered his hand to steady Jesus as Jesus made His way out of the tightly packed corner. Jesus placed a hand on Peter's head for balance as He stepped past the man.

Peter. A rock indeed according to the title that Jesus gave him.

I had to turn completely to follow Jesus as He moved toward Candence and Nebo, standing between two stone tables. One table held everything needed for handwashing and the other was covered with dishes for the meal.

The servants had the bowls and pitchers ready to ritually cleanse Jesus' hands. When He reached the servants Jesus greeted them with a smile.

"Nebo. Sit down," He said to the male servant.

Nebo's eyes widened in horror as Jesus looked at him expectantly.

"Sit down," Jesus repeated gently.

My eyebrows raised. Nebo was red with embarrassment as he set his bowl and pitcher on the table. He sat, careful not to rest against the luxury of a pillow.

Jesus removed the burgundy cloak from His shoulders and let it fall upon the floor.

"Sit down as well, Candence," Jesus said. He undid His belt and removed His outer tunic.

I frowned as He plopped His outer garment on the floor and wrapped His belt around His inner tunic.

Candence set a large pitcher of water on the floor and cautiously sat beside Nebo.

The disciples whispered amongst themselves as Jesus grabbed beige towels from the handwashing table against the wall.

I looked at Magdalene. Did she understand what He was doing? Noticing me, she simply shrugged and looked back to Jesus, who was tying a towel on His waist.

Jesus knelt in front of Nebo, who stared at Him with his mouth agape. Jesus was holding a wooden bowl and pitcher.

At the main table, Peter coughed rather obnoxiously.

Jesus began washing the servant's feet.

I put a hand to my mouth. Aunt Mary, in the corner, smiled tenderly as she gazed at her son. Salome, beside my aunt, whispered loudly to Aunt Miriam and Mary Alphaeus who nodded in agreement. Uncle Clopas scowled. Near them, Joanna and Susanna stared with blank faces.

My attention returned to Jesus, who gently washed the servant's feet. I looked to see the reaction of the Twelve. On the right-hand beam of the table, Bartholomew stroked his beard. Philip, beside him, frowned. Andrew was looking at the sidewall as if that was where the action was displayed. James Zebedee grimaced and Thaddeus and Simon whispered to each other. Toward the table's center beam, James Alphaeus' mouth was a giant hole, waiting for flies to enter. Thomas spoke in his ear. Matthew tilted his head to the side in interest. On the left-hand beam, Judas' eyes were no larger than slits. John looked down at his hands, while Peter's face was quite red.

Magdalene, beside me, angled toward Jesus. Lazarus' expression was stoic.

I looked back. Jesus had dried Nebo's feet. With a cheerful smile He now was washing Candence's feet.

The disciples' comments and questions grew louder. Jesus made His way to the head table, His back to me. "All of you." Jesus looked at the Twelve. "Come out from behind the table and sit so I may wash your feet."

The Apostles looked at one another, most likely waiting for the first to dare do so.

Silence.

At last, James Alphaeus rose, quickly followed by Matthew. They sat in front of the table. Uncle Clopas let out a growl-like sound. The rest of the Apostles reluctantly followed, except Peter, who shifted from a reclining position to sitting, so that his arms were crossed over his chest as he glared at his fellow eleven.

Jesus washed James Alphaeus' feet, then Matthew's, and then John's.

"Peter," Jesus said, moving closer to the main table.

Peter looked up at Him. "Kyrios," Peter croaked. He cleared his throat. "Do You wash my feet?"

Jesus nodded. "What I do now, you do not yet know, but you will know later."

Peter leaned back and grabbed a cushion, as if to hide himself. "You will never wash my feet."

Jesus loudly sighed. "If I wash you not, you will have no part with Me."

Peter's eyes widened. He looked around the room, striving to find words. "Kyrios!" He threw the cushion from his lap and stumbled up. "Not only my feet, but also my hands and my head."

"He that is washed needs not but to wash his feet, but is clean wholly," Jesus said as Peter hopped over the cushions to get out from behind the table. "And you are clean." Jesus looked back at all of His disciples. "But not all."

Gasps echoed against the large room's limestone walls.

A cry rose in me. I wondered if He meant me. Was it still my barrenness? "Who among us is unclean?"

"Has someone failed to ritually purify themselves?"

The disciples murmured as Jesus cleansed Peter's feet. After finishing, He rose and moved on to James Zebedee. James Alphaeus and Matthew helped Him wash the rest of the Twelve's feet.

I adjusted my position as I waited for whatever else was to come. I supposed I should be used to Jesus altering our traditions. Instead of simply having the servants help us cleanse our hands, *He* chose to wash our *feet*. Only when I lived as a rich woman in Bethany did I have my feet washed, and always by a plain servant. As a young girl in Nazareth, I washed my own and Ima's feet.

Soon enough, all of the Twelve had their feet washed, and Jesus ordered them to go in pairs to wash the rest of the disciple's feet.

Peter walked toward Lazarus, Magdalene, and me with a basin full of water, Judas behind him. Peter set the bowl down in front of Lazarus first.

"Judas, grab a towel," Peter commanded as he pulled Lazarus' feet into the bowl. Judas scowled and retrieved a towel.

Judas pushed the towel into Peter's face without a word.

Peter shoved his hand away. "I am washing the feet. You can dry them." He moved in front of me.

I awkwardly surrendered my feet to Peter who plopped them in the basin, not caring that water splashed out onto the rug. He washed them with diligence, though. He worked quickly but thoroughly. His hands roughly rubbed my soles, causing them to tingle. The cool water felt refreshing.

I looked to Judas, who stared sourly. I glanced down, feeling uncomfortable.

"Come, Judas." Peter pulled the bowl from under my feet, allowing them to drip on the floor, and set the bowl before Magdalene.

"I am not a dog," Judas growled.

"Just dry her feet. The water from them is seeping into the carpet."

"I am not drying a barren woman's feet! Is it not enough that I have touched a man's?"

Peter pointed to Magdalene's and put her feet into the bowl. "*Dry her feet*," he said through clenched teeth.

"I will do it." Lazarus tugged the towel from Judas' hands.

"Laza — " Peter started, angrily.

"I will do it," Lazarus repeated, taking my feet and gently patting them dry. He looked into my eyes, communicating his annoyance at Judas. All I could do was thank our heavenly Father that Lazarus stepped in when he did, or else a fight would have broken out. All because of my lowly, barren, female feet. A familiar bitterness seeped into me as Lazarus went on to dry Magdalene's feet.

I refused to look directly at Judas, but from the corner of my eye, I saw him return to the head table. Anger rained on me and my mind battled to forgive him.

Thankfully, time passed quickly as Jesus and the Apostles cleaned up. I watched Jesus put on His outer garments, draping His dark cloak on one shoulder.

Soon, Jesus and the Twelve were again reclining at the head table. Servants began bringing the dishes to them from the side tables.

"Do you know what I have done for you?" Jesus's authoritative voice resounded throughout the large room. "You call Me 'Master' and 'Kyrios,' and you say well, for so I am. If then, I being your Kyrios and Master, have washed your feet, you also ought to wash one another's feet."

I rested my chin in my left hand, knowing He was directing this to all of us. He was asking me to be a servant to all others. Had I not done enough? Was I not a mother of all those gathered here?

My gut rolled with discomfort. Would that nagging feeling ever leave? Now I needed to wash other people's feet? Even Judas', who refused to wash mine?

"All of you, dip your herbs in the salted water," Jesus said. "Remember the events of the first Passover. Remember the tears of the Israelites in Egypt. Recall your own tears presently."

We obeyed Jesus.

"Blessed are You, Adonai our El, King of the Universe, who creates the fruit of the earth." I prayed with the rest of the congregation.

I dipped my leaf of rue in the saltwater and chewed the bitter herb. I would dip a second time at a later part in the meal. My stomach growled, wishing for more than this meager amount.

Jesus's face was a mix of troubling emotions. "Amen, amen, I say to you," He continued. "One of you will betray Me."

My eyes widened. We all looked at each other as if trying to find a Roman soldier in the crowd.

"Is it I?" Magdalene asked immediately.

"Is it I?" John wondered.

"Could it possibly be me?" Thomas said.

"Kyrios, surely it is not I?" Everyone spoke at once.

Peter leaned over the table, past John and toward Jesus, looking into the Master's eyes with great intensity. "Kyrios, who is it?"

Jesus sighed, plucking a morsel of bitter rue from His plate. "It is he whom I will reach, morsel dipped."

My heart began to beat faster and faster as I watched Jesus dip the spindly herb into a small wooden bowl of salted water. Typically, it would be an honor to dip from the same bowl as the guest of honor. I looked across the length of the main table for any sign of who this betrayer could be.

Jesus' hand froze in front of Judas.

"Is it I, Rabbi?" Judas asked in his smooth voice as he looked at the green sprig in front of him.

His gaze skimmed to Jesus and back to the herb.

"You have said it," Jesus said.

Judas took the herb from Him. Chewing slowly, he then swallowed.

"Why does he eat of it?"

"Surely this means something else."

"What you are going to do, do quickly," Jesus said in a stony tone I had never heard from Him before.

Judas looked around briefly and grabbed his mantle from behind him. Rising, he stepped behind Thaddeus and Simon, dodged around Matthias, and fled the room, disappearing as he set down the staircase.

Magdalene leaned into me. "What do you think of this?" she whispered.

I gulped. "The Master may wish for Judas to buy something for the feast…"

"Esther, you and I prepared the feast ourselves. There is nothing we lack."

"Or the Master wishes for him to give something to the poor. It would be fitting to give to the poor on this special night."

Jesus broke the murmuring as Nebo placed the unleavened bread, covered by a fine linen cloth, in front of Jesus.

"Little children, I am with you only a little longer."

I clenched my teeth as I listened to Jesus' odd words.

"Where I go, you cannot come."

Nebo departed, his eyes humbly lowered.

"A new commandment I give to you: That you love one another as I have loved you."

Was this not what He had been teaching us all along?

"As I have loved you, you also must love one another. By this shall all men know that you are My disciples, if you have love for one another."

An impossible frustration overwhelmed me, and I felt that I could not bear any more uncertainty. He spoke as if He was saying, "Farewell."

Peter asked my question for me. "Kyrios, where do You go?"

Jesus lovingly reached for Peter's arm. "Where I go, you cannot follow Me now, but you will follow later."

Peter leaned in closer, past John, looking up into His eyes. "Why cannot I follow You now? I will lay down my life for You."

"Will you lay down your life for Me?" Jesus asked. "Amen, amen, I say to you, the cock will not crow till you deny Me three times."

The candlelight flickered as Peter drew back, shaking his head. Embarrassment and bemusement reflected on his face, which was now red, almost purple.

I shifted against the cushion, trying to shake off my discomfort. I could not understand. Was this some sort of prophecy? It could not be. Peter was Jesus' leading Apostle. Peter would never deny the Master.

The disciples watched silently as Jesus uncovered the three sheets of unleavened bread. The matzah; the bread of affliction with its pale, coarse surface.

Nebo and Candence presented several dishes at the head table. A large silver platter that held the roasted paschal lamb. More bitter vegetables. The second pitcher of ritual wine: The Cup of Judgment.

"A new king, who knew nothing of Joseph, came to power in Egypt. Thus he enslaved the Israelites and made their lives harsh through servitude and humiliation. This is the basis for the Feast of Unleavened Bread which we commemorate with these different rituals tonight," Jesus said. "John, My youngest Apostle, begin the story of the first Passover."

John looked at Peter and then at Jesus. I wondered if Peter's face was actually red or if it was the dim lighting.

After a moment, John nodded, shifted his position, and began. "Why is this night different from all other nights? Because we were once slaves, and we are slaves no more." He spoke reverently. "Tonight, we eat matzah instead of bread and we eat bitter vegetables, dipping them twice. We recline instead of sitting up straight. This night is different from all other nights because this is the night our ancestors went on the Exodus from Egypt, from slavery to freedom. We celebrate Passover because of what Elohim did for us when we left Egypt."

John and the Twelve continued explaining the meaning behind the Passover meal with traditional stories and parables. We listened to the familiar reasons for this meal: how the blood of the lamb is what saved our ancestors from the Angel of Death; the bread was matzah because our ancestors had no time to let it leaven when fleeing Egypt; the bitter herbs reminded us of the bitterness of slavery which was our life before Adonai delivered us.

"Blessed are You, Adonai our El, King of the Universe, who creates the fruit of the vine." Jesus said the blessing over the Cup of Judgment, symbolizing our deliverance from slavery. Nebo and Candence filled everyone's cup. Jesus drank and we all followed.

I sipped from my wooden goblet. The same undiluted wine.

Nebo brought a bowl of water to Jesus so the Master might cleanse His hands once again.

We sang Psalm 113 and Psalm 114.

Praise Adonai. Who makes a barren woman to dwell in a house, the joyful mother of children.

Did these words ring true for me? For there were some fools like Hezekiah and the Romans who I did not want as my children!

"Blessed are You, Adonai our El, King of the Universe, who has sanctified us with His laws and commanded us to wash our hands."

My cousin's beard was freshly trimmed for the feast, and His walnut-colored hair fell in waves below His shoulders. His face was serious and full of purpose.

Jesus took a piece of matzah from the platter in front of Him and said a blessing over it, beginning the ritual. "Blessed are You, Adonai our El, King of the Universe, who has sanctified us with His laws and commanded us to eat matzah."

He broke the matzah in two and lifted the bread, looking at it intensely. As if the bread were alive.

"Take and eat." Jesus' voice encompassed me. "This is My body, which is given for you."

My mouth dropped as He held up the matzah.

In memory of Him? We were faithful Jews, remembering the first Passover and our salvation from Egypt. How could He ask us to do this in memory of *Him?* That was not matzah, though. He called that bread His body!

He could not be serious. It could not be literal. Surely this was a parable. But was that not what we wondered in Capernaum?

Jesus lowered the matzah. *The bread of life.* Disciples, Ima, for one, had left us at such a claim. How could they eat the very *body* of Jesus?

Jesus handed half of the bread to John, who broke off a piece and handed it to Peter. Andrew followed. Likewise, on the other side, the matzah passed from Thaddeus to Simon and to the other disciples gathered.

My mind felt foggy as the matzah made its way to me. It was in my hands after Lazarus had partaken.

That roughly textured unleavened bread cracked as I snapped off a little piece. As I chewed, I expected something unusual to happen, but nothing did. It was the same as it always tasted. Tasteless. A cracker-like substance that lacked any flavor and was not particularly enjoyable to eat.

It certainly did not taste like flesh. *Blessed be Adonai for that!*

I handed the bread to Magdalene who accepted it. The bread continued to make its way around the room. There seemed to be just enough for Nebo and Candence.

Jesus raised His hands, signaling for the main feast to begin. Nebo came forward with more matzah. Surely, that could not also be His body.

The rest of the disciples and I were in a sort of daze. Usually, chatter and laughter began at this moment, but I was afraid to speak. Even if I had the courage to, I was not sure I would be capable of it.

Andrew cleared his throat, eyeing the vegetables in front of him. I saw him glance at Jesus, who was already spreading the fruit and nut paste onto matzah.

My mouth watered as I watched. Andrew followed Jesus' example and began to fill his plate, eyeing the tempting Passover lamb. Soon, all of the Twelve began to eat the full part of the meal.

When all of those at the head table had taken their share, it was time for me, Aunt Mary, Magdalene, Nebo, and Candence to come around. We filled the plates of the rest of the disciples with food from those dishes. As Aunt Mary served the lamb, my stomach curled with anticipation.

I myself served the celebratory, fruity wine to each disciple. It was not any of the four ritual wines, but purely for festivities. By the time Magdalene and I sat down, having completed our task, I was famished. Beside us, Lazarus spoke with Matthias and Stephen as the chatter in the room increased in volume.

"I am satisfied with this night's feast. The food smells delicious," Magdalene said as she cradled her plate like a baby in her arms.

"Indeed," I said. "What would we have done without you, Magdalene?"

"You would have been perfectly capable as you have Rabboni's mother." Magdalene smiled, jerking her head toward Aunt Mary in the corner.

"And if the Master's mother was not among us, you do not think we would be able to manage?" I tried to be light-hearted, but still felt distracted by Jesus' last words.

She tapped a finger to her chin in playful recollection. "I suppose you would be likely to succeed."

"Likely?" I feigned a smile.

Magdalene giggled as I forced a chuckle.

"And what are you women laughing about?"

I turned at my husband's voice.

"We are at a feast. It is a time for laughter." I gave him a real smile, hoping to see a smile from him in return. But no.

"He seems joyous in one moment," Magdalene said of Jesus as she piled celery, parsley, lettuce, and paste onto matzah. "And the next, troubled by suffering."

I slapped my hand to my knee. "Tell me! Either of you. What does Jesus mean by Judas betraying Him?"

"First, tell me what He means by us eating His very body," Magdalene said, her lips wilting into a thin line. My shoulders relaxed as I realized I was not the only one troubled and perplexed by Jesus' words.

Lazarus was silent.

"Judas has always struck me as overly ambitious when it comes to our salvation," Magdalene finally said.

"Perhaps." I raised my shoulders, biting into my customary sandwich. In truth, I never gave much thought to Judas. He was just another Apostle. "Are we not all overly ambitious for the kingdom? You are being vague, Magdalene. What do you really mean?"

"What I mean is, he is like the Zealots; wishing for the Messiah to bring about revolution." Magdalene sipped wine. "Rabboni has not done such a thing. He has built no army and has no intention to overthrow the Roman Empire."

I thought of my father and Barabbas and other men who had attempted a rebellion against Rome. All of them were squelched.

"*Rather,*" Lazarus said. "He has built an army of disciples with the intention of overthrowing our stony hearts and giving us hearts of flesh."

I tilted my head back, surprised at my husband's wisdom as he referenced the prophet Ezekiel. Lazarus' words had been few but meaningful since his return to life.

"Master, I hear You made quite an entrance into Jerusalem last week," Matthias said loudly, gaining our attention. "I was saddened to have missed it. I was tending to my sick mother."

Jesus seemed to be staring at the opposite wall.

"Yes, so many people believe in You, Kyrios!" John called.

"I heard King Herod wishes to meet You," James Zebedee bellowed, raising his cup in the air.

"That is not a new wish. King Herod has wanted to meet Him for years," Bartholomew pointed out.

"I do not think the people could get any more eager to touch You," Thomas said. "Even today when we journeyed from Bethany to Jerusalem. You saw how many followed us from the Temple to the upper city. All hoping to partake of this Passover meal with us."

"It is the Sanhedrin we need to worry about, not the people," Matthew said, peering at Jesus.

"I do not know who is more upset: The Pharisees or the Sadducees?" Twirling a cup, James Zebedee spoke with his mouth full. "The Pharisees do not like being called out for their stupidity and arrogance, while the Sadducees do not even believe in eternal life — how can one work with groups such as these?"

"Let us just pray that Annas will not do anything rash," Matthew said.

"It is Caiaphas who is high priest this year — not his father-in-law," Bartholomew corrected.

"And who is it that influences Caiaphas?" Andrew spoke. "His father-in-law." He slammed his cup on the table.

"Greedy family," I heard Peter mumble.

"Annas and Caiaphas would be fools to try anything, given the people's infatuation with the Master," Thomas remarked.

"Does this trouble You, Master?" John leaned in against Jesus' chest, like a child to his father. "It certainly troubles me."

Jesus looked at John and then at all of our expectant faces. "Do not let your hearts be troubled. You have faith in Elohim; have faith also in Me." John pulled away and Jesus crossed His legs. "In My Father's house there are many dwelling places." His face relaxed as He said those words. "If there were not, would I have told you that I go to prepare a place for you?" He gazed into each disciple's eyes.

Inwardly I spoke to Jesus as I picked at my food. *I have faith in You. I trust in You, Kyrios. Open wide the gates of the kingdom that Lazarus saw!*

"I am the way and the truth and the life."

My heart leapt as warmth spread beneath my skin. Yet my hands were clammy with a strange fear.

Jesus spoke slowly and clearly. "*No one* comes to the Father but by Me."

"Kyrios," Philip called from down the table, his curly hair falling over his eyes. "Show us the Father, and it is enough for us."

Jesus looked to Philip. "Have I been with you for so long a time and have you not known Me? Philip, he that sees Me sees the Father also. Do you not believe that I am in the Father and the Father is in Me? Otherwise, believe for the very works' sake."

Jesus spoke a mountain of words, but I found myself grasping only a few.

He was one with Adonai. He was the Son of Elohim.

Some of His words were comforting, and I soaked them up like the desert sand at its first glimpse of rain. I craved more.

He spoke of the Holy Spirit. He said that we would have shalom. He said that we would see Him even though the world would not. He told us that He was the vine, and we were the branches. He connected it all to the love of the Father. Then He told us about the hatred the world may have for us, and I could not help but think of the scribes, chief priests, and Pharisees, and how they hated Jesus — so it would be the same for us? But Jesus was with us, and only a few persecuted us. The Temple guards may have attempted to arrest Lazarus, but they were not able to do so because the people loved Jesus.

Then Jesus spoke of a sorrow so great that I could not comprehend. He said that for a little while, He would no longer be with us.

My food hardened in my stomach. I forced a sip of wine and adjusted my position again. Anguish started to fill me, but it was then topped with comfort as Jesus told us that our sorrow would turn to joy, just as a woman whose pain in labor, disappears once the child is born. Once again, He offered us eternal life.

Jesus prayed for us, interceding on our behalf to the Father. I was awed. He seemed to open the mysteries of the universe, but these mysteries were too great for me. The disciples whispered words of confusion and disappointment and fear.

"Just Father," Jesus cried, emotion caught in His throat. He looked at us with earnest, almost pleading eyes. "The world has not known You, but I have known You and these have known that You have sent me."

I was captivated.

"I have made known to them in Your name, and I will make it known, that the love with which You have loved Me may be in Me, and I in them."

Jesus was renewing our relationship with Adonai. The promised Messiah was here, and we were to be one with Him. A sigh escaped my lips as I reflected on His words — on His promises of our unity with Him and the Father and this Holy Spirit.

Eagerness and excitement overtook my fear. The kingdom was here. He had come as promised. Because of Him, I would be one with Elohim, just as He said those years ago in Nazareth. That the Spirit of Adonai was upon Him. He indeed was what He claimed. He had come to show us the Father and to give us the Holy Spirit; to join into communion with Elohim.

My appetite soon returned as I ate lamb. The rest of the meal was accompanied by joyful chatter and loud laughter. Jesus even beckoned the servants to join us. By the end of the great meal, I was filled and satisfied with the rich meat and abundant wine.

"We pray that He who establishes shalom in the heavens grant shalom for us, for all Israel, and all of mankind, and let us say, Amen." Jesus blessed the meal we had received, deeming it time to partake of the third cup of ritual wine.

I did not desire any more wine, as my head was hurting by then, but it would only be a few more sips.

It was Peter this time who poured the cup of Redemption. This cup symbolized the blood of the Passover Lamb, reminding us of our redemption from the hands of the Egyptians. Nebo and Candence filled the cups of all other disciples seated.

Jesus took His cup — a silver one, the finest of them all — and lifted it above His head in thanksgiving. "Blessed are You, Adonai our El, King of the Universe, who creates the fruit of the vine."

Lifting it higher, He gazed at the cup with the same intensity as He did when blessing the matzah. "Drink from it," He said to us. "All of you, for this is My blood of the covenant, which shall be shed on behalf of many for the forgiveness of sins. And I say to you, I will not drink of this fruit of the vine, until that day when I will drink it with you new in the kingdom of My Father."

He took a sip.

My right elbow was propped against a cushion. I looked at the cup in my left hand.

His body and blood. The new covenant. Our covenant with Adonai was marked with the blood of the Passover lamb. I again remembered Capernaum.

> *This is a hard saying.*
> *Who can listen to it?*
> *He speaks of cannibalism!*

I heard my blood pounding in my ears. I did not understand it. It made no sense. But I could not leave Him for this. He was offering us eternal life.

My hands circled the cup. I sipped.

Accepting that I did not fully understand, I looked at the disciples' faces. Stunned. Many looked down at their laps. Others seemed to be staring at absolutely nothing. Some stared at their own cups of wine.

"Thomas, pull out your flute so we may sing the psalms." Jesus looked at us pleasantly. And so we began singing the lively tune. The 115th psalm.

> *Not to us, Adonai, not to us*
> *But to Your name give glory*
> *Because for the sake of Your mercy and faithfulness*

The songs were joyful but long. My eyes felt heavy as the night went. The sound of Lazarus, beside me, singing with his whole heart relaxed me. I was dreadfully sleepy.

When we finished, I waited expectantly for the fourth cup to be poured. But Jesus rose. "Arise. Let us go. We depart to the Mount of Olives."

With that, the ache in my head grew worse.

The disciples and I looked at each other in confusion at His abrupt closing. Why did He skip the last cup? The Passover was not complete without the cup of Restoration. That was the cup in which we remembered our people being made one with Adonai.

Chapter 35

As David went up the ascent of the Mount of Olives,
he wept without ceasing.
2 SAMUEL 15:30

I tightened my green veil around my head as we walked downward, past the houses of the chief priests. Light and music poured from the windows of the affluent homes. I adjusted my mantle around my shoulders.

My husband walked ahead of me with Thaddeus and my brother Simon. Magdalene was at my left, her face softly lit by the light from the clay oil lamp she carried.

Servants walked around the houses, seeing to the Passover celebrations. A hint of anxiety wafted over me. What if Jesus was in danger, after all?

I stiffened as we passed the house of the high priest, Caiaphas. It was more of a palace than a house, with its substantial stone walls, pillars, and variety of courts. Smoke from a contained fire billowed from an outer courtyard.

My anxiety dissipated as we left behind the houses of the chief priests. Clearly, no one was looking to harm Jesus this night.

We began our descent down a series of thin stone steps leading to the lower city in the curve of what was called the Valley of the Cheesemakers.

"Master!" John gasped.

The disciples came to a halt and I nearly ran into Lazarus.

"Are you alright, Master?" I heard Philip say, far ahead of me. He started chuckling.

"I am well. I am well." Jesus let out a laugh, but it was not His usual heartfelt laugh. After all the years I had known Him, it sounded forced to me, but I concluded that He simply tripped while walking down the steps.

"Keep moving," James Zebedee said, loudly, so we would all hear.

Peter growled something that I could not understand as the southeastern gate came into view. Beside the Pool of Siloam, it was known as the Fountain Gate. Roman soldiers strolled up and down the city walls. They gave no care to anyone leaving the city but stopped to inspect and question anyone entering.

Passing through the Fountain Gate, embedded in the stone wall, we made it to the base of the Kidron Valley. I glanced at Magdalene beside me, looking at the small light emanating from her clay lamp.

"Were you wise bringing flasks of oil with you?" I questioned light-heartedly, referencing one of Jesus' parables.

Shadows shifted on her face. "I may be vigilant, Esther, but I am far from a virgin."

"That is beside the point, Magdalene." I lowered my voice as I yawned. "Like the wise virgins in the Master's parable, we are ready for the bridegroom to come."

"I would say He is already here," Magdalene mused, looking straight ahead. Though I could not see Him past the heads of the disciples, I knew she spoke of Jesus.

We walked along the dirt path in the Kidron Valley leading to the Mount of Olives. To our left, I could see the grand Temple glistening pearly white and gold in the moonlight.

Our group was unusually small tonight. Some of the disciples were still at the guest house of Nicodemus, sleeping or cleaning up the Passover meal. The rest of us were with Jesus and the Twelve heading toward the Garden of Gethsemane. We were going there to pray as Jesus so favored, though I did not know how much praying I could do. My eyelids felt heavy as bricks.

Now at the foot of the Mount of Olives, the Kidron Valley was behind us. Though it was already deep into the night, the sound of musical celebration still echoed from the city.

A group of drunks came running down the mount, laughing obnoxiously as we began to climb.

Multiple breezes rustled my garments. My fingers danced, enjoying the softness of the light wind. We made a turn up the base of the mount, a stone olive press marked the entrance to the garden that Martha now owned.

I caught a quick glimpse of Jesus' face as we turned. He seemed somber for a bridegroom. His eyes were not raised hopefully at the stars as if He were speaking to our Father in Heaven. Instead, they watched the shadowed path of rocks, grasses, leaves, and olives that had fallen to the ground.

"His mood did appear to decline once the meal was over," Magdalene commented. The other women had stayed with Aunt Mary in the upper room. Perhaps I should have done the same. I could fall asleep in an instant, but I wanted to stay near my husband and Jesus.

My foggy mind had many thoughts about that night's Passover meal. It jumped from Jesus washing feet, to Judas, to eating Jesus' body and blood, to Jesus eliminating the fourth ritual cup of wine.

Then there was the sort of "farewell" Jesus gave us. Surely, He would not be taken up to Heaven in a chariot like the prophet Elijah!

The twisted branches of olive trees stretched above us, further defining the entrance to the garden. Coming upon a grassier area, I felt the dew reaching for my ankles.

Still trying to stay awake, I stopped with the rest of the disciples. Jesus turned to us. We were about thirty in number. We heard a man's ecstatic hooting ring in the distance. A drunk.

"You sit," Jesus said. "While I go over there and pray." He pointed at a large, flat rock, a stone's throw away. "Peter, James, and John will come with me." He walked, those three behind Him. Salome would be reeling with pride if she saw her two sons following the Master so specially.

Glancing back at the rest of us, Jesus said, "Pray, lest you enter into temptation." I tried to read His face in the darkness, but He turned away again. I chose to give little heed to the meaning of His words as it was so common for Him to say strange things.

Lazarus brushed against me. "Do not go leaving this garden alone." He looked at me and his sister sternly. "You wanted to come along, so you must stay however long the Master wishes."

I nodded my head curtly, pulling my mantle tighter.

His face gentled, but stress was evident. "Stay by me, wife." He placed a warm hand on my arm for a moment, then turned and settled against the trunk of a rounded olive tree as the other disciples scattered about, choosing their places to sit.

Lazarus looked up at me, expecting me to join him.

I glanced at Magdalene.

"I will be over here, praying," she said, motioning toward a rock the size of a barrel. "Tell Lazarus not to fear. I will be in his eyesight."

I made my way to my husband, chills running up my arms. I settled myself on the moist, dirt ground which the roots of the tree plunged from. Wetness seeped into my garments but I did not complain.

Lazarus put his arm around me, warming me a bit as I watched the rest of the disciples settle. They whispered, but slowly, silence fell. I could still hear the noise of the city from here, and the insects buzz lightly, plus the occasional hoot of an owl.

I raised my head from Lazarus' shoulder to glance at Peter, James, and John a distance away at my far left. Their shadowed figures kneeled.

In front of them was Jesus, who I believe also kneeled, supported by the enormous rock, flat enough to be a table.

My head fell back against Lazarus' shoulder.

I should pray.

That was my final thought before sleep came.

"Could you not watch one hour with Me?"

I was startled awake by Jesus' voice. It was soft yet audible at this distance. Shivers ran down my spine as I lifted my head from Lazarus' shoulder and looked toward my far left.

Jesus was standing above Peter, James, and John, who were asleep. The shadow of one of the three stirred and that disciple clumsily stood.

I looked around. All the disciples were sleeping. I dared not move my position lest I wake Lazarus.

"Watch and pray that you enter not into temptation." Jesus said. "The spirit indeed is willing, but the flesh weak." His voice was like the soft echo of thunder.

Jesus muttered to Himself as He walked away from the three disciples, and back to His original position by the rock. I was not entirely sure, but it looked like He was shaking...or *weeping*. Perhaps my eyes deceived me. I decided that He was simply engulfed in prayer and that I would observe Him from that distance.

He crouched against the rock, He raised His hands to the sky, and then dropped them. His body collapsed as if the life had left Him.

He fell down upon the rock, prostrating Himself.

My breath stopped for a moment, but slowly and unsteadily, Jesus rose, and walked toward Peter and the sons of Zebedee. Passing them, He came closer to me and the rest of the disciples. I could hear His gasps.

My eyebrows knit in concern as His image became clearer. Magdalene's oil lamp was the only one still burning. Jesus paused, to take in Magdalene's sleeping figure.

He looked at me.

I jolted. Beside me, Lazarus rustled, but still seemed wrapped in sleep.

The light from Magdalene's lamp caressed the face of Jesus. I saw a drop of blood trickle down His face, sliding from His brow as if it were sweat. I wondered if He hurt Himself, but I saw no cut or injury. I gingerly removed myself from under Lazarus' arm and stood, to go to Jesus.

No longer on the damp ground my legs felt the chill.

At my movement, Jesus turned and shuffled back to where He had been praying.

I opened the bolt of my door to my beloved, but he had turned aside and was gone. I thought of Solomon's song. *My soul melted when he spoke. I sought him and found him not. I called and he did not answer me.*

Jesus nearly stumbled.

I released a shaky sigh, unsure of what to do. What if He was ill? Should I alert the others? I did not wish to disturb Him, but I yearned to speak with Him. Yet, He did not seem to want to speak with me.

Instead, He seemed engulfed in some interior chaos. Crisis? Battle?

I looked at the sleeping disciples.

Shivering in the cool night air, I clutched my hands together. I looked at the snaked branches of the olive trees. Their leaves rustled in the breeze.

Father in Heaven, I do not know or understand why Jesus is in such agony, but He told us to pray, so I beg of You to protect Him. I know You will protect Your Son. You will add days to the days of the king; His years even to generation and generation! I prayed the 61st psalm. *He abides forever in the sight of Elohim. For You have been my hope; a tower of strength against the face of the enemy...*

I stood in this position of prayer, not sure how long I was there. My heart beat wildly. I should have done something, but what?

Lazarus was soundly asleep. What hour was it? It must have been deep into the night by now. I could not see the moon through the thick tree branches.

"Lazarus," I whispered, nudging him.

"Esther?" He startled awake immediately. "What is wrong?" He made a quick survey of his surroundings. "What is it?"

"I...I do not know. It is Jesus. He is...I think He may be ill."

Slightly dazed, Lazarus got up and peered at Jesus across the garden. He was almost lying atop the rock.

"He is just praying," Lazarus said, rubbing his eyes.

I shook my head. "No. Wait! Watch. He is rising."

The two of us stared as Jesus lifted Himself from the support of the rock. With an agonizingly slow movement, He staggered toward us.

A few other disciples woke and began whispering to each other.

Jesus stood across from us again, near Magdalene. His face was once again aglow in the light of Magdalene's oil lamp and I saw several drops of blood slide down His brow. His eyes rolled back. His face reflected His distress.

Then the lamp was extinguished, and darkness settled in, masking Jesus' expression.

"Rabboni?" Magdalene mumbled.

Lazarus left my side and went to Jesus, stepping over sleeping disciples. "Master?" What is it?"

I heard men's voices and footsteps. My gaze darted to my right, to the light of torches. I looked back to Jesus, now standing perfectly straight, although He had been a drooping flower only a moment previously.

"Behold," He said. "The hour is at hand, and the Son of Man will be betrayed into the hands of sinners."

I gulped.

He spoke louder, waking more disciples. "Rise, let us go."

I trembled.

"Behold, he is at hand who will betray Me."

There was a group of Temple guards coiling around the trees. Their torches lit up the night and their swords. The clubs held firmly in their hands terrified me.

Jesus walked past the cluster of disciples, toward the guards.

"Jesus…" I moved toward Lazarus and Him, but Jesus did not acknowledge me.

I reached Lazarus' side and asked, "What is happening?"

"The Temple guards!"

"Why are they here?"

"*Master!*" James Zebedee's voice clearly bellowed from behind me. "Peter!"

"Whom do you seek?" Jesus calmly asked.

"Jesus of Nazareth," a Temple guard grunted with cold eyes, strutting toward my cousin. The guard's face was lit by the torch in his hand making his cone-shaped helmet shine.

"YHWH," Jesus replied simply.

I fell to my knees on hearing the divine name which we were not to utter. *I AM.* Adonai gave this name to Moses at the burning bush. Even the guards fell to their knees, but rose as quickly as they went down.

"Whom do you seek?" Jesus asked again.

"Jesus of Nazareth," the same Temple guard grunted.

"I told you that I AM He." He looked back at us disciples, who stared at Him in fear. "So, if you are looking for Me, let these men go their way."

A familiar voice called to Him. Its usual smoothness cracked as he spoke. Judas walked toward Jesus. Hatred burned within me.

Judas placed a hand on Jesus' shoulder. "Hail, Rabbi!" He laid a dreadful kiss on Jesus' cheek.

Jesus sighed. "Judas, do you betray the Son of Man with a kiss?"

Judas took a step back, wiping his mouth and fiddling with the collar around his thick neck.

The guards started toward Jesus who was as vulnerable as a lamb ready for slaughter.

"Kyrios, shall we strike with the sword?" James Zebedee yelled.

A Temple guard grabbed Jesus' arm.

"No! Master!" Peter rushed from behind me, running towards Jesus.

Simon and Thaddeus also rushed forward, their fists raised, ready to attack as the guards attempted to bind Jesus' hands and arms.

Others followed, but Lazarus stood firmly in place, despite the screams.

Magdalene darted toward the troubling scene. "Rabboni!"

Lazarus called after her.

I shrieked, reaching my hands out. What could I do?

The sound of Peter drawing a sword cut though the shouts. He sliced a man's ear.

"Put up again your sword into its place," Jesus said loudly, almost fiercely. "For all that take the sword shall perish by the sword. The chalice which My Father has given Me, will I not drink it?"

Peter hesitantly lowered his sword.

I remained frozen.

The man Peter struck was on the ground holding his face. The disciples and guards practically trampled him.

"Jesus!"

"No!"

"Master!"

"Peter," Jesus repeated. "Stop. No more of this." He reminded me of the storm He calmed at sea.

Temple guards surged toward us. The disciples moved back in terror as swords pierced the air.

"Grab Lazarus as well," the leading guard said. "The priests would like that."

"Run!" James Zebedee screamed. Followed by several others, he sped by.

"Oh, you better run!" A guard sneered.

Lazarus grabbed both me and Magdalene.

"Go! Go! Go!" Peter yelled. We did so, running.

"Do *not* stop," Lazarus yelled as he pulled me.

Sprinting disciples led the way as I gasped behind them. We ran up the Mount of Olives, stopping in a large cluster. We heard only the sound of our panting. With the moon and stars in the opening above us, each person's terror was visible.

In the west was the Temple and the shining tops of affluent buildings, including Herod's palace.

"Most of the gates are closed at this hour, or at least guarded," Philip said.

"Where shall we go?" Andrew's head shot upward after staring at the ground.

"Should we go to your sister's house?" Bartholomew asked Lazarus. .

"Fool!" Simon exclaimed. "They wanted Lazarus as well!"

"Do not go calling him a fool." Philip stepped closer to Simon. "It is a reasonable idea. The last thing we need is you and your Zealot ways — "

"He is no longer a Zealot!" Thaddeus pushed against Philip's chest and the three of them started bickering.

"I knew this would happen. I knew this would happen! The signs were evident." Matthew threw his hands in the air. "I told the Master not to go to Jerusalem. We all warned Him!"

"Blast those Sadducees," Thomas said through gritted teeth.

"We should go to Caiaphas' house." John focused on Peter and the other disciples.

"Did you not see? They arrested Him. They were ready to arrest us too," Thomas sniffed.

"I say we return to Nicodemus' guest house. That is where the others are," Andrew gruffly said, sweat dampening his old tunic.

"Nicodemus is on the council of the Sanhedrin! What if he betrays the Master?" Peter shook his head sadly.

"Judas already betrayed Rabboni," Magdalene cut in. "Nicodemus will be an asset to us. He can plead for Jesus' release."

"Judas..." James Zebedee growled.

"I agree with John. We should follow the guards. They will go to Annas' house — or to Caiaphas. Probably throw Him in prison or have a trial," Peter said.

Peter, Andrew, James, and John formed a little cluster.

"Is that even legal?" Matthew put a hand to his chin, making a *tsking* sound. "To have a trial at this hour? And to have it at their house and not the Temple? It is Passover of all nights!"

"That is why we should speak to Nicodemus," Magdalene urged. "He will know how to handle this."

"Nicodemus!" Thomas scowled. "Man is a coward. He will probably turn us all over."

"He is a disciple, like you and me!" I stepped beside Magdalene, looking up at Thomas, my boldness expanding with my emotions. His eyes glared down at me, past his thin, long nose.

"Death has no hold on the Kyrios." Lazarus firmly said his first words.

"Death? When did death have a part in all of this?" Bartholomew cut in. "You do not truly think they will kill the Master?"

"It would be illegal," Matthew told him. "They would need the approval of Rome for capital punishment."

"That has not stopped the priests from stoning blasphemers and sinners."

"Jesus is neither of those," I whispered.

"They could stone Him in secret," Thomas mumbled. "Or just rile up a crowd."

"You have seen the people. They adore Rabboni, even against the chief priests' wishes," Magdalene said, gasping for breath as she spoke.

"That is why they snatched Him at night," Philip decided. "They are doing it all in secret."

"The Master is as famous as Caesar himself," Simon told us. "It will not be a secret for long."

"They could accuse Him of treason!"

"You think they will take Him to Pilate?" I asked.

"He would be executed immediately. Pilate does not even give a glance at any of the rebels brought to him."

"The Master is no rebel!"

"All of you hush," James Zebedee shouted, turning from the cluster of Peter, John, and Andrew. "We have decided what we shall do."

"Since you are one of His favored ones, eh?" Thomas snarled. "What makes you the new master?"

"I never said — "

"You and John!" Bartholomew added. "Seated at the Kyrios' right and left hand!"

"Well, apparently, the Kyrios is a criminal!"

"Let me finish!"

"I do not have to listen to you!"

"You are just a stupid fisherman!" Thomas yelled at James Zebedee.

"And what are you? The king of clay pots?" James Zebedee shouted back.

"Stop it!" Magdalene yelled. "Stop. We cannot act like — "

"This is what we shall do!" Peter interjected. "Join us if you would like, or go camp out on the Mount, or Bethany, or wherever you choose…I do not care. Those who will stay by the Master's side will return to the city. Let us follow those guards."

"If we go back through the Fountain Gate, they could arrest all of us at once."

"If we go through any gate, they could arrest us at once."

Peter started walking southwest. "Come, brothers. We will go together and if they arrest us too, they arrest us too." Peter and John headed down the mount.

"I am going through the Sheep Gate!" Bartholomew decided.

"That is all the way on the other side of the city!" James Zebedee shouted.

"Which will be far away from Caiaphas' house!" Bartholomew looked back at the other disciples. Our group started to split apart.

I turned to Lazarus. "Husband, the guards were after you. Will they not be after you as we enter the city?"

"There is nothing to fear," he replied. "If I die again, it will be for the Kyrios."

"Rabboni would not have you rise from the dead only for you to now be killed!" Magdalene argued.

"Perhaps we *should* return to Bethany," I said.

"Or you can join *us*." Simon crossed his arms over his thick chest. He, Thaddeus, Thomas, and James Alphaeus were the only ones left. The others had chosen different paths.

"Tell them, James." Thomas looked at the small man.

"There is another way into the city," James Alphaeus said, stepping toward us. "We can take Hezekiah's tunnel." He looked nervous. "It will lead us straight into the Pool of Siloam. Right where we need to be by the upper city. It will be close to the high priest's palace, but we will not need to pass any gate or checkpoint — be it Roman or Jewish."

"Hezekiah's tunnel." Lazarus leaned toward the disciple. "Is it not filled with water from the Gihon spring?"

"It is. But we can wade through it." James Alphaeus fiddled with the tassels on his cloak. "It should not get any worse than thigh deep."

"Thigh deep!" Magdalene shook her head.

"I do not like bodies or streams of water," Lazarus said, a groan in his voice.

"I do not like the dark." Magdalene shivered.

"And I do not like small spaces." Simon flexed his large hands. "Or the cold! But this will be our safest route into the city."

Lazarus clamped a hand on James Alphaeus' shoulder. "Then lead us."

Chapter 36

The rest of the acts of Hezekiah, with all his valor,
and how he constructed the pool and conduit and brought
water into the city, are recorded in the book of the chronicles
of the kings of Judah.

2 KINGS 20:20

"You have never traveled through it?" I glanced at the small hole, surrounded by dark rock, and looked back at James Alphaeus and the disciples. Light reflected off of the roofs of the city of Jerusalem.

"No. I would never enter it just for enjoyment," James Alphaeus said.

"I have my lamp," Magdalene said. "And I even have a flask of extra oil, but we have nothing to light it with."

"I have a piece of flint," James Alphaeus said.

We all looked at him in amazement.

"You just happen to carry a piece of flint in your pocket?" Simon crossed his arms over his chest. It was true. This quiet, little disciple was full of surprises. "And you also just happen to have a map of underground Jerusalem as well?" Simon was being sarcastic, of course.

James Alphaeus shrugged. "I do not have a map. But I like to be prepared."

"Thank Elohim for that!" Thomas gave him a brotherly nudge on the shoulder.

After lighting the lamp, Magdalene cautiously moved toward the opening of the tunnel. "Now, how can we be certain this is safe?"

"We cannot." James Alphaeus twiddled with his tassels.

"For the love of Israel," Magdalene breathed.

"I do not know if I will fit in there." Simon stared ahead warily. He looked at Thaddeus, Thomas, and Lazarus. "We are tall men."

"I will lead the way, then." Of course James Alphaeus would.

Magdalene refused to be the last, so Thaddeus offered to be the last one.

"And I will go second, behind James Alphaeus." Thomas stood behind James Alphaeus.

"The women can stay in the middle if it suits them."

"We will carry our sandals." James Alphaeus pulled his off with one hand. "And keep your mantles no lower than your waist, lest they get wet. And I will take the lamp."

We followed his example. I bent low to remove my leather sandals, tied my mantle tightly around my head, and wrapped the ends over my shoulders. I shivered at the thought of the tunnel.

James Alphaeus was already inside. The light of his lamp softly touching the walls, his body descended and disappeared. My toes curled over the damp, loose earth beneath us.

Thomas went in after James Alphaeus.

I went next. Magdalene would walk between Lazarus and me, and Simon would follow my husband.

I lowered my head and stepped into the dirt-covered structure. My feet tingled as they met a steep decline. After a couple of steps, the ground turned from dirt to stone. I barely saw the back of Thomas' square head or the figure of James Alphaeus below me. I carefully walked downward.

When Magdalene gasped, I turned. She walked as if into a pit of snakes. "Take courage," I said. "Thus says Adonai, when you pass through the waters I will be with you."

She moved forward.

I soon heard the splash of water. "This is where the tunnel becomes level," James Alphaeus called over his shoulder. "But also where we reach the water. Prepare yourself." Thomas clumsily tumbled into the little stream. I followed after him, water rushing over my feet and swirling around my ankles. I looked downward, but could hardly see, even with the lamp James Alphaeus held. Water flowed in a pale reflection of browns and dark greens.

When we came upon a smaller tunnel, James Alphaeus turned left into it. "This way is south!" He called. The sound of rushing water grew louder. There was a strong current streaming toward us from the north.

"Where is all of this water coming from?"

"Directly from the Gihon spring!" James Alphaeus answered.

Rushing waters reached to my hips.

"Are you certain this is safe?" James Alphaeus did not seem to hear Magdalene's repetitive question.

I used the black stone wall to support myself. My feet slid on the muck. I could hardly move without the side walls hitting my shoulders. The men would not be as blessed and would have to walk through sideways. The ceiling was a couple of heads taller than I was. The men would have to bend.

"Thaddeus!" Simon yelled from behind me. "Ah!"

"What is it?" I looked back to see Magdalene looking over her shoulder as well.

"He ran into me!"

"I cannot see!" Thaddeus growled in return.

"Adonai, you will bring my soul out of trouble!" I thought of the Psalms.

"It is up to my waist, Esther! My waist!" Magdalene exclaimed. "I think I am going to slip! I will slip."

"Hush and calm yourself!" Lazarus ordered. "You must not panic, sister. I do not like this any more than you. If you slip, I will catch you."

I stumbled at a dip in the path and steadied myself on the wall. The waters pushed against my back. Droplets landed on my face. I held my sandals at head-level. My mantle was mostly soaked.

"James Alphaeus," Thomas said. "Tell me, why is this called Hezekiah's tunnel? It is more like a river."

"A channel, you could call it." James Alphaeus' voice was muffled. "King Hezekiah built it many, many years ago — before the exile — to bring water into the city when Jerusalem was under siege by the Assyrians. You will find a whole system of waterworks below the city."

The tunnel carved slightly to the right.

"How did you come to know of these waterworks?" I called out to James Alphaeus.

"Our little Galilean! The farmer with secret knowledge." Thomas exclaimed, patting James Alphaeus on the shoulder. Thomas then pressed one palm against the side of a wall.

"Family tradition," James Alphaeus said. "My late father, Alphaeus, and his father before him. Storytellers."

"Jesus is a good storyteller," I mumbled and then asked, "Do you think they will release the Master?"

All was silent except for our feet wading through the river. At least we were traveling downstream.

"We can pray, can we not?" Thomas said darkly. "And have faith." He did not sound convinced. The current had slowed.

Thomas halted suddenly and I almost fell against him.

We all slowed. I felt Magdalene breathing down my neck.

"James?" Thomas asked cautiously.

"Silence yourselves. There is a sinkhole here. We cannot let anyone hear us from the streets above." He continued forward.

I craned to see a hole in the ceiling, about as wide as a mule. It was covered by diagonal metal stripes that I expected to see people passing over, but it was pure darkness.

We continued, our path snaking sharply to the right. Then sharply to the left.

"You would think we were walking in a circle," Thomas said.

"We are not. In fact, this must be it!" The water was knee-deep. "Look ahead and see," James Alphaeus added.

I squinted. There was indeed an opening. The thought of fresh air made my stomach spin with excitement.

Soon each of us was wading through the knee-deep water of the Pool of Siloam. I took a deep breath, lowering the hand holding my sandals.

James Alphaeus walked the edge of the rock-cut pool and hopped onto the smooth stone ground. He smiled back at us, exhausted but satisfied.

He and Thomas helped us climb out. I shivered as a breeze passed over me.

There were noises above us. Men walked about the city, even at this late hour. I looked up from the rectangular cistern we were in.

James Alphaeus set the lamp down to put his sandals back on. Thomas squeezed water from the hem of his tunic. I adjusted my soaked mantle and struggled to put my sandals on my wet feet.

"We should split into groups," Simon decided, walking to the front of the group.

Thomas pulled at his tunic. "I am sure we do not look suspicious." He raised a sarcastic brow.

"James Alphaeus and Thomas should go first," Simon decided. He rubbed his hairy arms.

"First?" Thomas glared at him. "As bait?"

James Alphaeus put a hand on Thomas' shoulder. "As courageous disciples of the Master. We all need to get to Nicodemus' guest house."

"Unless the whole house is under arrest," Thomas said.

"Once you reach the top of these stairs, you will see the Temple. Do not go that way. Head west, to the upper city, close to the exterior wall. If we do this, we should reach the Essene Quarter far from Caiaphas' neighborhood."

James Alphaeus and Thomas hurried up the steps. When they reached the top, they did not hesitate but disappeared into the streets.

Simon told Lazarus and myself to go next. He, Thaddeus, and Magdalene would follow.

Lazarus put a hand on my back. "Rise up," he said. "To battle against it."

I smiled at that phrase we shared and hurried up the stairs, my sandals squeaking. As I ascended, the grand Temple loomed in the distance on the northern side of the city, hundreds of small houses bundled beneath it. The cold from the water felt unbearable. Lazarus and I shivered as we hurried forward.

Close to our right was the Fountain Gate. Thankfully, we turned to our left and crossed a main road. Laughing drunk men passed by. I heard a woman shouting. A couple of Roman soldiers strode by, not giving much notice to their surroundings. We crossed the street swiftly and began walking through a narrow road up the east side of the upper city. The houses were packed together, and people were on the roofs. Some stood in their doorway to watch us pass. I shuddered at a giant black spider on a wall.

The houses increased in size and we crossed one more main road to reach Nicodemus' manor house and Nicodemus' guest house beside it.

Lazarus ran to the door and banged on it.

The door opened just a crack.

Andrew's voice questioned. "Who is it?"

When Lazarus announced it was us, Andrew opened the door. "Quickly! Quickly!" He glanced down the street.

"Thank Elohim, you have arrived safe!" Susanna flung her arms around me. The other women followed, embracing me. "Where is Magdalene?"

"She should be right behind me." I tried to breathe, looking at the multitude of disciples gathered in the large room.

"You are wet!"

"I cannot believe you took Hezekiah's tunnel!" Philip spoke to James Alphaeus and Thomas.

"It seemed the safest route."

"We passed through the Sheep Gate unnoticed!" Bartholomew told them, pulling at his beard. "I told you, you should have come with us!"

"Peter and John! They were the only two to enter through the Fountain Gate. They could be arrested as well for all we know!"

"Where is Aunt Mary?" I looked around frantically. I could only imagine the emotions of a mother whose son was arrested.

Magdalene walked in.

Susanna put a gentle hand on my shoulder as Mary Alphaeus took my soaked blue mantle. "Your aunt went out with your other relatives; Clopas and his wife. Nicodemus went with them."

"Nicodemus!" Magdalene trudged toward us. "What did Nicodemus have to say about all this?"

"He is a part of the Sanhedrin but did not know of the arrest," Susanna explained. "He knew they disliked the Kyrios but he was shocked to find that they arrested Him in the middle of the night."

Mary Alphaeus took Magdalene's water-soaked mantle and set it with mine.

"He reasoned that they took Kyrios to Caiaphas or would at least put Kyrios in a cell overnight in Caiaphas' palace," Susanna continued.

Magdalene shuddered. "Caiaphas has prison cells!"

"I am sure he has many of them." Salome set a hand on her hip.

"Surely this is not legal," Magdalene continued. "Arresting Rabboni at night. And arresting him during the festival. And if all of the members of the Sanhedrin were not even gathered — "

"They will be able to do whatever they want. Caiaphas and Annas," Joanna said softly.

"Can we charge the Sanhedrin for breaking the law, then?" Magdalene put a finger to her pointed chin, her eyes narrowed in thought.

"What do you suppose we do?" I said dryly. "Go to Pilate? We do not want Rome involved with this."

"Perhaps *we* should leave the city," Joanna said. "My husband is Herod's steward and would be able to help us."

"We do not want Herod involved, either! Surely you of all people know no one can trust that man," Salome said.

"If the people knew of this — the crowds of pilgrims — they would rise with us," I said. I glanced at the men. "Or with them, at least."

"Esther, have you not learned violence is no method?" Magdalene looked at me sharply.

"I never said the word 'violence,'" I quickly said. "All we need is the people to show they protest this evil scheme to arrest Jesus! The way the people blocked Lazarus when he was among the guards."

We women argued.

"There is nothing we can do at this hour!"

"What of Mary? Are we to sleep while she goes in search of her Son?"

"Kyrios knew He was not safe! He knew Judas would betray Him!"

Lazarus caught my eyes. He stood in silence but when our eyes met, he walked to me.

"Wife, listen to me. You and I are going to pray. I care not if the others join us or not. But that is the only good we can do right now. Pray at my side." He surprised me with the force he used when gripping my arm.

We had not prayed together since our nuptial week. Even when following Jesus, the two of us never prayed together. I agreed with him.

"Where two or three are gathered together in His name, there He is in
the midst of them," I said, although Jesus was not in our midst. "What shall
we pray?" I looked up at him.

"The way He taught us. Our Father," Lazarus began, pulling me with
him to a corner. "Who art in Heaven, hallowed be Your name. Your kingdom
come. Your will be done on earth as it is in Heaven." The sound of arguments
lessened as several of the women joined us. I could hear James Zebedee still
yelling at Andrew, and Salome trying to add to the argument. Thomas spoke
frantically to James Alphaeus.

"Give us this day our daily bread and forgive us our debts, as we forgive
our debtors. And lead us not into temptation. But deliver us from evil. Amen."

My stomach wrenched. How was I to forgive the trespasses of the chief
priests? Of Judas? Would Jesus forgive them?

My back was sore from leaning against a stone wall in Nicodemus' guest
house. Half of us were down here and the other half were in the upper room.

All was quiet. All was dark.

Susanna sat near to my left and Lazarus and Magdalene were at my right.

I had not been able to sleep. Fear clawed at my heart and a terrible
resentment for all of the disciples raged like a sandstorm in me.

What were our assets? Nicodemus, a frightened Pharisee who had little
authority with the Sanhedrin. Loud fishermen. Bickering children. Cowards.
That is what we all were. Like little mice hiding in a hole in the wall. And
while our Master, Jesus, was bound and arrested. We had no idea where He
was. Peter and John, Aunt Mary, and my relatives had yet to return.

Jesus. Jesus. What will they do to You? I prayed to the Father that Jesus be
quickly released. Then we could flee Jerusalem and continue our travels.

Someone rapped at the door.

"For the love of Israel!" Philip moaned.

"We are done for!"

"Let us in! Let us in!" John's voice cried from the other side.

Joanna lit an oil lamp as Andrew hurried to the door.

"Wait! Wait!" Bartholomew rose unsteadily. "What if the Temple guards
are right behind them?"

"So we will just lock my son out in fear that some are following him?"
Salome croaked. "Andrew, open that door," she commanded.

Andrew was hesitant, then lifted the lock from the door.

Aunt Miriam strode in, Aunt Mary close to her side. Peter, John, and Uncle Clopas fell in behind them.

Andrew slammed the door shut.

The disciples rose and ran toward them.

I raced to Aunt Mary. I grasped her trembling hand as we walked to the center of the great room.

Everyone was sweaty. John's mouth hung open as he breathed heavily, while Peter swayed as he looked to the ground.

"Peter!" When Andrew reached for his brother, Peter swatted at his hand. Peter looked as if he was about to be sick.

Uncle Clopas stared at the ceiling as if he was trying not to cry. Aunt Miriam touched my shoulder.

"Well, where is He? Where is the Master?" James Zebedee yelled.

I felt my blood pumping. Was Jesus dead?

More disciples flooded downstairs.

"What happened?" Simon marched toward them.

"Say something!"

"I...denied Him..." Peter moaned, stumbling. "I..."

"Peter." Andrew reached for his brother again. "What happened?"

"I denied Him!" Peter yelled in his face, running up the stairs to the upper room.

"Peter, wait!" Thomas sprinted after him.

"I want to be alone! I denied Him!" Peter roared.

"Speak, John!" James Zebedee put a hand on John's sweat-soaked shoulders.

John stared blankly at the lot of us. "They are taking Him to Pilate.

"At this hour?"

"During Passover?"

"Why?"

"To kill Him?"

"What did they do?"

"How did this happen?"

John pulled from James Zebedee's grasp. "They accused the Kyrios of blasphemy. At dawn, they will take Him to the procurator."

Peter ran down the stairs, Thomas following him. When Peter ran into a large clay basin it crashed into pieces on the mosaic floor.

Peter continued moaning. "Leave me alone!" He ran to the entrance, unlocked the door, walked out, and shut it behind him.

"Let him go. Let him go." James Alphaeus said.

Susanna brought a jug of water to John who drank quickly. She then gave water to Uncle Clopas, Aunt Miriam, and Aunt Mary.

John told us, "Peter and I followed the guards at a distance. They took Him to the house of Annas, who accompanied them to the house of Caiaphas…Jesus was on trial…they accused Him of so many things…being mad…lying…magic…being the devil…blasphemy!" John wiped his mouth with his sleeve. "When…when they asked Jesus if He was the…the Messiah… Jesus said what He had said in Gethsemane — He pronounced the Divine Name."

"YHWH," Aunt Miriam innocently whispered. A few disciples looked at her in shock.

"They spat on Him," John continued, gulping. "They hit Him…and pushed Him…" I was frightened by the images his words evoked. "They said that…that they would take Him to Pilate…so that…so that they can…have Him executed!"

"No!"

"Adonai have mercy! Will they come after us too?"

"What do we do?"

"Is it not already nearly morning?"

"Where is the Master now?"

"They are holding Him in a cistern," John explained. "A prison owned by Caiaphas."

"I hear it is a sewer!" Philip groaned.

"What about Peter? Why did he keep saying — " Magdalene started.

" — Do you remember what the Master said at supper? About Peter denying Him three times? That is exactly what he did. Peter denied Him three times. He was recognized as a disciple — and he feared that he too would be condemned." John put his face in his hands, his voice coming out muffled. "I do not know if he will ever forgive himself…"

"They cannot kill Jesus!" I whispered to Aunt Mary, forgetting Peter as I gently squeezed her hand. "They will not!"

"Of course not," Simon said to us. "Jesus is the Son of Elohim. If Jesus does not want to be killed, then He will not be killed! His power is too great."

"But remember what He said," John added. "For the past weeks — months! He seemed to know that the chief priests were after Him — "

"We all knew the chief priests were after Him. Where is Nicodemus?" Thomas looked around.

"He is in his house, hiding." Uncle Clopas growled his first words of the night.

"I should have known that Judas would do this," James Zebedee shouted.

"He had been disappearing a lot, of late." Thaddeus crossed his arms.

"How can he live with himself after what he has done?" Matthew looked at each of us.

I released my hold on Aunt Mary's hand, wishing not to overwhelm her. She stood with her eyes closed.

"What are we to do now?"

"What if they kill Rabbi?"

"They cannot! They just cannot. Elohim forbid it!"

"They are going to kill all of us too!"

"Stop talking like that!"

"Wake up to reality!"

"Will not the people rebel?"

"We should fight."

"How can we?"

"Pilate is not known for his mercy."

"Surely, they will see sense."

"Doubtful."

"Of course, they will."

"Did you see how they hurt Him?"

"What if they scourged Him?"

"They have no right!"

I backed away. Tears burned my eyes. My head felt like it was spinning. My pounding heart was about to burst.

He was the Son of Elohim, was He not? Why was this happening? If He was indeed omnipotent, then why would He allow this?

I looked at the shards of the broken clay basin, spread across the floor. My faith felt like that broken basin. All that I thought I knew about Jesus — about our Father — was shattered.

Chapter 37

Though harshly treated, he submitted and did not open his
mouth; Like a lamb led to slaughter or a sheep silent before
shearers, he did not open his mouth.

ISAIAH 53:7

Dawn was approaching. It had been a few long hours since Peter, John, and my brethren returned with the news that Jesus was being taken to Pilate. Peter had yet to come back since his hysterics about denying Jesus.

John and we women were in an entranceway of Nicodemus' guest house, and ready to leave.

"Make sure no one follows you when you return," Matthew warned.

I felt annoyed.

"If you can, return immediately, once you know the sentence," Simon told us.

I pursed my lips in frustration.

Philip shook his head. "I tell you again, this is not wise."

I gulped down my feelings of irritation.

"Keep your headpieces tight around your face, lest you be recognized," Bartholomew advised.

A growl of sorts escaped from me. I could hold it back no longer. "You are cowards!" I wept. "*The wicked man flees when no man pursues. But the just, bold as a lion, shall be without dread.*"

The disciples looked surprised at my repeating the proverb.

Susanna put a hand to my shoulder, but I shrugged it off.

"It is simple for *you* to go, Esther," Thomas said. "*You* are not one of the Twelve."

"Eleven," Thaddeus muttered.

"Adonai will protect us," Aunt Miriam stated confidently.

"The same way He protected Jesus." Simon laughed bitterly.

"Silence your tongue, for once, Simon!" I let out, having kept my emotions in.

"Esther." Lazarus stood beside me, as I started weeping. "Stay here with me," he said. "You are in no mood for this. You know I would accompany you if I could..."

"Of course, *you* would come if you only could, but we have discussed this. You are a wanted man. Nicodemus said they are plotting to kill you as well. You *must* stay in here." I crossed my arms.

"Stay here with me, then. Do you understand the terrors Rome is capable of? You do not look well for — "

"Of course, I do not look well!" I snapped. "My cousin is being held in a cistern filled with sewer waste, waiting to be taken to the Roman governor!" I stared at Lazarus. "I *must* be there. Daylight approaches and every woman is willing to come with us. Aunt Mary is going to stand beside her son, and I will stand with her. And do not dare speak of the terrors of Rome! Jesus will be set free. I am certain of this."

Lazarus frowned. I had almost forgotten what his face looked like when he smiled.

"We are leaving," Susanna said.

"Go, then," Lazarus said.

He knew me. I lifted my chin, refusing to look at the Apostles and other disciples. I glanced behind only when I was out in the street, and saw Andrew swiftly shut the door.

I stepped beside Aunt Miriam. Magdalene slowed down to walk with us. Susanna, Joanna, and Salome were in front of us, and John and Aunt Mary in front of them. We headed east toward the chief priest's neighborhood.

The crowds were already thick when the light of the sun was just touching the sky.

We continued down the hill of the upper city. My head pounded as hard as my heart — beating with the agonizing fear of what could come.

Dear Elohim of our fathers, You spared Isaac when You tested Abraham. You protected David from Goliath and Daniel from the lion's den. Do likewise for Your Son, I beg of You, Adonai. I beg of You as my own Father!

The sun was visible by the time we reached Caiaphas' house, which was even larger and grander than Nicodemus'. A long stairway led to an entrance.

Two servant women walked down the steps, bundles in their arms.

"Excuse me!" Magdalene stepped forward. "Where is Jesus? Is He imprisoned here?"

The two women looked at each other. They had reached the bottom of the stairs.

"He was in the cistern over there." One motioned to our right. "Across from the high priest's house."

"Where is He now?" John asked.

"They have taken Him to Pilate," the other servant said blankly. The pair of them hurried away.

"Already? At this early hour!" I let out a shaky breath.

"Then we shall go to the Antonia Fortress," Salome decided.

I watched Aunt Mary grip John's arm and say something to him. He nodded as she released him and walked up a couple of stairs toward the chief priest's house.

"Aunt, He is not there anymore," I called, but she continued up the hill to the mansion, then stopped. She kneeled on one step, running her hands along the stone as if she were caressing a cat.

"What is she doing?" I asked Salome, whose only response was a humming sound. My aunt turned around, tears glazing her cheeks. "This is where my son walked up and down multiple times last night and this morning."

Her hands shook as she leaned down and kissed the step, bordered by fresh grass. I looked up, my eyes following the route of the long staircase. I imagined Jesus, bound as He was in the garden.

John helped my aunt rise. When she was steady on her feet she said, with feeling, "Never forget this, nor any place that He walked, for each of these spots will always be holy."

We set our eyes and feet north toward the Antonia Fortress. Its towers were blocked from view by the large Temple.

A pair of Roman soldiers walked by. I did not hold back my glare as I watched the up-and-down motion of their silver helmets as the soldiers trotted forward. We followed them through the streets, into the busier sections of the city.

More people emerged from the buildings as we approached the vendors and money changers in front of the Temple.

As I took in the high walls of the Temple, the strong, familiar stench of animal and sweat hit my nose.

Birds screamed in their cages. Sheep, goats, and cattle moaned in their captivity. They were to be purchased and sacrificed.

"Doves! Lovely doves!"

"Precious stones!"

"Make an offering!"

"Purchase your sacrifices for the feast."

Irritation wafted over me as I thought how Jesus drove these money changers out of His house. As we passed the western wall of the Temple, my senses became alert to the name of Jesus.

"Blasphemer."

"They are awaiting His trial!"

"Caiaphas and the lot of them."

"Yet another prophet killed off."

I looked at Magdalene, my eyebrows shoved together.

The four cubed towers of the Antonia Fortress loomed. It was like a palace, mounted on rock. The red capes of soldiers above us caught my eye. They walked between the towers, while several lines of soldiers secured the exterior of the fortress, awaiting the command of their centurion.

Did Jesus not heal a centurion's servant?

Jews in traditional head coverings crammed through the large entrance-way and into the main courtyard, calling Jesus' name.

"I have never been this close to the Fortress," Joanna said, ahead of us.

"Neither have I. Are there usually this many people?" Susanna asked.

"No." Joanna looked back over his shoulder. "Only when there is a trial. At Passover of all times."

Hearing the word 'trial,' I felt faint.

"And where is my Jesus?" Aunt Miriam was short, making it impossible for her to see past anyone.

"Is He already in the court?"

Joanna wailed in response, making the hair on my arms spike, despite the rising heat.

I gasped and stumbled backward.

Jesus! He was bound and bloody.

Surrounded by a dozen Temple guards, He emerged from the wide entrance of the fortress onto the paved road. Half the guards yanked Jesus forward as the other half pushed the crowds out of the way.

"Move it! Move it! Let us through."

"Let the prisoner pass!"

"Respect the chief priests."

The Sanhedrin and other Pharisees and Sadducees followed the guards, their beards hanging far down their chests.

I had never seen Caiaphas, but I knew him instantly. His thick turban and heavy black and white vestments, gold neckpiece, and purposeful walk gave him away. He expected each man to move out of the way for him, and each man did so.

"Jesus!" Magdalene called as someone pushed her.

Jesus looked our way. His face was covered in bruises in the same way a leper is covered in ulcers. His hair was damp with sweat and oil. Blood streaked His face.

I was horrified.

His tunic was torn. His hands were bound in front of Him, blood seeping from His wrists. I lowered my gaze. No sandals; bare and bloodied feet.

I cried out as did the women around me.

But the guards and crowd were not grieving. "Who is the king of the Jews now, eh?"

"You are Satan himself!"

"Kill Him off, is what I say."

A Roman soldier shoved past. "Out of the way! Out of the way! Let them pass!"

Fear and rage joined in me as I watched the Roman push people aside. Confusion and terror cut into me as I saw *my own people* yelling death wishes at Jesus!

Forgive. The word popped into my mind. My gaze wandered to the Roman soldiers who were pushing the crowds out of the courtyard.

Blood rushed to my head and I ignored that most frustrating word. *Children.* No! Not all could be children of our heavenly Father! Not these men!

"Young man." Salome tapped the shoulder of a boy in front of her. "What are they going to do to Jesus?"

The boy looked annoyed but answered. "Pilate is sending Him to King Herod. Since Jesus is a Galilean, Herod will decide His fate."

Was that a good or bad thing? Rumor was that King Herod wished to meet Jesus. If Jesus performed a miracle, all would believe He was indeed the Messiah. Now was the time for Jesus to reveal another great miracle. Perhaps Herod would see that Jesus was released.

We followed the mob toward King Herod's palace, on the western side of the city.

Frustrated and tense I had no option but to wait and pray with the others.

Jesus was sent back to Pilate without a verdict from Herod.

Aunt Mary looked mortified. She had hardly spoken as we followed her beloved son from Herod's palace back to the Antonia Fortress. She pulled her mantle from over her head to her shoulders.

"If Herod was merciful to the Kyrios then surely Pilate will be as well. Clearly neither of them wish to condemn Him." Susanna was hopeful but her usually bright face was dimmed.

"It does not sound to me that Herod was merciful," I pointed out. "Only that he wanted nothing to do with Him."

"Did you see Jesus?" Magdalene strode next to us, her face red. "That purple cloak they forced on His shoulders to mock Him!"

"Every man mocks Him," Salome said sadly.

"His face. . ." Magdalene avoided our eyes. "It looked like someone had carved into His cheek!"

I could imagine the guards and priests yanking Him as they returned to the procurator.

"We have walked the length of the city by now," Salome heaved. We kept walking. My patience was thin as the noise increased. Had people nothing better to do during the Feast of Unleavened Bread than to watch the trial of an innocent man?

Surely it was the will of our Father for Jesus to live. He would be released soon without a verdict.

Once again we started up the many steps to the Fortress with its looming towers. The day got hotter.

John looked back at us, his usually young face appearing older. Creases dented his forehead. He put his arm around Aunt Mary as we reached the two curved stone doors to the outer courtyard.

With much pushing, we entered and stood against a back wall.

The rectangular courtyard stretched in front of us, filled with onlookers. Mostly men. Some wore a tallit. Some stood on the long porch opposite us. Some were servants. Some were Roman soldiers, their helmets removed.

Pontius Pilate appeared on the main porch. He was bald and wearing a rich red robe over a spotless white tunic. Gold rings glittered on his fingers. I immediately spotted Jesus, in the purple cloak. Romans dragged Him up the steps.

"I cannot see." Aunt Miriam was distraught.

"Nor can I," Salome said.

"Pilate is silencing us," Magdalene said fiercely. She was the tallest of us.

The noise lowered to that of an eager whisper as we readied ourselves for Pilate's words. "You have presented to me this man as one that perverts the people," Pilate shouted, his voice loud, aggravated, and impatient. "Having examined Him before you, I find no cause in this man in those things where you accuse Him."

Relief flooded my being at those wonderful words. Then I again tensed as the crowd made known their dislike.

Pilate yelled over the voices of anger. "As Herod found no cause in this man, nothing worthy of death is done to Him." Pilate's voice was drowned by shouts of displeasure.

"Punish Him!"

"Jesus is a liar!"

"He is a false prophet!"

"Blasphemer."

I shuddered.

"Therefore, I will chastise Him and release Him."

The crowd continued their howls of dissatisfaction.

"Free Him!" Magdalene yelled. "Free Jesus!"

A man in front of me turned around and narrowed his eyes as he peered into mine. I averted my gaze.

"Look at her eyes." He nudged the man beside him.

I turned away.

"They are green. Very bright green. Surely she is the barren wife of Lazarus."

My breath caught in my throat.

"Get away, man. Get away." Salome looked at them.

"Is your husband Lazarus? Do you follow that man, Jesus?"

I was unable to speak.

"They are all His followers. Look! I have seen that one in the Temple with Him! It is His disciple."

Other men turned to look at us.

John stared back at them, his face white.

"Get out of here."

A Temple guard came near us, his pointed helmet far above our heads.

"They are Jesus' disciples."

"Fools!"

"They should be flogged as well."

"Get out of here. Get out of here." The Temple guard lifted one hand, the other holding his spear. He pushed my shoulder. "We do not want you here."

"Leave." The men assisted the guard as they roughly grabbed and pushed us out.

"Every supporter of Jesus! Get them out!"

Some man yanked me toward the entrance of the courtyard. I looked around and saw a chief priest with a couple of Temple guards who were roughly grabbing John.

If they have persecuted Me, they will also persecute you. Jesus had said this to us. But why did there have to be persecution at all?

"Stupid women."

"Probably all prostitutes."

"It is unlawful for women to travel in the company of that man."

I stumbled over my feet as I was practically carried out of the courtyard. Shoved out of the door, I gripped Salome and started accounting for each woman to ensure she was safe.

"Aunt Mary!" I touched her arm. John had his arm around her.

She gulped, putting a hand to her stomach. "I am fine, Esther."

I touched my face, astounded that I was so easily recognized by my eyes.

"They are rigging the crowds!" Salome groaned.

"Hush," Joanna said. "We can still hear Pilate from here." She raised her chin high to listen.

"I find no cause in Him. But you have a custom that I should release one prisoner unto you at Passover." I heard Pilate.

My shoulders rose upward.

"Whom will you that I release to you? Barabbas or Jesus, the one who is called Christ?"

I turned to Magdalene. "Barabbas is a Zealot. Lazarus was tied up with him. As was Jesus. Barabbas was trying to start a revolution and wanted Jesus to be the leader. Jesus denied his request and Barabbas attempted to start a riot by himself."

"Release Barabbas," the people shouted.

"Jesus!" I screamed with all my might as did the other women. "Jesus! Release Jesus of Nazareth. He is innocent."

Our words bounced off the exterior walls, diluted by the crowd of howling demons.

"Barabbas!"

"Release Barabbas."

How could they support a murdering, thieving bandit against the resurrection and the life?

"Barabbas! Barabbas! Barabbas!"

Through the entranceway, I saw angry fists raised. All of us women continued to yell our Kyrios' name, but there was no hope of us being heard.

A couple of Roman soldiers looked at us quizzically.

"Attend to the crowds," a centurion yelled.

"Jesus," I persisted, but weakly.

Susanna bravely ran closer to the entrance and practically jumped in order to see.

To my side, John still held his arm around Aunt Mary. They said nothing. Tears slid down Aunt Mary's face and John looked like he was going to vomit.

Was the entire world against us?

My rage toward the Roman Empire had burned intensely in me before, and it still burned. Yet more and more, I felt a horrid hate for my *own people!* These Jews. Our priests. Our Pharisees. Our leaders. Caiaphas. Annas. The Temple guards. Barabbas. I hated them!

Susanna walked back toward us, her hands tightly clasped at her chest. "He released Barabbas."

I put a hand to my head.

"Crucify Him!"

"Crucifixion."

"Crucify Him!"

My mouth dropped. *Father! No!*

"Elohim have mercy on us!" Magdalene followed Susanna back to the entrance.

"They will not allow this. Pilate will not allow this. It is unjust!" I whispered. Salome and Aunt Miriam mumbled their own quiet prayers.

Magdalene ran toward us. She clasped Aunt Mary's hands.

"They are not going to crucify Him!" She exclaimed.

"Praise be Adonai."

"Pilate is having Him flogged."

I took a faltering breath. Flogging. Never could I wish flogging upon Jesus, but I would accept any fate less severe than crucifixion.

"They often flog prisoners before crucifying them," Joanna said, horror in her pretty face.

"No! Pilate did not say they were crucifying Him." Magdalene lifted her pointed chin with determination. "The procurator may simply wish to appease these crowds with a flogging. An alternative to death."

"Then let it be so," I agreed.

"When He is released, we will be ready to care for my beloved boy," Aunt Miriam said, looking up at us.

I glanced at the people spilling out of the entranceway.

"I have…never seen a man scourged," Susana whispered.

"I have seen it several times in the synagogue," Salome told us, a hand at her hip.

"Those are light floggings," Joanna explained. "This…they will use a flagellum."

"Where will they carry out the sentence?" I asked.

"In the east court," Joanna said, adjusting the veil on her head. "We simply need to follow the people."

John stepped forward with Aunt Mary and we followed them through the entranceway to the fortress. No one stopped him. The crowd inside had lessened. Either all the people had left the fortress together or were going deeper into its court to witness the scourging.

I surged forward after John and Aunt Mary.

Sparks of tension buzzed inside me as I hurried through the large court toward the northern side of the building. Governor and officers were no longer on the porch.

We entered through the northern door to a smaller court. Stone pillars sprouted from the center like barren trees in the desert. My eyes immediately focused on Jesus, stripped down to His inner tunic. A wave of sickness passed through me as I saw tunic and skin already torn from a whip. I wondered if they scourged Him last night.

They dragged Him toward a tall pillar, not giving Him a chance to walk on His own. Some people cheered while others waited in stoic silence. Other women, like myself, were in tears.

I saw the covered heads of the Pharisees and Sadducees. Surely Caiaphas and Annas included. They had a front seat for the show. Hypocrites, just as Jesus said they were.

My eyes followed the several Roman soldiers who clamped Jesus' wrists to the pillar with chains. Jesus leaned His forehead against the very tip of the pillar, just taller than Himself.

On seeing the whips that the soldiers' waved, I felt sick. That was a flagellum. Half a dozen whips attached to one. Each tongue holding its own set of spiked balls.

Father! Father! Your Son!

Counting in Greek, the soldiers began their attack.

My eyes slammed shut as the whip dug into His flesh. I opened my eyes to see fresh blood dripping down His back.

More strikes came upon Jesus. The whip dug into His skin like claws and pulled His flesh out as if they were shoveling dirt.

I moaned.

They ripped apart His flesh. Jesus groaned like a beaten animal.

Father! Father in Heaven! Hallowed...hallowed...hallowed be Your name!
Your kingdom come! Father! Send these horrific sinful goats to Gehenna! Disown
those who harm Your own Son!

Tears streamed into my mouth. I started to choke on them. I was dizzy. Blood trickled to Jesus' ankles. He gripped His chains.

I shook as I imagined His pain.

The sobs of my companions echoed as the soldiers counted their strikes.

I had the urge to run at those soldiers and claw their backs; to strike them; spit on them; yell in their evil faces; kick their legs; punch their stomachs; send them to where there was wailing and grinding of teeth.

Jesus could not still wish for me to forgive them. Not as my own children. I hated these soldiers and these men who shouted for Barabbas over their own Messiah!

Aunt Mary wept in total silence. John had a hand to his face, perhaps wincing, crying, or both. Magdalene wrapped her arms around Susanna and Joanna, her tan veil sliding down the back of her head. Aunt Miriam stared with her mouth wide open as Salome and Mary Alphaeus gripped each other.

I roughly rubbed my nose. The lashes continued.

"I thought they would release Him immediately when the scourging was finished," I said to Magdalene. We were in the outer court of the Antonia Fortress.

No one had kicked us out of the court. Magdalene and I switched veils so she had my green one and I had her tan-colored one. We hoped that the plain-colored veil would not draw attention to my eyes. I felt my face, stiff and dry from all my tears and I brushed aside a loose strand of hair that stuck to my forehead.

"They nearly killed Him," Mary Alphaeus said in her high-pitched voice.

"We have John and all of us women," I said. "We will carry Jesus if we must — back to the guest house — where we will tend to Him."

Joanna put her fingers to her trembling lips. "I fear that we will be attacked on our way to the guest house. Look at these people. They will kill Him themselves if they get the chance."

The crowd was tense. I could feel their impatience and anger. I tried to ignore it, but I could not help hearing their harsh words to one another:

"They should let Him be crucified."

"Did you see the man?"

"The scourging was punishment enough."

"It is never enough until these false prophets are killed."

I urged we leave Jerusalem with haste and go to Bethany, where Martha and Mary could assist us. "They have all that we need to see to His wounds."

Aunt Mary and John had been most silent this whole time, almost paralyzed with shock.

"Martha and Mary will be horrified at the sight of Him," Magdalene said.

"We all are." I looked at the porch, far ahead of us.

Magdalene grabbed my arm. "Here He comes! Pilate!"

The marble porch in the front of the fortress was lined with pillars, each engraved with Roman art of curves and swirls. Pilate walked purposefully toward the center of the porch, his red cape dancing behind him.

My stomach felt like there were crickets inside it, flapping their wings, trying to escape. I shifted my weight from my right leg to my left. We had been standing there for at least an hour.

Pontius Pilate raised his hands, motioning us to be silent. I strained to hear his words.

"Behold, I bring Him forth to you, that you may know that I find no cause in Him. Behold the man!"

My eyes darted to the porch to see a soldier on each side of a hobbling man, slowly making their way toward Pilate. I squinted, trying to see clearly from so far away.

My mouth dropped. My companions gasped.

Jesus was small from this distance, but His torn flesh, His blood, was evident. The purple cloak from Herod was loosely attached to His shoulders.

"Father Abraham." Magdalene gasped. "Tell me, what is on our Rabboni's head?"

A wreath of thick needle-like points was pressed into His head.

"Thorns," Susanna whispered, despite the yells of both approval and mockery from the crowd.

"Who did this to my nephew?" Aunt Miriam's mouth hung open.

"The Roman soldiers." My voice was flat.

"Crucify Him!" a man yelled behind me, causing me to jump.

"No!" I looked back at the man in disbelief. "Have they not done enough to Him? Have — "

"Crucify Him!"

"Crucify Him!"

"Take Him yourselves and crucify Him!" Pilate's voice pleaded.

"We have a law, and according to the law He ought to die!"

"He made Himself the Son of Elohim!"

Pilate grabbed Jesus by the arm and pulled Him to an inner court. The people continued to yell.

"Crucify Him!"

"Let Him be crucified!"

The horrid words were mimicked by the entire court. People pushed angry fists through the air and the crowds shuffled about. Some tried to shove their way forward.

"Crucify Him!"

"Crucify Him!"

My lips mouthed the word "no," but no sound came out.

"Shall I crucify your king?" Pilate shouted at the top of his lungs as he strode back onto the porch.

Jesus was pushed by a guard until He stood beside Pilate.

"If you release this man, you are not Caesar's friend!"

"Whoever makes himself a king, speaks against Caesar."

I pressed my hands to my cheeks. "How dare they now invoke Caesar! Tiberius is the enemy! What of the kingdom of Heaven?" I pulled my fingers downward. "Is Israel no longer possessed by Elohim? Cursed be all of them and cursed be Caesar!"

"Hush yourself, Esther," Magdalene scolded me sharply. "Do not let them hear you."

Aunt Mary was simply motionless, and Aunt Miriam stood solemnly beside her and John, her mouth hanging open.

"Why? What evil has He done?" Pilate surprised me with his persistence.

"Crucify Him! Crucify Him!" People pressed forward, jumping and pushing. "Crucify Him! Crucify Him!" They chanted, raising their clenched fists.

"I am innocent of the blood of this man. You look to it!" Pilate sounded defeated.

My mouth dropped again. I heard shouts of acclamation.

"His blood be upon us and our children!"

Oh Father, do not allow them to do this! He is your Son!

But I could not hide from the truth nor convince myself of anything else. My hope of Him being released was gone. Jesus was going to be crucified.

Chapter 38

Dogs surround me; a pack of evildoers closes in on me.
They have pierced my hands and my feet...

PSALMS 22:17

Magdalene attempted to embrace me, but I stood stiffly, unable to return the gesture. My eyelids drooped with exhaustion and despair. Shaking myself alert, I raised my eyes to the sun. Late morning. It felt like the day should be over by now, but it was not even noon.

Aunt Mary urged us not to wait at the entrance of the Antonia Fortress with the crowd and chief priests. "We must be near Him through every moment," she insisted.

So, we stood by a sidewall of the fortress where the prisoners were supposed to be.

I heard a frightened scream. "Please! I am innocent! I promise! It was not me!" The voice did not belong to Jesus, but rather another prisoner, dragged by three Roman soldiers. Long hair covered his face.

"I am not a bandit," the man yelled.

One soldier kicked him. Two more soldiers forced a wooden beam behind him, pushing it into his back. They roughly tied the man's wrists to the edges of the beam.

"It was him." The man indicated a man next to him, also being pushed on a beam.

"No! You know what you did," the other man responded.

"I know I am innocent — "

"We both know that you — "

"Shut up!" A Roman shouted, fiercely jabbing the first man in the stomach.

They both whimpered as they were pushed forward, arms spread and tied to what would be the beam of their own cross.

And then there was Jesus.

With one soldier holding His arm, Jesus hobbled out of a small entranceway. His beaten body made His shoulders hunch.

He turned in our direction and gazed upon us for a precious instant.

He smiled.

I blinked. No. He could not have smiled.

Yet He looked as if He was in complete control. As disabled as He was, He walked toward the soldiers waiting for Him with His cross. Something about Him showed He had the same authority as Pilate. Control. Confidence.

I gaped. Soldiers came up behind Him and pulled the purple cloak off Him, making Jesus wince. Then, they shoved His tunic over His head so that He wore the withered garment, then they placed a beam on His back. Jesus willingly placed each of His wrists on the wood and allowed the soldiers to tie them to the beam. His back was now attached to the wood and His arms were stretched out wide on each side of Him.

"Come, king of slosh and scum!" a soldier mocked. "Let us anoint You before all of Your people."

I started as he whipped Jesus in the stomach. Jesus' face strained with the impact as He made a small step forward.

"Get moving," another soldier hissed as Jesus stumbled.

John and we women followed closely, consumed with sorrow.

Jesus was hunched and breathing heavily. I lifted my hands in helpless alarm as He collapsed, His face on the ground.

Horrid shrieks of laughter came from the soldiers.

"Here! Here He is!" A man ran toward Jesus.

"They are bringing Him out."

"Let us watch this one crawl."

"Are you still a king?" a man said with scorn.

"Look at Him now!"

"Blasphemer!"

"Cursed worshiper of Satan!"

"Save Yourself if You are so great!"

Jesus' chest heaved. Aunt Mary gripped my arm, then let go. She walked toward her son.

Trickles of sweat ran down my body.

The soldiers were too occupied laughing and joking as Aunt Mary went to her Son, who had steadied Himself on His feet once again. His and His mother's eyes met. No words were spoken.

Was this the role of a mother? To have no control over her son's sufferings? To stand by and watch silently as her child walked to His death?

"Keep moving," a guard grunted, nudging Jesus. Jesus struggled, yet had the strength to continue.

Aunt Mary returned to us. A soldier mimicked Jesus, his lips in a mocking pout.

More people came as we passed the grounds of the Antonia Fortress, and entered the streets of Jerusalem.

Elohim's Son. Elohim's Son.

I clutched my sweaty hands and inwardly screamed at Jesus. *Adonai? Father?* My insides twisted like long, thick worms. I did not know if I wished to hide, run, yell, or disappear.

Father! Father!

Sparks beneath my skin shot in all directions. Why did I feel so suddenly repulsed by the thought of the all-holy Elohim? Was it the Father's abandonment of His child?

I touched my womb. I would never abandon my child!

Jesus kept walking, though "walking" seemed too generous of a word. People gave Him evil, disgusted looks. They shouted curses and foul words of mockery.

A group of children gawked at Jesus as He passed and a woman shook out a carpet from her window, stopping to stare.

I clasped a hand over my mouth as Jesus weakly stumbled and fell to His knees.

"What is happening here?" a man with dark skin and even darker hair asked me.

Magdalene spoke for me. "They are killing Rabboni! Jesus!" Tears trickled down her cheeks. "I know Him, the Messiah — He did nothing wrong."

"I have heard of this man," the man said. "I thought people revered Him. Why are they going to crucify Him? Is He not some prophet?"

Magdalene opened her mouth to respond, but a soldier pushed her to the side and grabbed the man. "You! Help Him! Help Him carry His cross."

The man shook his head. "I cannot — "

"Oh yes." the soldier smirked. "You can. Now get moving!"

The man looked at Jesus and then at his hands, surely wondering how to help Jesus carry the cross when Jesus' body was attached to it.

Another soldier, with his spear, cut the beam from Jesus' wrists. Forcing Jesus up, the soldiers set the wood perpendicular on Jesus' right shoulder.

The man was forced to carry the other end of the cross. He put his arms around the back of the beam, and they walked the narrow, crowded street.

Vendors in the marketplace were selling their ropes, herbs, bread, knives, leather, and clothing. I slid against the rough, stone walls as people bumped into me. One man threw a rotten apricot at Jesus' head. Those nearby burst into laughter.

I buried my face in my hands. Salome's warm hand gently touched my shoulder. I looked at her blankly and proceeded forward.

One woman rushed past me, toward Jesus. Removing her undyed veil, she lifted it to His face and cringed. She started wiping His face with the veil until a soldier pushed her aside.

The woman clutched her veil and watched Jesus pass.

"Rabboni," Magdalene murmured beside me.

"I know, dear," Mary Alphaeus said comfortingly.

"No! Did you see her veil?" Magdalene pointed but the woman was gone.

"Rabboni's face was on the veil," Magdalene exclaimed.

"She wiped His face with his veil…of course it…" Susanna said quietly.

"His image was on it! His holy face."

I looked back to Jesus, squeezing through the crowd. I tried to muster enough strength to keep going, but it was like swimming through cow dung.

He fell yet again, His face flat on the hard ground. The man helping Him carry the cross stared at Jesus on the ground and bent down, trying to help Him.

Soldiers continued to whip Jesus, shouting for Him to get up. For a moment, I thought He was dead. He was not moving. But then I saw His head stir and with the help of the man, He slowly rose.

I edged closer to Him, hearing the whimpers of my companions near me.

Eventually, we were beside Jesus. He raised His eyes to ours. Jesus' face was now but a cubit away from mine. I wept more, seeing His cuts and gashes up close. The thorns from His wicked crown almost covered His eyes. His lips trembled and He gasped for breath.

For the first time this morning, He spoke. Though His body was broken, and He spoke in barely a whisper, His tone was strong.

"Daughters of Jerusalem," He said as we sniffled, sobbed, and panted.

Daughter. Daughter of the Holy City. Daughter of Zion. Belonging to Adonai.

Jesus swayed, trying to keep His balance beneath the weight. The man pressed into assisting Him was close to His back. "Weep not over Me, but weep for yourselves, and for your children."

My eyes burned.

Such is my beloved, and he is my friend, Daughters of Jerusalem. As the Song of Solomon said. *The keepers that go about the city found me. They struck me and wounded me. The keepers of the walls took away my veil from me. I* adjure you, O Daughters of Jerusalem, if you find my beloved, tell him that I languish with love.

Love? Our Beloved was sentenced to death. Indeed, I was languishing.

"For behold," Jesus said, "the days shall come where they will say, 'Blessed are the barren, and the wombs that have not born and the breasts that have not given suck.'"

Would I one day rejoice because I had no children to mourn over?

"Then shall they begin to say to the mountains, 'Fall upon us,' and to the hills, 'Cover us!'"

I thought of the scriptures I had studied so vigorously. Hosea. *The sin of Israel shall be destroyed; the bur and the thistle shall grow up over their altars. They shall say to the mountains, "Cover us," and to the hills, "Fall upon us."*

"For if in the green wood they do these things, what shall be done in the dry?"

Wood that was green was moist and could not burn like wood that was dry. Ezekiel lamented at Jerusalem, the useless vine, before it was destroyed.

Jesus continued to walk to His death. We passed out of the city through the Gate of Judgment. Judgment. Judgment upon them all. Soldiers and priests. Liars. They were the blasphemers.

If any man will come after Me, let him deny himself, and take up his cross daily, and follow Me.

Jesus spoke of such things. It was not supposed to be literal.

For whoever will save his life, shall lose it; for he that shall lose his life for My sake, shall save it.

The crowd was smaller now that we were out of the city. I looked up, seeing Golgotha. My stomach churned. I knew all too well what occurred on that skull-shaped heap of rock. I could see the deep imprint of the sullen eyes in the rock, the thin lines of the skull's nose, and its devilish mouth.

Jesus was ahead of us, His wobbly feet making their way up the incline. Each step He took seemed to take longer and longer…

He fell.

"Jesus!" I shrieked as He dropped to the ground.

Soldiers whipped Him on the back as Jesus pushed on His bloody hands. Now on His knees, the man forced to help Jesus, grabbed His hand. The man had one hand on the wood and the other on the broken Jesus.

Jesus at last stood.

I felt Magdalene squeeze my hand. I pulled it away. In rage and sorrow, I did not know how to share this agony with Magdalene. We walked up the small hill. The uneven ground scuffed against my sandals and the edge of my foot scratched against the rock. My calves burned and my back ached.

Jesus stumbled again, fresh blood dripping down His legs. This time, Jesus did not have to try rising. Now that He had reached the top of the hill, two soldiers dragged Him toward beams of wood protruding from the earth, rocks on either side.

A soldier ripped off Jesus' garments, causing Him to cry out in pain. More soldiers tore and divided up His garments, laughing and sneering.

Jesus said not only to forgive them but to *love* them?

No. Not after tearing His body to shreds and forcing Him to carry His cross. Pilate and all those soldiers. Those who scourged Him. Mocked Him. Those who massacred our people. Those who killed my abba. Those who terrorized us. Those who raped Susanna. Those who took Simon's wife. Those who frightened our children. Those who stole our livestock. Those who intimidated us for pleasure. My fellow Jews. And my own leaders. Caiaphas. Annas. Sadducees and Pharisees.

Forgive.

Pharisees stood straight as if they were simply performing a ritual sacrifice at the Temple. Long tassels dangled at the ends of their cloaks. They looked like the hypocrites they were.

Men. Even women. My own people, egging on the soldiers.

I heard the dreadful sound of the Kyrios crying in pain. He was lying on the ground, His arms sprawled out alongside Him.

A soldier drove a nail into His hand. Blood sprayed from Him. I almost passed out. The sound of the mallet vibrated off the hill.

I remembered when Jesus and I were teenagers, so long ago; when I would hear Him and my uncles and cousins hitting a mallet on a nail; when Jesus was an unknown carpenter. It would excite me to hear my brethren working, for it meant that Jesus was near. But it now stirred only sorrow and anguish. I shocked myself with how intensely I sobbed. I did not even cry like this at Lazarus' death.

More groans of pain came from Jesus as they nailed His other hand to the beam.

I turned away from the dreadful sight, knowing that they were striking more nails into Jesus' flesh — in His feet.

Looking up, I saw the two criminals already hanging from their crosses.

It took several soldiers to adjust the cross Jesus was on so it was steady. The wood of the cross was stained with His blood. His hair was almost black with His blood. Thorns still encircled His precious head, but most of the blood on His face was dry.

His head fell to one side. His arms stretched behind Him, His hands just above His head. Blood trickled down His arms.

The rest of His body held the now familiar pattern of blood. Blood dripped down to the stony ground.

People gawked. Did they not know the great tragedy of this hour?

"Father," I barely heard Jesus pant. "Forgive them, for they know not what they do."

I wondered if a stone struck my head.

I do not hate them. The young Jesus said to me and our brethren.

Blessed are the merciful, for they shall obtain mercy.

But I say to you, love your enemies and pray for them that persecute and calumniate you.

Forgive us our debts, as we forgive our debtors.

Father, forgive them, for they know not what they do.

Father! Father!

I shook.

For if you will forgive men their offences, your heavenly Father will forgive you also your offences. But if you will not forgive men their offences, neither will your Father forgive you your offences.

And who is my neighbor?

For whoever will do the will of my Father that is in Heaven, he is My brother, and sister, and mother.

And your Father who sees in secret will repay you.

And call none your father upon earth, for one is your Father, who is in Heaven.

And when you shall stand to pray, forgive, if you have aught against any man; your Father also, who is in Heaven, may forgive you your sins.

Be merciful, as your Father also is merciful.

And when he was yet a great way off, his father saw him, and was moved with compassion, and running to him fell upon his neck, and kissed him.

He who honors not the Son, honors not the Father who has sent Him.

As the living Father has sent Me, and I live by the Father, so he that trogo Me, the same also shall live by Me.

Do you not believe that I am in the Father and the Father in Me?

In this is My Father glorified, that you bring forth very much fruit, and become My disciples.

I am friend and I am Father. Believe me that I am in the Father and the Father is in Me.

There is no mother without the Father, Esther. As My Father in Heaven loves all His children, so too a mother loves all children of the Father.

I approached His cross.

YHWH.

To my surprise, the Roman's did not push me away. They just continued their mockery.

I could reach out and touch the cross, I could have touched Jesus' feet at the level of my head, but my flesh recoiled.

I looked at the soldiers. Opposite them were the Pharisees and further away, Caiaphas and the Sadducees.

"Shall these be my children as well?" I asked quietly, only to look back at Jesus' torn and bloodied feet. I wondered if Jesus could hear me. I strained my neck to look up at Him. I felt His shadow upon me.

He nodded. Or perhaps I imagined it. But something firm, strong, and good welled inside of me. I realized what it was. It was a part of my will and a part of my faith.

Slowly, without even thinking about what I was doing, I leaned toward the cross, beneath His bleeding feet and kissed it with my dry lips.

"I will love them," I said. "As You have loved me."

Chapter 39

*On that day—oracle of the Lord G*OD*—I will make the sun set*
at midday and in broad daylight cover the land with darkness.

AMOS 8:9

Touching my mouth with one hand, I worshiped His most precious blood.

I backed into someone and turned around, startled. It was a Temple guard.

He did not pay me any attention but walked forward and shouted, "You that would destroy the Temple of Elohim, and in three days rebuild it, save Your own self."

"If You are the Son of Elohim, come down from the cross." One man passed by the cross and spit at Jesus.

I looked at these men with something new inside me. Forgiveness.

"He saved others; Himself He cannot save," a chief priest mocked.

"If He be the king of Israel, let Him now come down from the cross, and we will believe Him," a Pharisee shouted.

"Yes, then we will believe in Him," another laughed.

"He trusted in Elohim; let Elohim deliver Him now if He will have Him…" one of the criminals next to Jesus yelled, joining in the mockery.

"For He said, 'I am the Son of Elohim.'"

If only they knew that He was in the Father and the Father was in Him! I looked at the Jews yelling at Him and the Romans who were casting lots on the ground, shouting and drinking.

Our Father, forgive them. They do not know what they do. Forgive us our debtors as we forgive our debtors.

As I rejoined my company I started to repeat the "Our Father" prayer that Jesus taught us. Magdalene now approached the cross and venerated it as the people stared and yelled insults. No one bothered her as no one bothered me, likely finding us harmless.

The sky darkened. It matched my emotions.

I stood thinking of the words of love I said to Jesus.

For almost thirty years, I had tightly held my hate, judgment, and condemnation, only now to forgive these children when they performed the most horrendous of crimes. It was said that the greatest thing a disciple could do for the master was follow his teachings. At last, in His last hours, I followed Jesus. My eyes blurred with tears.

I gazed at His stretched-out body. His ribs were visible, and His muscles strong yet strained; firm from His years of carpentry and building.

How long would it take for Him to die? Three days? I would stay there as long as it took. Sabbath began at sundown. Would these soldiers stay here on the day of Adonai?

Time passed slowly. Salome, Mary Alphaeus, Aunt Miriam, Joanna, and Susanna each took their turn to approach the cross and kiss it or the Master's feet.

Overcome by tears, I turned to Magdalene who leaned into my embrace. I felt her warm tears fall on my face.

Hardly any of us said a full sentence, but rather wailed uncontrollably and groaned like women in labor.

Aunt Mary was the last of us to go to Jesus, John faithfully beside her. I fingered my dark blue mantle. It was fully dry from last night's excursion through the waterworks.

John had one arm around Aunt Mary's shoulder, and the other supported her as she stood, surely trying not to collapse with grief.

"Woman," Jesus called out. We all looked. "Behold, your son."

Woman. Like in Cana, it was not said to demean or blame her. It was to claim her for what she was. Woman. That she had a son. That she was a mother. "Behold, your mother."

Aunt Mary leaned in closer to John, resting her head on his shoulder.

When Aunt Mary and John returned to our vigil post, we embraced her and kissed her. Lines of tears shone on her face. Mary put an arm around each of us, then put a hand over her heart.

We stood for a long time. Salome was ready to collapse, and I did not blame her. My feet were sore. We sat on the hard ground, and stared at our Kyrios, adoring Him silently, and praying to Adonai, our Father, for assistance.

I spoke to Jesus in my heart and was slightly comforted when I told Him about all my confusion and sadness.

My Jesus, I cannot believe this is happening. How terrible this day is! I do long to be in Your presence, but not here as You hang on a cross! I wish to escape all of the suffering, even though I know mine is nothing compared to Yours.

Tell me why, Jesus. If not as my master and teacher, then tell me as my friend and cousin. Why are You being crucified? It is You who taught me that Elohim is Father — our abba. Why would Your abba make You the object of scorn and mockery? Why give You to us, only to take You away from us? You are the

Messiah, are You not? I have seen You multiply food, heal lepers, change hearts, calm seas, and raise people from the dead. You brought my Lazarus back to me. Why then, do You not save Yourself? I do not ask this in the tone of mockery the Pharisees and other Jews have, but in innocence and confusion. Why?

You forgive them without restraint. And now I too do so, though I do not understand. Am I not doing what You asked of all of us? But now the Messiah is supposed to deliver us. Look at us. Look at You. Subject to the power of men.

It was far past noon, coming upon the ninth hour.

Several of the Pharisees had left. Many of the Jews who were gloating had also left. A few Temple guards remained with some chief priests, often looking back at our cluster of women. Nicodemus arrived and stood alone near the bottom of the hill. The soldiers, of course, remained, seeming not to paying any attention to their surroundings as they drank. They played games, their laughter echoing off Golgotha. Yet they took turns at anxiously glancing up at the darkening sky.

Clouds were thick and the light from the sun was blocked, so much so it seemed to be late evening, though it was only mid-afternoon. Jesus was cast under the shadow of the sky. He and His cross. My lips trembled and chills ran through me.

Jesus twisted His head in agony.

"Eli, Eli, lema sabachthani?" Jesus cried. He mixed His Hebrew and Aramaic. The 22nd Psalm.

Why have you forsaken me? Far from my salvation are the words of my sins. O my El, I shall cry by day, and you will not hear, and by night, and it shall not be reputed as folly in me.

I wept again as I looked at His misery.

"This one is calling for Elijah," one man told a chief priest, pointing at Jesus.

"I thirst," He then groaned.

My mouth was dry, too. Next thing I knew, a soldier was sticking a spear with a sponge attached to it up to Jesus' mouth.

"What is the soldier giving him?" Joanna asked.

"Vinegar," Aunt Mary responded without taking her eyes off her son. "Bitter, bitter wine."

I cringed.

After the sponge touched Jesus' lips, He turned His head away, and the soldier pulled back the spear.

"It is probably mixed with a narcotic," Salome said.

"Did you say narcotic?" Mary Alphaeus looked quizzical.

"Myrrh or something of the sort. They give it to the crucified to ease the pain," Salome explained.

"How thoughtful of them." I could not resist sarcasm.

"Let us see whether Elijah will come to deliver Him," a bystander called.

But Jesus was not taken from the cross. The weight of His body on His arms seemed to be getting heavier and heavier, and His breathing more and more ragged.

Father, You have the power to save Him! Save Him!

"The Temple guards and priests keep looking our way," Salome said. She tried to adjust her position on the rocks. "See how they speak with those Roman soldiers?"

"They probably recognize that we are His disciples," I suggested.

"I do not like the way they are looking at us."

"It is finished," Jesus sighed loudly in obvious relief. I stood up with the rest of the women and folded my hands to my chest.

At that moment, two Roman soldiers came toward us, striding purposefully.

"You!" The leading guard said, pointing at me.

I looked down as Magdalene gripped my arm.

The leading guard grabbed my other arm, causing me to gasp.

"Look at me, woman! You are the one with the green eyes."

I looked to the lead guard in panic.

"It is as they say. The wife of Lazarus the Zealot." The guard tightened his grip on me as he looked back at his companion.

"Are you certain?"

"It is what the Pharisee said. This is the woman they pointed to. They say her eyes give her away."

"My husband is no Zealot!" I cried. "He is a man of shalom!"

"Let us take her then."

"No! No!" Magdalene held me.

Joanna cried out.

"Please," John said. "She is but a woman. She has caused you no trouble." A guard pushed John away.

"Her husband is a criminal and rebel. She will be set free when we find him."

"A storm is coming." A Roman soldier near Jesus' cross yelled at them.

"Quickly then." Their hands clamped on my arms like chains. I looked around frantically unsure of what was happening.

"Esther!" Magdalene screamed.

"Father," Jesus cried from above us. "Into Your hands, I commend My spirit!"

The sky darkened. Thunder bellowed.

The hands on my arms fell away as the wind raged. The ground beneath us started to move.

I fell flat on my back. The roughness of stone scratched my skin. Dizzy and unable to think, the world shifted around me. I trembled as the earth jolted. The sound of screams, shouts, cracks, and crashes enveloped me.

Then it was quiet.

I looked up, shaken although the earth was still. I turned to Jesus. His head drooped, and His chest no longer moved up and down with life.

It *was* finished.

Rising, I looked around. The two Roman guards were still on the ground. One appeared to have passed out.

"Run, Esther," John urged. "This is your chance! Run."

I dropped my mantle and immediately sprinted down the hill. I fell on the cracks and crevices in the ground, rough rock scratching my ankles and hands. But I kept running. As I moved toward the city, I saw smoke rising in different spots. Trees had fallen, and rocks spilled randomly upon the earth.

I slid through the Gate of Judgment.

The city was chaos.

I ran into a Pharisee. Not looking him in the eye, I pushed past him.

Buildings were crumbled and people walked or ran around frantically. Some lay on the ground, and I supposed that they were dead or unconscious from the quake.

As I passed down one side street, toward the hill to the upper city, I heard a faint sound amidst the shouts.

"Help."

I turned around sharply.

No. An inner voice told me to keep running.

But the voice persisted. "Help me."

I saw the glint of metal in the rubble from a fallen stone house, I moved closer and gasped. A man was partially buried beneath a large stone.

I moved even closer and recognized the shine and the red of his uniform. A Roman soldier. I wanted to run to safety. Was he not of the people who crucified my Kyrios? Jews hurried by, perhaps not noticing him. Even a Roman on his horse trotted by but did not stop to help his fellow soldier.

I closed my eyes. What if all the Romans knew of my green eyes like the ones on Golgotha?

Father forgive them, they do not know what they do.

Woman, behold your son.

Without any further contemplation, I ran toward the buried soldier as if he were Jesus, or Ima, or Magdalene, or Photina and her son, Victor. I bent to determine his condition. One of his legs was stuck.

Weak eyes gazed up at me. Young eyes. He had to be no older than eighteen. He was young enough to be my own son.

"Fear not," I said in a soothing voice — or so I hoped. "It is good that you have your helmet on." I gave a small smile. "It may have saved your life by saving your head."

He just groaned in response, his hands reaching toward the large stone that held him captive. I realized I was not strong enough to move it by myself.

Jesus. Father. Help me help your son!

I looked around. People hurried past, tripping over or dodging fallen materials.

My eyes settled on a wooden beam that must have been a part of a roof before the earthquake. I climbed stacks of rocks and grasped the beam with both hands. It was heavier than I expected and reminded me of the cross that Jesus had carried, but I pulled it, feeling a splinter slice under my skin as I made my way to the fallen soldier.

"Woman," the soldier groaned. "Jew."

"Yes. I am woman and Jew." I said as I pushed the beam beneath the large rock. I set the middle of the beam on a smaller stone. "I will push this rock off of you, using the beam as a lever. But you must pull out of it quickly, for my strength is small."

He gulped. With all of my might, I pushed down. It worked better than I thought it would, and the soldier squeezed out from beneath it.

I dropped the stone, worn out. I wiped the sweat from my forehead.

My heart filled with pity as I looked at the man's broken leg, reminding me of Victor's broken arm.

"What is your name?"

A tear slid down his cheek. He looked so vulnerable and innocent. "Justus," he mumbled. Both of his hands reached down toward his broken leg.

"May I pray over you?"

Justus let out a bitter laugh. "I care not, woman."

I carefully placed my hand on his leg. He flinched. Easing my touch, I said, "In the name of Jesus Kyrios, be healed of your affliction." I kept my eyes focused on his youthful eyes.

Justus stood on both feet. I jumped, surprised the soldier could move. Justus stared at me with furrowed brows. "Jesus who was crucified?"

"Yes," I said. "Know that the kingdom of Heaven is near to you." It felt so strange to speak of Jesus' message and act like I was still a disciple when my Master was dead.

"Who are you?" Justus leaned toward me, wiping the dust from his face.

"As you have said." I straightened my shoulders. "Woman."

With that, I left him, breaking again into a run. I continued up the hill to the upper city. I navigated around pilgrims and darted around street corners. No one found my sprinting unnatural, given the recent storm.

Many houses, from small cubes to tall, lavish structures of manor homes, had fallen roofs or crumbling walls.

I picked up my speed as my eyes fell on Nicodemus' house. I banged on the wooden door of the guest house.

No one opened.

I banged again, only now taking a look behind me. No Roman soldiers and no Temple guards. I slapped my hand on the wood, panting like a dog.

"Who is it?"

"Esther!" I cried.

The door opened and I fell inside. Andrew slammed the door behind me.

"Esther!"

"What has happened!"

"Lazarus, your wife has returned!" James Zebedee yelled.

Lazarus raced down the stairs, across the mosaic floor, and grabbed me. "What has happened, Esther? Are you well? You have blood on your face! And hands!"

"Yes," I said. "Yes. I am…I am well enough…"

"Speak, woman. Tell us what has happened."

"We heard they are crucifying the Master."

I told them that Jesus was dead. More disciples appeared.

Peter rushed to me. "He is dead?"

I nodded, trying to breathe. And asked if they had known about the storm.

"The earthquake? Yes!"

"Ah. It struck right just as He died." I looked into their ashen faces.

"I told you! I told you that is what it was!" Peter looked at the disciples. "Where are the others?"

"They are still at the cross. They...I...."

"Esther," Lazarus said gently. "You came alone."

I nodded. Tears cascaded down my dry cheeks. "Lazarus," I said. "Lazarus. They...the Romans...they tried to arrest me. They — they want to kill you, Lazarus!"

Lazarus did not look entirely shocked. "Did they hurt you?"

"No! I was able to get away right as the storm hit. They were thrust to the ground."

"Did anyone follow you?" Andrew asked, looking at the door.

"No. No," I cried. "No one did. I...Lazarus. They want to kill you!"

"Because he is a disciple?" Thomas looked at me, rubbing his thin nose.

"No. I do not know why. They...they called him a Zealot. A rebel. For some reason, Rome thinks Lazarus is a criminal...I think...I think it is the chief priests doing, so that Rome may punish you, Lazarus!" I started to cry.

Lazarus did his best to comfort me, but I pulled away. "They want to kill you. They want to kill you. They knew I was your wife because of my eyes! May Elohim curse these eyes!"

"You must leave Jerusalem!" James Zebedee said. "They will surely come here in search for you."

"They could be searching for all of us!" Bartholomew exclaimed, tugging at his unruly beard.

"No," Peter said. "You must stay here for now. It is nearly the Sabbath." His bushy eyebrows furrowed. "Your wife is in no state to travel. It is safer here."

"They have no proof you are a Sicarii!" my brother Simon cried. "You are not one!"

I turned to Lazarus. "Yet your father had enough connections. Syrus' punishment could fall on you." I banged my fist against Lazarus' chest.

"Not since I relinquished my title," Lazarus said. "All that my father owned now belongs to Martha!"

"Surely, they would not arrest Martha, then!" I said.

"No! No! I do not know!" Simon pushed his fingers through his hair.

I sobbed, pulling away from the lot of them. Finding a corner by a stone table, I bent over, shaking. Lazarus was behind me. Yet I could not hear what he said. Nor could I feel his touch.

Chapter 40

She [Jerusalem] weeps incessantly in the night, her cheeks damp
with tears. She has no one to comfort her from all her lovers;
Her friends have all betrayed her, and become her enemies.

LAMENTATIONS 1:2

We sat in total silence in the upper room. My head rested on my knees, pulled to my chest. I longed for sleep yet felt that I might never sleep again. Lazarus leaned against the wall. His face was ashen and unmoving.

The lamps were lit and ready for sundown. The Sabbath would begin at any moment. James Zebedee looked out a latticed window, ready to announce its beginning.

Knocks, yelps, and slams suddenly sounded downstairs.

"Andrew, I swear..." Came Salome's croaking voice. "I will blast the door off its hinges myself!"

"You do know what happened, do you not?" It was Mary Alphaeus' high-pitched voice.

"Careful." Susanna's gentle voice sounded without a hint of joy.

"We made it just in time for the Sabbath!" I heard John say. "Let us go to the upper room."

"Lazarus! Esther!" Martha was close to shouting. "Tell me they are here!"

Mary of Bethany suggested she calm down.

Magdalene stood in the doorway of the upper room. My green veil sluggishly fell down her head. Her tunic was covered in dirt and blood. She held two blue mantles. One was mine. I had not realized I was not wearing it.

Martha and Mary pushed behind her.

Then the other women.

Lastly, John and Aunt Mary.

"Lazarus," Martha cried, marching toward us.

Lazarus stood, but I felt weighed down and unable to move.

"Lazarus. Hezekiah is after you. Listen to me!"

"Explain slowly, Martha. Please!"

Mary walked behind her sister, carrying her alabaster jar of ointment. It held the nard that she anointed Jesus with just a week ago.

431

The other disciples got up and moved about, bumping against one another and talking rapidly to each other. We were like chickens squawking and waddling in a small pen.

Martha spoke with a new ferocity. "O Abraham, I cannot believe the man! I never even see Hezekiah; it is as if he was not my husband. O Abraham. O Abraham. All because of a ring?" Martha held up her family gold signet ring. "A ring! I would give the whole inheritance to *him* if he would just keep his mouth shut and not spread rumors to Rome! They want to kill you, Lazarus. *Kill* you. And the bastards will use any method possible."

"*Who* is trying to kill him?" Simon asked. "The priests? Or Rome?"

"Both! The priests and the Herodians are seeking his life. They use their enemy to pursue it," Martha rattled on. "O Abraham! Hezekiah has betrayed his own brethren. I never should have built that hospice. I never should have been chosen as woman of the household. O Abraham! O Abraham!"

Magdalene handed me my dirt and dust-coated blue mantle with a tired hand.

"Sister!" Lazarus said to Martha. "Why have you come to Jerusalem? Now that Passover is over, should you not be in Bethany — "

"I needed to return to Jerusalem! O Abraham, Lazarus! When Mary and I heard that the Master was taken to Pilate this morning and was then hanging on a cross, we came immediately! And who was finally home in Bethany? Hezekiah! O Abraham, forgive my household for harboring a hypocritical Pharisee like him!"

"What has Hezekiah done?" I tried to put the pieces of her account together.

"He spoke with the chief priests. They killed Jesus so it was time to take out the next one: Jesus' dear one whom He raised from the dead. Hezekiah gave them all they needed. Lies! Lies! O Abraham, lies. Now, the chief priests have reported to Rome that Lazarus is a Sicarii just like our father Syrus. There is evidence all about the house. They want to crucify you next, Lazarus!"

"My husband is innocent!" I cried, now standing.

"As was Jesus!" Martha yelled, tears spilling from her eyes.

"The soldiers knew you as my wife," Lazarus looked at me. "Because of your eyes."

"May Adonai curse my eyes, then," I declared. "I will pluck them out if I have to."

Mary shuddered.

"You will need to leave the city at once." Martha stepped closer to Lazarus.

"The Sabbath is upon us. I cannot leave," Lazarus said. "And if they kill me, they kill me. Death has no hold on me."

"Well, it does on us," Magdalene said. "I have told you before, Lazarus! You are proof that Rabboni is the Messiah."

"*Was* the Messiah!" Thomas yelled.

For a moment, I thought Magdalene was going to tackle Thomas, but Mary grabbed her arm.

I looked to Mary and Magdalene as Martha kept speaking hurriedly to Lazarus.

"Why do you hold ointment?" I looked at the alabaster jar Mary held.

"Martha and I were on the Mount of Olives when the earthquake hit. By the time we reached Golgotha, Jesus was dead! I saw men walking out of their tombs, as Lazarus had done. And they headed for the city just like any ordinary living men. They were *living*, I tell you. Jesus may have died, but the Father is still working miracles. When we reached Golgotha, we hardly had any time to anoint the Kyrios' body." Mary released Magdalene's arm.

"Where was Jesus buried?" I asked. Would His body rot with other Roman criminals?

"Joseph of Arimathea — a member of the council — put Rábboni in his tomb, by permission of Pontius Pilate himself. Nicodemus helped," Magdalene explained. "They had spices and ointment to bury Rabboni. Clearly, not every priest and Pharisee wanted Rabboni dead."

"Praise be to the Father that Jesus had a proper burial," I said.

"It was not proper! I would have anointed Him properly," Mary said, looking at the vessel in her hands. "B-but there was no t-time."

"What are we to do now?" I asked. "Do you think Rome is searching the city for Lazarus because they think he is some...some..."

"Some Zealot leader like Barabbas!" Martha's face was red.

"The Sabbath has begun!" James Zebedee bellowed. "The Sabbath has begun!" He turned from the window.

"Hush, James, lest the whole city hears us," Matthew said.

"We must begin our Sabbath meal. Shall we, Mother?" John looked to my aunt, Mary.

She used the Gentile word for "amen." She said it simply, but firmly. "*Fiat.*"

"What is our faith anymore?" Thomas asked the lot of us.

I had no desire to discuss this any further.

"Mustard seed," Thaddeus mumbled.

"Not even." Matthew held his head in his hands.

I offered grapes and dates to each disciple. Some had no appetite, while others were hungry as wolves.

One day had passed since Jesus' death. "I did not get to anoint Him! He said to anoint Him with my oil for His burial! I never anointed Him!" Mary of Bethany clutched the alabaster jar of nard to her chest.

Martha said they could go to the tomb after the Sabbath if they must, before returning to Bethany.

I did not want to think where Lazarus and I would go. Until sundown tonight, we were stuck in the upper room with the rest of the cowering disciples.

"Miriam, I say we leave at first light tomorrow morning," Uncle Clopas said.

"Are we to leave my sister-in-law, Mary?" Aunt Miriam asked.

"She now belongs to the care of John." Uncle Clopas growled. "I do not think it is safe for us to travel to Nazareth right now. We should get out of this city, but somewhere only a day's walk from here."

Aunt Miriam suggested Emmaus.

"Do you think your family would host us?" Uncle Clopas looked at his wife, who did not respond.

"Emmaus," Uncle Clopas said. "Just west of here." He ripped the grapes off of the vine with his teeth.

"Now that He is dead, our faith is dead." Thomas walked toward the center of the room with heavy feet.

John sat on the floor beside Aunt Mary. "Are we that weak? To not trust Him?"

"I do not think I can stand another one of these discussions," Salome groaned. She was on a mat against the wall.

"Trust Him? I do not think the Master planned on dying." Bartholomew suggested.

Magdalene disagreed. "I think He did plan on it." She sounded annoyed. "He spoke of it several times. Surely you remember."

"I should have asked Him what He meant when I had the chance." Philip shook his head. "He said the Son of Man would be killed, but I was afraid if I questioned Him, He would just say, 'Do you know Me so little, Philip?' Well yes, I do know Him so little!"

"And He said He would be raised." Magdalene said.

"Literally? Like Lazarus." Thomas glanced at my husband, who gulped.

"Yes. He raised Lazarus. He can do anything." My sister-in-law Mary sounded hopeful.

"He *is* the resurrection and the life!" Martha voiced.

"Was that a metaphor? A parable?" Philip pulled at his hair. "Just as He is the bread of life? The good shepherd?"

"There is no telling with Him!" James Zebedee dramatically said.

"I never actually understood a word He said." Bartholomew practically yanked his beard off his face. "Perhaps He was not the Messiah after all."

"You are saying we followed a fake?" Andrew's eyes widened.

"We clearly must have missed *something*. Maybe that is it."

"Explain all the miracles," Matthew challenged. He *hissed* like a snake.

"I am just pulling out ideas! Trying to make something of all this." Bartholomew tugged at his beard as he rocked back and forth.

Aunt Miriam shook her head at me, not wanting any food.

"Where is Peter?" James Zebedee asked.

"Loitering downstairs," Andrew drawled. "Refuses to speak or eat."

"Did you hear that?" James Alphaeus' wide eyes looked at the door leading to the staircase. "Someone just opened the main door."

"It is probably a servant."

"Did you hear a knock?"

"We are done for."

"It is the Sabbath — they would not arrest us today."

"Everyone shut your mouth."

"Nicodemus!" Magdalene walked to the Pharisee as he entered the upper room. "Please, come in." She acted as hostess.

"Thank Elohim it was only you!" Thomas exclaimed. "Unless..." He narrowed his eyes.

"Enough, Thomas!" Simon pressed a hand to Thomas' chest. "We can trust the man. Nicodemus is not going to hand us over."

"He has proved himself a true disciple," Matthew said.

"I would not go that far," Simon said darkly. "How can we be disciples of a dead man?"

"Please," Nicodemus insisted. "I have...some unfortunate news. I thought it best to tell you before you hear it on the streets."

"I am staying in here as long as you will allow me, Nicodemus," James Zebedee crossed his arms. "Not nearly ready to go out on the streets."

"Hush, James, my son." Salome sat up from lying on her mat. She looked hopefully at the Pharisee. "What news do you bring?"

I dreaded hearing of any more disasters. I thought of Job, who had to face disaster heaped upon disaster.

"Judas is dead."

My stomach dropped as I turned my head to the Pharisee. A horrid silence sat among us, far louder than a hundred Roman soldiers galloping on their horses.

"I do not believe it," Thomas finally said.

"You do not believe anything!" James Zebedee growled.

"Was he killed?" Philip asked.

"By his own hand" Nicodemus heaved.

"His own hand!"

"What do you mean by this?"

"He hung himself." Nicodemus looked away. "You could see him from the chief priest's roof; dangling from a tree just off the Kidron Valley."

I put a hand to my throat as if my neck had a rope around it.

"How terrible."

"May he burn in Gehenna!"

"Do not talk like that!"

"I am leaving!" Thomas shouted, scooping his mantle from the floor and leaving the room.

"Thomas!" James Alphaeus pattered after him. "Wait!"

"Me too! I am going home."

"I am not daring to leave this house."

"They are after us next."

"It is the Sabbath!"

"I tell you, now is the time to leave. They cannot take us on the Sabbath."

"Rome can do whatever she wants."

"Go then! Forget us."

"What if we can still follow the Master's teaching?"

"That the kingdom of Elohim is here?"

"The Son of Elohim is dead!"

"They have also posted guards at the Kyrios' tomb." Nicodemus struggled to be heard above the bickering disciples.

"How can this be?" Simon grunted. "Did they think we would steal His body and claim He rose from the dead?"

"That is exactly what they think."

I looked past the disciples, now all standing, and saw Aunt Mary and John, still seated. Aunt Miriam, Susanna and Joanna were with them. None spoke.

I walked over and set a platter on the carpeted floor. Aunt Mary looked at me, the gentleness in her face a complete contrast to the rigor of all others.

I wished to say something, to comfort her, to ask her something. Would my voice sound like a squeaky mouse?

My eyes watered. It was her own son who had died, yet each disciple spoke carelessly of Jesus, as if she were not in the same room. How many times had they shouted, "He is dead! I do not think I believe any longer. He was false. I am leaving."

How could she stand it?

"My children," Aunt Mary said, just loudly enough for me to hear. John and us women looked up at her as if we were children. "Graces will be shed on all, great and little, especially upon those who seek them."

"Esther, come here," my husband said. He was with Nicodemus, Magdalene, Martha, and Mary.

Nicodemus looked at me warily and then at my husband and sisters-in-law. "I have news concerning…concerning you, Lazarus."

"I have been told," Lazarus said stiffly. "The chief priests are plotting to kill me."

"And they have Rome involved," Nicodemus continued.

"They claim Lazarus is a secret Zealot like our father was," Mary said. She frowned. Only recently had she discovered that her father aided Sicarii.

"Both Hezekiah and Barabbas swore to the chief priests that Lazarus continued Syrus' work."

"Barabbas as well!" I groaned. And *he* was the man who was freed instead of Jesus!

"I suggest you leave the city." Nicodemus looked from Lazarus to me. "Both of you. Your green eyes give Lazarus away."

I looked down at the floor to hide my eyes.

"They will come searching for you, I am sure. If not Rome, then the Temple guards. And Mary and Martha best return to your father's house. To keep suspicions away from your brother."

"We will leave tomorrow after we properly anoint the Kyrios' body."

"Husband," I said shakily. "Where are we to go? What are we to do?"

"Be not afraid," he replied. "Death has no hold on us."

"You will flee, though, brother?" Magdalene touched his arm.

"We who hope in Adonai will renew our strength," Lazarus said. "We shall take wing as eagles, we shall run and not be weary, we shall walk and not faint." He looked at me with confidence.

That was the first time I had seen his smile since his return to life.

I returned the smile to him in pure joy. I was thankful for this gift of my husband, despite the sorrow that surrounded us. "Let us leave tomorrow as well," I said.

Chapter 41

But the LORD sent a great fish to swallow Jonah, and he
remained in the belly of the fish three days and three nights.

JONAH 2:1

"You have the nard?" a voice whispered.

"And I have the extra spices."

I quickly sat up. It took great effort to open my eyes, as they were plastered shut from my tears the night before.

The light in the upper room was dim and the floor was covered with the sleeping bodies. A few disciples sat or stood against the wall. Simon looked at me from across the room. He was one of the many unable to rest.

I turned my focus to the women whispering by a wall, then threw my slept-on mantle around my shoulders, stood, and stepped over disciples to reach the cluster of women. Actually, I believed I stepped *on* a disciple, but I prayed it was only a shoe or clump in a blanket as opposed to a hand.

"Martha!" I whispered. "Were you going to depart without saying goodbye?"

"Of course not." She turned from the women to look at me. "Mary and I are going to the tomb with the others. We will return to Nicodemus' guest house and then we return to Bethany."

"I want to come with you."

"I do not want you to come with us, Esther." Martha sounded decisive. "You and Lazarus are too precious."

"Some of us are attempting to sleep," James Zebedee's muffled voice rose above the cacophony.

"Forgive me," I said.

"Let us go downstairs."

I followed the women to the main chamber of the first floor. We settled in the center of the large room.

"Where is Aunt Mary?"

"On the balcony," Susanna said.

"The balcony?" I raised a brow. "I thought she would accompany you."

"She wishes to stay. She is in an unusually pleasant mood. Despite what has happened to her son."

"Has she voiced any explanation for this?"

"She has hardly spoken a word. Only that she wishes to remain alone on the balcony."

"She will not have a problem being alone," Magdalene said, pulling her sister Mary under one of her arms. Mary clung to her jar of nard as if she was carrying a child. "The Twelve will not even poke a head out the window."

"John would," Mary said. "And they are now Eleven."

"Or even less," Salome croaked bitterly.

"John is sleeping and has no need to join us." Martha examined the group. "How many of us are there? Seven? We can look after each other." Salome, Mary Alphaeus, Martha and Mary of Bethany, Magdalene, Susanna and Joanna.

"What of Miriam? Where is *that* woman?" Salome put a hand to her hip as she leaned back.

"She and Clopas are preparing to leave for Emmaus," Joanna explained. "It is Miriam's hometown."

"Let us not be idle." Martha clasped her hands together, determination in her expression. "The light of day is already upon us."

"Our Father be with you." I touched their hands. "Walk with wisdom." My eyes blurred at the thought of Jesus' dead body, His blood dried on His skin. "Lazarus and I plan to leave before noon when most all of the pilgrims will be leaving Jerusalem. We will blend in well with the crowds."

"We will be back before then," Martha assured me. "No matter what, disguise yourself." She looked at me pointedly and then exited the door. Joanna closed it securely behind them.

Alone, I blew out a long breath and locked the door.

Three days since His death.

I glanced at the mosaic on the floor, and grabbed a small oil lamp from one of the decorative tables against the wall. I used the lamp to illumine the array of tans, browns, blues, greys, and maroons that formed a geometric design of the mosaic.

I lost myself in the colors.

"Esther."

I smiled at Lazarus as he descended the stairs. "I thought you would still be asleep," I said. "We have a busy day today."

"I have been awake all night," he said.

I raised the lamp to his face. "I was certain you were asleep."

"Perhaps for a moment. Since my return to life…" Lazarus shrugged slightly.

I lowered the oil lamp, holding it with both hands at my chest. The warmth of the small fire in it gently brushed my neck. I breathed in the scent of the burning olive oil.

"You smiled for the first time yesterday." I rubbed my finger over the heated clay. "Since your return to life."

He frowned.

"Will you smile again?" The burning flame was diminishing. A line of white smoke rose from the vented opening.

"Everywhere I look." He spoke slowly. "Since my return to life, I see souls choosing Gehenna."

I winced at the thought of that fiery place.

"Gehenna," Lazarus whispered. "How can I smile after what I have seen?"

He had shared so little with me about what happened when he died. I was surprised.

"They hear the word of Adonai, yet they reject Him."

"You should have seen your sisters and the other women, all eager to go to Jesus' tomb," I said. "Though many have rejected Him, they have not."

"Do you remember the parable of the sower?"

I did.

"Some fell by the wayside, but birds of the air came and ate them up. That is the one who hears the word of the kingdom and does not understand it, so there comes the wicked one and catches away that which was sown in his heart," I recited.

The flame from my lamp extinguished, yet we were not left in darkness. The morning sun had gently eased in. "Think of the people who shouted hosannas and waved palms at the Kyrios' entry into Jerusalem this past week. Where are they now? Their faith has been snatched from them."

The smell of the burnt oil lingered, tickling my nostrils.

"Then, some seed fell on stony ground. That is one who hears the word and immediately receives it with joy. Yet he has not roots and his faith lasts only for a time." Lazarus gulped, shifting his weight from one foot to the other. "When there arises some tribulation or persecution because of the word, he falls away. There are many souls like that in Gehenna. You and I are witness to that. We have seen people drop everything to follow Jesus and then leave. See how many have left us after His death."

Tears filled my eyes as I stared at his sullen face. Uncle Clopas and Aunt Miriam would leave for Emmaus. No one knew where Thomas was. And Ima left us with many others, far before Jesus' death.

"And others fell among thorns. That is the one who hears the word and the care of this world and the deceitfulness of riches chokes up the word and he becomes fruitless. You remember that rich man who came to Jesus — and several others — they could not let go of their wealth. As for me. It took months for me to finally give up mine."

"Yet you did renounce your wealth and title for Jesus." I swept a foot toward Lazarus. "Do not forget, beloved, that the seed sown on good ground is the one who hears the word and understands it, who indeed bears fruit."

Lazarus' face was hard as he looked down at me. "I have not forgotten. I only mourn those who have rejected Him, despite hearing His word."

The smell of fresh unleavened bread wafted over us from the kitchen. Nebo and Candence must have been preparing it.

"Forgive me, Esther. Forgive my mood. You do not deserve me and my sulking."

"I forgive you a hundred times over," I said immediately. "As, by the Father's grace, I have forgiven all."

"All?"

"The Romans. Each one of them. The man who killed my Abba. The ones who tortured and killed Jesus. Hezekiah and the Pharisees, I forgive. Actually, every soul that has wronged me in any way. I forgive them. And I will take them to myself as my children. As my Aunt Mary does. They say she even spoke to the soldier who pierced Jesus' side at the cross. She spoke to the man and he confessed that he believed Jesus was the Son of Elohim."

Lazarus raised his eyebrows. Since he knew me to be a woman of resentment and judgment, I sensed it unlikely he would believe this new me, but that was not so.

"You, Esther, the motherless wife, has become the mother of many. At this strange time."

I placed one hand over my heart. "I had ears but did not hear. At His cross, I *heard* for the first time. My eyes *saw* for the first time."

"Your eyes light up when you speak. Beautiful olivine eyes."

"Cursed eyes." I returned the oil lamp to its place on the stone table. Looking back at him, I asked, "Where do you suppose we will go? North towards Damascus? South toward Arabia? West toward Egypt?"

"Wherever Kyrios tells us, although being in this house makes me feel like I am back in the tomb." He looked up at the tall limestone walls, the many windows giving nice natural light.

But the Kyrios was gone. "Peter should arrange a meeting — for the Twelve — Eleven — for whoever is left," I said. "They are loitering here with no direction."

"This is only the third day since His death."

"Long days." I frowned.

I woke myself from my dull thoughts. "The Sabbath is behind us. I must do some sort of work before we leave the city."

"You will wear your veil over your face, so none can recognize you."

I looked back at my husband and nodded. After all that had happened, I was surprisingly calm. From Hezekiah's tunnel to Jesus' crucifixion. Sneaking out of a city did not seem as daunting.

Andrew hurried down the stairs.

"Is someone guarding the door?"

"Guarding…" I muttered under my breath, deciding to let Lazarus speak with him.

I saw Candence, and scrawny Nebo at work in the kitchen, preparing the day's bread.

"It smells good in here," I said, clasping my hands in front of me. They glanced at me and returned to their work.

I saw at least a dozen loaves on a wooden platform against the wall. Nebo crouched and slid more dough into the oven's opening with a wooden shovel.

"Our numbers are decreasing…we will not need as much food." I walked over to Nebo who was by the oven.

He looked up at me, flour powdered on his face. "Master Nicodemus alerted us of the decrease."

"What may I help with? Surely there is always something to do." It was still the Feast of Unleavened Bread.

He looked around, pulled the wooden shovel from the oven, then rose and looked at me respectfully. "Candence is kneading the dough over there. Would you grind the grain?"

I nodded, thankful for their humility. My stomach curled with hunger at the fresh smell. I made my way across the small kitchen to Candence, who knelt in front of a platform, on which a large trough sat. With her sleeves rolled up past her elbows, she rolled the dough roughly inside the trough, pressing against it vigorously.

"Candence," I said, kneeling beside her. I grabbed a handful of grain from a sack and plopped it on the grain mill. "How do you fair?"

The servant paused. She did not look at me, and then resumed rolling and punching the dough.

"I...I am well."

I took a wooden peg to grind the grain with. On the wooden platform beside me was an enormous pot of freshly ground flour, a jug of water that towered above a bottle of oil, and some salt. No leaven.

"These days have been eventful," I told her, unsure if I should even be trying to make conversation.

"Yes, my lady."

I released a breath, my hand making the familiar circular motion.

"I saw the women preparing to go to the tomb," Candence said.

"Yes. Yes." I tried to move the mill faster, but it would take hours to make enough flour just for the rest of today's bread. "I wish I could have accompanied them."

"I wish I could have as well."

I stilled my hands and turned to her. She did not look my way.

"If only you had asked," I said. "Surely, you would have been allowed to accompany them."

"No." She shook her head timidly, her small nose wrinkling in a sniffle. "My work is here."

There was silence between us. Whatever flour I had ground, I placed in the jar, a whiff of the flour bombarding my nostrils.

"The Master was kind."

I looked to Candence again. She leaned back from her work and looked at her lap. Her flour-powdered hands still rested on the trough.

"Nicodemus?"

She shook her head, wiping her eyes with her arm. "Jesus, the Kyrios."

I did not realize how devout these servants truly were to Jesus.

"He washed my feet," Candence barely whispered as she gingerly added more water to her dough.

"Nebo!" An elderly voice entered the kitchen. I turned and made eye contact with Nicodemus. He touched his heavy head-covering and peered at me. "Ah, the wife of Lazarus!" he said frantically.

"Yes?" I wiped my hands together to get the flour off of them.

"Praise to Adonai! Nebo! Fetch Lazarus of Bethany. Bring him here at once."

"Sir? What is the matter?" I stepped toward the Pharisee, examining the sweat on his face and his grey-white beard that also glistened with perspiration.

"Candence," he spoke to his servant. "Prepare food and water for a journey. For several days."

She rustled about behind me, but I did not take my eyes from Nicodemus.

"Sir..." I began.

"Lazarus," Nicodemus said, not looking at me. I turned to see Nebo leading Lazarus into the kitchen. Candence took several circular loaves of unleavened bread but dropped one due to her frantic motions.

Ignoring this, I listened to my husband speak.

"Nicodemus. What is the cause of such urgency? Are you not well?" Lazarus asked.

"I am fine." Nicodemus put his hands to his chest, wiping them on his dark, outer garment. "It is you I worry for."

I gulped.

"I was summoned by the chief priests," Nicodemus heaved. "This morning, when the Sabbath was completed. I have just returned and...you must know it is no longer a secret that I am a disciple. They know that all of you are here in my guest house."

I listened intently.

"I went to Caiaphas' house as requested," Nicodemus continued, some of his words slurring together. "If only Joseph of Arimathea was with me at that moment. They told me of the shame I brought them, and offered me to spy for them on you and the disciples."

I sucked in a breath.

"And?" Lazarus asked.

"First and foremost, they wanted to pay me...to, well, betray you the same way Judas betrayed the Master. They offered me silver if I would hand Lazarus to them."

I gasped at Lazarus' name.

"I do not know what their plan is exactly; if they alerted Rome or not. They know you are here, and they could be coming for you this instant — I do not know. But they could take you to Pontius Pilate and condemn you for assisting rebels."

"Are any of the disciples' safe? Is Caiaphas after all of the Kyrios' followers?" Lazarus wondered.

"I...do not know. I do not think they have the right to arrest me or the disciples unless they made a riot or commotion."

"But Lazarus has," I said dully.

"I suggest you leave now and with haste. Do not go to Bethany. They will look for you there as well."

"Lazarus!" Simon walked into the kitchen. "What is this about? Why all this secrecy and haste when you left the upper room?"

"Esther, grab your veil and our mantles. There is no time to bid farewell. Speak to no one," my husband instructed. I obeyed, darting out of the kitchen and up the stairs. The disciples were all awake now, loitering about the room, many sitting sadly, as they were yesterday. I refused to make eye contact with any of them. Magdalene's tan veil was on the floor. She still had my green one. Grasping her veil, my mantle and Lazarus' mantle, I left.

Aunt Mary was coming inside from the balcony. For a moment, she smiled at me. I smiled back, and then forced myself to turn and leave. It was not a proper goodbye, but it was better than none.

As I ran down to the lower room, I saw Lazarus speaking to Nicodemus and Simon.

"See to my sisters!" Lazarus said to Simon, on seeing me. "If they have need of anything."

Simon nodded frantically. I embraced and kissed my brother.

Lazarus looked at the Pharisee who gazed back with acute sadness. "Thank you, Nicodemus."

He turned to me. "Wife, are you ready?"

"Yes." *My heart is ready, O Elohim. My heart is ready.* "Rise up. To battle against it." I gave what I hoped was an assuring smile to Simon as Candence handed a satchel to Lazarus, who slung the long leather handle over his shoulder. I followed him across the mosaic floor, and after Andrew unlocked the door, Lazarus led us out.

It felt like a giant wave hit me as we started walking quickly down the street. People were everywhere. I threw my veil over my head and carried both Lazarus' mantle and mine around my shoulders.

I took Lazarus' arm.

Servants carrying supplies passed us. Others pulled stubborn oxen. Still others, clothed in rich purple, hurried through the wealthy quarter. I noticed Lazarus was heading in the opposite direction of Caiaphas' house and the other houses of the chief priests. He took us northward.

A beggar called for mercy in the name of Elohim.

"Which gate are we taking?" I held onto Lazarus' arm.

"The Gate of Judgment."

It was a wise choice. It was the least used of the gates of Jerusalem because of its nearness to Golgotha.

I panted as he picked up the pace again, the houses becoming smaller as we went downward, very close to each other due to lack of space. We made sharp turns, and I could see the wall of the city. I glanced behind me to see that we had already far passed Herod's palace. Its tiled orange roof sparkled, but that was nothing in comparison to the shining white of the Temple far ahead.

A man with a white lamb on his shoulders emerged from his house, likely to offer the unblemished animal for First Fruits — the last sacrifice finishing the feast of Passover. Someone passed us with a tray of unleavened bread on his head and a woman dumped a pot of dirty water through her window. Another man with a lamb pushed a child, probably his son, toward the Temple.

It was a cool morning, despite the heat caused by our fast pace. We followed the wall of the city which blocked the sun for now.

As we came closer to the market, the number of people increased. Still following the wall, we saw men with carts and mules. The vendors in the marketplace beckoned us to buy their dates or precious stones. I shifted the weight of Lazarus' mantle on my shoulder.

I covered my face with my veil. The Gate of Judgement came to view. It was a foggy mist for me. I was wary of the street Jesus had carried His cross through.

Lazarus allowed no time for rest. Roman soldiers on white steeds stood observant by the gate. One soldier shouted at a merchant who was trying to bring in his cart of supplies. A money changer sat at his booth. Stalls of salt and produce were behind him.

We walked under the arched stone gate with ease. Ahead was the hill of Golgotha. Lone halves of crosses stood. No criminals hung on them that day.

Few people were in this rocky quarry. I eased my grip on Lazarus. My feet were scratched by the rough piles of rocks. Soon, we could see the small hill of tombs.

Though we had stopped running, my heart was still quick with the knowledge that Jesus' body was so near.

"Lazarus, may we stop by His tomb? Just briefly?"

Lazarus looked back at me. "I wish to…"

"Then let us!"

He nodded his approval and I blew out a breath of gratitude. As we turned around the edge of Golgotha, we looked at the variety of tombs. I did not know if we would be able to tell which belonged to Joseph of Arimathea.

"Nicodemus said guards were posted at the tomb. I did not think of this. Perhaps we should leave," I said.

"No," Lazarus responded. "Look there!" He pointed at a tomb with the rock pulled away from it. "See — the remains of a fire they made, and one guard must have left his helmet!"

"Are you sure this is Jesus' tomb?" I was confused. Would the women be inside anointing His body?

I pulled my veil from over my eyes.

"Look at the inscription here in Hebrew," Lazarus said as he reached the sepulcher with the missing stone. "It bears the name Joseph of Arimathea. This must be it."

Wonder overcame me. The quietness was eerie.

Lazarus glanced back at me as he bent down into the tomb. I put a hand to my mouth. Without thinking, I dropped Lazarus' mantle outside the entrance. The inside was damp but had some light falling in from outside, scattering the darkness. I passed through the large interior.

It was empty.

All of Jesus' burial linens were lying on a stone slab in the back chamber, a slab I had assumed Jesus' body would be lying upon.

I hurried past my husband and knelt before the slab. The linens were heavily marked with dried blood and smeared with oil.

"Did someone take His body?" Emotion rose in my throat like bile.

"Why would they take it and leave the linens? No one has taken it, Esther."

"How can you be sure?" I looked back at Lazarus, who was bending over a shattered clay pot.

"These are spices. One of the women must have dropped it."

I walked over, breathing in the pungent scent of myrrh. "The women are no longer here…"

Neither of us spoke, then:

"He is alive, Esther."

I refused to look at Lazarus. I was stunned and almost immobile. Finally, with effort, I met my husband's eyes. The light of morning streamed through the tomb's entrance. I looked back at the empty slab, the shroud draping it.

"Alive," I murmured.

"I was raised from death, Esther." Lazarus stood behind me. "You witnessed it."

I placed my hand on the slab's cool stone. Goosebumps ran up my arms.

"He is risen," Lazarus said.

"Where is He, then?"

Lazarus did not know.

A ringing filled my ears and my eyes blurred. I steadied myself on the stone slab, and tried to grasp what had happened.

Quickly, though, a rush of joy hit me. I kissed the stone of the tomb. Lifting my face, I gently cheered. I smiled, filled with belief.

I threw myself into Lazarus' arms and cried, "He is risen!"

Lazarus laughed with me and lifted me off the ground. "He is! He is risen, indeed."

Chapter 42

He received dominion, splendor, and kingship; all nations,
peoples and tongues will serve him. His dominion is an
everlasting dominion that shall not pass away, his kingship,
one that shall not be destroyed.

DANIEL 7:14

We sat in a stable attached to some villagers' humble home in Shiloh, Samaria. It was evening. My feet and calves screamed from the day's journey. Yet my previously parched mouth was moist, and I was content with the restful night awaiting us.

"I am impressed Shiloh boarded us. We are Jews after all. *Criminal* Jews," I said lightheartedly.

"They put us in a stable," Lazarus said. "I think they meant to insult us." A large black cow behind him breathed heavily.

"The only payment you gave them was your wool mantle." I tapped my fingers on my knees. "What else can we expect in return?"

I leaned back in the hay, my mantle wrapped around me. "I wonder where Jesus is now." If He had truly risen, then He was as real as Lazarus was, sitting beside me. "Perhaps He is with the disciples in the upper room as we speak. I wish we had not left. But you are safe here." I glanced at the chickens as well as the donkey beside me. A lone lantern hung from the low ceiling. "Rome will not think to look for us first in Samaria. They will begin in Bethany and Judea and then go straight to Galilee where all the rebels tend to come from."

"Perhaps," Lazarus said. "But I would think they would come *here* first," he remarked. "Samaria is a good place to hide for a Jewish bandit. But I doubt they are sending out search parties for us. Perhaps if they found me walking around the Antonia Fortress in Jerusalem or wandering around Caesarea or Tiberias, they might arrest me. But Rome has more important things to do than track down one supposed bandit."

"Your father knew a network of bandits." I looked at him pointedly. "Your head may be more valuable than you think."

"Jesus was innocent. As am I. I care not what happens anymore." He rubbed his nose.

"Where will we go after Shiloh?"

"As far as Cyprus if we have to. Esther, we finally get a night of privacy."

"If you do not count the animals, yes," I laughed, glancing at a sleeping goat.

"Did you not say Jesus was born in a stable?"

"That is the story my Uncle Joseph and Aunt Mary told me. They even placed Him in the manger." The donkey in front of the manger looked back at us on cue, its mouth full of hay.

"Born in humility and died in humility," Lazarus mused, putting his arm around my shoulder.

"Go and do likewise."

I started. That person speaking was not Lazarus. The stable gate was closed.

But Jesus Himself stood inside, gazing at us with a smile larger than a full moon.

Lazarus and I both rose clumsily. And then fell to our knees.

"Jesus!" I cried.

"Kyrios, it is You!" Lazarus buried his face in the straw on the ground.

I trembled as I dared to look into Jesus' eyes. They were the same as I remembered. Brown, bronze, and glowing, as if roasting embers were inside them. The rest of His face was clean. A beard covered His jaw but was not extensive. His brown hair was tame with just a hint of auburn in the dim lighting.

He looked at us with relaxed brows and calm muscles. "Get up, Lazarus. Esther."

I stood, feeling a current was issuing forth from Jesus, like heat rays from the sun.

"Kyrios Jesus," I said, looking at His new white tunic. "May I...touch You?"

Jesus laughed softly. "Yes, you may touch Me, My dear one."

I slowly took His left hand as Lazarus took His right.

His hand was soft and uncalloused, but my fingers touched a strange edge. Looking closely, I saw the large hole in His hand. I dropped His hand in terror. I could see through that hole the way I would see through a window.

"The marks from the nails remain with Me," Jesus said, His eyes warm like the stable. "As they shall remain a part of the paschal mystery."

I had so many questions for Him but could not think of one to ask.

Lazarus cradled Jesus' right hand like a babe and Jesus reached His left hand for me. Chills pricked my spine as I felt Jesus' breath on my face and His hand on my shoulder.

"Come. Let us sit." Jesus ushered us forward.

I took my blue mantle and set it upon the straw. "Sit here, Kyrios."

He nodded, accepting my modest offering.

I curled my hair behind my ear, Magdalene's tan veil piled next to me on the straw. Lazarus and I sat across from Jesus.

To be with Him again felt so familiar, yet at the same time, totally strange. I glanced at the holes in His feet, crossed beneath Him.

"What do you will us to do next, Kyrios?" Lazarus asked, gazing intently at Jesus.

"You are to continue what you started the day you became My disciples."

"Proclaim the kingdom of Heaven," Lazarus concluded, gripping his knees as he sat on his heels.

"May we join You and the disciples?" I asked. "If You return to Galilee! If we are with You, Jesus, Lazarus will be safe."

"Some will witness in Galilee, but others in Judea, Samaria, and then to the ends of the earth."

"And You will be with us as we go, will You not?" I asked hopefully.

"Yes," Jesus said. "But I will not join you in the way I used to. I have told you that I am leaving so the Spirit of truth may come. When I ascend to My Father, the Holy Spirit will come upon you and will guide you."

My lips puckered. "Jesus...what does this mean? You will no longer be on this earth?"

"I will be here in the breaking of the bread. And remember: I am in the Spirit and the Spirit is in Me."

"I am still confused, Kyrios." Lazarus looked at his hands folded in his lap.

"Why did You die?" I asked. "Why so painfully?"

"Listen, my children." Jesus looked at us confidently as He folded His hands together. "Think of the Scriptures. You have both studied the Torah and the psalms and the writings, and the prophets."

I inclined toward Him, relishing His presence. My heart stirred with warmth.

"You know My Father's covenant with David. He swore to David His servant that He would make his dynasty stand forever and establish his throne through all ages. My Father swore an oath to David. He said, 'Your offspring I will set upon your throne.'

"He foresaw and spoke of my Resurrection. That neither was I abandoned to the netherworld nor did my flesh see corruption. My Father raised Me up in the Spirit.

"Both Jews and Greeks are under the domination of sin. As it is written, 'They are all gone aside. They are unprofitable together; there is none that does good, no not one.' But now the righteousness of Elohim has been manifested apart from the law, though testified to by the law and the prophets.

"As prophesied in the Torah, I would conquer Satan, crushing the head of the serpent. That, as Isaiah said, I would make an offering for sin. As a servant, suffering, I bore the sins of many and interceded for their transgressions. That, as prophesized by Ezekiel, I would give you a new heart; and My spirit within you so that you walk in My statutes. That, as said by Jeremiah, I would make a new covenant with you — not like the covenant I made with your ancestors the day I took them by the hand to lead them out of the land of Egypt. But this is the covenant I make with the house of Israel after those days. I place My law within them and write it upon their hearts. See that I forgive their iniquity and no longer remember their sin…"

It was far into the night when Jesus finished speaking, and I knew He had given us but a drop of the depths of reality. I stared at Him, amazed, my lips slightly parted and my heart rising in exultation.

"We are ready, Kyrios," Lazarus said. "Let us go out and proclaim this truth! I will go to the ends of the earth!"

Jesus smiled. "First, Lazarus, you must be clothed with power from on high. I will ascend to my Father so that the Spirit may come. The Apostles will receive the Spirit in Jerusalem, but I am outside of time and place. The Spirit will come upon all of My disciples — so it shall be for you here."

"Where shall we stay, then? If men are after my life?" Lazarus looked earnestly at Jesus. I leaned toward our beloved Kyrios, ready for His answer.

"I protected you from the hand of the Egyptians, and I protected you when you wandered in the desert to the promised land. So too, will I protect you, Lazarus and Esther. Be not afraid. The Spirit will give you the knowledge of when to go and what to do."

"Jesus!" I said quickly, my eyes widening with fear. "You sound ready to leave us."

"I will never leave you — even till the end of the age, I will be with you. That is why I have given you My body and blood, so I may be one with you, and so even though you cannot see Me, you know I am with you."

I looked at Lazarus with tears in my eyes. He patted my hand comfortingly. Looking back at Jesus —

"He is gone!" Lazarus exclaimed.

The stable felt utterly empty without Him. Though there was hardly a square cubit of extra space, Jesus' absence was far too evident. It was as if the sea had no water, or the sun had no light.

"I know where we will go," Lazarus said, turning eagerly to me.

I raised a brow.

"It is not far from here. Let us go to Sychar."

"Where Photina and Victor live?"

"Yes, we could reach them by sundown tomorrow if we walk quickly enough!"

"And ask them to harbor criminals?" I asked doubtfully.

"If they are our brothers and sisters in the Kyrios, then we need not fear. Faithful Samaritans have shown more trust in Jesus than we Jews!"

"I wish Jesus were still here with us. I want to hear Him tell us more about the Scriptures."

"You forget," Lazarus said, a bright smile on his face. "He is here with us presently."

"Then together, let us speak more with Him!" I rose, my heart ready for a night of prayer.

Epilogue: 35 CE

However, be on your guard and be very careful not to forget
the things your own eyes have seen, nor let them slip from your
heart as long as you live, but make them known to your children
and to your children's children...

DEUTERONOMY 4:9

If joy could make a sound, perhaps it would be that of a yelp — not one of fear or pain — but a cry of bliss, just as Lazarus and I cried out when the Spirit came upon us in Sychar of Samaria. Perhaps joy also sounded like sweet music. Like those memories of the Levite choir singing in their deep tones at the Temple, or Thomas playing his flute when we traveled with Jesus during His ministry. The sound of joy passed on as laughter. A satisfying laugh from Lazarus after a period of refused smiles. The memory of Susanna's easy giggles and those of the women disciples.

If joy could be touched, then it might feel like a sea breeze that passed over Lazarus and I when we took a ship across the Great Sea to Cyprus. It could feel like the rays of the sun warming my back when standing on the shore of that large island. It could even feel like sweat running down my back after I finished working with textiles, collecting flax, dying fabrics, weaving, sewing, and mending, which I did for businesses in Kition. Joy was the warmth that came from praying the "Our Father," crying out to Jesus, and acknowledging the presence of the Spirit.

If joy could be tasted, then I think it might taste like the body and blood of Jesus. The breaking of the bread that we shared here with Jews and Gentiles alike. The coarse, dry bread, that was the very flesh of the Son of Elohim. The wine that warmed my tongue and fell down my throat, alerting me of the presence of the Kyrios.

If joy could be smelled, then I might say it would smell like the carpenter shop next door to Lazarus and me, reminding me of Nazareth. The pure, fresh scent of an orphaned baby, born of a Roman prostitute, that I got to care for. It could also smell like salt and rope and spices drifting toward us from the port. The smell of parchment; papyrus dipped in ink, in which we heard news of Jerusalem; of the works of Peter and the Apostles, and this new man called Paul.

If joy could be seen, then, it would be seeing Jesus everywhere. I saw Him in my husband as he worked beside the Cyprian people at a textile factory. I saw Him in the Cyprians who looked at us with eagerness and respect; those who sought a glimpse of the man whom Jesus rose from the dead. I saw Him in the rich merchants who came in and went out at sea; in the laborers, sailors, servants, and slaves. I saw Him in the tax collectors and the prostitutes. I saw Him in the many green-eyed women of Greece, Crete, Rome, Germania, and Galatia. I saw Him in the Roman soldiers who passed through the city, unaware that the "Eleazar of Kition" they saw, was the one they knew as "Lazarus the Zealot."

Most of all, I encountered joy in the innocence of children.

"*Mitera* Esther!" Hector whispered to me, poking his head around the corner of the mudbrick home. I stilled my hands on the wooden spindle, my fingers aching from the repetitive motion. Mitera Esther. They called me "mother" in Greek. A title that never ceased to tender my heart.

"What is it Hector?" I looked at the child. "Step forward so I can hear you."

With great hesitance, Hector stepped toward me, looking sheepishly over his shoulder. "It is story time," he said quickly, looking over his shoulder once again.

I smiled, lowering the spindle to my lap. "Is it that time already?" I looked at his hands gripped tightly together. "I thought you enjoyed story time," I said, setting the spindle and basket of wool on the table beside me. "You look afraid."

Hector raised his chin. "I am not afraid."

"Oh," I said pointedly. "You are not afraid." I rose, grabbing my tan veil so that it settled evenly on my head. Magdalene's veil. A remnant of my sister-in-law.

Hector looked at his feet.

"You do look...what is the word...?" I feigned thinking as I tapped a finger to my chin. "Embarrassed." I stood up, taking my blue mantle and resting it over one shoulder.

Hector opened his mouth to protest and then dropped it. "I am twelve years old now. I have come of age and...not many men listen to your stories."

"I see." I put a hand on his shoulder, motioning him out of the traklin. We walked into the courtyard where younger children played. I looked downward. "We need a *man*," I emphasized the word. "To oversee the storytelling. We need a devout young man like yourself to keep watch over the children.

And remember, some of those children down the street can get naughty. I will need your help, eh?"

Hector looked at me, a clear battle in his mind.

"Alright, young man," I decided. "Let us go. You said it is story time. Help me gather the children. Let me get my baby." I walked through the traklin to the little cradle of sleeping Aurelia.

"Look at you!" I exclaimed, gazing down at Aurelia. "You are already awake and ready for story time too!"

The child's bright blue eyes looked up at me. She was about six months old now. I swept her up in my arms and held her to my breast. I kissed her soft head, covered in fuzzed brown hair.

Glancing at Hector, I walked into the courtyard. "I will start gathering the little ones in here." Nodding, Hector jogged out of the house.

"Children," I said to the two little ones running in circles. "It is story time. Get on the rooftop now!" Only Aurelia was mine, but the other children came to play in Lazarus and my courtyard. We had become the mother's mantle of Kition.

They screamed in delight and hurried up the thin stairs to the small flat roof. Lazarus and my home. One courtyard. One traklin. One bedroom. One rooftop. Just what we needed, despite our many guests.

I swayed Aurelia in my arms and dabbed at a bit of spit at the corner of her mouth. I gingerly carried her up the thin stairs to the roof to see children running through the streets from different directions toward me.

"Mitera Esther!" children called, hurrying through the courtyard and up the stairs. We met here every day at the ninth hour, beneath the awning that Lazarus built to block the fierce heat of the sun. This time was perfect as it was the same time Jesus died and the time just before mothers would need help with supper

Looking down, I was surprised to see Lazarus walking along the street, a donkey behind him loaded with sacks of what I assumed was flax on each side of it. Sweat glistened from his brow and pride filled me as I thought of his hard work in the fields and in the factory. He enjoyed humble work and humble wages, as that is when he felt closest to Jesus.

"What is today's story?" he called up at me. A child patted the side of his donkey as he ran past Lazarus.

"Yours." I gave the simple reply with a one-sided smile as I turned toward the children gathered beneath the twigged and linen awning.

Jesus Himself spoke to them, through me. I smiled, looking at Aurelia's sweetly innocent demeanor and at the children seated and ready to begin.

Jesus, my dearest friend. Do not leave my side!

I envisioned His smiling face, knowing that He was closer to me than my own heart. *You said that he that sees Me sees the Father also. May You be a Father to all of these dear children.*

Hector issued commands, telling the children where to sit. Some of the younger ones sat in the older one's laps. They sat on mats that Lazarus and I had prepared. I lowered myself carefully on a short wooden stool, adjusting Aurelia's position in my arms.

"Mitera Esther! May I hold Aurelia?" One girl begged, hands folded at her chin.

"You may," I said, gently easing her into the girl's steady arms.

"What is today's story?"

"Mitera Esther, look at my finger! I cut it!"

"Wait for me!" one child called, hurrying up the stairs with all her might.

"I will tell you the story in a moment." I patted one's arm. "Yes," I said, looking to another. "That is quite a cut you have on your finger."

"May I sit on your lap?" A tiny girl asked hopefully.

"No. I told you, no more sitting on my lap." It started out as a good idea, but the children became indignant if they were not on my lap. They all struggled for their shining moment in the storyteller's arms.

"You did all the work your mothers gave you before coming today?" I looked at each child. Close to two dozen of them.

"Yes," many said in unison as others nodded proudly.

"Good. Good. You know, Jesus was always a good child. He was obedient to His parents, but He was also a dear friend to me and the other children."

"I wish He was my friend," an older girl said.

"Oh, but He is!" I lifted my hands in excitement. "We cannot see Him, but He is with us, even till the end of time."

"Is He sitting with us right now?" one asked.

"Yes," I said.

"Is He above me, sitting on the awning?"

"He is."

"What about in my house?"

"He is everywhere!" I laughed. "Most importantly, He dwells within you."

"Me?" one asked as if a king just requested to dine with him.

"Yes. All of you." I examined their round cheeks and big eyes. Their small hands moved about with energy, whether they were tapping their thighs or touching their faces. I kept the girl who was holding Aurelia in my focus. Praise Jesus, Aurelia was not crying today.

"Now, let us get started with today's story." I adjusted my position on the stool.

"I liked the one you told yesterday when Jesus rebuked your sister-in-law," Hector said, his legs crossed.

"But remember what I said. Martha is a lovely woman. Jesus has rebuked many people, including myself, and including His closest Apostle, Peter."

"What does rebuke mean?"

"She told us yesterday!"

"It means scolding someone," Hector explained. "Or disapproving of what someone has done."

"Enough of yesterday's story," I continued. "I have an exciting one for today. It also occurred in Bethany where my sisters-in-law live."

"Are Martha, Mary, and Magdalene in the story?"

"Yes, they are, but Lazarus is the main character this time."

"Lazarus!"

"I like him!"

"People follow him around."

"Lots of people like him."

"I like him as well." I smiled. "Now," I said, clapping my hands together. "I am going to tell you how Lazarus died." I paused for effect, watching the confusion spread on their faces. I held up a hand as one child started to question.

"How he died...and was raised to life again!" I said slowly, my heart warming at the wonder in their expressions.

"Raised to life again?"

"He died?"

"How can you be so sure?"

"How did he die?"

"How do you know he came back to life?"

My mouth curved into a wider smile, stretching my cheekbones. I looked at each child one-by-one. "I saw it through my own eyes."

Author's Note

Through Esther's Eyes was created with much research and study. Still, what I have learned is hardly a drop in the ocean. I pulled sources from historians, modern biblical scholarship, the *Catechism of the Catholic Church*, and the Catholic study of Sacred Scripture. My professors, Dr. Kelly Murphy from Central Michigan University and Dr. Edith Covensky from Wayne State University have led me in my research. One of my main sources, Miriam Feinberg Vamosh, wrote *Daily Life at the Time of Jesus* and *Food at the Time of the Bible*. I also took information from *Scripture Footnotes (The World of Jesus)* by George Martin. I learned a lot from *The Nazareth Jesus Knew* and other resources from Nazareth Village. The works of the ancient Jewish historian, Josephus, was very insightful, as was the *Ignatius Catholic Study Bible New Testament.* Then there is Pope Benedict XVI and his work, *Jesus of Nazareth.* I also took inspiration from the *Apostolic Letter, "Mulieris Dignitatem"—Pope John Paul II on the Dignity and vocation of women on the occasion of the Marian year.* Then, *Jesus and the Jewish Roots of the Eucharist* and *Jesus and the Jewish roots of Mary* by Dr. Brant Pitre were valuable. Dr. Scott Hahn's book, *The Lamb's Supper*, was very enlightening. These are but some of my sources.

The storyline for this novel is totally fictional. Though I explored and used real people and recorded words from the Bible, nothing that occurs in this novel should be taken as doctrine or truth, other than that Jesus walked on this earth, died, and rose for *you*! And we must not forget that Mary is our mother! Otherwise, Esther's story is simply the expansion of my imagination and personal meditation on Sacred Scripture. There is no evidence whatsoever that Jesus had a cousin named Esther. There is mention that Jesus had "brothers" and "sisters," but with a correct reading, this may have referred to cousins.

There are so many "Marys" in the gospels, that I took Mary, the wife of Clopas, and named her Aunt Miriam. Mary Magdalene is simply called Mara or Magdalene. Then there is Mary of Bethany, Mary Alphaeus (who could be the "other" Mary in the gospels), and Aunt Mary, the mother of Jesus. I could have called Jesus by His Aramaic name, "Yeshua," but many English-speaking modern Christians call Jesus by the "Holy Name of *Jesus*," my hope is to restore reverence to the Name. Many of the names that are in the novel are the Greek version of the names as opposed to the original Hebrew because I want to keep them consistent with the modern translation of the gospels, translated into English. Still, to give the reader a little taste of Hebrew and Greek, I added words like "Ima" and "trogo."

Traditionally, Jesus, Mary, and Joseph lived in their own home in Nazareth, but I put them in the same complex as Uncle Clopas and his family for easy conversation and interaction with Jesus' extended family.

There is no evidence that Lazarus of Bethany had a wife. There is no historical or biblical evidence that Mary Magdalene was sister to Lazarus, Martha, and Mary. Much of what I took for Lazarus' family, including the names of his parents are based on legends and a very small amount from the writings of Venerable Catherine Emmerich.

Any words that Jesus speaks are either based on one of the gospels or have come from my own personal prayer conversations with Jesus.

Any words spoken by Aunt Mary are based on the gospels, Marian apparitions, and my own personal prayer conversations with her.

With Jesus, Mary, and Joseph,
Jacqueline St. Clare

Glossary

Abba: Hebrew word for "Father" or "Daddy."

Adonai: Hebrew word for "Lord."

Apostle: Greek word for "to send forth."

Aramaic: The language that Jesus spoke.

Centurion: Roman commander in charge of 100 soldiers.

Chair of Moses: A seat of honor in the synagogue; typically for the rabbi or honored speaker.

Cubit: A measurement that is close to eighteen inches.

Day of Atonement: (Yom Kippur.) The high holy day of repentance for the Jewish people. As part of the Temple ceremony during Jesus' time, a high priest would sacrifice an animal as a symbolic way of restoring the relationship between God and the people.

Diakonia: Greek word for "to serve."

Dinar: A silver Roman coin that has Caesar's image on it.

El: The Hebrew word for a "god" or "God."

Elohim: A name for God first found in Genesis.

Essenes: A radical sect of Jewish men who lived celibately in a community in the desert.

Fiat: Greek word for "yes" or "amen."

Feast of Lights: A non-pilgrim feast that celebrates the rededication of the Temple at the time of the Maccabees. It is known in modern day as "Hannukah."

Feast of Pentecost: Also known as the Feast of Weeks, this feast commemorates the giving of the Torah to Moses, celebrated 50 days after Passover. Only men were required to attend the feast in Jerusalem.

Feast of Tabernacles: Also known as the Feast of Booths, this feast commemorates the Israelites journey through the wilderness under the Lord's protection. This is just after the Day of Atonement (a high holy day of prayer and sacrifice).

Feast of Unleavened Bread: A seven-day commemoration in which no leaven is eaten. Preceding it is the Feast of Passover. The Israelites had no time to let their bread rise when fleeing Egypt. Thus, they eat unleavened bread (matzah) in memory of that.

Gehenna: A valley near Jerusalem where waste is burned. Jesus often references Gehenna as the place of punishment/Hell.

Gentiles: Non-Jews.

Hebrew Shekel: Worth about two dinars and is used in the Temple, particularly for the Temple tax.

Ima: Hebrew word for "Mother."

Kyrios: The Greek word for "Lord."

Levite: A priest and/or assistant at the Temple.

Matzah: Unleavened bread prepared at Passover. Bread without yeast; the Israelites were not able to let their bread rise since they left Egypt in haste.

Mikveh: A "bath" for ritual purification, often hewn from stone.

Mitera: Greek word for "Mother."

Mohar: What the groom gives to the family of the bride; the bride-price.

Passover: All Jewish families went to Jerusalem for this feast to celebrate the Angel of Death passing over their ancestors in Egypt. It commemorates the Israelites freedom from slavery through the prophet, Moses. This is a 24-hour period feast proceeding the Feast of Unleavened Bread.

Pharisee: A Jewish sect that consists of typically rich Jews who strictly follow the Torah and the law of Moses. They have long tassels on their cloaks to show their devotion to God. They serve as rabbis or even chief priests.

Prutah: Also known as a mite, it is the smallest unit of currency; a copper coin.

Rabbi: A learned man and a leader who studies the Torah.

Rabboni: Another name for "rabbi."

Sadducee: A Jewish sect that does not believe in the resurrection of the dead. The Sadducees are very rich and mostly make up the chief priests. Many Jews dislike the Sadducees because they get their riches from Rome and are "in league" with Rome.

Sicarii: A radical group of Jewish Zealots. They carry curved daggers beneath their cloaks and strike and kill Romans in mass gatherings, and then disappear in the crowd.

Shalom: The Hebrew word for "peace;" a greeting.

Sheol: The Jewish land of the dead. It is not Heaven or Hell but is similar to the underworld in Greek and Roman religions.

Tallit: Jewish prayer shawl that men wear over their heads.

Tetrarch: The leader of a small province. For example, Herod Antipas is the tetrarch of Galilee, by order of Rome.

Todah: Means "thanksgiving" in Hebrew. It is a type of peace sacrifice offered in the Old Testament and remarkably correlates with the thanksgiving sacrifice of the Catholic Holy Sacrifice of the Mass.

Traklin: A main, common room that is inside many simple homes.

Trogo: Greek word for "chew" or "gnaw."

Zealots: A Jewish sect that holds the attitude and disposition of zeal that the land of Israel belongs to God and not to Rome. Many Zealots used increasingly violent and revolutionary methods until the fall of Jerusalem in 70 CE.